The New Encyclopedia of Stage Hypnotism

Ormond McGill

Crown House Publishing Limited
www.crownhouse.co.uk

First published by
Crown House Publishing Ltd
Crown Buildings
Bancyfelin, Carmarthen, Wales, SA33 5ND, UK
www.crownhouse.co.uk
and

Crown House Publishing Company, LLC
6 Trowbridge Drive, Ste. 5, Bethel, CT 06801, USA
www.crownhousepublishing.com

First published 1996: reprinted 1997, 1998, 1999, 2000,
2001, 2002, 2003, 2004, 2005, 2007

British Library Catalouging-in-Publications Data
A catalog entry for this book is available
from the British Library.

13 digit ISBN: 9781899836024
10 digit ISBN: 1899836020

LCCN 2002117315

**Anyone using any of the techniques described in this book does so entirely
at his or her own risk: the publishers cannot be held liable for any loss,
damage or injury whether caused or suggested by such use or otherwise**

Printed in the United States of America

Also by Ormond McGill

The Encyclopedia of Genuine Stage Hypnotism
The Art of Stage Hypnotism
Professional Stage Hypnotism
Hypnotism and Mysticism of India
Hypnotism and Meditation
Religious Mysteries of the Orient (Ron Ormond co-author)
A Better Life Through Conscious Self-Hypnosis
Psychic Magic
How To Produce Miracles (also in Signet Paperback)
Entertaining With Magic
Science Magic: 101 Tricks You Can Do
Balancing Magic and Other Tricks
Alfred Binet On Hypnotism
Power Hypnosis Hypnotherapy
Real Mental Magic
Grieve No More, Beloved

ORMOND McGILL
Dean of American Hypnotists

Advisory Board: American Council Hypnotist Examiners (ACHE)
National Guild of Hypnotists (NGH) Washington Hypnosis Association
(WHA) Staff: Hypnotherapy Training Institute (HTI)

Dedication

This book is dedicated to the memory of my delightful wife

DELIGHT McGILL

whose bright spark of creativity has contributed so much to the art of stage hypnotism

Table of Contents

Foreword

No man in the history of hypnotism has had more impact on stage hypnotism than has Ormond McGill. Hundreds of professionals have profited by his works.

In 1947, Ormond McGill wrote his original *Encyclopedia of Genuine Stage Hypnotism*, which was published by Abbott's Magic Company of Colon, Michigan. The book has gone through five editions and has become known as a "bible" for stage hypnotists. It presents his work in the field from 1927 to 1947.

In 1970, he wrote *The Art of Stage Hypnotism*, which presented his work from 1947 to 1970. The first edition was published by Lloyd Jones Magic Limited of Oakland, California, and the second edition by Borden Publishing Company of Alhambra, California. The book is now out of print, and is a collector's treasure.

A check with the Library of Congress in Washington, DC, reveals that no copyright was ever obtained on the original book, and in 1977 a revised, copyrighted version of the first edition was published, entitled, *Professional Stage Hypnotism*.

Currently, Ormond McGill has written this masterwork on Stage Hypnotism, which is all-inclusive of his previous works combined with much new, up-to-the-minute material added for today's mastery. Its coverage is encyclopedic in scope: Part One dealing with Mastering Hypnotising and Part Two dealing with Entertaining With Hypnotism, providing a book that is paramount in its field.

Ormond McGill was a pioneer in presenting hypnotism on television, and his contemporary work in hypnosis has earned him the reputation of "the Dean of American Hypnotists", through an international reputation gained by his many performances and his excellent books on magic, hypnotism, meditation and mysticism, East and West. During the last decade, Ormond McGill, in addition to his stage performances as a certified clinical hypnotherapist, has turned his attention to instructional seminars introducing innovative techniques of Power Hypnosis Hypnotherapy.

I am pleased to write the Foreword to *The New Encyclopedia of Stage Hypnotism*, which joins the ranks of classical literary achievements in the domain of hypnotism. As the late Percy Abbott (ABBOTT's "Magic

Capital of the World" original publishers of the first edition) stated back in 1960, "Ormond, you and I will pass away, but there will always be an *Encyclopedia of Genuine Stage Hypnotism.*"

I believe it!

Gil Boyne, President,
American Council of Hypnotists Examiners (ACHE), 1994

Ormond McGill on television with Art Linkletter in 1944, proving "People Are Funny" on the national Linkletter show.

Preface

This book has been long in the process of research, assembly and finally production. Gil Boyne in the Foreword to this book outlines the history of previous works by the author which have in themselves contributed to this compendium or encyclopedia of stage hypnosis. Work began on this project during the mid nineteen-eighties and the last piece of new material was added in early 1996.

This book could only have been produced by Ormond McGill whose personal knowledge of the subject is unsurpassed by any other living soul. Ormond at the time of publication is in his eighty-second year. During his life he has been an avid observer of the world about him and the people who populate it. He has been blessed with a memory for detail which is quite staggering. It is this wonderful memory of the hypnotic acts that he has witnessed coupled with an enquiring mind that have provided him with the knowledge to enable him to produce this outstanding work. Add to this his awe-inspiring knowledge of the world of magic, ESP and eastern religions and you have a recipe for something very special indeed.

Whilst Ormond is probably best known in North America, he has travelled the world widely, both performing and training others in his art. In 1995 he visited London, England, and conducted a number of workshops there. On the last night of his visit he gave a demonstration of his skill as a stage hypnotist by presenting his "act" to over one hundred students from his workshops. No one left the auditorium that evening without a profound respect for a true artist and a supreme performer. Later in 1995 he was the star guest of the National Guild of Hypnotists where he again presented his act but this time also with a number of his magic routines added for good measure. These shows left many of us hoping that we could be half as good as Ormond one day but, please God, long before we have reached his age!

Some of the acts and techniques described within the book are from Australia, England, Italy and other countries outside North America. It is therefore perhaps fitting that the production of the book itself should have been a collaborative venture by people and organisations from several nations. The author of course is an American, and indeed a major part of the original editorial work was undertaken by Abbott's Magic Company of Colon, Michigan. Further work was then undertaken by The Anglo-American Book Company in Wales.

I should, on Ormond's behalf, like to thank all those who have contributed to this book through the acts they have performed and the information they have provided that has made it possible. He would also like me to mention Glenys Roberts, Christopher Gough, David and Karen Bowman who contributed their time to the final production of the book and a great big thanks to Mark Williams for his wonderful artwork for the jacket.

The cosmopolitan nature of the development of this book has led to a number of problems with presentation and the English language. Winston Churchill, when Prime Minister of Great Britain during the second World War, described Britain and America as "one nation divided by a common language". This book originally written mainly in American English is here presented in British English. However, as far as has been humanly practical all expressions unique to the American English have been retained.

Over the years there has been a great deal of criticism of stage hypnosis in various countries and territories within countries. Often this criticism has been based on ignorance or fear. I hope that this book will to some extent help to redress and dispel such criticism. Throughout this book the author constantly reminds the reader of the need for ecology in what he does and integrity in its application. Total respect for his subjects has always been paramount in Ormond's performances. He also reminds us that cheap laughs are easy to get, but a skilled and professional performance is far more highly valued by your audience.

Finally, as much of my background in hypnosis has been in its clinical application, I hope that the book will go some way towards persuading my medical colleagues that whilst hypnosis has great potential in entertainment it actually has far greater potential when applied to healing. It is now well understood that many of today's ills in the western world are associated with stress and the ever quickening pace of life. Often the pressure of modern living leads to breakdowns in health which clearly can be diagnosed as being psychosomatic in nature. In many cases hypnosis offers a really powerful and effective alternative to drug therapy. For the skilled eye and open mind this book also provides a number of clues as to how easily this may be achieved.

Thank you, Ormond, dear friend, for investing so much of your time and energy in producing a truly wonderful book. God bless you, and may the cosmic force be with you.

Martin Roberts PhD
Cranfield University, England

Part One

Mastering Hypnotism

Preface

FASCINATION. From time immemorial Mankind, under one name or another, has been fascinated by hypnotism. Like magic, hypnotism is shrouded with mystery for it presents the magic of the mind, and this is the most astonishing magic in the world. It is the magic of YOU. Stage hypnotism ranks among the most wonderful entertainment mediums for it is entertaining,with you observing others doing what you could do. It is a very personal form of entertainment. This book shows you how to become a master of that entertainment.

Every journey commences by taking the first step. Stage hypnotism is no exception to this fact. *The New Encyclopedia of Stage Hypnotism* maps your way to mastery of the art. Part One gives you the "know how" of mastering Hypnotism. It provides some background in understanding hypnotism and suggestion, and shows you how to develop hypnotic power. Then it takes you along, step-to-step, in learning how to hypnotise, and tells you what to do. Then you must put into practice what you learn, for with experience comes expertness. Part Two of the book shows you how to use that expertness to entertain with hypnotism.

The ability to hypnotise flawlessly comes with practice. The importance of practice in hypnotising cannot be over-emphasised. For that purpose, your first objective is to obtain subjects who are interested in your work and are willing to experiment with hypnosis. Through application you become skilled in the technique.

The New Encyclopedia of Stage Hypnotism teaches you both how to hypnotise and how to present a hypnotism show. Even though you have never hypnotised in your life, if you follow these instructions you will succeed and will become a hypnotic entertainer.

You will find these instructions combine the practical with the scientific. You learn to hypnotise by a gradual approach of advancing from experiments in waking hypnosis on to the deeper phenomena of hypnosis. This is a sensible way to learn hypnotism as the lighter stages of hypnosis are more readily induced than are the deeper trance stages (with most people).

Training by this progressive method of hypnotising shows the new students how to effectively use suggestion while you train your subject(s) in how to be hypnotised.

By following this procedure of performing simple tests first, you will find you will be able to hypnotise more people successfully, as through this handling your subjects will gain confidence in your ability, and you will gain confidence in yourself.

ADVANCE THROUGH THESE FIVE STEPS:

1. *Knowledge of hypnotism*
   Be sure you understand what you are to do before attempting to hypnotise anyone. Go about your work in a competent manner so it is obvious that you know what you are doing.

2. *Perseverance*
   Success in hypnotising comes with experience in hypnotising. As a new student, do not expect to hypnotise everyone you try. You may succeed immediately with the very first person or you may not. If you do not succeed at once keep right on trying, for as sure as the sun shines you will eventually find a subject who responds. So persevere. You cannot fail if you follow these instructions carefully. And once you have hypnotised one or two persons you will soon find that you can influence the majority with whom you work.

3. *The first hypnosis*
   Hypnotising successfully your first subject is the initial goal you must achieve. Just keep in mind that a good hypnotist might possibly try ten persons and not hypnotise one of them for a variety of reasons depending upon the situation. On the other hand, with different people under a different situation, the whole group might be hypnotised. You must learn to expect this variation in responsiveness. In time you will minimize it.

   In this training, learn your processes as well as you do your ABCs. Then proceed directly to practising with people, as often as you can. You are bound to succeed. Once the ice has been broken and you have successfully hypnotised a few persons, you will have confidence in yourself, and you will be amazed at your own success.

4. *Understanding the power of suggestion*
   The skillful use of suggestion is the "key" to effective hypnotising as it is both the means of producing the state of hypnosis and of controlling the state it produces. Indeed, it is the key to understanding hypnotism, as hypnotism is a hyper-suggestible state of mind. In such regard, speak positively and directly to your subjects. In this text,

careful attention is given to how to present suggestions that influence, i.e. the power of suggestion.

5. *You cannot fail*

    If you perform correctly, there is no such word as fail. Study conscientiously and you will be on your way to a successful career in hypnotism.

Ormond McGill
Palo Alto, CA
1993

Introduction

Stage hypnotism provides fascinating entertainment. It combines the mysterious with human interest producing a behavioural programme that is amazing, amusing and thought provoking.

Properly presented stage hypnotism provides quality entertainment which emphasises the work done in medical and academic fields, and lifts the science of hypnotism to the status of an art.

Few forms of entertaining are more basically appealing than the hypnotic exhibition, as people like people; and, as the hypnotism show is devoted entirely to audience participation entertainment, the show is very interesting to watch and every programme is different since the cast on stage is different.

There is something so warmly human, and at the same time verging on the magical which causes hypnotism to stand unique on the entertainment spectrum. An audience will be literally convulsed with laughter in watching the fun-filled antics of hypnotised subject on stage; a few minutes later, that same audience will lean forward in their seats staring in wonder at the mental phenomena unfolding before their eyes.

The hypnotism stage show is an action show based on the greatest wonder and mystery of all the human mind. Hypnotism demonstrates the magic-of-the-mind.

This book provides consecutive instructions in how to become an expert hypnotic entertainer presenting a remarkable programme for all manner of performing situations. The performer will find a wealth of information for presenting successfully stage hypnotism. The non-performer will find a wealth of knowledge about the psychology of hypnotism and its practical application, as stage hypnotism provides the opportunity to acquaint thousands of people with the science/art through the medium of entertainment. Making knowledge entertaining is the best way to learn.

However hypnotism must never be regarded as a toy that one plays with. The human mind is a delicate instrument which must be handled with great care. The hypnotist has a legal and a moral obligation to approach the performance of hypnotism in a completely ethical manner and to appreciate that the most important person in his (or her) presentation is the subject(s) and not himself.

Chapter One
Understanding Hypnotism

Before you can learn to do anything well, you have to have some knowledge of what you do. And so ...

What is Hypnotism?

Hypnotism is much like electricity. No one knows for sure just what it is, but we use it anyway. Assuredly it has power. Basically hypnosis may be regarded as a state of mind conducive to subconscious behaviour rather than more normally regarded conscious behaviour. Hypnotism is the means of inducing that subconsciously responsive state of mind. Possibly hypnosis is best understood by regarding it as a way of programming the mind so that it functions through the automatic nervous system rather than the sympathetic nervous system of the body, as is most noticeably the case in everyday behaviour.

Gaining some understanding of the characteristics and theory of hypnosis will both make you a better hypnotist and provide interesting material to explain to your audience during the course of your show. The more you can educate while you entertain the better stage hypnotist you will be.

Characteristics of Hypnosis
Absolute Fixation of Attention

According to experiments published in the *American Journal of Psychology*, entering the state of hypnosis consists in gradually limiting the field of attention until a perfectly concentrated and unvarying focus is reached. Attention in the waking and hypnotic state is represented, in one case, by a wide curve with a broad hump in it (as illustrated in Graph A), representing the fact that we are conscious to many different stimuli at the same time in varying degrees of intensity with the peak of the hump at the focus of attention, and, in the other case, by a single spikelike peak in an otherwise flat curve (illustrated in Graph B). Entering hypnosis has resulted in so narrowing the field of attention that only a very small range of stimuli is perceived, and this range is determined by the suggestions of the hypnotist.

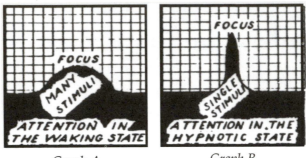

Graph A   Graph B

Hyperacuity of Senses Within the Field of Attention

Numerous experiments on seeing, hearing, feeling and other sensory perceptions show that they are much more accurate and active when attention is directed to them in the hypnotic state. The logical powers of the mind are also greatly enhanced, and deductions may be performed with remarkable accuracy. The comparison between the waking and hypnotic state is the same as the comparison between a shotgun and a rifle.

Artificial Control of Reflexes and Subconscious Nervous Activity

By hypnotic suggestion the pulse rate may be altered, an area of the body anaesthetized, menstrual periods be regulated, time of childbirth determined, and such automatic bodily functions controlled.

Loss of Autonomy Resulting From Diminishing Conscious Control

The hypnotised person elects to relinquish his autonomy and chooses to allow the hypnotist to direct his course of action, as long as the suggestions presented do not run counter to powerful tendencies or the moral nature of the subject. When such suggestions are given, the subject either refuses to respond to them or frequently will "awaken" from the hypnosis.

Susceptibility to Posthypnotic Responses

Suggestions given under hypnosis for actions to be performed after the subject awakens will be performed, if the subject was deeply enough entranced, often with amnesia resulting, provided that these suggestions do not violate the conditions mentioned in the foregoing characteristic.

From a study of the characteristics of the hypnotic state here listed, it is obvious that whatever method is employed to produce hypnosis, it must include factors that will produce hyperacuity of the faculties of the individual hypnotised, and which will give control over subconscious nervous activity, simultaneously providing a response to the posthypnotic influence.

Some Theory on Hypnotism

There was a time in the history of hypnotism when the practice was shrouded in much mystery and it was believed that the hypnotist was all-powerful with complete dominance over the subject.

Then the pendulum swung to the opposite extreme and there was a tendency to oversimplify hypnotic phenomena as being entirely induced by the subject in himself. The role of the hypnotist being relegated as being scarcely more than a "recording" presenting the suggestions.

Today, the pendulum of understanding of hypnotism has sought the middle road in regarding both the hypnotist and the subject as important factors in the production of hypnosis. It is a dynamic situation developed between hypnotist and subject.

In other words, the hypnotic situation can be regarded as one of cooperation and trust between hypnotist and the subject in which each has a special role to perform to achieve together a most remarkable mental condition of the state of mind termed hypnosis (trance).

In relation to stage hypnotism, there are mainly two facets of the phenomenon of pertinent interest: 1. Waking Hypnosis (Waking Suggestion Experiments); 2. Artificial Somnambulism (referred to as Hypnosis). Both of these facets call into action the subconscious phase of mind. Hypnosis can be considered a means of producing a trance and/or trancelike state which can be regarded as a "shift of consciousness". Most Waking Hypnosis calls into action behaviour prior to the complete shift of consciousness while Somnambulistic Hypnosis calls into action subjective behaviour after the shift of consciousness has occurred. However, this shifting from objective consciousness to subjective consciousness can be of such a subtle nature that it is often difficult to differentiate between the two, other than by observation of the intensity of the phenomena produced. There is a blending, which is why the stage hypnotist will often find it to his advantage to start with experiments in Waking Hypnosis prior to proceeding on to deeper phenomena. Such provides a learning process, enabling the mind of the subject to move gracefully from conscious to subconscious activity.

Basically hypnosis can be regarded as a state of mind produced by the transference from one level of consciousness to another; a state with capacities for mental activities distinctly its own directly keyed to the automatic nervous system rather than the sympathetic (central nervous system), as was previously observed, productive of the state of mind of somnambulism, i.e. subconscious behaviour.

When somnambulism occurs in spontaneous form it is known as "sleep walking" or "sleep talking". The close alliance between natural somnambulism and hypnosis is obvious from the fact that but a few suggestions from the hypnotist will readily capture the attention of the natural somnambulist, and, through establishing a rapport, quickly transfer the former into hypnosis. The somnambulist then responds to the directions of the hypnotist.

Hypnotising may be said to be a means of deliberately induced somnambulism in the subject. It is well termed "artificial somnambulism". Possibly it could be more accurately referred to as "guided somnambulism".

The point of a rapport developing between the hypnotist and subject is important to consider as it is universal to hypnosis in providing the avenue of communication to the altered level of consciousness produced by the hypnotising process. It may be said that an en-rapport relationship exists throughout hypnosis, either between the subject and hypnotist in the case of hetero-hypnosis or with the subject with himself in the case of self-hypnosis.

Unique as the state of mind of hypnosis is, it is not an isolated function of mind. Manifestations of it are found in all walks of life and in all phases of society, from the most primitive to the most civilised. Native trance dances, voodoo and hexing are primitive applications of the state; faith cures, ecstasy and miraculous healings are religious applications; psychosomatic medicine and psychotherapy are psychological applications of the state. Each and all are at their roots the same, each being but a different road that leads to artificially induced somnambulism. This state of mind is characterised by extreme suggestibility focused strongly in the direction of the special suggestions played upon it.

A study of hypnotism will reveal some of the phenomena observable in a variety of abnormal psychological states as found in the insanities, i.e., delusions, illusions, hallucinations, catalepsies, personality alterations, etc. The major difference is that in insanity these mental aberrations are the product of a mind "running wild", as it were, while in hypnosis such phenomena are produced under control and as directed ... and there is a complete integration of the subject's personality at all times. A study of the phenomena of hypnotism reveals many of the remarkable things the human mind is capable of accomplishing.

Chapter Two
The Power of Suggestion

Suggestion, in the hypnotic sense, is the subconscious realisation of an idea. The mastery of the effective use of suggestion is extremely important to your success as a stage hypnotist, as suggestions as previously mentioned is both the means of inducing the state of hypnosis and of controlling the state induced.

Suggestion provides the means of directing the subconscious phase of mind, so the more you become aware of the nature of the subconscious, the rules of suggestion operation and how to give suggestions that influence, the more expert hypnotist you will become. These thoughts on the power of suggestion will be helpful to your mastery of stage hypnotism:

The subconscious part of our mind may be likened to the storehouse of our memories. It is not unlike the "memory bank" of a computer in operation. It is where every experience we have had from earliest infancy to the last hour of life is filed. Recent research in hypnosis even reveals the possibility that memories of previous lifetimes are filed therein. These memories, however, are not passive; they are vitally active, each forming a thread in the texture of our personality, the total of these impressions being the nature of the individual.

The subconscious is also a dynamo. It is dominated by emotion, and emotion is the driving force of life. It is the energy source for conscious thought and action and for the performance of the vital functions of the body. The subconscious plays the role of supervisor over our body's physical processes. Digestion, assimilation, the circulation of the blood, the actions of the lungs, the heart, the kidneys and all the vital organs are controlled by its agency. The subconscious never sleeps; indeed, during sleep it seems to be more alert and active than it is during our waking hours, and is on constant vigil to protect the individual.

The two facets of mind, conscious and subconscious, are in perpetual interaction. If we consciously think a thought (idea) and cause it to be accepted by the subconscious, the idea will spontaneously go into action to produce its effect. If it is a beautiful thought, we are so much the better. If it is a diseased thought we are so much the worse, because, unlike consciousness, the subconscious has no selective power. Whatever is presented to it is accepted and automatically acted upon. It is in the process of this transformation of a thought into an element of our life that we make use of the power of suggestion. Since the phenomenon is a normal part of the mind's action, we can easily find evidence of its working in our daily experiences.

Remember this rule of operation: every suggestive idea which enters the consciousness, if it is accepted by the subconscious, is automatically transformed into a reality, and it becomes an element in one's life. This rule is constantly manifested in stage hypnotism.

The thoughts we think determine not only our mental states, our sentiments and emotions but also the delicate actions and adjustments of our physical bodies. Trembling, palpitation, stammering, blushing and the variety of pathological states which occur in neuroses are all due to modifications and changes in the blood flow, in muscular action and in the working of the vital organs. These changes are not voluntary and conscious ones; they are determined by the capacities invested in the subconscious phase in our mind, and come to us often with a shock of surprise.

If we can get the subconscious to accept an idea, realisation follows automatically. But, for any idea to so enter subconsciousness it must be charged, to a greater or lesser extent, with emotion. This is where so many of the "thinking fads" fall down, for it is not the thinking of ideas that is of paramount importance, but the emotional drive that is given to the thought!

For this reason, ideas that are directly associated with our personal interest are the ones most likely to carry the greatest suggestive influence. Ideas related to health, success, money or a goal in life dear to our heart all carry emotional impact, and the greater the degree of emotion attached to it the more potently the Power of Suggestion can affect it.

The ready acceptance or rejection of an idea by the subconscious depends largely on the associations connected with the idea. Thus, an idea is most readily accepted when it ties in with similar emotionally charged ideas already seated within the mind, and tends to be rejected when it is contrary to ideas previously established.

Suggestions, it will be observed, are seen to be emotionally charged ideas, and this fact brings to attention another operating process of the power of suggestion: A suggestion is accepted when it is not countered by other suggestions already established in the mind.

If this operating process is true, how then is it possible for a person who has unwanted ideas (such as various bad habits) firmly established in his mind to make use of suggestion to counteract them?

On this point, we must look upon the subconscious as a tide which ebbs and flows. In sleep, it seems to submerge consciousness altogether, while at moments of full wakefulness the tide is at its lowest ebb. Between these two extremes are any number of intermediary levels. When we are drowsy, dreamy, lulled into a gentle reverie by music, etc., the subconscious tide is high. On the other hand, the more wakeful and alert we become the lower it sinks. The submergence of consciousness causes an outcropping of the subconscious. Hypnosis does this in a controlled manner.

This "outcropping of the subconscious" are desirable times in which to effectively implant suggestions in the mind and have them become part of one's personality. During such times contrary associations do not seem to take place, and established suggestions in the mind lose their strength to resist the influx of new suggestions. The power and emotional drive of hypnotically inspired suggestions are such that the enrooted unwanted suggestions may be weeded out from the soil of mind and fresh ones planted, so that on the resumption of normal consciousness a new "flower of thought" will be growing in place of the old.

This brings us to another important process in the operation of suggestion: whenever the will is in conflict with an idea, the idea invariably wins the struggle.

You can prove this for yourself by performing a little experiment.

Take a plank of wood, about six inches wide and twelve feet long, and place it on the floor of your room. Now, try walking along the plank from one end to the other. You can do it easily. Now, take that very same plank and place it over the canyon between two tall buildings and try walking over it. You take a few timid steps out upon it; and, unless you make a hasty retreat, your life is in danger. Why this change in your reactions?

The new position of the plank has aroused in your mind the suggestion of the idea of falling, an idea that is coloured with the emotion of danger to your life. Immediately your subconscious goes into action and accepts the idea of a possible fall. With your will you try to battle against the impulse to fall. Logic tells you that you have just walked over that very same board so there is no reason why you can't do it now just as you did before. But, reason about it as you will, the more you think about not falling, the more the counter-idea that you will fall is aroused. Were you to stubbornly persist in taking the risk, you could lose your life.

As the famous French autosuggestionist, Emil Coué expressed it: "We can now see that not only is the will incapable of vanquishing a thought, but that as fast as the will brings up its big guns, thought captures them and turns them against itself."

This process has been called "The Law of Reversed Effort": when the imagination and the will are in conflict, the imagination invariably gains the day. In the conflict between the will and the imagination, the force of the imagination is in direct ratio to the square of the will. Thus, the will turns out to be not the commanding monarch of life, as many people would have it, but a blind Samson, capable of either turning the mill or of pulling down the pillars.

Hypnosis provides an excellent means for programming the subconscious as it succeeds in avoiding this conflict between our ideas and our will. It replaces wrong thoughts by right thoughts, literally by not resisting the unwanted thoughts, but by overpowering "bad" thoughts by "good" thoughts. This procedure in no sense devaluates one's "will power", it merely relegates it to its proper place.

Will is under the direction of our consciousness; and, for it to operate effectively and efficiently, it must be in harmony with the ideas rooted in the subconscious. Of itself, will power can never uproot any subconsciously implanted ideas as it does not have that capacity. However, it can locate the ideas that are unwanted, it can locate thoughts that are needed, and it can direct the deliberate process that will result in an injurious idea's removal and the implanting of a new and desirable one in its place.

It must be always remembered that the foregoing process of using conscious to benefit oneself in such regard can take place only through it cooperation with the innate capacities of the subconscious mind. Hypnosis provides our gardening tools for the successful cultivation of the fertile field of the subconscious to raise a full crop of better living and personal achievement.

NOTE TO HYPNOTIST: This information relative to subconscious mind and how suggestion psychologically performs is presented not only to increase your understanding of hypnosis and how it operates through the power of suggestions but equally is useful in providing you good patter material to use in your show, as the more you can inform your audience correctly on these matters, the more significance your show takes on, as you develop your skill as a stage hypnotist.

Chapter Three
Presenting Suggestions that Influence

Suggestions carry an amazing amount of influence. An incident is told of a college student who was killed by its power. At a fraternity initiation a young man was blindfolded, and, after the usual emotion arousing proceedings, was told that he was to have his head chopped off. His head was then placed on the block and viciously the knife slashed into his neck. It was actually only a wet towel, but the victim died of heart failure. His subconscious had accepted the idea that the knife was real, and when the towel descended it ended his life just as death would have followed a genuine decapitation.

The fact that suggestion can produce physical responses in our body can be easily shown by simply thinking of a sour lemon, and noticing how the thought spontaneously starts the flow of saliva within the mouth. Or think of itchy sensations about your body, and feel the itches commence. During your hypnotism show you can even use these simple experiments to illustrate to the audience how suggestions operate.

But not every person who takes part in a college initiation, as above described, would die as the result of the damp towel striking across the neck. This brings us to a basic law in the operation of this power. Every suggestive idea which enters the consciousness, if it is accepted by the subconscious, is automatically transformed by it into a reality and becomes an element in our life.

In the qualifying phrase, if it is accepted by the subconscious, lies the heart of the power of suggestion. There are ways to present suggestions that will cause them to be most accepted; in such are found the secrets of how to present suggestions that influence.

Timing

Proper timing of the presentation of a suggestion by the hypnotist is important. In other words, you do not usually want to tell the subject that something is happening before it has happened. A good rule is that if you see indications that a certain reaction is going to take place at any moment, then you can suggest that it is taking place. Otherwise, and often this is preferable, you should introduce the event as a future possibility and work up to its occurrence more or less gradually.

Repetition

Repetition is the driving force of suggestion. It is cumulative in its effect. Further, it prevents the hypnotist getting ahead too fast and out of proper timing in giving his suggestions to the subject, as well as having a certain monotony about it that is, in itself, hypnotic in effect.

Delivery

Proper delivery of the suggestions is likewise fundamental to their acceptance. In this regard, tone, inflection and phrasing all have their places, the major purpose of all being to focus the subject's attention on the suggested phenomena desired to occur. There are instances when a rapid-fire barrage of suggestions is indicated; conversely, there are times when a slower pace of insistence will prove most effective. There are times when it is well to challenge the subject to try to resist the influence, the very inability the subject finds in not being able to do so enforcing the effectiveness of the suggestion. And there are times when the very opposite of challenging is desired, an earnest persuasion providing the best suggestion.

How is one to know which delivery is best? In that "knowing" comes mastery of the art. Experience will be your teacher.

Means of Increasing the Influence of Suggestions
A. Combining of Suggestions

The combining of suggestions is compounding in effect. For example, to tell a subject that his arm is rigid and that he cannot bend it, but that when you snap your finger his arm will instantly relax and will drop into his lap, and when it falls into his lap he will go even more deeply into hypnosis is a compounding of suggestion. Notice how each suggestion used in combination reinforces the next building towards the desired response.

B. Training the Subject in Suggestive Responsiveness

Every individual has a certain potential to be influenced by suggestions. This potential may be increased or decreased by training through a graduating response to suggestion. If the suggestions succeed, the suggestibility ratio is increased; if they fail, the reverse is the case. For this reason, it is often well to train subjects in successful suggestive responsiveness by allowing them to proceed from simpler tests gradually on to the more difficult.

C. Voluntary Actions to Increase Suggestibility

A voluntary response to a suggestions has an influence in increasing an involuntary response. In the practical application to the performing hypnotist, the use of this principle lies in instructing the subject to do certain things that he must comply with before presenting hypnotic suggestions. For example, to sit down, to place his feet flat on the floor and rest his hands in his lap, etc., doing this or doing that, as the case may be, in relation to the performance. Obedience to such commands tends to get the subject to act upon your suggestions uncritically, which has a carry-over effect to the acceptance of your subsequent hypnotic suggestions.

D. Deep Breathing to Increase Suggestibility

This is a further refinement of a voluntary action increasing suggestibility in this case, deep, rhythmic breathing on the part of the subject, as requested by the hypnotist. Further, deep breathing floods the brain with oxygen producing a slight dizzying effect, producing a state of mind more open to suggestions.

E. The Counting Technique

Giving a certain number for the occurrence of a suggested action is effective in causing its response to occur. People are used to things happening at "the count of three". The principle of stating that a suggested effect will occur at such and such a time on cue, as it were, often intensifies the suggestive influence.

F. Nonverbal Suggestions

These consist of all suggestive influences exerted by the operator other than verbal suggestions, i.e., such processes as gestures, body movements, breathing, pantomimes, etc., for example, the gestures of the hands in passes toward the subject carry such suggestive influence. The use of nonverbal suggestions is very important to the hypnotist, and their use should be developed to become an intimate part of his suggestive pattern combined with verbal suggestions.

G. Mass (Group) Suggestions

The influence of suggestion upon a group is frequently more marked than when working with a solo subject. The element of self-consciousness is eliminated when being part of a crowd; also the factor of imitation is present. Seeing the suggestions working upon another has a strong effect favouring its working upon oneself.

NOTE TO HYPNOTIST: Come to have a great appreciation for words. Words form the backbone of suggestions. Words are "triggers to action". That is, we have become so conditioned to words that our response to them is automatic. The principles given in this chapter are important to your work as a stage hypnotist. The more effectively you learn how to present suggestions the more masterful a performer you will become.

Chapter Four
Your Hypnotic Power

Basically there are two ways of hypnotising: 1. Using the physiological method of the human energies (mesmerism); 2. The psychological method via suggestion. For most powerful results, these methods should be combined. This process of combining the physiological with the psychological is recommended throughout this text. It will make you a master stage hypnotist, as this combination gives you "Power Hypnosis".

A hypnotic power resides within you to influence others. Everyone has the power. It is an influence which you can learn to exert under volitional control. As a stage hypnotist, you learn how to use this power for sensational effects upon the stage.

Power Hypnosis is the influence of mind upon mind, so, to understand its operation, you must first learn some things about the nature of mind. Mind is nothing tangible; it is nothing you can place your finger on; it is present in everyone. You know you have a mind, but do you really know what you have?

Mind is a process for producing thoughts, and thoughts are things. In other words, thoughts are forms of energy arranged in certain patterns. Some refer to such as "thought forms". The more effectively you learn how to use your mind, the more powerful the "thought forms" you can produce, and powerful "thought forms" carry influence even across space.

The brain acts like an electrical transformer in stepping up the current, while the nervous system provides the wires which conveys the current throughout the body. Mind produces thoughts which the brain amplifies. The stronger the amplification the more powerful are the thoughts which can influence others directly.

The operation is like the process of induction, in which two coils of wire are spaced apart. One coil is electrically charged with an impulse and it is transmitted through space to the other coil. Each resonates to the same tune, as it were. In the Orient, the concept is presented in a more romantic manner. Mind is likened to a lake of still water. The hypnotist causes ripples to occur in his lake and the person towards whom his thoughts are directed obtains similar ripples in their lake.

Some have called this powerful transmission of thought from one person to another "thought projection". The mental energy used appears to be of two types: magnetic energy (referred to as "raw energy") generated within the body and telepathic energy generated within the mind. The raw energy gives the power while telepathic energy gives the direction. The two work together as a unit in applying Power Hypnosis. The operation of the two energies in combination is what Mesmer referred to as "animal magnetism". Mesmer may have been off on some of his theories, but beyond question he was a great hypnotist.

A "thought form" is mental energy with a purpose. In the case of stage hypnotism it is Power Hypnosis used to produce striking hypnotic results upon the stage with an eager audience watching. For a "thought form" to be powerful it must be charged with energy, and that energy comes from the hypnotist. Actually, it comes from the body of the hypnotist, for it is a physical thing. That is, it is physical as far as your method of producing it and experiencing it is concerned, although I rather suspect there are more subtle aspects involved as well. However, as this is a practical book in demonstrational hypnotism, you will be given a physical exercise to develop the energy. Do this:

Begin by looking upon your body as your personal reservoir of energy collected from the universe. Consider your body as functioning like an electrical condenser to store energy, which may be discharged for specific purposes, as directed by the mind. The purpose you are learning to use it for is to hypnotise profoundly your subjects.

Now, close your eyes and think of the universe as being like a great ocean of energy, and you are like an inlet of that ocean. The energy of the universe is there for your taking, to use it as you will. Energy is vibration and vibration is motion.

Sit in a chair, extend your arms in front of yourself, and start shaking your hands vigorously. Shake them in any direction, any way they want to go. Just shake them wildly, in absolute freedom. You start with effort, but soon the shaking will become effortless, and it will seem to occur almost by itself. As you do this, allow your mind to grow calm and experience yourself as the shaking continues. The time will come when it seems that it is no longer your hands that are shaking, rather it is *you* who are shaking both inside and outside.

When you become the shaking rather than just doing the shaking, you will begin to feel yourself filling with energy; an energy that somehow seems both mental and physical, at one and the same time. After you have become the shaking of your hands, and have had enough of this activity for awhile, relax your hands in your lap, and rest a bit. You are now ready to perform another associated process which brings the shaking to your entire body, in an automatic way, bringing you great quantities of this vital energy.

Stand erect, close your eyes, and allow your whole body to vibrate. You will find this easy to do, as you have already started the energy flowing throughout your body. So, now just allow your whole body to become energy, allowing your body to melt and dissolve its boundaries. Just stand relaxed, loose and natural. You do not have to do anything; you are simply there waiting for something to happen; all you have to do is cooperate with it and allow it. The cooperation should not become too direct, it should not be a pushing; it should remain just an allowing. You will find that your body will start making movements on its own. What movements it makes depends on you; all persons are different. Possibly your head will twitch and your body will start shaking in different ways. Just allow it to take on the shaking freely, and shake any way it wants to go.

Possibly your body will make subtle movements like a little dance, your hands move, your legs move seemingly on their own, and your entire body starts shaking with subconscious movements all over, and all you have to do is allow the shaking to happen. The energy is very subtle, so do not resist it. Just allow it to develop on its own; and, as it does, think of the shaking as being the energy of the universe coming into you.

When you have had enough of this automatic shaking of your body just stop. You can stop anytime you please. Now, stand still with your eyes closed and breathe deeply and fully while directing this energy towards your brain. Visualise your brain as glowing like a ball of energy, and from the brain passing through every nerve of your body, permeating every fibre of your being.

Use your imagination in doing this. In your mind's eye see the energy you have brought into your body flowing throughout your entire body. You are alive with energy. Never be afraid to use your imagination. Imagination is the creative power of the mind. Everything starts in the imagination. Now, how do you feel? You will feel yourself alive with vital energy. Test it for yourself:

Extend your arms and direct the energy into your hands, and you will feel your fingers tingle, as though an electrical current were passing out of them. Bring the fingertips of each hand towards the other, spaced about an inch apart. You will experience the flow of energy between your hands. Touch your fingertips together in front of a black cloth; then separate them a little, and move them back and forth an inch each way. Observe what is there. You will see lines of "misty radiance" flowing between them.

This is the "raw energy" of the hypnotist. When you place on this energy telepathic energy (thought forms) the latter riding piggyback, as it were, it is then that you have Power Hypnosis.

Telepathic energy is the product of thought. Every thought produces an electric-like discharge in the brain, and an electrical discharge produces a wave. A thought wave is much like a radio wave, only more subtle, and it can be transmitted through space from one person to another. When this transmitted "thought form" is powered by the raw energy applied to the hypnotising process, the result is Power Hypnosis.

Telepathic energy is not difficult to produce, as its production is an automatic function of mind. Every thought produces it. However, it can be strengthened by attention and will.

In relation to Power Hypnosis, attention means holding the thought consistent and centred in the mind. Will means to direct the thought to go where you want it to go to produce the effect you wish to produce. Both processes are deliberately directed by the hypnotist causing an induction of thought from one mind to another; and/or the ripples of the "lake" of one mind upon the "lake" of another. You have learned how to generate the raw energy in yourself. Now learn how to most powerfully project the completed "thought form" into the mind of the recipient.

The more effortlessly you project the thought, the more effectively it will be transmitted. That is, do not concentrate hard upon the thought and try to push it out by an effort of will into the mind of the other person, pushing mentally as though you were trying to move the thought that way, for thought does not travel through three-dimensional space. Thought goes through hyperspace. Or, if you can understand it better, you could say that thought goes through the fourth dimension. In other words, it is here and then it is there instantly.

Will is not used to push the thought; will is only used to form the thought and place it in the centre of the mind where it is visualised. This means you mentally picture what you want to occur in the mind of the recipient of the thought (the one you are hypnotising). If you wish, you can visualise it as ripples of your thoughts occurring in your own "lake of mind" and then similarly picture the same ripples forming in the "lake of mind" of the other person. Always employ imagination in the process. The more clearly you can form the mental picture of the happening, the stronger will be the influence. This is the induction process. It is optional, but I have found it effective to include a mutual hand shaking suggestion experience just prior to inducing group hypnosis.

Perform the action of violently shaking the hands as a mutual action. In doing this, the subjects can be told to hold in their minds the thought of being receptive to the energy while you (as the hypnotist) hold in your mind the thought of being projective of the energy to the subjects. This shaking hands in unison creates both a bond of friendship and trust combined with a resonance occurring between hypnotist and subjects resulting in a dynamic hypnotic situation.

NOTE TO HYPNOTIST: Learn to perform the processes given in this chapter well. Practise them often. They will increase your stature from being just another stage hypnotist to being an outstanding stage hypnotist.

To summarise, Hypnotic Power resides in using in combination, within your mind, the triple processes of **visualisation, affirmation, projection**:

1. In visualising, hold the image of precisely what you wish to occur in your mind, as you wish it to occur in the mind of your subject.
2. In affirmation, verbally, and mentally, suggest what you visualise as occurring in your visualisation.
3. In projection, think of what you visualise in your mind as occurring simultaneously within the mind of the subject(s).

Such is your hypnotic power. Not only does it help you on a physiological level, it equally helps you on a psychological level, as you are bound to more effectively present your hypnotism show when you *think* this way.

Chapter Five
Résumé of Hypnotic Phenomena

Phenomena of Hypnosis

In response to direct and specific suggestions the hypnotised person may be rendered happy or sad, angry or pleased, liberal or stingy, proud or humble, pugnacious or passive, bold or timid, hopeful or despondent, insolent or respectful. He may be made to sing, to shout, to laugh, to weep, to act, to dance, to shoot, to fish, to preach, to pray, to recite a poem or expound a theory.

The expressions of the subject in response to the suggestions is most significant, as its very earnestness is profound. The attitudes and gestures are equal to the best effort of an experienced actor.

The hypnotised person is not acting a part in the ordinary sense, as he believes himself to be the actual personality suggested. The subject will impersonate to perfection any suggested character with which he is familiar, such as a movie star or television personality.

One of the most striking and important functions of hypnosis is the prodigious memory that may be produced. In all degrees of hypnosis, this exaltation of memory is phenomenal. It is possible to revive recollection of circumstances and impressions long past, the images of which have been completely lost to ordinary memory, and which are not recoverable in the normal state of mind. All the sensations which we have ever experienced have left behind them traces, often so slight as to be imperceptible under ordinary circumstances; but hypnotic suggestion, addressing itself to the subconscious memory banks, as it were, can bring them to recall by the suggestions of the hypnotist.

Everything learned in life can be remembered in hypnosis, even when apparently it has long been forgotten. Indeed, those who give credence to reincarnation claim that even memories of past lives may be brought back under the suggestions of the hypnotist.

Memory may also be obliterated, such as causing the subject to forget his name and condition in life. The subject may even forget entire periods of his life at the suggestions of the hypnotist.

Sense delusions as illusions or hallucinations may be induced by hypnotic suggestions, for instance, when a chair is taken for a dog, or a broom for a beautiful woman, a noise in the street for orchestra music, and a pencil for a cigarette.

Try these experiments with illusions: play on a real piano. Then suggest that a table is a piano and play on that. Ask the subject which piano he likes the best, and he will choose the real one. Give your subject an empty glass and tell him it contains a shot of whisky, and that he must take care not to burn his throat as he swallows it. The ensuing endeavour to handle the imaginary liquor is often followed by catching of the breath and coughing.

An hallucination is the perception of an object which does not exist, as for instance, when you suggest to a subject: "Sit down in this armchair" where there is really no chair at all; yet the hallucination is so perfect that he seats himself in the imaginary chair, as though it were a real one.If you ask him if he is comfortable in the chair, he may reply: "Not particularly, I would prefer one that is more comfortable." It seems incredible than a hallucination can be so real that a person would assume an attitude so strained, but it is so.

Hallucinations of all the senses and illusions (delusions) of every conceivable kind can be readily suggested to a subject in deep hypnosis. Just how real these effects are to the subject is evidenced in experiments where the image of the hallucination has been caused to be doubled by a prism, magnified by a lens, and in all ways behave optically like a real object.

In suggesting an hallucination, say that of a bird, the suggested approach of the "bird" causes contraction of the pupil, and vice versa. At the same time, there is often convergence of the axis of the eyes, as though a real object were present.

The hypnotised person will eat a potato for a peach, or drink a cup of vinegar for a glass of champagne. He may be thrown into a state of intoxication by being caused to drink a glass of water under the impression that he is drinking vodka; or he may be restored to sobriety by the administration of gin under the guise of an antidote for drunkenness. In these cases, the expression of the face, induced by the suggested perception, corresponds so perfectly that a better effect would scarcely be produced if the real article were used.

Various physiological effects can be produced in the state of hypnosis. A subject can be caused to cry and shed tears on one side of the face and laugh with the other. The pulse can be quickened or retarded, respiration slowed or accelerated, and perspiration can be produced all by suggestion. Even the temperature of the body can be affected. If a subject is told he has a high fever, his pulse will become rapid, his face flushed, and his temperature increase. Or if a person is told that he is standing on ice he feels cold at once: he trembles, his teeth chatter, he wraps himself up in his coat, and sometimes even "goosebumps" develops. Hunger and thirst can be created, and other functions increased or retarded.

The mind can be so concentrated upon a physiological process as to stimulate that process to normal activity, so as to produce curative effects and even to produce pathological effects. For instance, a blister can be caused on healthy skin by applying a postage stamp and suggesting that it is a mustard plaster; or placing upon the skin a key or coin, with the suggestion that after waking a blister will appear at the spot where the key or coin was placed, and of corresponding size and shape. The key or coin is then removed and the subject awakened, having no conscious knowledge of the suggestion given; but, at the appointed time, the blister appears.

On the other hand, blisters and burns have been annulled by suggestion. Local redness of the skin is easily produced by suggestion, and can be seen to appear in a few minutes by watching the subject.

Several senses can be influenced by suggestion at the same time. For example it is suggested to the hypnotised subject that he is holding a rose. Immediately the subject sees, feels and smells the rose. When an illusion or hallucination is positive, the subject believes he sees what does not exist; when it is negative, he fails to recognise the presence of an object really placed before him.

The cessation of the function of any sense organ can be induced in the same way as a negative hallucination. The sense organ affected loses its functions. A suggestion to the contrary restores the function. It is certain that blindness and deafness induced this way are of a mental nature, for the fact is the organ involved actually performs its functions, although the impressions do not reach consciousness level. In the same way, the sight of one eye can be suspended while the other sees as usual.

The production of reddening and bleeding of the skin in hypnotised subjects, suggested by tracing lines or pressing objects thereupon, puts in a new light the accounts of the stigmata of the cross appearing on the hands, feet and forehead of mystics. The physiological effects of which hypnosis is capable serve to show the power of the state.

Posthypnotic Phenomena

The sense of time appears to be an innate mental power. Posthypnotic suggestions make use of the "time sense" in which the suggestion given the subject is instructed to commence after the hypnotic session has terminated.

Some extraordinary experiments can be performed using posthypnotic suggestion. For instance, it can be suggested that he (or she) will perform such and such an action at a certain time; whether in one or twenty-four hours, or 1000 or 2000 minutes, or a month or even more remote periods. The time-memory of the subconscious is remarkable. A case is reported in which the subject was told to make the sign of the cross after the lapse of 43334 minutes. In spite of the fact that the subject had forgotten all about the suggestion, the action was performed right on schedule.

In using posthypnotic suggestion, the mind is directed to perform a certain action at a certain time, and the idea is then dismissed from the mind; but, if the subconscious has been properly impressed, at the definite time (or reasonably near it) the action will be performed, although neither the thought of the time nor the idea of performing the action may have been in the mind from the moment the resolution was taken and was put on one side to make room for other ideas. In presenting "time-sense" experiments, the performer can use posthypnotic suggestions to demonstrate phenomena that truly savours of magic.

It is suggested to the subject that, at a time when a certain signal (cue) is given, a certain event is to take place. The moment the signal occurs the subject, who until then seems in a perfectly normal waking condition, will experience and perform the effect of the suggested event. As an illustration, suggest to the hypnotised person: "When you awaken you will feel perfectly normal in every way, but when I touch the lobe of my ear you will experience an irresistible impulse to leave your chair, walk to the centre of the room and stretch yourself. You will have no memory whatsoever of this command when you awaken from the hypnosis, but the moment I touch the lobe of my ear you will do as directed as an automatic and unconscious action". Awaken the subject, and shortly touch the lobe of your ear and watch what happens: he will respond exactly as you suggested in the trance and often will be surprised that he did what he did. Such is the nature of posthypnotic suggestion.

In the same manner, you can re-hypnotise your subject by the posthypnotic command that, when you give a certain signal, he will immediately return to the hypnotic sleep. This principle is used in presenting the effective stage demonstration of "Instantaneous Hypnotism" in which you tell your subject that, when you point your finger at him, no matter what he is doing, he will go instantly deeply asleep in hypnosis. The test can be performed with a group of subjects at the same time. All of the effects which may be obtained with a subject while in hypnosis, may be equally obtained with responsive subjects using posthypnotic suggestion.

Chapter Six
Questions and Answers about Hypnotism

Before you start learning how to hypnotise it is well to gain some answers to pertinent questions about hypnotism in general. This will prove not only pertinent information for yourself as a hypnotist but also provide answers to some popular questions others are bound to ask you. Some answers can even be incorporated in your show patter.

Q. Who Can Be Hypnotised?

Every human being who is mentally sound can be influenced, some speedily and others with repeated trials. The degree of influence varies with the individual. Some persons are capable of responding to deep somnambulistic phenomena including posthypnotic effects, while others will only respond as far as muscular catalepsy tests, such as "Hand Locking", etc.

On average, approximately one person in five may be classed as a natural somnambulist, that is a subject who has the ability to enter profound hypnosis on a first trial. Twenty percent of the population being somnambulistic isn't a bad percentage for the stage hypnotist to work with, especially when somehow somnambulists like to attend hypnotic shows and enjoy being hypnotised.

Q. What Constitutes a Good or Bad Hypnotic Subject?

First, it must be understood that being a good or bad hypnotic subject has nothing to do with being a good or a bad person. Factors of intelligence, sex, character, even emotional stability have little or nothing to do with it. In a way, the ability to be hypnotised and/or use hypnosis is a talent. It is the capacity to reach through to the subconscious phase of mind; of entering another level of consciousness with its own laws of operation uniquely different from those with which we are more daily acquainted.

Q. Does hypnotism weaken the will?

This question is a hangover from superstitious times when a Svengali type of hypnotist on stage appeared to dominate his subject, making it appear that they were weak-willed puppets. Actually the domination was more an illusion of the stage situation than a fact, as subjects tend to enter into dramatisation as they feel the performer wants them to react. Remember, always, that a stage situation is a stage situation.

As to hypnotism's weakening the will, will has very little to do with hypnosis. Hypnotism not only does not weaken the will, but through its clinical use it is possible to even strengthen and develop traits of character usually associated with willpower, i.e. increased determination of purpose, better concentration, more forceful personality and self-confidence.

Q. Is a weak-willed person easier to hypnotise?

Actually, not! The very factors that go into making a determined, forceful personality are the ones most needed for the successful induction of hypnosis. Generally speaking, weak-willed persons are those incapable of seriously holding thoughts sufficiently for the successful pursuance of any idea. As such they are poor hypnotic subjects.

Q. Can a person be hypnotised against his/her will?

As was mentioned in the answer to a previous question, will has little to do with hypnosis. Hypnosis is more an emotional matter. Expectancy, faith, belief, imagination and even fear are factors that are productive of an hypnotic state of mind. The fearful or scaring approach has been used to produce hypnosis in some instances. A forceful dramatic approach sometimes triggers a rapid hypnotic response.

The turn-of-the-century hypnotist Sydney Flower cites an example of how stage performers can occasionally make use of this principle to produce an "instantaneous hypnosis demonstration", as a timid subject comes on stage. He writes in 1900: "The fact is that fear creates a bewilderment in a person so that it is possible to drive home a positive suggestion swiftly and with such force that it is instantly obeyed, producing hypnosis on the spot.

"In such an instance, a subject will come upon the stage goaded on by the laughter of his companions who dare him to try it. He is filled with lively apprehensions. The hypnotist by reason of his experience can instantly detect such signs of fear in the countenance of the man. He knows that if he can catch him off guard and drive home a forceful suggestion he can plunge him immediately into hypnosis.

"Therefore, the hypnotist steps forward to the edge of the stage and as the subject gets one foot upon the stage, the performer suddenly claps one hand on the back of the subject's neck, which appears to the audience to be merely an eager method of helping the man up the stair. Actually, it has the effect of still further bewildering the subject; and, without giving the latter further time, the hypnotist brings the palm of his other hands with some force against the chin of the subject producing a sudden jarring. This has the effect for the moment of deadening sensibility. It creates a slight roaring in the ears, and the subject feels his senses reeling. At this moment the hypnotist sharply commands: "Sleep! You are going instantly asleep!" In many cases this method is successful, and the subject's eyes roll back in his head, and he is plunged into somnambulism."

Sydney Flower writes for another age. Interesting and occasionally effective as these impulsive methods are, they cannot be overly recommended for contemporary hypnotists. We live in a democratic age. People, in general, like the way of freedom in choice of action. In order not to give false impressions of hypnosis in general, the modern performer does well to concur with current public sentiment, which is to secure the willing consent of all subjects before attempting hypnotising. Such is the way in the Western World.

Q. Is it possible for a hypnotist to make a subject perform an immoral act?

On this question most authorities agree that a person's moral code under hypnosis remains unchanged. Just because a person is hypnotised does not imply they have become another individual in any sense whatsoever. What moral scruples the subject has in his normal state of mind he will exhibit under hypnosis.

Q. Are women more easily hypnotised than men?

Not necessarily. The sexes are about equal in their responsiveness to hypnosis. While the greater emotional nature of women can frequently make them somewhat more susceptible to hypnosis unless this motivation is handled properly, the very emotional quality of females can produce a self-consciousness that is resistant to suggestions. Men, on the other hand, tend to accept the experience in a more matter-of-fact way and often more readily comply with directions.

Q. Does intelligence aid hypnosis?

College students make excellent hypnotic subjects and they are certainly intelligent. However, it is not so much intelligence that is a factor towards hypnotic responsiveness as it is an innate desire to explore unknown realms. And the human mind is the greatest mystery of all.

As the famous physicist Steinmetz once stated: "The next great frontier for man to explore will be the depths of his own mind."

In relation to hypnosis it is the creative mind that is most responsive. Artists, musicians, actors, persons who visualise well generally make good subjects. Working with people of such nature is excellent for the hypnotist. But he must always remember to keep his show in keeping with the level of intelligence of his audience.

Learning How to Use
the Power of Suggestion

Chapter Seven
Initial Hypnotic Training

Having absorbed the foregoing, you are now ready to begin at the beginning to become a hypnotist. For practice, the first thing you need are people (subjects) to hypnotise. The more you practice hypnotising the more expert you will become.

It is not difficult to find people who are interested in experimenting with hypnosis, and who will be willing to work with you. In such practice be as professional as you can, and naturally do not mention you are just learning. Your initial concern is to train yourself in how to hypnotise and to train your subjects in how to be hypnotised. The three tests given in this chapter provide a good beginning. Perform the tests in sequence.

Test One: Muscular Relaxation

A good way to start is to associate hypnosis with relaxation. Comment that through hypnosis excellent relaxation may be obtained which is good for health. Explain that many people think they know how to relax while actually they do not. You propose a test to see how well they can relax, and provide a little training in relaxation.

Have the volunteer take a seat and raise his left arm to a right angle position in front of his chest; then extend his right forefinger and place it under the centre of his left palm. (See Fig. 7.1.) Tell him that he is to concentrate on relaxing his left hand and arm completely, so its only support is the extended right forefinger.

Figure 7.1

> NOTE TO THE HYPNOTIST: In this positioning you have produced a situation simultaneously requiring concentration and relaxation which is relative to the hypnotising situation.

When the person is confident that his left hand and arm is completely relaxed instruct further: "At the count of three withdraw your right forefinger." Count "One, two, three" and see what happens.

Figure 7.2

Figure 7.3

If the subject has correctly followed instructions, the moment he withdraws the support from under his left hand that arm drops to his lap. (See Fig. 7.2.) It demonstrates that he is able to relax at will. On the other hand, if the left hand remains before the chest it is obvious that he has not followed instructions and has not relaxed. (See Fig. 7.3.) In the instances where the subject does not relax and drop his arm on the instant, repeat the test until the desired response is obtained.

NOTE TO HYPNOTIST: The performing of this test is very important as it commences training the subject not only in relaxation but in following your instructions. Further, it produces a state of concentrating on one action while relaxing on another which is conducive to the hypnotic state. This test can even be used a first experiment with a group of persons on stage when commencing a show.

Test Two: Drawing a Person Over Backward

This is a "Posture Sway Demonstration". Use it following the first test in training a new subject in hypnotic responsiveness. Explain to the subject learning how to be hypnotised that another curiosity of mind is the fact that, when an idea of action is concentrated upon, it will realise itself in unconscious movements (motor responses). Psychologist William James termed this psychophysiological effect ideomotor action.

NOTE TO HYPNOTIST: Ideomotor action can be easily demonstrated by using a pendulum. Hold the pendulum (a weight tied to the end of a string). Hold the pendulum in your hand in front of yourself and keep your hand still while you think of the pendulum moving back and forth or around in a circle. Without conscious movement on your part the pendulum will commence swinging in response to the thought. The Pendulum Experiment can even be used as a stage demonstration in which each person is given one to operate. The results are quite interesting.

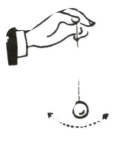

In using ideomotor action response to performing the posture sway experiment of drawing the subject backward do this: Have the person stand erect with his feet together. Explain that this experiment will demonstrate how unconscious muscular action will develop in direct response to thought, and he will feel an inclination to fall over backwards. Inform him that you will be standing behind him and will catch him when he falls. He is perfectly safe and is to allow himself freely to fall right over backwards into your waiting arms.

Advise that he is not to try to fall; neither is he to resist falling. He is merely to be relaxed and passive, and is to think of the idea of falling backward which you will suggest to him. Explain that he will experience a decided drawing sensation which will pull him right over backwards.

Now, request that he close his eyes and relax his body. You can ascertain that he is doing as directed by placing your hand on his shoulder, and pulling him back slightly. If he is tense, tell him to relax more. If he moves easily, he is ready for the test. Step behind the subject and place your right hand at back of head and your left hand on the left side. Tilt his head back a bit so it rests against your right hand, at nape of neck. (See Fig. 7.4.)

Now, in a low persuasive voice suggest: "In a few seconds you will begin to feel an impulse to fall … a sensation of falling right over backwards. Just let yourself go, falling right over backwards and I will catch you. You are beginning to feel it now. You are beginning to fall, fall, fall right over backwards into my arms. When I withdraw my hand from the back of your head, you will slowly fall right over backwards into my arms." (See Fig. 7.5.)

Figure 7.4

Figure 7.5

As you give these suggestions, slowly slide your left fingers from his forehead along the side of his head while you slowly withdraw your right hand from the nape of his neck. These actions amplify the effect of the suggestions.

NOTE TO HYPNOTIST: The words you give to a subject in hypnotic experiments are known as "suggestions" which are ideas that produce an unconscious rather than a conscious response. The correct way to present suggestions is to speak in a calm positive tone. Keep your voice gentle, but at the same time let there be no doubt as to your authority, and that you expect what is suggested to occur. To achieve this effect, visualise in your mind the reaction you expect, as you affirm with your words (suggestions).

Continue your suggestions: "Now you feel the influence getting stronger … it is drawing you back. You are falling backwards … falling backwards." As your suggestions thus continue, soon your subject will commence to sway, and will shortly topple over backwards into your arms. As he falls, be sure to catch him, and immediately help him to regain his balance.

Test Three: Drawing a Person Over Forward

Perform this test immediately following the previous one. The success of the former assures the success of this experiment. Briefly explain that ideas concentrated upon will affect the sense of balance in any direction. Request your subject now to stand relaxed facing you, as you place your hands upon his temples and he looks into your eyes. (See Fig. 7.6.) Explain that this time the influence will draw him over forwards.

Figure 7.6

NOTE TO HYPNOTIST: As the subject looks into your eyes, fix your own gaze directly upon the root of his nose, looking him straight between the eyes. This is know as the "hypnotic gaze", and you will find you can concentrate much better by fixing on one point rather than trying to look into both of the subject's eyes. As far as any observers are concerned, it appears that you are looking the subject directly in the eyes. You will use this technique often during the hypnotism show.

At this point tell your subject to concentrate on your suggestions pulling him over forward this time, and that soon he will find himself falling forward right towards you. Still resting your fingers on his temples and looking him squarely between the eyes, move your left foot back a step and slowly and lightly draw your fingers along the sides of his head toward the front, at the same time bending your body backward a bit at the hips allowing your two hands to come together in the front of his forehead in this action. Then slowly separate the hands, hand forward, and again place your fingers along the sides of his head repeating the lingering stroking motion.

During this forward drawing motion keep your gaze centred on the root of his nose and suggest: "Now you feel a drawing impulse causing you to fall forward. Fall forward ... fall forward and I will catch you." Your subject will respond. (See Fig. 7.7.) The test completed, help him to regain his balance.

Figure 7.7

NOTE TO HYPNOTIST: In all tests where you gaze at the subject watch the eyes. If they remain fixed and intent you can be certain of success. Fixity of attention is important in all such experiments. If the subject's eyes waver from yours, stop the test at once and explain that he must keep his gaze riveted upon yours at all times. Then proceed with the test.

These Posture Sway Experiments demonstrate ideomotor action. They show how an idea of motion centred in the mind leads unconsciously to motor action (muscular response) in the body, i.e. in this instance the presence of the idea of falling causing the fall, in the direction concentrated upon. The process can be used for hypnotic induction. (See Chapter Seventeen.)

The subject's own reaction to these experiments is interesting. He knows he did not deliberately try to fall over, yet he did. To him the sensation is as though an outside force pulled him over. This sensation of an outside force operating develops because suggestion produces an involuntary effect. The actual fact is that the influence which caused him to fall originates in his own mind and imparts automatic movements to his muscles producing the suggested results. Of such nature is The Power of Suggestion. Suggestions are ideas which when centred in the mind (concentrated upon) stimulate the imagination and lead to involuntary effects.

NOTE TO HYPNOTIST: You are learning how to skillfully use the power of suggestion and implant influential ideas into the subconscious. Learn how to perform well these initial experiments with the subjects you work with in practising the art. And succeed with each test you perform before carrying on to the next. Hypnotising is a progressive process of one success compounding upon the next.

Chapter Eight
A Milestone in Personal Influence

Locking the Subject's Hands Together

This test is of sufficient importance that a chapter will be devoted to it. Its successful mastery represents a milestone in your training as a hypnotist. Likewise the test can become a featured demonstration upon the stage.

"The Hand Locking Test" was first introduced to the public by the famous French pharmacist turned psychologist, Emile Coué. Coué became internationally known through his classic suggestion phrase: "Every day, in every way, I am becoming better and better." He is recognised as the father of autosuggestion, which is another word for waking suggestion and/or waking hypnosis. Coué performed the test upon every patient in his clinic and, if it did not work for them, they were dismissed from treatment until it did.

Waking suggestion and Waking Hypnosis are synonymous terms. Such refers to the state of mind the subject is in when the tests are performed. Perhaps the term "Waking Hypnosis" is the most apt, as, in participating in these experiments, the mind of the subject is gradually led from a waking state to an hypnotic state via a path that is easily followed. In learning how to hypnotise, perform this Hand Locking Test following your mastery of the tests presented in the foregoing chapter.

Modus Operandi for Performing the Test

Ask the subject to stand facing you and put his hands together with the fingers interlocked, as shown in the drawing. Ask him to push his hands tightly together, to make his arms stiff, and to think he cannot take his hands apart.

NOTE TO HYPNOTIST: The subject must treat the experiment with solemn seriousness, making up his mind that his hands will become fastened together. The experience is one that shows how, by concentrating on an idea of a muscular response, the response moves from a conscious (voluntary) action to subconscious (involuntary) action.

Now place your hands on those of the subject and ask him to look you straight in your eyes. Impress upon him that he must not look away and, should he do· so, command him to continue to look into your eyes. Meanwhile, centre your gaze upon the root of his nose (between his eyes) with a firm concentration, keeping the subject's attention steadily fixed upon you. Suggest to the subject:

"Squeeze your hands tighter and tighter together. Think of how tightly they are becoming locked together … so tightly together that you cannot take them apart!"

While your hands are on those of the subject, press firmly upon his hands to emphasise your suggestions that his hands are firmly fastened. Also, make passes down his arms and off at the hands. Repeat the operation until ready to give the suggestions that the subject absolutely cannot take his hands apart!

You can now remove your hands from those of the subject, as you keep telling him that he cannot take his hands apart no matter how hard he tries! Keep repeating the suggestions that his hands are fastened together so tightly that he cannot unlock them try as hard as he will. Suggestion gains and holds it strength by repetition. Continue the suggestions:

"Now you will find your hands are fastened tightly together. They are stuck, stuck tight! They will not unlock try as hard as you will. Pull! Pull! Pull hard! They are stuck ... they will not come apart no matter how hard you try!"

Give the suggestions in a forceful manner, throwing more and more energy into the process until the climax is reached in a challenge when the subject is told that he cannot take his hands apart!

Observe the subject's eyes as he performs this test. When you note a sort of "giving up" intensity of expression you will know your suggestions are sinking home. The subject will tug and tug and find himself unable to unclasp his locked-together hands. The demonstration having proved successful, you know unlock the subject's hands by a reversal of the suggestions.

After the subject has proved to himself his inability to unfasten his hands, clap your hands together making a sharp sound, and say positively: "All right now, the influence is going away. Relax. You can take your hands apart now!" Immediately, the concentration being broken, he will find he can now separate his hands.

Occasionally the subject's hands will have become so tightly fastened together that they will not separate even when you tell him to relax and take them apart. In such an instance, simply take his hands in yours and quietly suggest: "All right now. Just relax, relax your hands. I will count slowly from one to three, and at the count of 'three', your hands will come right apart." Then count: "One, two, three", and at the count of "three" suddenly clap your hands, and his hands will then separate easily.

Once you have learned how to successfully perform "The Hand Locking Test" on a subject you can proceed to performing other experiments which will be described in Chapter Eleven. First, however, it may be well to study the following two chapters as they will give you some depth of understanding of the Art of Waking Hypnosis.

NOTE TO HYPNOTIST: Naturally, you must not expect to influence every person upon the first trial. You are in training. Becoming an expert hypnotist takes time. Practice and perseverance are the roads to success. The more you perform these tests, the more effectively you will handle them, and the more people you will be able to influence. If you affect people with these tests, you can equally affect them with other more advanced tests. The same influence that enables you to draw a man backward and forward or fasten his hands together will enable you to accomplish many remarkable things. You cannot master these principles too thoroughly.

Bear in mind that the study of hypnotism unfolds the laws of personal influence. A man who sways multitudes by the charm of his voice and charisma is no less a user of the power of suggestion than is he who fastens another's hands together. Both operate under the same law. The study of hypnotism forms a remarkable background for the development of a personality that is forceful, dynamic and charming. Such qualities the successful stage hypnotist must possess.

Chapter Nine
The Art of Waking Hypnosis

Hypnosis can be regarded as an induced state of mind that is not sleep (unconsciousness), but is a state of mind of altered consciousness in which suggestions bypass the critical faculties of normal consciousness and automatically go into action.

When the conditions are right, hypnotic effects can be accomplished in the waking state without benefit of formal hypnosis. We will consider this phenomenon in some detail.

Hypnotic suggestion produces subconscious realisation of ideas (thoughts), which is to say suggestion produces its effect via the subconscious mind rather than the conscious mind.

The blanket terms of "conscious mind" and "subconscious mind", while popular, are a bit arbitrary. Modern psychology no longer tends to adhere to such two-part division of mind but rather prefers to consider mind as a whole operating in constant variation: sometimes that which has been subconscious surfacing to become conscious and vice versa. Hypnosis provides a means of causing this manifestation whilst under control. Actually, the influence of suggestion is constantly about us presenting ideas to which we respond spontaneously in varying degrees.

As an example, in a crowded room someone yawns. The yawn acts as a suggestion and soon many people will be seen yawning. The yawn comes not as a deliberate action on the part of anyone, but entirely as the result of the suggested effect. This subconscious responding to yawning can be effectively incorporated into hypnotising methods.

Experiments in Waking Hypnosis can be produced among people in daily life as well as upon the stage. These are interesting to observe: while on a crowded bus, during rush hours when the driver is under pressure and in a preoccupied mood, say to the bus driver: "An odd thing has just happened, you are unable to tell me the name of the next street." The driver does his utmost to remember the name of the street and call it out, but is unable to do so. Your unique way of giving the suggestion has temporarily produced the hypnotic effect of amnesia in this regard, all accomplished in the waking state.

It will be observed by the student that many of the effects obtainable in deep hypnosis may also be produced in Waking Hypnosis. Indeed, through your skill at using Waking Hypnosis will come your skill in presenting suggestions that influence which will lead to complete mastery of the art of hypnotising.

Here is another test you can try. In the presence of several people, crack and break open a perfectly fresh egg. Make a wry face and exclaim: "Whew, this egg smells rotten. I wouldn't eat it for a hundred dollars." Now pass the egg around and let everyone smell it. Some of the people present will agree that the perfectly good egg has a most offensive odour. Others will agree that it even looks bad.

Now these people have been temporarily persuaded into believing that the fresh egg is bad. They most certainly have not been placed into a trance, in any sense of the word, yet through these suggestions (via Waking Hypnosis, as it were), they are exhibiting, in this limited form, true hypnotic phenomena.

As you study hypnotism, you will come to appreciate more and more the fact that the state is characterised by heightened suggestibility and that the subconscious phase of mind can only perform deductive reasoning. That is, it believes and accepts without question whatever premise is presented to it, to which premise (suggestion) it reacts with remarkable logic, acceleration and lack of criticism.

Consider the case of "the egg that smelled rotten". You made a positive statement (a suggestion) of apparent fact which your hearers accepted totally. You by-passed their critical factors, substituting your own. Respect of your judgement caused them to believe what you said even before they smelled the egg. Psychologically observe what happened:

Having minimised their ability to judge the egg fairly, you asked them to judge the egg. They judged the egg, not with their own critical factors, but with yours. They were in a state of mind in which your judgement superseded theirs. You gave them an illusion that a good egg was bad, and had an offensive odour; others that the egg even looked bad. By this experiment you altered two of their senses: that of smell and sight, all accomplished in the waking state.

While you had not produced formal hypnosis in any person, you had definitely produced hypnotic phenomena by this application of Waking Hypnosis which clearly shows the close overlap of such with deeper trance states; such being of great use to the stage hypnotist. For in truth, many effective experiments can be produced on subjects without deep hypnotic induction at all.

It is well for the student to appreciate the power of Waking Hypnosis, as its application can be valuable in many ways in stage performances. Likewise, its usefulness can be applied in many other activities, as will be mentioned in a later paragraph. Here is another example of its effect as an experiment in daily life:

You are the boss in an office. As you pass your secretary you surprisingly intrude upon her preoccupied frame of mind by stating: "Miss so and so, would you mind standing and turning around just once? There is something about that dress you are wearing that puzzles me." You have here set up an episode that develops into Waking Hypnosis.

The secretary follows your instructions and turns about. You gaze at her critically for a moment. "Hmm," you remark, "I wondered what was wrong with that dress, now I know." With no further comment you exit from the scene.

Despite assurances from others in the office that her dress is quite in order, she will be certain that her dress is too short or too long, or too small or too large, that it bulges or doesn't bulge in the right or wrong places. And the longer the secretary wears the dress, the more she will question her judgement as to the dress's fitness. When her ability to judge is sufficiently minimised, she will substitute what she believes is your considered judgement for her own. With Waking Hypnosis you have implanted a suggestion so firmly that she will not be satisfied until she changes the dress.

And having changed the dress, she will rationalise her actions by saying to herself: "Well, I never did like that dress in the first place." But the rationalisation has no basis in fact. The suggestion you presented had a hypnotic effect all accomplished in the waking stage. Of such is the power of suggestion.

Let's consider a few further examples from normal life in Waking Hypnosis. A child hurts itself. It runs to its mother who kisses the sore spot to make it well, and the pain is gone.

In the summertime, you are enjoying the weather. Suddenly someone says: "Wow, it's hot!" and in a moment or two, you notice that you are perspiring profusely and are not at all comfortable. And it never occurs to you that the suggestions precipitated and brought on the perspiration. Waking Hypnosis.

You are a non-smoker and have been talking in earnest conversation with some person who has been smoking. You never gave the matter any thought until later someone remarks: "You sure got your lungs full of cigarette smoke that time. I don't know why you didn't move. You were in the direct line of a cloud of smoke all evening." Suddenly your lungs strike you as being congested, you taste tobacco in your mouth most markedly and you actually feel ill. The idea never occurs to you that you felt perfectly fine up until the suggestion was presented, calling your attention to an occurrence you personally do not like. Waking Hypnosis has produced its effects.

In every case, notice how the critical factor of the mind has been bypassed and a substitute judgement used. Here are the rules for obtaining Waking Hypnosis; the same principles apply whether used for specific demonstrations upon the stage or in daily life:

1. The mind of the subject must be locked around a given idea. From these examples just considered, the crying child with the hurt is certain that, if mother kisses her, the pain will disappear. The suggestion of the uncomfortable weather suddenly made you uncomfortable and perspire, just as your attention being directed towards the cigarette smoke that you normally do not like makes you feel ill immediately when prior to the suggestion you never gave it a thought. And in the case of the secretary, she is certain that the judgement of the boss is infallible in the case of her dress and is influenced accordingly until his judgement is accepted as being her own judgement. The people present at the egg experiment are certain that the first person who passed judgement on the egg was correct. They experience the effects as suggested accordingly. Waking Hypnosis. In all of these examples/ experiments, the minds of the people have locked themselves around a specific idea.

2. To cause the human mind to lock around a given idea, suggestions in this state (Waking Hypnosis) must be given with complete confidence and absolute assurance. They must leave no room for doubt. If doubt creeps in, the suggestion usually becomes ineffective. Therefore, present the suggestions in a manner that implies that what you have said is inevitable of happening as the coming of the dawn. Leave no room for doubt, and the power of suggestion will be potent.

3. For suggestion in Waking Hypnosis to be effective, it must be presented in such a way that the suggestion will be accepted without causing the critical faculties of the mind to be brought into action. The fine use of language (semantics) is extremely important to the hypnotist. It is in the way he phrases his suggestions and the way in which he presents them that his skill as a master hypnotist develops. Such handling brings consent, and consent is always necessary in any hypnotic effect.

Words are your major means of conveying suggestions to your subject. Words automatically release mental sets – learned responses of repeated spontaneous (unconscious) reactions in the mind of the listener. It has been said that the proper word spoken in the right way at the right time can change the world. As a hypnotist, learn to use words well and appreciate their power! Such is the real art of Waking Hypnosis.

4. For a suggestion to be effective in Waking Hypnosis, it must be one that the subject wants and/or believes possible, or at least doesn't object to. If you give a suggestion that is objectionable, the critical faculties of the mind are brought into play, and the suggestion will be rejected. Always try to present your suggestions in such a way as to play on the subject's wants. As an illustration:

Any person suffering pain wants relief. Such a person is apt to quickly accept the suggestion for alleviation of his distress, but resist those that would bring on more. Let the subject hear those words which he is anxious to hear. Don't tell him that he won't hurt any more as such brings critical factors to bear; rather frame your suggestions in this manner: "Now that you are relaxed, you will find that what bothered you a moment ago doesn't bother you now. Isn't that right! All gone! Now when I have you open your eyes, hold on to your relaxation and nothing will bother or disturb you further. Open your eyes and notice how good you feel!"

Such is the way of the trained suggestive therapist. And it works because the subject's mind becomes locked around an idea to which he is receptive. This applies to the use of suggestion as it applies to all conditions and situations you will meet in the conducting of your everyday affairs. Be positive and confident, lock the mind of the person you wish to influence around your ideas, and you will be successful.

NOTE TO HYPNOTIST: These examples of the operation of suggestion in every-day life can be used as interesting patter inserts for the stage hypnotist. They help explain to the audience what hypnotism is all about, and the more this is under-stood the more purposeful will be the performance.

Chapter Ten
Waking Hypnosis on the Stage

The experiments in Waking Hypnosis you have learned to perform in your initial training, i.e., the "Falling Backward and Forward Tests" and the "Hand Locking Test" can all be effectively used upon the stage. In such regard, here are some further Waking Hypnosis Tests that will be found useful.

Harry Aron's Arms-Rising-and-Falling Test

This test is one the entire audience can try prior to inviting subjects upon the stage to participate in the hypnotism show, those who found they could perform it well being invited to come on stage and experiment further with the power of suggestion to which they responded. The test is performed in this manner:

"This is an experiment everyone can try, at the same time, to see how well they can respond to suggestion. We will use your extended arms to show you how the power of suggestion operates automatically. Since you are going to extend your arms out in front of yourself in this test, everyone stand up. This will allow better freedom for your arms to move. Stand up, everybody." The audience stands. You continue:

"Now extend your arms out in front of yourself with your right hand turned down and your left hand turned up. Notice that your arms are perfectly even. Now close your eyes and concentrate on these suggestions." Wait until everyone in the audience has complied and all are standing with both arms outstretched in front as directed, and eyes closed.

"Now as you stand with your arms outstretched and your eyes closed, imagine there is a heavy weight attached to your right wrist, and that weight is so heavy it commences to pull your right hand down, down towards the floor. The weight is so heavy, down, down it pulls your arm. Let your right arm move downward with the heaviness you experience as you concentrate upon it.

"Now think of your left arm, and imagine there is a balloon filled with helium gas fastened to your left wrist, and as the balloon rises into the air

57

your left arm follows it and moves up, up, up. Your left arm is so light it rises up, up, up into the air."

As you perform this demonstration keep a watchful eye upon the audience, and you will quickly spot the persons who responded most forcefully to the suggestions. Many will be standing with right arm lowered and left arm raised. To end the test: "Hold your hands where they are and open your eyes. Look all around you and observe the variety of responses to suggestion."

You will find it will cause quite a reaction in the audience. Some will have responded greatly, others only slightly, and still others not at all, but everyone will find the reactions amusing. Let the audience respond until the murmurs die down, then state, while they are still standing: "Those who found they could respond well to the suggestions, if you would to like to learn more of how to control your body with your mind, I invite you to come on stage as members as the committee."

Many will come forward who responded well. Usher them to seats upon the stage, and you will have filled the chairs with suggestible subjects for your show. As they come forward, motion to those remaining in the audience to resume their seats.

Hands and Fingers Testing

"The Rising-and-Falling-Arms Test" splendidly illustrates the operation of the power of suggestion in a visual manner. A variation of this test is to have the subject and/or subjects stand with arms outstretched with the palms of the hands facing each other about a foot apart. Eyes are closed and it is suggested that the hands are magnetically attracted to each other, which attraction is causing the hands to move closer and closer together until they touch palm-to-palm, the suggestions being given: "Your hands are pulling together, together, together until they touch." The subject will soon find himself standing with the palms of his hands pressed together.

A miniature version of the foregoing test can be performed in which just the extended forefingers of the subject move together. In this, the person is asked to interlock and clasp his hands and extend his forefingers. This position brings the forefingers about an inch apart from each other. Have him keep his eyes open and watch what happens as you suggest that you are going to crank his fingers together until they touch. Begin making cranking motions in front of the extended fingers; sure enough they will begin slowly moving towards each other until their tips touch.

This stunt works very well, as the position of the extended fingers place them under muscular tension so the suggestion "they are being cranked together" is quickly followed. The stage hypnotist does well to take advantage of physiological conditions to aid his demonstrations.

Australian hypnotist Franquin uses the posture sway experiment to commence his show. He has the subjects stand in a row on the stage; going behind each in turn he performs the test. If the subject responds quickly he is given a seat on the stage. If a subject does not respond that person is immediately dismissed. This provides an excellent way to dismiss the worst and keep the best.

American hypnotist Dan LaRosa uses this process in a reverse manner in having the subjects stand at the front of the stage. He performs "The Drawing Forward Test" on each in turn with those responding being invited to go up on stage and take a seat, those not responding being dismissed.

A variation on the Franquin/LaRosa testing is to have the row of subjects stand before their chairs and close their eyes. You give suggestions that they are falling backwards to take a seat in their chairs. Those who respond are kept; those who do not are requested to leave the stage and watch the show from the audience. Always make your dismissals courteous.

Experience in the handling of Waking Hypnosis is of great value to stage hypnotists. Also, it is important from the subject's standpoint as it teaches him how to gradually respond to suggestion. Frequently it is really too much to expect a person to drop into deep hypnosis without some preliminary training.

NOTE TO HYPNOTIST: As a student learning how to hypnotise, in practising it is most likely that the majority of the Waking Hypnosis Tests you perform will be on solo subjects. But, as you advance in your training, the time will inevitably come when you will both use them on stage and with the audience to get your best subjects on stage. These group demonstrations work well for that purpose. Further methods to secure the most suggestible people in the audience on stage for your demonstrations will be found in Chapter Eight of Volume Two.

De Waldoza's Show of Waking Hypnosis

Danish hypnotist De Waldoza presented his entire show with Waking Hypnosis without once mentioning hypnosis, sleep or trance. His show was routined in this manner: The performance opened with the comments that the exhibition would actually be in two sections (without intermission), the first section being devoted to experiments in so-called mind reading and the second section to the power of suggestion. De Waldoza then invited a spectator forwards to blindfold him, and had the party hide an object amongst the audience. Gripping the wrist of the spectator, the mind-reader then led the man directly to the hidden object. The test was then performed with some other spectators, each being simply asked to concentrate upon where they had hidden the object as he gripped them by the wrist, and the object was found each time successfully. Such demonstrations are well known to magicians as muscle-reading (Hellstromism), a most effective feat requiring skill and sensitivity. Hypnotist Franz Polgar is another expert performer with this type of work. Likewise Kreskin.

Following these initial demonstrations, De Waldoza invited a committee of spectators upon the stage whom he offered to show how they could accomplish such a feat. First, each person was handed a watch on a chain to hold, and, as they dangled it in front of themselves, he asked that they concentrate on thinking it swinging from left to right. The dangling watch moved accordingly. Next they were asked to think of it moving around and around in a circle, which it did. The performer explained that such motion was the result of thought unconsciously producing motion in the pendulum. This will be recognised as a stage show application of The Pendulum Experiment mentioned in Chapter Seven under ideomotor response.

The entertainer then invited various members of the committee to stand before him and showed them how this unconscious motion could be transferred to movements of their bodies as he caused them to fall over both backwards and forwards. Finding an especially responsive subject, he asked the party if they could strongly feel the influence of the pulling sensation? When they confirmed, he told them now to follow exactly that same pulling sensation in whatever direction it might pull them; to follow it right along and it would pull them directly along to find the hidden object just as he had previously done. The subject was blindfolded, and an object hidden amongst the spectators. De Waldoza took his hand and asked him to make himself receptive, and just move along as he felt the pulling influence. The subject slowly began to move first in one direction and then in another, then gradually moved with more assurance and stepped forward, going among the spectators pulling the performer behind him, and found the object. The effect was electrifying. The feat was then repeated with a second volunteer spectator as well.

The committee was then dismissed, and De Waldoza gave a brief explanation about the power of suggestion which would be featured in this second section of the show. He requested all in the audience who wanted to try an experiment to lift their hands above their heads and clasp them firmly together, with their fingers interlocked. He then performed the "Hand Fastening Test" on the entire audience. Many were affected. These persons he requested to advance forwards to the stage that he might release their hands for them. People from different parts of the audience marched forwards with their hands locked tightly together above their heads, and each in turn was released and then ushered to a seat on the stage. Thus he obtained from the audience the individuals most responsive to the influence of suggestion.

From this point forward, De Waldoza made use of many of the Waking Hypnosis Experiments described in the next chapter of this book along with those used in a full stage presentation.

It was a splendid show and a fine testimony to what entertainment values can be achieved entirely with waking suggestion without once resorting to Sleep Hypnosis. It is truly amazing the extent of the phenomena that can be produced by waking suggestion. Most hypnotists are familiar with the muscular phenomena, but in addition all manner of sensory effects and alterations can be produced. Wietzenhoffer provides this list as examples:

1. *Gustatory effects*
   a. tasting of salt
   b. tasting a glass of plain water as sweet
   c. anaesthesia of taste for sweet (a piece of sugar rendered tasteless)

2. *Olfactory effects*
   a. smelling the odour of roses
   b. perceiving the odour of violets in a plain piece of paper
   c. smelling a pungent odour which makes the subject sneeze
   d. anosmia (loss of the sense of smell)

3. *Visual effects*
   a. seeing the colour red
   b. seeing everything in the room illuminated in red
   c. visualising a scene

4. *Tactile effects*
   a. causing an object held by the subject to become ice cold
   b. making the subject feel very hot or cold
   c. experiencing an itch

When producing sensory alterations, the operator need not restrict himself to one suggested effect at a time. As a matter of fact, by including two or more sensory modifications in your suggestions, one suggested effect may help in reinforcing the other. For instance, if you suggest to an individual that a glass of water is a glass of beer, you can reinforce this suggestion by also suggesting that he smells the odour of beer. Similarly, you can reinforce the hallucination that a potato tastes like an apple by making it also look and smell like an apple.

NOTE TO HYPNOTIST: In performing experiments in hypnosis of any kind, make it a rule always to specifically "cancel out" any suggestions which have been previously given. In other words, definitely conclude each test you perform and clear the subject of suggestion effects before proceeding on to a new demonstration. This rule applies regardless of whether or not the subject has given evidence of having responded to the suggested test.

Chapter Eleven
Further Experiments in Waking Hypnosis

Once you have advanced in your hypnotic training so you can lock your subject's hands together, you can proceed to try the following experiments in Waking Hypnosis. All make interesting stage demonstrations.

Stiffening the Subject's Leg

Have the subject place his weight on the leg you wish to make stiff, while you take hold of one of his hands. Tell him to look you straight in the eyes and think he cannot bend his leg. You perform this operation in a stooping posture, as shown in the illustration. When you rise, tell him to let his eyes follow yours.

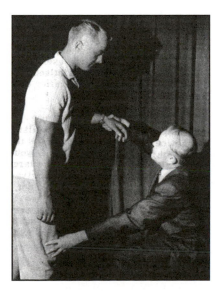

Now begin making a few passes down his leg with one hand, commencing about six inches above the knee and continuing downward to about six inches below the knee. While making these passes, state in a positive manner: "Now you will find your leg is getting stiff ... stiff ... it is becoming stiffer ... stiffer ... and you cannot bend it! You will walk stiff-legged!"

As you say the last words, rise. Keep your gaze centred on the root of the subject's nose, between the eyes, and pull him toward yourself causing him to walk stiff-legged.

After he has walked a few yards, remove the influence by clapping your hands together and saying, "All right. It is all gone now. You can bend your leg now. It is all loose and free. You can walk perfectly!"

Stiffening the Subject's Arm

This process is similar to that of stiffening the leg. Have the subject extend his arm and make his muscles tense by forming a fist. Take hold of his fist and pull it out towards yourself, as shown in the illustration.

Pull on the arm stretching it out as you affirm: "Your arm is getting stiff ... stiff ... stiffer ... stiffer ... stiffer ... and you cannot bend it try as hard as you will. Try. Try hard, but you cannot bend it. The more you try, the stiffer it gets. You cannot bend your arm!" After the subject has tried in vain for a few moments to bend his arm, remove the influence according to the preceding instructions.

NOTE TO HYPNOTIST: In presenting these tests in Waking Hypnosis, make certain the subject's gaze is always intent upon your eyes. You will find that as you proceed from test to test, as the subject responds to each, that you may conduct each test more and more rapidly. Often just a few sharp commands spoken in a positive manner will cause the effect.

Fastening Open the Subject's Mouth So He Cannot Close It

In this experiment, have the subject open his mouth wide, as you present these suggestions: "Open your mouth wide ... wider ... wider ... wider ... it is becoming stuck open so you cannot close it. It is impossible to close it try as hard as you will." After the attempt to close his mouth has resisted his best efforts, suggest: "Your jaw is relaxing now. Relax your mouth. You can close it now!"

Causing the Subject To Forget His Name

Stand directly in front of the subject, stare between his eyes, and when you notice his eyes become set begin stroking down the sides of his face and around his mouth, as you suggest:

"Your lips are becoming stuck fast together and you cannot open your mouth now. Your lips are stuck together so you cannot speak. Try to speak. See you cannot speak because you cannot open your mouth. Try, try hard! Tell me your name if you can. See, you cannot even speak your own name!"

The subject will try to speak, but his mouth remains tightly shut. Then move your fingers gently around his mouth and suggest: "Now your mouth muscles are relaxing and you can speak, but you still cannot speak your name. See you can speak now. Say 'Hello' to me (subject says "Hello"), but you cannot speak your own name; you can't even remember what it is!"

A sort of blank look will come over the subject's face. He finds that not only is he unable to speak his name, but somehow it eludes him, until you say: "All right. You can speak and remember your name now." He complies as a look of relief comes upon his countenance.

Stuttering Test and Name Amnesia

You can elaborate upon the "Forgotten Name Test" by performing it in this manner.

Select a subject who has been responding well to Waking Hypnosis. Have him seated in a chair as you lean over him, standing close to his left side. Suggest that his gaze is becoming fixed to yours. Watch his eyes and, when an expression of fascination begins to enter, ask him to repeat the word "MISSISSIPPI." He does, and you state firmly: "Now you will find you cannot again utter that word without stuttering over it, no matter how hard you try. Try, try hard, but you cannot say MISSISSIPPI without stuttering. You will stutter. MISSSSSSISSSSSSSIPPPPPPI. You absolutely cannot say Misssss-isssss-ippppppi without stuttering. Try and say it! Try hard!"

> NOTE TO HYPNOTIST: Present suggestions of this type with intensity, insist on their performance, and stutter yourself as you perform the test. Imitation is a powerful suggestion.

Once you have the subject started he will stutter all over the place on the word. Then softly say: "All right, you can pronounce the word clearly now. Say it. Mississippi … it is easy." The subject gingerly says it.

Then suddenly exclaim: "Close your mouth! Clamp it tight, tight, tighter!" Make stroking passes along his locked jaw, as you rapidly suggest: "Your jaw is locked tight shut, and you cannot open it! Try hard to open your jaw. You cannot do it!"

The subject tries to open his jaw and finds he cannot; you carry right on with further suggestions in this test: "You will find that you cannot speak even a single word try as hard as you will. You can open your mouth now, but you cannot speak a single word. Try! Try hard!"

The subject opens his mouth, but finds that now he cannot speak. You follow right on: "In fact, you cannot remember your own name now. You have completely forgotten your name. You can speak now. Say 'Hello' to me." The subject says "Hello," and you continue: "You can speak now but you cannot say your own name. You have forgotten it!"

Place your right forefinger directly in the centre of the subject's forehead and press in as you continue: "You cannot remember your own name, but you can speak now. What is your name? Try hard to remember it, but you cannot. Try! Try hard! You have completely forgotten your own name!"

The subject will develop a blank look on his face in realising that he has forgotten his own name. You can remove your finger from his forehead now, and ask him quizzically: "Just what is your name?" There is no reply. You continue: "All right, I will tell you what your name is." Give him some funny sounding name like Oswalt Flopper for instance, and repeat over and over: "Your name is Oswalt Flopper. What is your name? Your name is Oswalt Flopper! Tell me your name! Tell me your name! It is Oswalt Flopper!"

The subject will suddenly blurt out his name as Oswalt Flopper. Immediately clap your hands beside his ear and state: "All right. It's all gone now. You can remember your real name now perfectly. What is your real name? Relax and tell me your real name." The subject states his real name. The test is completed.

> NOTE TO HYPNOTIST: Observe "the confusion technique" used in this test. The success of one suggested response leads to the success of the following suggested response ... each compounds upon the other. Each part of the test leads directly to the next part with scarcely a pause between each. Your manner is aggressive, and the subject is kept under constant pressure as you forcefully pile suggestion upon suggestions.

The Hand-shaking Test

This test can be performed upon the entire group on stage at the same time. Face the committee and ask them to hold up their hands, allowing them to dangle from the wrists. Have them shake their dangling hands rapidly. Demonstrate this violent shaking of hands yourself, as you suggest:

"That's it. Shake your hands. Shake them faster and faster. Let them go any way they want to go! Let them shake and flop in any direction. Now forget about your hands. The shaking has become automatic. You cannot stop it! Your hands are shaking on their own! You cannot stop shaking!"

You will soon have everyone on stage shaking their hands vigorously. Now go to each subject in turn and bounce his legs up and down a few times as you suggest: "Your legs, too, are shaking right along with your hands. Shaking! Shaking! Shaking! You cannot stop the shaking!" Get all the group bouncing their legs along with their shaking hands.

Rapidly dash down the group, from one shaking subject to another, releasing each with a clap of the hands and the suggestion: "All right, you can stop shaking now. Stop shaking and be calm."

> NOTE TO HYPNOTIST: This moving directly from one suggested effect to another in a continuous flow is good technique. The suggested responses become associated with each other causing a confusion which amplifies each effect. Once you get your subjects responding to the various tests, you will find that just a command will cause the occurrence. Less and less formal "suggestion formula" is needed, and your performance will gather momentum.

Fastening a Stick to the Subject's Hands

Have the subject stand before you and tightly grip a stick. Have him grip a stick from underneath with the fingers folding on top, as shown in the illustration. Tell the subject that the stick is stuck to his hands and that he cannot release it from his hands try as hard as he will.

Suggest: "The stick is stuck to your hands. Try to thrown it away from you but you cannot. Try, try to throw it away ... but you cannot!"

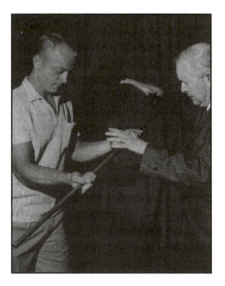

The subject's attempt to release his hands and throw down the stick causes an exciting drama. Try as he will he cannot release the stick until you state: "Okay now ... now your hands are relaxing their grip upon the stick and you can throw it away from you!" The stick is tossed to the floor with a clatter!

Making it Impossible for the Subject to Sit Down

Have the subject stand up from the chair. Tell him to look deeply into your eyes. Now tell him to make his legs stiff, and state: "I am going to count from one to three, and by the time I reach the count of three your legs will have become so stiff that you cannot sit back down try as hard as you will."

Count: "One, two, *three!*" and the reaction sets in. The subject finds that his legs have become so stiff that he cannot sit down despite his best efforts. The more he tries the stiffer his legs become.

After the subject has tried hopelessly for a few moments to sit down, remove the influence by clapping your hands and exclaiming: "All right … it is all gone now … you can sit down now! What a relief it is!"

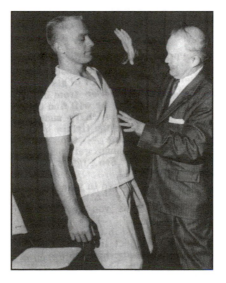

Making it Impossible for the Subject to Stand Up From His Chair

This test in Waking Hypnosis is the reverse of the foregoing. Have the subject look into your eyes while you gaze back at him, concentrating on the root of his nose. Tell him to think that he cannot stand up from his chair; that when you count "Three" he will find that he is stuck firmly to the seat of his chair, and he cannot get up try as hard as he will … that the more he tries the more firmly he will be stuck to his chair. Then say:

"Ready ... one ... two ... *three*! Now you cannot get up ... you are stuck tightly to the seat of your chair!" See the illustration:

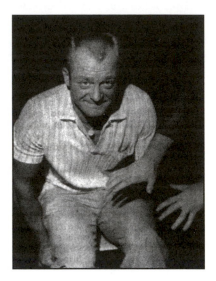

To conclude the test, clap your hands and suggest: "All right now, get up. You are released from you chair now. You can stand right up!" The subject stands ... the influence has been removed.

Variation and Amplification of the Various Tests

This is an important principle for the stage hypnotist. For example, when you perform the "Posture Sway Experiments of Drawing the Subject Backward and Forward", you can stand a responsive subject on one side of the stage while you stand upon the opposite. Face the subject and stretch out your arms to him, as he gazes into your eyes across space. Make pulling passes towards him and suggest: "You can feel a pulling towards me now. I am drawing you towards me. Take a step towards me. Walk towards me. Walk towards me. Come to me." Step by step the subject will be drawn clear across the stage to you. It is a dramatic experiment.

Another example of this principle of variation and amplification is in this handling of "The Hand Locking Test". Have all the subjects join hands together, and suggest that their hands are becoming locked together and the entire group is so entwined they cannot get apart no matter how hard they try. It is exciting to watch the line of subjects trying to get apart, as they mutually struggle. To end the test, suddenly clap your hands and suggest: "All right ... pull now and you can part suddenly and with a jerk!" The jerking separation is hilarious.

NOTE TO HYPNOTIST: Learning how to successfully perform Waking Hypnosis is great hypnotic training. Master the skill well. Then you can proceed on to trance induction. In performing all tests in Waking Hypnosis two principles should be applied:

1. Fix the subject's attention acutely on you to ensure his concentrating on the suggestions.
2. Visualise the subject responding precisely as you suggest he will. In other words, see it happening within your mind as you intend for it to happen, as you give positive affirmations for it to happen!

If you have succeeded in these tests you can readily influence your subject in all tests of such nature, such as fastening his hand to the wall so he cannot pull it free; gluing his feet to the floor so he cannot walk, etc. Your creative imagination will suggest numerous Waking Hypnosis tests which can be performed. These make fascinating tests for your stage presentation. You will learn how they are used when you subsequently study hypnotism show routining.

Learning How to Hypnotise
by Hypnotising

Chapter Twelve
Background for Hypnotising

You now move from Waking Hypnosis to Trance Hypnosis. Trance Hypnosis takes you into the realm of sleep which takes you into the realm of somnambulism. Somnambulism is the state of profound hypnosis in which amazing things occur which you can demonstrate on the stage.

Before studying how to induce Trance Hypnosis it is well to gain some understanding of the depth levels of hypnosis, the suggestion of sleep, the question of amnesia, the decorum of dismissing unwanted subjects, concluding the show, etc. This gives you important background.

The Depth Levels of Hypnosis

In relation to his work, it is well for the stage hypnotist to have knowledge of the associated phenomena of each depth level. It will increase the skill of successfully handling subjects on stage.

The degree to which a person will enter hypnosis depends upon (1) resistance or cooperation; (2) natural capacity or hypnotic training to enter/achieve the state; (3) motivation towards being hypnotised. To review these points:

1.   *Deliberate resistance of the subject to being hypnotised.*

The stage hypnotist can handle this matter by simply refusing to work with the subject who will not cooperate. There is little sense trying to hypnotise a person who deliberately does not wish to respond. In relation to stage hypnotism, this simply means the dismissal of such a subject from the show.

Hypnosis, at all levels, is basically a cooperative process between subject and hypnotist; subject willingness to being hypnotised being an important requisite.

Unconscious resistance to being hypnotised is another matter entirely. Such resistance can be based on a number of causes such as fear of being hypnotised, a dread of losing consciousness, a psychological "block" of one kind of another that makes entering the state of mind of hypnosis difficult for that person.

Such subjects can occasionally be dealt with by an intellectual approach, but the stage hypnotist rarely has time to go that route. Possibly a trained psychologist might have the time to remove such "blocks" in his or her office, but the stage situation simply does not afford that opportunity. Such subjects are best dismissed quickly. After all, there are plenty of good subjects to work with, so why work with those who are difficult?

2.   *Natural capacity to being hypnotised and training in hypnosis.*

Natural capacity for entering hypnosis seems an innate trait directly related to natural somnambulism. As you recognise, the person who walks or talks in sleep is a natural somnambulist. In definition, somnambulism is a state of mind in which an individual in the sleep state performs actions appropriate to the waking state. Natural somnambulists obviously make ideal subjects for the stage hypnotist to work with.

Approximately twenty percent of the population have natural somnambulistic leanings. However, that percentage can be much increased through frequently practising being hypnotised. Entering hypnosis can be a learned skill.

3.   *Motivation towards being hypnotised.*

The percentage of one person in five who can be hypnotised profoundly can be greatly increased through proper motivation to being hypnotised. The stage situation provides that motivation. That is why hypnotherapists and hypnotic researchers sometime fail to achieve the depth levels of hypnosis which the stage hypnotist does easily. Hypnosis on the stage is a fun situation which is largely effortless. We do thing best when we make the effort without effort. Further:

A reason the stage hypnotist often brings forth striking hypnotic phenomena is found in the motivation of the stage situation as mentioned, i.e. the bright lights, the music, the audience, the hypnotist's reputation, the expectancy of marvellous occurrences, group psychology. All are factors that bring about the deeper levels of hypnosis. In other words, the emotional charging of the stage situation brings about an emotional charging of the hypnotic situation. And most important of all, the subjects know it is a show they are entering into and willingly, without resistance, become part of the show. Such is why night club hypnotist Pat

Collins emphatically states: "If you can't be funny, don't come up." Being profoundly hypnotised is a matter of *letting go*!

The more the stage hypnotist can convince the volunteers they are in a safe place to let themselves go the more successful will be the show.

There are methods of scoring the depth levels of hypnosis. This Davis-Husband scale is possibly the best known:

Depth	Score	Test Suggestion and Responses
	0	
Insusceptible	1	Relaxation
Hypnoidal	2	Fluttering of the eyelids
	3	Closing of the eyes
	4	Complete physical relaxation
	5	Catalepsy of the eyes
Light Trance	6	Limb catalepsies
	7	Rigid catalepsies
	8, 9, 10	Glove anesthesia
	11, 12	Partial posthypnotic amnesia
Medium Trance	13, 14	Posthypnotic amnesia
	15, 16	Personality changes
	17, 18, 19	Kinesthetic delusions:
	20	complete amnesia by suggestion
Deep Trance	21, 22	Ability to open the eyes without affecting the trance
		Bizarre posthypnotic suggestions
	23, 24	Complete somnambulism
	25,	Positive visual hallucinations,
	26	posthypnotic
	27	Positive auditory hallucinations, posthypnotic
		Systematised posthypnotic amnesias
	28	Negative auditory hallucinations
	29	Negative visual hallucinations,
	30	hyperesthesia

By the use of this depth scoring method in relation to producible trance phenomena, the operator has a serviceable gauge of the depth of trance his subject is in.

Hypnotist Harry Arons has simplified this scaling by generalising it into six divisions:

1. Hypnoidal or lethargic stage
2. Light sleep
3. Sleep
4. Deep Sleep
5. Somnambulism
6. Profound somnambulism

The first three of the above stages are memory-retaining stages while the last three are amnesic or posthypnotic erasing of memory stages.

I have simplified this hypnotic depth scoring still further by citing only two divisions that are most practical for the stage hypnotist:

1. Waking Suggestion Phenomena (Light Hypnosis)
    … shifting of consciousness …

2. Hypnotic Phenomena (Guided Somnambulism)

In relation to this scoring, all phenomena listed on the Davis-Husband scale previous to Medium Trance (subject scoring of 13) and on the Arons scale of "3. Sleep" are regarded as Waking Suggestion Phenomena. I see no reason to hold differently than to simply regard all initial (light) hypnotic phenomena as waking suggestion (Waking Hypnosis); the phenomena unique to the trance state of hypnosis not occurring until a shift in the level of consciousness occurs and the subject enters the condition of guided somnambulism.

It is then, and then only, that some phenomena of the trance state become manifest in difference from waking suggestion phenomena, the dividing line between the two not being based upon memory or lack of memory, but rather by the subject's entrance into artificial somnambulism, which condition has capacities producible especially in that state of mind.

Hypnotism and the Suggestion of Sleep

Sleep is possibly the most frequently used word in the vocabulary of the hypnotist. It is classic and has been used for ages in the induction of hypnosis. This is so because the mind instinctively knows the pathway to sleep, as every night we go to sleep, and sleep leads to the subconscious phase of mind in which all hypnotic phenomena originates. In general, for the stage hypnotist the suggestion of sleep will be used more than any other, yet it is not absolutely essential to the induction, as normal sleep and hypnotic sleep are diverse states of mind, associated as they are. Possibly referring to hypnosis as entering the realm of sleep rather than going to sleep comes closest to the truth.

Psychologically speaking, sleep and hypnosis represent directly opposite states of mind: in sleep the attention of the sleeper is extremely diffused while in hypnosis it is extremely concentrated. Yet so closely has the state of sleep and hypnosis been associated through years of history (indeed the very word, hypnotism, coined by Braid, is derived from the Greek *hypnos*, meaning sleep or to sleep) that suggestions of sleep in relation to hypnotising are almost invariably given, and from the practical standpoint of the stage hypnotist the subject being asleep is almost synonymous with being hypnotised. Thus from both the standpoint of the subject's association and understanding of what being put to sleep means as well as from the audience's reaction to observing the phenomena, the suggestion of sleep is most important. So much is this true that most methods of hypnotising incorporate suggestions of "sleep" or "going to sleep" in their formula.

NOTE TO HYPNOTIST: Despite the fact that "Going to Sleep" is a powerful suggestion which the subject can relate to, it is not essential to the phenomena. Subjects can be hypnotised without mentioning sleep at all. The main essence for hypnotising without mentioning sleep is to establish some other causation focus that will motivate the subject to enter the hypnotic state. For example, the presentation can be along the Yoga line in which an association with meditation is employed. Or, it can be along the Voodoo line in which a state of spellbinding is suggested. During my years of performing in the 40s I made use of this latter approach, advertising as Dr Zomb. Such diversions of presentations of the expected cause of the hypnosis provides the showman with an excellent opportunity to make his show original and different.

Poster as used for my hypnotism show (1955) as Dr Zomb using a mysterious approach. Poster was designed for tour in Australia.

Hypnotist Paul Goldin made use of this diversion of hypnotic causation by advertising that hypnotism was not used in his show, but that his phenomenal performance was the direct result of the telepathic influence of his mind upon the minds of those who participated on stage. In such regard, hypnotist/mentalist Kreskin says there is no hypnosis, there is only suggestion, and presents his show under that guise. It is all a matter of presentation.

Hypnotist Dr Dean, in his night club presentations, uses this association with going to sleep most forcefully in his initial induction technique. As this is useful study for the performer desiring a rapid and effective method of hypnotising in such situations, I shall detail such a handling.

After a few words of introduction about hypnotism in general, it is explained that being hypnotised is actually a mental skill and that only about one person in five has the ability to go into deep hypnosis and be put to sleep. A group of subjects is then invited on the stage and it is explained that each will be tested in turn to see who amongst the group has the mental capacity to enjoy and enter this interesting state.

The group seated in chairs before the hypnotist are asked to concentrate on going to sleep and that they will now be put to sleep. Each subject is approached in turn and a rapid induction procedure is employed that is very direct and to the point, i.e., to concentrate their eyes, *to go to sleep*. Just as simple and direct as the suggestions are given with all the emphasis being on *go to sleep!"*

As the subject closes his eyes, his head is pushed down on his chest and the suggestions of "going to sleep, go to sleep now!" is emphasised. If the subject responds, the performer advances on to the next subject and repeats the process, quickly putting each in turn "to sleep." If a subject does not respond or resists the suggestions by keeping his eyes open or not seemingly going to sleep, that party is immediately dismissed from the stage without ceremony and the operator proceeds right on to the next subject; thus unresponsive subjects are rapidly removed from the stage and the responsive ones retained.

Now comes a subtle point in handling in which fractional hypnosis is employed to deepen the state. Obviously such a rapid process (except in cases of extremely suggestible individuals) produces only a light hypnosis, however to the audience the subjects seem very much asleep and the hypnotists proceeds exactly as if they were, as he announces:

"I am going to awaken you, one at a time, in just a moment … and then you will look into my eyes again; your eyes will become immediately very heavy and tired and will quickly close your eyelids and you will sink down deeply, very deeply asleep, *fast asleep*."

The hypnotist now goes to each subject in turn and suggests to them: "All right, wake up and look directly into my eyes." The subject opens his eyes and the hypnotist continues: "Your eyes are getting heavier and heavier very quickly now, your eyelids are closing down and you are going to sleep again, down, down more deeply asleep than ever. Deep down, sound, sound asleep. Sleep deeply!"

One by one this process of awakening each subject and then quickly rehypnotising them is employed. Should any subject not return instantly to sleep, this subject is dismissed from the stage as unwanted.

The hypnotist next addresses the entire "sleeping group" and suggests: "At the count of three you will all again awaken and will open your eyes and will look directly at me. As you do, your eyelids will close down quickly again and will return to sleep. Fast asleep; sleeping more deeply than ever.

"All ready, one, two, three, open your eyes now and look at me. Concentrate on my eyes. Already your eyes are becoming heavy again and are closing, and you are sinking down deep, deep to sleep. More deeply asleep than ever."

Any subjects that fail to reenter the hypnosis are further eliminated from the stage. This rapid awakening and rehypnotising process is then repeated two more times. The hypnotist then suggests his initial experiment (which is one of fast violent action) to the sleeping subjects.

Going to each down the line, one subject is told to stand up and sit down rapidly in his chair; rising up and sitting down over and over and that he cannot stop. Another subject is told to bend forward to the waist and touch his toes, and then to again stand erect and repeat the exercise. Another is told to toss an imaginary basketball into the basket over and over. Another goes shadow boxing. Another revolves his arms around and around. Down the line of the group the hypnotist goes until each subject is performing a repeated action of some kind. Should any subject not respond to the suggested experiment, he is dismissed from the stage.

Finally the subjects are stopped from their exercises and are returned to a sleeping condition ready for the performance of whatever tests the performer wishes to present in his show.

This technique of hypnotising will be found excellent for stage use (when you have a large group to work with) as it is fast and full of action and culminates in a series of many tests that entertain the audience. It is rapid and leads the subjects along from quickly induced light hypnosis to deep trance and finally into a response of violent physical action which, if successfully performed, prepare them for the performance of almost any type of test without being awakened from the "sleep".

Stage Dismissal Decorum

There is a divergence of opinion on this matter of dismissing unresponsive subjects from the stage. Some performers feel that it is best to allow the unresponsive subjects to simply remain where they are during the performance; concentrating their work with those who are responsive. Not infrequently it will be found that a subject who at first was unresponsive will subsequently become highly responsive. Also, such stage hypnotists feel that the psychological effect of subject dismissal, at the beginning of the show, is detrimental as it represents a sort of admission to the audience and the other subjects that the operator was ineffective.

I personally am of the opinion that this dismissal of unresponsive subjects depends much upon the situation in which the performer finds himself. For instance, if it has been difficult to obtain the group of volunteers, then to dismiss any of them is poor showmanship. On the other hand, if the stage is overflowing with more subjects than the performer knows what to do with, the dismissal of some will make little difference. Likewise the prestige of the performer is a factor in this dismissing of unwanted subjects: if he holds the respect of the audience, then whatever he does is accepted as the proper and right thing to do. Conversely, if his prestige with the audience is shaky, then he will certainly be wise to think twice before dismissing any person from the stage just because they do not prove immediately susceptible to his influence.

At all events, the decorum of subject dismissal must always be handled with courtesy and diplomacy. A device I have often used in such regard is to tell the audience, in advance, that I will test the subjects in order to retain the best on stage to demonstrate effective hypnotic phenomena, and if any are dismissed there is no offense whatsoever but merely an appreciation that they will enjoy the show more watching from the audience than participating on the stage. This approach works wonders, both from the standpoint of audience understanding, those that are dismissed and the subjects who will be retained on stage.

The Questions of Amnesia

As every hypnotist knows, many persons expect to be somehow "zapped out" when they are hypnotised. In other words, unless they "wake up" with a loss of memory of what they did while on the stage they feel disappointed and frequently state they do not believe they were actually hypnotised. As they express it: "I remember what I did and believe I could have resisted doing it, but somehow I didn't seem to want to."

Sometimes this ambiguous factor of hypnosis can be used as an interesting demonstration. For example, the hypnotised subject, following a striking demonstration, is aroused from trance and asked: "Do you feel you were hypnotised?" Often the person answers: "I don't think I was." or: "I don't know." These are truthful answers, for the hypnotic state can be bewildering to a mind not familiar with the state. What is amazing to behold is that after such a simple admission, when the hypnotist says: "Sleep!" the subject instantly returns to hypnosis and continues with further striking demonstrations in trance. The state of hypnosis is obvious to the audience, even if the subject does not know how to recognise his personal mental condition.

Amnesia is by no means to be regarded as belonging exclusively to hypnosis. Amnesia, in one form or another, is a daily experience for everyone. Who has not started to say something and had their mind go blank. Who has not driven a car down a freeway and then woken up to the fact they have missed their turnoff, having driven a considerable distance down the road without being consciously aware of the driving? Amnesia is a common mind experience and does not necessarily occur just because a person has been hypnotised. However it can be produced, while the person is in hypnosis, by suggesting it will occur. In other words, hypnotic suggestions to that effect can blot out the memory of what occurred during the hypnotic trance. Conversely, memory to hypnotic experience can be recalled by suggesting that it will be recalled.

Suggestion is the key to hypnotic amnesia. If you want the person to know what they did while hypnotised tell them they will remember; if you do not want them to remember tell them not to remember. This works most effectively, as hypnosis produces a state of mind that is hyper-suggestible.

Actually amnesia, according to most authorities, is not a criterion of hypnosis at all. Psychologist P.C. Young reports that he can find no evidence of spontaneous amnesia as a result of the hypnosis itself. Amnesia seems to be entirely a suggested effect, and he makes the following observations:

a. Amnesia following hypnosis varies greatly with the subject.
b. There is probably never total posthypnotic amnesia.
c. The extent of posthypnotic amnesia is a function of the method of testing.

Nonetheless subjects insist that they should have amnesia on awakening from hypnosis, and the practical way to satisfy them is to cause its occurrence as a posthypnotic suggestion.

> NOTE TO HYPNOTIST: I am of the opinion that due to the shifting of consciousness factor inherent in hypnosis that spontaneous amnesia does occur in some subjects (and not too infrequently). However it is a phenomenon that varies with individuals and is modified according to the expectation of the subject and the suggestions of the hypnotist. Likewise, the very suggestion of "Going to sleep" in the induction process is conducive to amnesia, as temporary loss of memory on going to sleep is a universal experience.

As a stage performer, I regularly conclude my show with these suggestions just prior to awakening the group and dismissing them from the stage: "You have had a wonderful experience on the stage tonight. In a moment I am going to awaken you and when you wake up you will feel just wonderful and well. And here is a very strange thing. When you wake up you will have no memory whatsoever as to what occurred on the stage tonight. It will seem to you that you merely dozed off to sleep and then awoke feeling completely refreshed. And when your friends tell you of the many interesting things you did, you will think that they are only trying to kid you. When you wake up, you will feel wonderful and well and will have no memory whatsoever of anything that occurred. All right, I will count from one to five now, and, when I reach the count of five, you will be wide awake and feeling fine." Thus awaken the subjects.

Remember, if you want amnesia you will have to especially suggest it. Sometimes it occurs spontaneously as a result of a presuggested and/or autosuggested expectancy on the part of the subject that such is going to occur, but this is an uncertain factor and is usually not sufficient. If amnesia is desired, it must be "set" as a posthypnotic suggestion.

As a stage hypnotist, it is well to always suggest amnesia, not that it makes your hypnosis any more intensive or effective, but, from the standpoint of the subjects being impressed themselves with the phenomena you have induced, it is important. I have frequently found it effective to suggest: "Like a dream, all the effects will fade and vanish from your memory and be entirely forgotten."

The living of a dream (somnambulism) is indeed very much like the hypnotic experience. There is a close simile here and these suggestions will be found effective.

NOTE TO HYPNOTIST: Relating the state of hypnosis to dream experience is sound psychology,as both hypnosis and dreams are subjective phenomena. Dreams contain the component of both remembrance and lack of remembrance, as the case may be. Further, dreams carry a tinge of the fanciful while still keeping within the bounds of the psychological.

On Concluding the Show

In addition to the above handling for concluding the show, the stage hypnotist can absorb his subjects in the performance of further posthypnotic experience that can be used as a climactic test. In this regard, I frequently use the posthypnotic suggestion of having the subjects' feet stuck to the stage. The subjects are then released, one by one, to return to the audience.

French hypnotist Paul Goldin makes use of an interesting posthypnotic ending to his show by suggesting that the subjects will see leprechauns hopping about their feet as they leave the theatre and that they will try to catch them for five minutes, after which they will all vanish and be gone entirely. This is interesting showmanship as it continues the show and holds audience interest even after the show on stage is over.

It will be found that such posthypnotic action combined with the posthypnotic suggestion: "You will remember nothing that occurred during the show" will produce amnesia effects completely satisfying the subjects that they were truly hypnotised. And if you want to be absolutely certain of it, tell the subjects, while they are in hypnosis, that they will know they were hypnotised when they come out of hypnosis.

If you wish amnesia, insist up on it

NOTE TO HYPNOTIST: Always make certain that a "cue" for a discontinuance of the posthypnotic experience is included in the suggestion, as one certainly does not want such as leprechauns tripping up the feet of persons for days afterwards!

In concluding this chapter on Background for Hypnotising, it is important to emphasise that the very factors of the stage situation that so readily produce hypnosis will often produce a hypnosis that is unstable. That is, unless continuously given attention by the hypnotist, the subjects will tend to drift from deep hypnosis to lighter hypnosis and even awaken on their own. The secret of maintaining continued trance on stage is to keep the subjects busy doing something, either of a mental or physical nature. This tends to stabilise the state.

Chapter Thirteen
A Basic Method of Hypnotising

You are now ready to deal with an altered state of mind, hypnosis and/or the induction of the hypnotic trance. The method given here is basic training, is simple to apply and concentrates on one suggestion of sleep. However, it does not produce sleep, it produces hypnosis. While the state of sleep and of hypnosis have become closely associated in the public's mind, technical analysis, via brain wave recording, show that hypnosis is actually more closely allied to awakeness than it is to sleep. Hypnosis is much like a super-awakeness, but in a limiting sense of what it is awake to, as such is determined by the suggestion of the hypnotist. Practice now this method of hypnotising. You will find it productive of a state of mind that is very wonderful.

The Hypnodisc

This method employs a Hypnodisc as the object for the subject to concentrate upon. This consists of a black and white spiral disc. It will be found on the following page of this book. Photocopy from book and mount on cardboard, then cut around the outside of the circle. It is ready for your use.

The Sleep Mood

This is a brief private session the subject does alone, prior to the hypnotic induction. It is designed to calm the mind in preparation for entering hypnosis. For this purpose, have the subject relax in a chair, close eyes, and repeat over and over mentally the phrase: "I am going to sleep. Sleep. I am going to sleep. Sleep. I am going to sleep. Sleep. I am getting sleepy. Sleep. I am ready now to go deeply to sleep in hypnosis. Sleep." Allow the person opportunity to perform this autosuggestion practice for five minutes before commencing the actual hypnotic induction. You are now ready to apply this method.

The Hypnodisc

The Hypnotic Induction

Step One

Have the subject take a seat in a comfortable chair, and relax back with feet flat on floor and hands resting in lap. Then use The Hypnodisc and hold the spiral surface facing the subject. Hold the disc in front of the subject above eye level, so he (or she) will have to stare upward in looking at it. Begin to revolve the disc in four or five inch circles before the subject, as shown in the illustration.

Tell him he is to concentrate his attention on the centre of the spiral and that, as you revolve it around, it may seem to start to spin and his eyes will go a bit out of focus. It will hold his complete attention as it commences the illusion of spinning. Continue revolving the disc before his upturned eyes and suggest in a low, monotonous voice: "Your eyes begin to feel tired. Your eyelids are becoming heavy, very heavy. Your eyes are becoming so tired they are getting moist … they are beginning to blink more and more. Your eyelids are closing now. Go ahead and close your eyes. Close your eyes and relax all over, and prepare to go to sleep."

As you repeat these suggestions over and over continue revolving the Hypnodisc around and around and around. Soon the subject's eyes will close.

Put the Hypnodisc aside.

Step Two

Place your fingers on both sides of subject's head with thumbs centred on forehead, as shown in the illustration. Now, move the thumbs slowly from centre of forehead outward over the temples, and repeat the process for two or three minutes. Keep the fingers still on the sides of the head, only moving your thumbs as you suggest with each stroke:

"Sleep ... sleep ... sleepy ... sleep ... sleepy sleep. You are going to sleep. Sound asleep. Go sound asleep. Sleep. Sleep. Sleepy sleep", etc. Continue these monotonous suggestions in a slow positive tone.

Step Three

As shown in the illustration, place the fingers of your left hand along side of subject's head with thumb of left hand resting on the temple. Leave fingers of right hand resting along right side of head. Now, move left thumb to centre of subject's forehead immediately under the hair line, and move the thumb down centre of forehead in a stroking motion until a little below bridge of nose. In doing this, keep right hand fingers still supporting side of head. Continue left thumb stroking downward from centre of forehead, and proceed to tip of nose. Repeat these processes for three minutes or so, while continuing the suggestions of: "Sleep ... sleep ... sleepy sleep", etc.

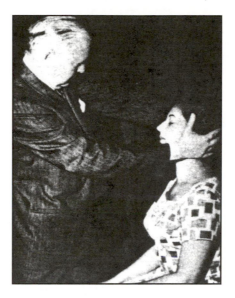

Step Four

Place thumb of left hand at root of subject's nose, with fingers resting on top of head, and make passes with right hand over back part of head down to base of brain.

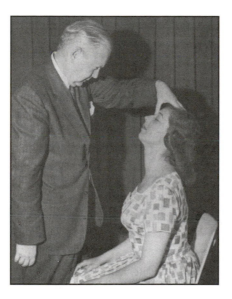

NOTE TO HYPNOTIST: All passes to induce hypnosis are made downward; those used to arouse the subject are made upwards.

91

Keep your left hand still maintaining its position, while right hand continues stroking down back of subject's head exerting a firm pressure. Continue these passes down back of head for three or four minutes, while suggesting:

"You are going to sleep. You are going to sleep now. Sleep. Sleep. Sleep. Go sound asleep now", etc.

Step Five

Stop passes now. Maintain same position with left hand, and repeat the following "sleep formula" in a low, positive, monotonous manner: "Your eyes are closed tightly ... you cannot open them. Your arms feel heavy. Your hands are motionless. You are so relaxed you cannot move. You are going sound asleep ... sound asleep ... sound asleep. Your head feels heavy ... your legs feel like lead ... you are so sleepy ... when I count 'three' you will go into a deep sleep. One ... two ... three ... you are sound asleep ... you hear nothing but the sound of my voice. You are sound asleep ... sleep!" You can now lean the subject's head backward and support it at the neck with right hand behind.

Continue repeating the "sleep formula" over and over for ten minutes. Some hypnotists continue it with advantage for double that length of time. At the end of Step One through Step Five, if the subject is not asleep in hypnosis, the work should be discontinued until another session.

This is a methodical way of hypnotising. It provides a detailed technique for your initial experience in hypnotising. In this practice you can take up to thirty minutes. There is no hurry in learning. However, you will find that many of your subjects will go into hypnosis in but a few minutes, in which case you can discontinue the long process of repeating the "sleep formula" over and over. As your results continue to improve, the length of time you give to each successive step in the process may be shortened, until you can accomplish all five steps inside ten minutes.

However, when first learning how to hypnotise, it is well to work slowly and thoroughly. Such will not only teach you more, but will also assure you a larger percentage of successes in your early experimenting. There is no need, at this time, to go further than inducing hypnosis. Now learn how to arouse (awaken) the subject from the trance.

The famous French Hypnotist *Emile Coué* the master of
autosuggestions who's self-hypnotic slogan of
"Everyday, in everyway, I am getting better and better"
is known throughout the world.

Chapter Fourteen
Awakening the Subject

Perhaps "arousal from trance" would be the more accurate way to express it, but "awakening from hypnosis" is the more conventional.

The awakening of the subject is just the reverse of the hypnotising procedure. It obeys the same rules of suggestion. It is important to awaken the subject pleasantly, so that he or she will feel even better than before the induction. Just keep in mind how you would like to be awakened if you were being brought back from sleep, and you will be on the right track.

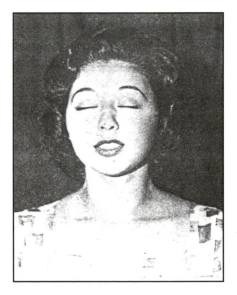

Just take your time in the awakening, and suggest it as a gradual occurrence. Some subjects may possibly "hang on" to the state for a bit, as they find it so pleasant. If so, let it be of no concern. Just take a little longer, and then insist it is time to come out of it now.

The suggestions for the awakening are handled in this manner: "In a moment, I am going to awaken you from hypnosis, and when you wake up you will feel wonderful and fine. You will feel good all over . . this has been such a pleasant experience for you. You will awaken feeling wonderfully refreshed.

"Now I will count from one to five and, by the time I reach five, you will be wide awake and feeling fine! You have had an absolutely splendid rest, and you're going to awaken in a few moments now full of vim, vigour, and vitality.

"All right, I am starting counting now ... and remember with every count you will slowly and gently awaken ... and when I reach the count of five you will be wide awake and feeling fine!

"So get ready to awaken now. One ... two ... three ... you are gently awakening ... four ... five. You are wide awake now and feeling *fine!*" Under the influence of these suggestions, your subject will gradually open his eyes, move about, stretch himself and will awaken feeling fine.

Note how gradual that process of removing the hypnotic sleep has been. How gentle and considerate it is. How the subject is "mentally set" for the awakening before it begins. He expects it. Notice how the process proceeds step by step. Notice how the suggestions are formed that the awakening from hypnosis will be a cause for feeling fine. Handled in this manner, the arousal from hypnosis will always be a pleasant experience for the subject.

NOTE TO HYPNOTIST: There is never any danger of the subject not awakening from hypnosis. Left entirely to himself the subject will spontaneously move from the hypnotic sleep into natural sleep and will awaken of his own accord just as he does on arising each morning of his life.

Chapter Fifteen
The Ormond McGill Method

This is my personal method of hypnotising that I have used for years. It will serve to advance your knowledge of how to hypnotise and give you additional techniques.

Have the subject take a seat and relax back. Take a position about two feet in front of him, and request him to look directly into your right eye. Indicate the eye into which he is to stare with a gesture of your hand. You, in turn, stare back at him, focusing your gaze directly upon his right eye. Tell him not to allow his gaze to wander, and to concentrate upon every thought you give him.

> NOTE TO HYPNOTIST: This right eye to right eye handling is effective, as it maintains a one-point focus while allowing you the opportunity to observe that the attention of the subject is unwavering.

The underlying secret that makes this method so productive of positive results is that, in its process, the hypnotist mildly hypnotises himself as he entrances his subject. Thus he experiences the same effect from the suggestions that the subject is experiencing and accordingly is able to properly time the presented suggestions.

Also, this process tends to place the hypnotist and subject in rapport with each other. As the hypnotist presents each suggestion series to the subject, he concentrates upon same in his own mind, visualising that he is projecting the sensation-ideas right along with the suggestive-words.

As an example of this handling: let's say you have come to the point where the eyes of the subject are becoming tired. You experience the tiredness in your own eyes, so you give and think your suggestions to the subject in direct relationship to how you feel yourself. Each reinforces the other. And, as you present the suggestions, you visualise a mental picture in your mind of what is occurring to the subject. With this understanding of the introspective aspects of this method you are ready to proceed with the hypnotising of the subject.

Suggest to the subject: "As you look into my eye, you will begin to feel a pleasant calm creeping over you as you release tension from all the muscles of your body. Relax the muscles of your head and face right on down through the muscles of your neck and shoulders. Every muscle of your entire body is relaxing, right down to your feet. You are becoming relaxed and calm. You are quiet and peaceful. You are becoming relaxed all over. All is quiet and serene. It is just as though a heavy velvet cloak were being draped over you. All is so quiet and calm."

As you give your suggestions, make short slow passes downward in the direction of your subject. Perform these in a sort of downward ellipse, starting with both hands in near to your face, then bringing the hands out and downward towards your subject, and completing the elongated circle by bringing your hands back again towards your face.

Make these passes unobtrusive, more to emphasise your subject's attention to your eye and suggestions than to cause notice of themselves.

Proceed with your suggestions: "Your eyes are becoming fixed ... set upon mine." Make a gesture from his right eye to yours. "How tired your eyes are beginning to feel. The lids are becoming heavy; they want to blink and close. How you want to close those tired eyes. But they will not close yet because they are set – looking directly into my eye. How your eyes burn and smart. How you want to close your eyes – they burn and smart. All right, let them close and get relief. I will count slowly from one to ten. With every count your eyes will get heavier and heavier until by the time I reach ten, or before, they will be tightly closed.

"Ready now ... one ... two ... your eyes are getting so very, very heavy they are beginning to close. Three. How heavy your eyelids are, you can scarcely keep them open a moment longer. Your eyes are closing. Four, five. Let your tired eyes close now. It feels so good to close those tired eyes. Six, seven. That's it ... close your eyes now. Eight, Nine, *ten*! Eyes closed ... all down tight together shutting out the light. Your eyes closed tight!"

NOTE TO HYPNOTIST: Time the giving of these suggestions to the manner in which your own eyes feel. Likewise, time in accordance to the reaction you observe in the subject as his eyelids wink, blink and droop. By the time you reach the count of "ten" his eyes should be tightly closed. If they are not, gently close the lids with your fingertips, as you suggest: "Close your tired eyes now, and let them rest."

Continue …

"How good it feels to close those tired eyes. It feels so good to rest them. They are shut tightly together, and are shutting tighter and tighter. So tight that they are stuck together. They are stuck so tightly that they will not open anymore. They are stuck shut together. Stuck tight!"

Place your right thumb in the centre of subject's forehead, and push downward towards the root of his nose, while gripping, at the same time, his right wrist in your left hand. Suggest: "You cannot open your eyes now no matter how hard you try. They are fastened tightly together. See how tightly they are shut. Try and open them but you cannot!"

The subject will try in vain to open his eyes; his eyebrows will rise and fall, but the eyelids will remain tightly shut. After the subject has tried to open his eyes for a few seconds, continue … "It's all right, just forget about your eyes … just let them rest … and let yourself rest … and go to sleep now. Just rest and go sound asleep. Go sound, sound asleep. Your eyes are resting, you are resting, and you are going sound asleep. So sleep!"

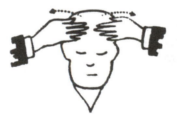

Now step behind your subject and make stroking passes over his forehead from the centre outward towards the temples.

Continue this stroking action, as you suggest: "Everything is becoming quiet and calm. You are so quiet and calm. You are so drowsy and sleepy. So just go sound asleep right now. It feels so good. Everything is fading away. You are going to sleep, down into deep sleep. Down, down deep asleep. Things are all getting farther and farther away, even my voice is getting farther away and, as it becomes more and more distant, you sink down deeper and deeper into sleep."

At this point, lower your voice and speak more and more softly, accompanying these suggestions of your voice getting farther and farther away. Then gradually resume your normal tone for these suggestions ... "You are going down deep asleep. Sleepy sleep. Sound, sound sleep. Sleep deep. Your muscles are all relaxed. Your head is getting heavy; it is falling forward on your chest."

Gently give the subject's head a push so it will fall forward on to his chest. Then begin stroking the back of his neck from the top of his head to the base of his brain. In this stroking process, locate the small depressed spot between the first and second vertebrae at the very top of the spinal column. Press firmly upon this spot with right forefinger. It produces a numbing sensation, as you suggest: "How numb everything feels. You are so drowsy and sleepy. So go to sleep. Sleep. Deep sleep. Your entire body is at rest now, so go to sleep."

Now place your hands in the centre of subject's shoulders (on each side) and press downward. Slump his body down in his chair as much as possible and suggest: "Your hands and arms are so heavy. So very, very heavy. You can feel them weighing heavily in your lap. And the fingers of your hands begin to tingle. And your legs, too, are getting so heavy. They are pressing heavier upon the floor, as you sink down deeper and deeper to sleep. Now your breaths are beginning to deepen. Breathe deep and free. Breathe deep and free. Breathe deep and free. And every breath you take is sending you down deeper and deeper to sleep."

Step back and observe your subject for a moment and note if the breathing is deepening. If so, it indicates that your suggestions are "taking hold". Next, step in close and place your nose close to subject's ear and inhale and exhale forcefully. Watch the subject closely at this point, and note that he picks up the rhythm of your breathing as his breathing becomes deep and full. Suggest ... "You are breathing deep and full.

Deep and full. Deep and full, and every breath you take is sending you down deeper and deeper to sleep. Go sound asleep. Go sound asleep … down, down into deep, deep sleep."

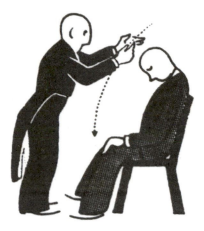

Move to the front of your subject now, and make long, slow downward passes from the top of his head to his lap. Make the passes close to his body but without contact. Suggest: "Sound, sound asleep. Sleep. See how limp and relaxed your arms are. They are limp like rags."

Pick up one of the subject's hands from his lap and let it drop back. Then push his hands from his lap, and they will fall limply to his sides. They dangle rag-like. Suggest: "Nothing bothers you in the slightest. Just sleep deeply and quietly. My voice seems very far away, and you are sleeping peacefully."

Pick up his hands and place them again in his lap, and press with your thumbs upon the roots of the nails of his second and third fingers, between the first knuckle and the nail. Make the pressure firm and even as you suggest: "As I press on your fingers you will go deeper and yet deeper to sleep. Way down *deep asleep*! *Way down deep asleep!*"

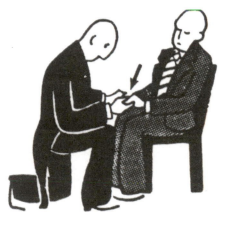

Pick up your subject's hands, hold them out free from his lap and let them drop. If they fall limply, completely without resistance, you will know you have induced profound hypnosis, and you can suggest: "Now, as you sleep, nothing will disturb you, and everything you do will increase the depth of your sleep. You will follow every suggestion I present to you. Nothing will bother or disturb you in the least, and you will continue going on down deeper and deeper to sleep in the hypnotic trance … asleep in deep hypnosis."

NOTE TO HYPNOTIST: This is a "progressive method" of hypnotising. The subject is led from response to response in a graduated series of suggested effects, ever progressing into deeper levels of hypnosis. Practise and master this method well as in its production you will learn a variety of subtleties that are hypnotic in effect. Likewise it is important to your subsequent work in entertaining with hypnotism.

Chapter Sixteen
The Relaxation Method

This is a subtle method of hypnotising. It is so subtle that frequently the subject is unaware that he is hypnotised even when he is. The method is performed entirely without suggestions of sleep. In fact there is no need to mention hypnotism at all, the subject's attention being entirely directed towards relaxation; yet a deep level of hypnosis is induced. If desired, the "Muscular Relaxation Test" described in Chapter Seven may be used as a prelude to this method of hypnotising.

First consider these two important aspects related to entrancement:

1. *Consent*. The consent of the subject (willingness) to be hypnotised is basic to the successful induction of hypnosis. This can be either a conscious acceptance or an unconscious acceptance. The operation can be summed up in the word, "expectancy".

2. *Communication*. There must be an avenue of communication (rapport) between the operator and the subject. Occasionally a subject can be hypnotised without a single word being spoken. If an understanding of the expected hypnotic condition occurring can be conveyed to the subject, the hypnotising technique can be successful even in

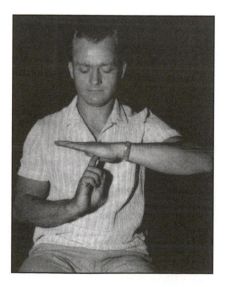

pantomime. This makes possible the hypnotising of persons who speak a foreign language unfamiliar to the hypnotist. Generally speaking however it is best that both the hypnotist and the subject speak (and think in) the same language.

Performing the Muscular Relaxation Test

You and the person you are going to hypnotise by this method sit opposite each other, and have a chat about relaxation. You comment: "I will show you a pleasant way of relaxing that will make you feel very good. The method is often used by doctors to relieve tension. The doctor would probably define it as concentrated relaxation of mind and body. It will make you relax and feel good all over. Would you like to try the experience?"

Obtain the subject's verbal consent that he (or she) would very much like to. You continue: "Okay then. As you sit in your chair right now, make yourself comfortable and relax. Let me take your hand for just a moment. Now, relax the hand I am holding as much as you can. Relax it so it becomes completely loose and limp. [Subject does as requested.] That's fine. You are doing excellently."

By noting the subject's response in relaxing his hand, as it rests in yours, you can immediately determine his state of mind in relation to following your suggestions. Insist that he become completely relaxed. When you sense that his hand is entirely relaxed, proceed: "Now, take a deep breath. Breathe in slowly and deeply. Hold your breath for a moment, now let it out slowly. [Subject does as instructed.] Very good. Now, once again take a deep breath, hold it, and let it out. It relaxes you. Now, let your eyes close and think of relaxing all tension from your body. [Subject does as instructed.] Fine. You are doing fine. Feels better already, doesn't it? Now, relax the muscles around your eyes; relax them so completely that they feel loose and limp. When you are sure your eye muscles are so relaxed that the muscles won't work, try to make them work, and you will find that they will not work at all, and you cannot open your eyes because the muscles of your eyes have become so relaxed. You are now achieving really deep relaxation."

At this point in this induction process, the subject has bypassed his "sense of judgement", which is his conscious mind telling him that he can close and open his eyes at will. If he should open his eyes, tell him that he has just proved that he has not completely relaxed his eye muscles as yet, as they still operate. Request him to concentrate further on the relaxation of those muscles so they become completely relaxed and will no longer function. Have him test his eyes, and if they remain closed proceed with these further suggestions: "Now that your eyes are closed and the muscles of your eyes are completely relaxed, you will find that you can now relax your whole body much more deeply than ever, and you feel wonderful. So extend that same feeling of your eyes relaxing down over your whole body relaxing. Just let the relaxation of your eyes flow down over your whole body. Extend that same feeling of complete relaxation right down from your eyes to the very tips of your toes. What a nice feeling it is to relax like this. You enjoy it.

"Now, here is something very interesting. When I ask you to, I want you to gently open and close your eyes. You can do this easily, and you will find that it will make you more relaxed than ever. In fact, it will make you ten times as relaxed as you are right now. All the other muscles of your body will continue being completely relaxed. Only your eyes will open and close gently when I tell them to.

"All ready, one, two, three … open your eyes gently … now close them … and relax ten times as much as you were before. Notice what a wonderful surge of relaxation this brings over you. Now, when you do that again, just double your relaxation this time, and you will feel as though you have a blanket of relaxation covering you from head to toes.

"Ready again … one, two, three … now open your eyes and now close them, and double the relaxation you had, and you will feel that blanket of relaxation covering you from head to toes."

Throughout this initial procedure, you have been holding the subject's hand in yours. follow with these suggestions: "Now, when I release your hand, it will drop like a limp rag into your lap, and you will be completely relaxed."

Release his hand and let it fall into his lap. You have induced hypnosis and are now ready to deepen the state by this technique. Suggest to the subject: "You have achieved a splendid state of physical relaxation but, if you can relax mentally as well, you will find it will make you feel a hundred times as good as you do right now. Here is how you can do it. When I tell you to, I want you to start counting backward, beginning with the number one hundred, and each time you say a number double your relaxation, and by the time you get to number ninety-seven, the numbers will have been relaxed right out of your mind. They will simply fade out and disappear, and you will not be able to find any more numbers. Now, relax deeply, say that first number, double your relaxation and watch what happens."

Subject says the first number.
"One hundred."

You instruct: "That's fine! Now double your relaxation and they will commence to fade away. Say the second number now."

Subject says the second number.
"Ninety-nine."

Continue on in this manner up until number ninety-seven. At this point you instruct: "And now they'll all be gone. All gone! You can't see any more numbers in your mind. You can't find any more numbers. They are all gone. That's fine. Now relax more and more with every breath you take, and notice how relaxed and wonderful you feel."

If the subject continues to count on backward from one hundred at this point, stop him with the suggestion: "You are doing fine, but stop now saying any more numbers. Relax in between the numbers. Relaxation will make them disappear. Now, I will pick up your right hand and drop it and, as I drop it, let those numbers drop right out of your mind at the same time."

Pick up his hand and drop it in his lap, as you suggest: "There, the numbers are all gone. The numbers have dropped right out of your mind. They are all gone and you can't find any more numbers. The numbers are all gone from your mind, and your mind as well as your body is now relaxed."

This process has placed the subject in deep hypnosis and has commenced amnesia, as exemplified in the "forgotten numbers sequence". Note that you have not stated that the subject could not remember any numbers, you have stated that he cannot find any more numbers. The fine use of language is the key to effective suggestion. Continue the induction process further by testing for increased amnesia as you suggest: "Now you are relaxed so completely both physically and mentally that if I asked your phone number you wouldn't be able to find it to tell me … would you?"

Subject responds with a shake of his head or a whispered "no". You have induced hypnosis with an amnesia response in this gentle way and you can now proceed to other hypnotic experiments from this point.

NOTE TO HYPNOTIST: In this method of hypnotising the entire attention of the subject is centred on the idea of achieving physical and mental relaxation. Hypnosis can be induced very effectively this way and, with some persons who object to the idea of "Going to sleep", which infers a loss of consciousness, the method will be found excellent.

Chapter Seventeen
The Ideomotor Method

This method of hypnotising uses ideomotor action as its *modus operandi*. It can be used effectively with one subject or with a group on stage. The method uses a conscious process of thought acting through unconscious muscular reactions in the body to induce hypnosis. The process is largely automatic in operation producing a sleep state of hypnosis, as sleep is psychosomatic. The very act of preparing to "go to sleep" spontaneously releases muscular tensions of the body so hypnosis can occur.

This process is presented in twelve successive steps. It gives the subject and/or subjects something to *think* about in each phase of the induction. All thoughts presented to the mind relate to comfort, relaxation and the pleasantness of going to sleep which lead from voluntary actions to involuntary actions, ultimately leading the subject into hypnosis. It is a circling method, commencing with mind affecting body and causing the body, in turn, to affect the mind, producing a hypnotic state of mind.

This is an easy method to use, as all the operator has to do is tell the subject what he is to think about, and the hypnosis occurs on its own. Objectively this is true, but subjectively it is not entirely, as throughout the process the operator holds in his mind the affirmed thought that by following the instructions the person will be hypnotised. This does two things:

1. It adds sincerity to the way in which the instructions are given.

2. It is the action of mind upon mind. In giving the instructions of what the subject is to *think* about, "see" in your mind each step, as an event occurring. It is Power Hypnosis. The method is applied in these successive steps:

Step One
Have your subject take a seat in a comfortable chair while you stand before him and give instructions telling him what he is to *think* about. Tell him to think of how comfortable his body is as it relaxes in that comfortable chair. Give him time to think about it. Ideomotor action starts in that direction.

Step Two
Tell him to think about yawning, and to actually yawn in this order:

1. Deliberately yawn. What starts as a conscious effort will soon trans-
    form into an actual yawn, as yawning is a reflex action. It sets the
    body in the direction of becoming sleepy. Complete the yawn.

2. Rest a moment. Think of another yawn. Yawn. Complete the yawn.

3. Rest a moment. Think of another yawn. Yawn. Complete the yawn.
    The mind likes to think in groups of three, as it is used to doing things
    that way. For example, (1) Ready, (2) set, (3) go!

Step Three
Hand a pendulum to the subject and have him hold it, dangling from his
fingers, with his arms outstretched before himself. Have him centre his
eyes upon the pendulum and think of it swinging back and forth.
Ideomotor action starts the swinging. In the event you are using this as a
group induction on stage, hand each person a pendulum to use. They follow your directions all together.

Step Four
Tell the subject that as he watches the pendulum swinging back and forth
he is to think of how tired it is making his eyes become and to close his
eyes when they feel tired. The staring at the swinging pendulum and the
thinking of how tired it is making his eyes starts the ideomotor muscular
reaction of the eyes becoming tired, and the subject's eyes will soon close.

Step Five
Tell him that now that his eyes are closed he is to think of his extended
arm, and how tired he is getting in having to hold it outstretched. The
physical fatigue of having to hold the arm up, accompanied by the
thought of how tiresome it is, will cause the arm to become increasingly
heavy. Ideomotor action goes into effect.

Step Six
Tell him to think of his arm becoming increasingly heavy, so that he can
no longer hold it up and must let it drop down to his lap. Think of his
heavy arm dropping down to his lap, and that when it hits his lap to relax
and think of going to sleep. Thinking of sleep starts the body going to
sleep.

Step Seven
Watch the subject as his arm falls to his lap, and when it hits his lap tell him to think of his hand relaxing and the pendulum dropping from his fingers to the floor. Ideomotor action causes the pendulum to be released from the fingers. When this method is used as a group hypnotic method, the line of swinging pendulums, which subsequently clatter to the floor, provides a spectacle. In presenting, lower the stage lights to blue and spotlight the swinging pendulums moving the light along the line, from subject to subject on stage. And it is fun to see the group yawn, yawn, yawn as the process proceeds. Even some in the audience will tend to pick it up and will yawn. Yawning is a powerful suggestion, as the mind is conditioned to associate it with relaxation and sleep.

Step Eight
As the pendulum drops to the floor, tell him to think of his whole body being relaxed as his hand is. Tell him to think of being relaxed right through his body, and of slumping down in the comfortable chair and going to sleep. Watch the subject as he slumps down in his chair.

Step Nine
Tell him to think of going to sleep and of his breathing becoming full and regular. Ideomotor action causes the response. Watch the subject's breathing deepen.

Step Ten
Tell him to think of his breathing slowing down in the same rhythm as he breathes when he is sleeping (his subconscious mind knows what this is without your having to gauge it), and to think that this sleep rhythm of breathing is causing him to go deeper to sleep in hypnosis. Watch the rhythm of the subject's breathing as it changes to the rhythm of sleep.

Step Eleven
Tell him to think of himself slipping and sliding down and down ever deeper into hypnosis … down and down into profound hypnosis. Ideomotor action produces sleep in this instance, hypnotic sleep, as that is the basic "mental set" to which the person is responding.

Step Twelve
Tell the subject to think he is in profound hypnosis, and that his mind and body are open to respond to all suggestions given. Take your time in using The Ideomotor Method of Hypnotising. At each step allow the subject full time to think of the physical processes his body is going through. Allow the reaction of each step to set in before going on to the next step. By so doing the climactic result will be to have your subject in deep

hypnosis and receptive to respond to whatever demonstrations you elect to present. The suggestions are presented in the same manner as the instructions in the induction. He is to think of them as occurring.

Hypnotism fun on the stage

Chapter Eighteen

The Master Method of Hypnotism

I wrote and published this method of hypnotising back in 1949 during my show business days as Dr Zomb. It was developed out of the necessity to have a method that would effectively produce profound hypnosis (somnambulism) in young women so they could sleep in a store window for hours without disturbance in performing the "Window Sleep" as a publicity feature of the show. The technique proved uniformly successful. I give it to you in detail for your study. The method employs four basic step: the **interview**, the **induction**, the **awakening**, the **rehypnotisation**.

The Interview

Seating yourself opposite the person who has volunteered to be hypnotised, explain to him (or her) that the process of being hypnotised is not mysterious, that any intelligent person can easily enter hypnosis, and that it will seem to be, as far as the experiencing is concerned, just another way of going to sleep exactly the same as they do every night of their life; only in this case they go to sleep by the deliberate concentration on ideas of sleep rather than by the usual process of going to bed.

Next, ask your subject if he has ever been tired and dozed off to sleep in a chair or on a couch? Most people have so, when he affirms, say that this experience of being hypnotised will be exactly the same; all he is going to do is simply to doze off to sleep, the only difference being that when he dozed off before he was physically tired, while, in this instance, you will make him tired and sleepy by having him concentrate on ideas of tiredness and sleepiness until he gently dozes off to sleep in his chair.

> NOTE TO HYPNOTIST: The psychological handling of the interview is highly significant: it removes the fear from the hypnotising experience and associates it with a familiar process.

In learning the method, read the text and study the photographs.

The Induction

Now, ask your subject to sit back comfortably in his chair, place his feet flat on the floor, rest his hands on his knees, and to concentrate his entire attention on your eyes. (The eyes are recommended as the "fixation object" to be employed in this hypnotising method because of their reputation and natural convenience. Used as here described, they will be found extremely effective.) You stand directly before your subject and gaze back intently into his eyes, but do not focus your gaze upon his eyes; rather look through him, focusing your eyes on an imaginary point about five feet behind his head. You will find this hypnotic gazing technique very compelling in holding the subject's attention, and yet it is not fatiguing to your own eyes.

Having captured the subject's attention, start your flow of suggestions and, as you speak, make gentle passes downwards in the direction of your subject. Perform these in a sort of downward ellipse, starting with both hands near your face, then bringing them out and downward towards the subject, completing the elongated circle by bringing your hands back again towards your face. Make these passes unobtrusive, more to emphasise the subject's attention to your eyes and suggestions than to cause notice of themselves.

Now suggest: "Just relax back in your chair, let every muscle of your body be completely at rest and keep your attention concentrated on my eyes … and forget about everything else except the one desire to go to sleep. Everything is beginning to feel so very, very comfortable. It just seems so good to thus relax and let everything go. Your whole body seems so warm and comfortable … and, as the pleasant warmth begins to penetrate through every muscle of your body, you are relaxing back more and more comfortably and pleasantly in your chair. Everything is so very pleasant, comfortable and warm."

NOTE TO THE HYPNOTIST: Notice how the suggestions up to this point concentrate entirely on bodily comfort, relaxation and pleasant repose.

"Now, as you relax back in your chair, your gaze is getting more and more concentrated on my eyes, and your eyes are beginning to become very, very heavy and tired. It is hard to keep those eyelids open; they are so very, very heavy and tired, but they won't close yet because you are concentrating so powerfully upon my eyes. But now though, as I count slowly from one to ten, they will begin to close. Close your eyelids anytime you wish as I count slowly from one to ten, shutting out the light. One … two! How very heavy and tired your eyes are. How they burn. They are so tired. So very, very tired. Three! Close them now, shutting out the light. Four! The eyelids feel just like lead. Like lead. Close them tight now shutting out the light, letting them rest. Five! Six! Eyes closing right down tightly together. Close them tight. That's it. Eyes all closed, shutting out the light. Eyelids closed tight together. Eight! It feels so good to just close those tired, tired eyes, and let everything be just quiet and dark. Nine! Ten! Eyes all closed tight together now, everything is all quiet and dark."

NOTE TO HYPNOTIST: Note how this section of the "sleep formula" concentrates on the closing of the eyelids. Most subjects will have their eyes closed by the time you reach the count of five, and almost invariably all persons by the time you reach the count of ten. Should it ever happen that your subject does not have his eyes closed by the last count, merely lean slowly forward, and with your fingertips gently touch the eyelids and close them down.

"Eyes all closed in darkness now. Now, go to sleep. Go deep asleep. Everything is gently drifting and floating gently by, and you are sinking on down, down, down deep to sleep. You are just floating and drifting gently as though on a cloud, and you are sinking on down, down, down gently to sleep. Go to sleep! Go deep, deep to sleep. How tired you are; every muscle in your body just calls for sleep ... wonderful, restful sleep that will take away every tiredness. How tired you are, so tired, so very, very tired. You need sleep so badly . . wonderful, restful sleep. So go to sleep! Go fast, fast asleep! You can feel that wonderful rest and relaxation creeping through your entire body, and you are drifting ... drifting ... and floating on down, down to deep, sound, wonderful sleep. Everything is just fading, fading, fading far, far away, down into deep, wonderful, peaceful sleep."

> NOTE TO HYPNOTIST: Notice how the suggestion in this phase of the induction concentrates on release from all tiredness and the peace and rest that can be found in sleep. Now comes a very important bit of technique: standing at the side of your subject, whisper your suggestion directly into his ear.

"Go deep asleep now! That's it, go deep asleep! Sound, sound asleep! You are sinking on down and down into a deep, sound sleep. Go deep asleep now! Go sound asleep! You are breathing deeply. You are breathing deep and free. Breathe deep and free. Your breaths are coming in deeper and deeper, and every breath you take is sending you on down deeper and deeper to sleep."

Watch your subject carefully at this point. If his breathing begins to deepen in response to your suggestions you can begin to gauge the depth of the hypnosis that is starting to develop. Stand up now and speak while standing behind your subject: "nothing can disturb you. All is so quiet and calm. Breathe deeply and go deeply to sleep. Your muscles are all so very relaxed that your head is beginning to get very, very heavy ... so

heavy it is nodding forward onto your chest. Your head is nodding forward … it is falling forwards onto your chest."

Watch your subject's head: if it nods and falls limply forward onto his chest, proceed right on … Otherwise continue longer with your suggestions of sleep and relaxation and gently push his head forward onto his chest. Then place your hands, one on each side of his shoulders, at the sides of the neck, and push down firmly so his body tends to slump down into the chair.

Next exert pressure, with your right forefinger, between the top two vertebrae; these are easily located as they stand out prominently due to the bent forward position of the subject's neck. as you thus press firmly, forcefully suggest: "Go to sleep now! Go fast, fast asleep!"

Next, place the tip of your right forefinger directly on the bridge of the hypnotised subject's nose and press in firmly as you continue to forcefully suggest: "Go to sleep! Go deep, deep to sleep!"

Now take the subject's hand in your and press firmly on the base of the nails of the first two fingers of his hands, and forcefully suggest: "Sleep! Sleep! Go deep to sleep!"

In this technique, you are making use of pressure upon the so called hypnogenic zones, and the suggestions given, at this time, should be commanding and forceful. You are now ready to apply a most effective bit of technique. Suggest: "Your jaw is slackening now. The muscles of your face and jaw are relaxing completely. Open your mouth just a bit. That's it. Open your mouth … just a bit."

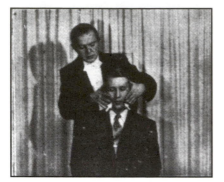 

As you give these suggestions, run your fingers gently down each side of the subject's jaw and continue your commands until you get the desired response and the jaw hangs slackly open.

"Keep your mouth gently open now and inhale very slowly a deep, deep breath. Inhale now ... that's it ... a deep, deep breath. Now hold it. Hold it! Hold it! Now exhale slowly, very, very slowly. Slowly, slowly exhale, exhale. Inhale now, inhale deeply, very deeply. Hold it! Hold it! Now exhale slowly, very slowly. How sleepy you are becoming, how very, very sleepy. Go deep, deep to sleep. All right now, inhale again; inhale deeply. Hold it, and now exhale very slowly. Exhale very, very slowly ... and go deep, deep to sleep. Inhale ... that's it. Now exhale ... and go deep, deep to sleep. And again, inhale deep, deep, very deep ... hold it ... and go to sleep as you exhale so very, very slowly. Go deep, deep, deep asleep."

You have employed a technique here that is physically sleep inducing and combined with your suggestions is virtually irresistible. Stop your commands of deliberate inhaling and exhaling at this point and watch your subject closely. In many cases, the deep breathing will continue on automatically. Continue the suggestions: "Sleep, deep now. Wonderful restful sleep is all that matters. Nothing can disturb you or bother you in any way. Nothing can awaken you. Every breath you take is sending you on down deeper and deeper to sleep. Breathe deep and free, and go sound to sleep. Deep, deep asleep."

Notice that emphasis at this stage of the induction has been concentrated on the breath control of the subject. Your subject should by now be thoroughly relaxed. Slumped down in his chair with head resting limply on chest and his breathing coming in slow and deep, to every appearance deep asleep. You are ready now to commence some physical stimuli and muscular responses.

"A warm sensation is coming into your body, and you can feel a tingling in your fingertips. A tingling exactly how the nerves feel when they go to sleep in your hand. That tingling is becoming very strong. Now, it is passing up from your fingers over your hands and on up your arms, and you are going deeper and deeper to sleep. Go deep, deep to sleep! Now, your fingertips on your lap are becoming very, very restless. It is hard to keep them still, they are getting so restless. They want to move up from your lap. Your hands are becoming very, very light … they are lifting right up from your lap into the air. Raise your hands right up from your lap into the air. Raise them up. That's it! The muscles are automatically pulling them up. Up! Up! Right up from your lap into the air. Now, your hands are moving up to touch your forehead. Touch your forehead with your hands. And when your hands touch your forehead you will be sound, sound asleep in deep hypnosis. Sound asleep. Touch your forehead now with your hands and sleep … sleep in deep sound sleep."

Notice in this phase of the induction you are testing for a direct hypnotic response, and the quality of same will indicate the depth of trance you have induced thus far. Whatever the response, keep your suggestions continuous until the subject's hands leave his knees and eventually reach his forehead. You have an important bit of technique here that bridges often the difficult boundary between normal consciousness and complete hypnosis.

Remember to always force these movement responses. If your subject resists movement of his hands and arms as you command, then gently lift his hands up and get them started in their movements; on releasing the hands they will then continue on of their own volition.

This is the vital secret of hypnotising difficult subjects: when they do not respond automatically, then you must force somnambulist. Once you have your subject's hands touching his forehead, suggest, "Sleep deeply now, and when I say three, your hands will fall limp as rags to your sides and you will be fast, fast asleep. One, two, *three*."

Here is another splendid indicator of your subject's depth of trance. If his responses are positive and immediate, you can proceed rapidly. If slow, uncertain or sluggish, then retard your technique and continue with repetitions of the suggestions you have employed up to this point: always build towards quick, spontaneous and automatic responses to your hypnotic commands.

Next, take the subject's right hand in yours and start it revolving around and around in a large circle (see illustration overleaf). With every

119

revolution suggest: "You are going deeper and deeper to sleep. You are deep, deep asleep. You are fast, fast asleep. Deep, deep asleep. Fast, fast asleep. Deep, deep asleep. Fast, fast asleep. You are deep, deep asleep"

Let go of his arm now and it will continue revolving of its own volition. You can use this revolving arm indicator to judge how best to present hypnotic suggestions to your subject from this point onward, i.e., if the arm continues revolving on around and around by itself, when you release your grip, you can feel assured that you have induced deep trance, and are working with a spontaneous type of subject from whom you can secure hypnotic responses with very brief commands. If the subject's arm continues on revolving after you release your grip, as the result of your verbal command to that effect, it is indicative that his subject is best handled through repetition and careful understanding of all command. If the subject still does not respond, it indicates that you are working with either a lethargic type of person or that the trance is not yet deeply enough established for the following of hypnotic command: in which case, patiently continue with your previous sleep developing suggestions until you get the desired reactions. Follow with your suggestions: "Your arm is revolving around and around by itself … nothing can stop it, and you are deep, deep asleep. Your arm is beginning to get heavy now; it is falling down to your side. Falling to your side … limp as a rag. You are deep, deep asleep."

Your subject's arm will fall to his side almost at once and will dangle limply. Stand behind the subject now and start revolving his head around and around and around, move it first over to the right side, then on around to the front, the left side, back, right side again and so on. Continue on moving it around and around and around and then gently remove your hands and it will continue on its circular movement of its own volition. Sit back quietly for a few moments and watch the head in its revolutions … And then suggest: "Sleep deep now. Sleep deep and sound in a complete and dreamless sleep. You will follow perfectly every suggestion I present to you. Sleep deep now! Your head is stopping its rotations and is coming to rest comfortably on your chest. Sleep deep now and follow perfectly my every suggestion."

Take your subject's arm and hold it outstretched as you command that it is stiff in that position and cannot be bent. All of the subject's efforts to move his arm will prove in vain. Command the arm to drop, and it instantly falls to his side. Your subject is entranced now in the somnambulistic condition of hypnosis and will follow your hypnotic commands.

Strive next to deepen this somnambulistic condition by directly developing a sensory response. Suggest: "It is beginning to get very warm in this room. It is getting so very, very warm that you are becoming uncomfortable. It is becoming positively hot in this room; it is so warm and so hot, that you are very, very uncomfortable. The heat is making you very restless. You are beginning to squirm about in your chair; you are so hot and uncomfortable. You are so hot and uncomfortable. Wipe away the perspiration from your forehead; wipe away the perspiration from your forehead and relieve that heat."

Carefully watch your subject's responses: continually barrage with repetition of your suggestions, and get the subject to react as freely and spontaneously as you possible can.

"It is so hot in that chair that you want to stand up from it and get cool. Stand up from your chair now and get cool. Stand up from your chair now and get cool. That's it, stand up and get cool."

When you have your subject standing, suggest: "Ah, it is so nice and cool now that you are standing. All is so nice and cool. All of the heat is gone now, it is so nice and cool, and you are sleeping so deeply and comfortably. Your body is going limp and you are falling back into your chair fast, fast asleep."

Grip your subject by his shoulders as your give these suggestions and gently lower him into his chair.

Notice how, step by step, you have gauged your hypnotic induction technique until its culmination results in complete hypnosis. This principle of training the subject in the art of being a somnambulist is an important procedure in obtaining deep hypnotic responses.

Having thus hypnotised your subject, remember these four important techniques to assure continued perfect results:

1. Between each test with the subject, continue to give suggestions that he is sleeping deeply, and that every breath he takes is sending him continuously on down deep and deeper to sleep. (Breathing being a continuous process, this association of the deepening of sleep with breathing is a very powerful factor in "setting" the trance.) such repetition of suggestions will keep the subject from slipping out of the trance as sometimes occurs as the result of physical movements.

2. Only give one suggested response at a time, allow its complete occurrence and then remove the suggestion before giving another command. By such technique you can avoid all possible complications that sometimes arise from conflicting suggestions being present.

3. In giving suggestions to the hypnotised subject, present them in a positive and commanding fashion. Always make your commands direct and to the point!

4. Before removing the subject from his hypnotic state, give these suggestions: "Remember, the next time you try entering hypnosis with me and look into my eyes, you will at once become very sleepy, your eyes will close, and you will go immediately deep to sleep in the hypnotic trance. Remember, when you look into my eyes you will go immediately fast asleep."

These suggestions act as a posthypnotic suggestion and start "conditioning" towards instant hypnosis when the subject works with you. Such a technique will save you much time in subsequent hypnotisation when working with that particular subject.

The Awakening

Having hypnotised your subject, you are now ready to remove the trance. Continue your suggestions along these lines: "You are fast asleep now. It has been a most wonderful, restful and healthful sleep. And when I awaken you, in just a few moments, you will awaken feeling wonderful and well. I will count from one to five, and with every count you will slowly awaken, and by the time I reach the count of five be wide, wide awake. And you will awaken exactly as you do every morning of your life after a night of sound, dreamless slumber. You will feel fine and refreshed; all has been just a pleasant, dreamless sleep. You will feel fine and refreshed at this night's sleep of sound, dreamless slumber. Remember, you will awaken exactly the same as you do every morning of your life after a night of deep, sound, healthful sleep. And you will awaken without memory of anything whatsoever; when you awaken it will seem exactly as though you have merely closed your eyes, dozed off to sleep, and then awakened feeling refreshed, wonderful and well."

Deep hypnosis calls for amnesia on awakening and, to get amnesia, demand it!

Forcefully suggest and insist that the subject will not remember anything of the hypnotic experience on awakening. Don't pull your punches in giving suggestions. All too frequently hypnotists are inclined to feel that possibly their subjects have not reached a deep enough stage to develop amnesia so rather than risk a failure of their suggestions, they temper their technique. Such is the wrong approach. Come what may, always forcefully suggest the results you want!

"All ready now, it is almost time to begin thinking about getting up … but you are sleeping so deeply and comfortably it is hard to even think of the idea that you will soon have to wake up from this deep, wonderful sleep. But it is morning now, so you must soon wake up. I am counting now… One, you are beginning to wake up. My, how sleepy you are, but you must wake up. Two! Like a dream the curtain of sleep begins to lift. Sleep is slipping and fading away, and you are beginning to wake up. Wake up. Three! Your eyes are opening now. See the light. It is morning. What a wonderful night of sleep you have enjoyed. Wake up. Four! Wide awake now. Five! Wide, wide, awake, that's it! Wide awake now, and you feel just fine!"

This is unquestionably one of the most important developments yet conceived for the removal of the trance. Note how the suggestions are designed to associate the hypnotic sleep with the awakening from normal sleep. It not only awakens the subject gently and pleasantly, but the technique actually deepens the degree of trance during the awakening process which invariably tends towards complete amnesia.

The Rehypnotisation

Having awakened your subject, immediately, before the person is even fully aware that he is awake, request him to again stare into your eyes and repeat the hypnotising process. Hypnotise your subject by exactly the same process you made use of in the first induction, but this time you will find results will occur much more rapidly, so you can proceed accordingly.

This is a vital point in the training of a somnambulist. To awaken your subject and let him rationalise about his hypnotic experience removes much of the somnambulistic training you have developed so far but, by plunging immediately into rehypnosis, you deepen immeasurably his hypnotic responses.

Having deeply rehypnotised your subject, give these suggestions prior to his second awakening: "Remember, when you wake up you will have no memory of your hypnotic experiences. You have merely dozed off to sleep in your chair but, when you awake you will see a chair in front of you, and you will immediately walk over to that chair and sit down in it and then you will go instantly fast to sleep."

Repeat these instructions three times to make sure they are firmly "set", and then awaken your subject.

Following the response to your suggestions, the subject will at once leave his chair, walk over to the other, seat himself, and will instantly go to sleep. Standing beside him now, forcefully command: "You are sleeping deeply now ... and, remember, from this time on, whenever I snap my fingers in front of your face, as you stare into my eyes, you will go instantly to sleep. Remember, no matter what you are doing, or where you are ... whenever you look into my eyes and I snap my fingers in front of your face, you will go instantly fast, fast to sleep."

Quickly awaken your subject. Let him rest for a few moments, then suddenly stare into his eyes and snap your fingers in front of his face. Instantly he will drop off into deep hypnosis, and you have thus "conditioned" him to become hypnotised on the "cue" of snapping your fingers.

Having so put him to sleep by this instantaneous method, awaken him and try it again. Immediately he reenters hypnosis, and you have a trained somnambulist, the ultimate aim of this hypnotic technique.

NOTE TO HYPNOTIST: You now have in your possession one of the most per-fected and detailed methods of hypnotising that has ever been developed. There are insights and "bits of business" here that has taken years of practical experi-ence to create. "The Master Method of Hypnotism" will be found of equal value to hypnotise on the stage as it is in private practice. Of course, when applied to the stage performance the processes must be telescoped and speeded up, as time is a factor in stage hypnotism since audience attention must be maintained. Generally, speaking, the stage hypnotist invariably makes use of more rapid pro-cedures than does the private hypnotist. On stage, hypnotism must entertain.

A Pot-pourri of
Hypnotising Methods

Chapter Nineteen
The "Eye Blinking" Method

This method will be found useful in hypnotising people who find it difficult to concentrate fully on ideas on sleep. The essential thing about the "Eye Blinking Method" is that it provides activity to hold the subject's attention throughout the induction by having him open and close his eyes, as the hypnotist counts. The subject does this in rhythm with the counting.

Have your subject seat himself in a comfortable position, and explain to him that you want him to go to sleep. After he has become passive, have him look directly into your eyes while you gaze intently at the root of his nose (using the "hypnotic gaze", as you have learned).

Now tell him that you are going to count slowly and that as you say each number you wish him to close his eyes, then to open them and be ready to close them again by the time you say the next number. For instance, you slowly count: "One, two, three, four". At each count, the subject is to close his eyes and open them in between counts. He is to keep his eyes focused on yours throughout the process, even when they are closed.

Start counting now slowly and in rhythm, and you will find that as you continue the counting, the period during which the subject's eyes remain open becomes shorter and shorter, and finally instead of the eyes opening there will only be a movement of the eyebrows while the lids remain closed.

Many subjects will go into hypnosis via this method by the time you have counted to only fifteen or twenty, and it is rarely necessary to count over one hundred.

When you find the eyes are closed and the subject does not seem able to open them, instead of continuing with the counting begin to say, in exactly the same rhythm and tone as your previous counting: "Sleep. Sleep. Sleepy. Sleepy. Sleep. You ... are ... going ... to ... sleep. Fast ... fast ... asleep. Asleep. Sleep. Sleepy. Sleep ..." etc.

Soon the subject's head will drop forward, and you will notice he is very drowsy. At this point you can commence some of the head stroking passes, as previously explained, while you suggest "the sleep formula" to your subject until hypnosis is achieved.

The Hypnotic Party: The Classic "Drunk on a Glass of Water" Experiment

Chapter Twenty
The "Visual Imagery" Method

This method employs a mental-picturing process. As a stage demonstration it is presented in this manner:

Stand before the committee of subjects with their eyes open and ask them to visualise the following familiar objects: first a house, then a tree, next a person and finally an animal. One by one you name these, and as these subjects achieve the visualisation and can mentally picture each object in their mind, they are to lift a hand to indicate.

When the entire group has succeeded, ask them to close their eyes and now visualise, in their "mind's eye", seeing themselves as sitting in the chair upon the stage exactly as they are, except the image of themselves that they visualise has his or her eyes open.

Now tell the group that each person is to concentrate on the image he or she sees, and that all of your comments will be directed towards the image and not themselves personally.

Now perform "Eyelid Fixation" on the image, in which the subjects visualise themselves as being able to open their eyes. Ask the subjects to lift their hands when they see the image with its eyes stuck tightly shut. Tell them to have the image try to open the eyes but be unable to do so.

An observation of your subjects at this point will reveal an outer physical inability to open the eyes precisely as it is visualised within the mind. Continue challenging the image to open its eyes a bit longer, and then suggest: "The image you see of yourself is forgetting about its eyes now and is relaxing back comfortably and is going to sleep. See the image go to sleep in your mind."

The next step in this unique hypnotising technique involves moving directly into the induction relationship with the subjects personally. This may be done by stating: "Now you are feeling just like the image, going deeper and deeper asleep and the image is disappearing and you are the image."

From this point forward, proceed into your regular hypnotic sleep formula until the desired hypnotic state is induced in the committee. This method will be found very effective as it removes all self-consciousness and disassociates each subject from guarding against anything personal occurring as the experiences seem to be happening to an inner image they conjure up in their mind rather than to themselves. They will be hypnotised before they know it. The method works equally well with a solo subject as with a group.

Chapter Twenty-One
The "Clock Dial" Method

This method of hypnotising may be used with a solo subject or with a group on stage. It requires a 12-inch-diameter circular card on which are numbers from 1 through 12, around the outside edge, forming a clock dial. Draw the numbers large and clear.

The subject is to hold this clock-dial before himself, and it is explained that he is to start on number one and to concentrate upon it; and, as he does so, he is to inhale deeply and say the word "sleep" out loud. He is then to exhale while still looking at the number, and proceed to say the words "deep sleep."

This performed, he is then to advance his eyes on to the next number on the dial (number two) and, while looking at this number to inhale twice and say the word "sleep" twice. He then exhales twice and repeats "deep sleep" twice. He then advances his eyes to number three and inhales three times, repeats the word "sleep" three times, exhales three times and repeats the words "deep sleep" three times. This process progresses around the clock dial, advancing from number to number until, by the time he would reach number twelve, he would be inhaling and exhaling twelve times and saying the words "sleep" and "deep sleep" twelve times. The process requires close attention to perform correctly, and becomes increasingly difficult as the numbers advance. It is wearying to the subject. Very few persons get beyond the fifth or sixth number before closing their eyes and heading towards sleep. The process causes a desire to get it over with, and entering hypnosis is the alternative which the hypnotist encourages with his barrage of suggestions emphasising such feelings.

The process employs a "confusing technique" in that, while the subject is moving his attention from number to number around the clock dial, as directed, you, standing behind him, keep up a continual barrage of whispered suggestions close to his ear. Suggest: "As your eyes concentrate upon the numbers, as your eyes move along ahead from number to number around the clock dial, as you inhale and exhale deeply, and repeat the words 'sleep' and 'deep sleep', it is sending you on down to sleep in deep hypnosis. It is becoming more and more difficult for you to see the numbers, and they begin to blur to your vision. The numbers are blurring and your eyes are becoming so tired they are closing. You are getting very tired of doing the whole thing; you just want to get it over with. So just close your eyes now and let the card drop from your hand as you drop down into sleep, hypnotic sleep. Go to sleep, etc."

Continue such suggestions until the subject's eye close, and he drops into the sleep of hypnosis. It is important that you give these suggestions in "low key" so they are little more than a murmur in the background so as not to intrude too consciously on the attention of the subject in the process he is performing. As the method proceeds, you will note the subject becoming increasingly lethargic as he advances from number to number on the clock dial. When this occurs, you can make your suggestions more specific telling him that his eyes will close and he will go to sleep, the card will drop from his hand, etc.

When performing this method as a stage demonstrations, Clock Dial Cards are passed out to everyone in the group, and the technique is performed in union with all eyes moving from number to number on the card, while you present the "sleep suggestions" standing centre stage.

Chapter Twenty-Two
The "Light and Shadow" Method

This is an unusual method of hypnotising which employs light and shadows. The subject is seated in front of a lamp. Use a bright light which shines directly into his eyes. To ease the glare, he is requested to close his eyes. Have him lean his head back so the muscles of the neck will be drawn tight and taught.

Experiment with the process yourself and you will find that even though the eyelids are shut, light can be noticed as a sort of reddish glare as it penetrates through the closed lids.

This is a quiet method of hypnotising, and in it very little verbal suggestion is used. Thus, as you proceed with the technique keep your gaze fixed on the top of the subject's head and concentrate of the mental suggestions that the subject is getting drowsy, and finally is going to sleep. In this method, whatever stages of hypnotic sleep you wish to develop in the subject, i.e., relaxation, heaviness of limbs, drowsiness, sleep, etc., don't speak them: *think them*!

Next, hold your hand in front of the subject's closed eyes, about two inches from his face, casting a dark shadow over them. This shadow is held for a short time and is suddenly removed. The effect of this is to bring within the closed eyes of the subject a sensation of darkness jumping to diffused redness. Repeat this light and shadow process several times. Sometimes make the shadow-to-light effect fast, and sometimes perform the action slowly. Occasionally you can draw your hands off to each side of the face, and the shadow will pass in that direction. Vary the process, but always keep the effect of shadow-to-light, shadow-to-light following a definite pattern in rhythm. Continue this process for about three minutes.

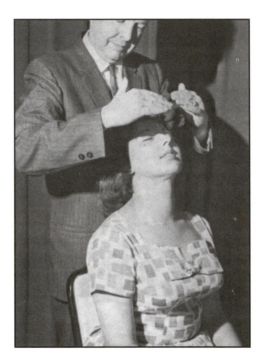

Then gently, very gently, make passes over the face of your subject, occasionally touching his cheeks lightly here and there. Rub the forehead softly, and then continue with more of the non-contact shadow passes in front of his face. Sometimes open the fingers of your hands as you pass them in front of the closed eyes, this produces a flickering effect. This flickering shadow effect is decidedly hypnotic. Then again close the fingers and make the shadow solid and black. Sometimes use just one hand in making the shadow and sometimes both. Make passes now over the body of the subject going from the face as far down as the stomach. Then make passes down over the shoulders and chest, sometimes touching lightly, and sometimes without contact.

As you continue with this process, you will notice that your subject will develop a marked quivering of the eyelids, and that the head will frequently fall forward on the chest or shoulder; you can assist this by gently pushing it forward on the side opposite from which you wish it to fall. The muscles of the mouth will also become somewhat drawn, and the breathing deepens and quickens.

Your subject's head having fallen forward on his chest and his breathing having become deep and regular, turn out the light and softly, so softly that your voice is barely a whisper that can be heard only by the subject, commence giving your "Sleep Formula" of verbal suggestions.

Chapter Twenty-Three
The "Body Rocking" Method

Have the subject stand facing you and look into your eyes, as you fasten your gaze on the root of his nose. Then place your hands on his shoulders and in a tone of authority state: "I am going to put you to sleep. I want you to relax, and you will feel your body become very light. You can feel it happening now! You must feel it for you are going to sleep! You cannot help yourself for you are going to sleep! Deep sleep!"

Now begin to rock the subject's body gently back and forth easily and slowly while keeping your gaze fixed upon him. Continue your positive barrage of suggestions that he is going to sleep! That he cannot help himself for he is going to sleep, etc.

Continue the rocking motion to-and-fro until you note his eyelids begin to droop, then command forcefully, *"Close your eyes and go to sleep!"* Next place your hand over his closed eyes and repeat: "Deep sleep. Deep sleep. Nothing will awaken you until I command you to awaken. You are sound asleep!"

This method was used by Dr Herbert Flint during his Victorian age stage shows. He was a big man with a forceful demeanour. It worked well for him. Some persons respond excellently to the command approach.

Chapter Twenty-Four
The "Loss of Equilibrium" Method

This method of induction has been made popular by Gil Boyne who uses it frequently in his practice. It is an authoritative hypnotising method. Begin by standing facing the subject and place your left hand on his shoulder. Gain full attention and begin the process.

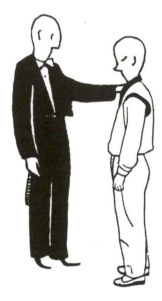

Now rock the subject gently back and forth and from side to side. If he does not seem to relax, pick up his left hand and drop it to his side. Insist that he let it drop. As soon as he allows his arm to swing, take your left hand off his shoulder and compliment him: "That's fine now! Now you've got it!"

Repeat the same procedure with his left hand. Say: "Fine. Now you're relaxing." Replace your left hand back on his shoulder and rock him gently.

"Now I want you to become absolutely quiet. Do not move or speak. I know you understand what I say, so don't nod your head or try to help me. Just remain passive and follow my suggestions, and you are about to enjoy a very pleasant and relaxing experience.

"Your ability to be hypnotised by this method depends upon your ability to concentrate your attention upon a small spot. In this case, the spot will be my little fingernail. Focus your eyes on my little fingernail and concentrate your entire attention upon it. Don't allow your eyes to leave it for a moment."

At this time, hold your right hand about six inches from the subject's eyes at a position that forces him to roll his eyeballs upward in an eye-straining position.

"Your goal is to relax your entire body, from head to foot. To achieve that goal, I want you to take three long, deep breaths. Each time you exhale I am going to say the words: 'Sleep now!' However, I do not mean sleep in the usual sense such as sleeping at night. Hypnosis is much more pleasant and relaxing than normal sleep. 'Sleep now' will be your cue for deep relaxation. Every time you hear me says the words 'Sleep now', just let a wave of relaxation sweep through you from the top of your head to the tips of your toes".

"All right. Now, as you continue to stare at my fingernail, take the first long deep breath." Move your hand down to the subject's eye level. "Inhale." As he inhales, move your hand up to its original position. "Hold it. Hold your breath. Hold it!"

Pause …

"Now let it all out. Exhale." Go right on down with your hand again. "Now take a second long, deep breath, even deeper than before." Raise hand. "Hold it in. Hold it. Hold it."

"Now let it all out. Exhale, and go right on down with it to sleep. Sleep now." Lower hand. "And now take a third long, deep breath. Inhale." Raise your hand, and do not lower it this time as you tell him to exhale. Keep it in a raised position so his eyes have to stare up at it. "Now let the air out of your lungs and relax even more. Breathe normally. I am going to pass my hand down over your face, and as I do it will cause your eyelids to close. As I count from five down to one, your eyelids will become heavy, droopy, and you will be drowsy and very sleepy. Keep looking intently at my little fingernail all the time as though nothing else existed except your eyes and my little fingernail. At the count of five you start going down into a deep hypnotic sleep. Number five. Your eyelids are so heavy, droopy, drowsy, and you feel so sleepy.

"Number four. Your eyes become more and more tired with every number you hear." Slowly lower hand.

"Number three. Your tired eyes are ready to close." Hand is now at eye level.

"Number two. Your eyes are so heavy, droopy, drowsy and sleepy and are closing now. Closing. Closing." Your hand is now at subject's chin level.

Before you say the final number, shift your left hand which has been on the subject's right shoulder to the back of his neck. Grasp him firmly as you say "Number one" and pull him suddenly forward so that his forehead rests upon your shoulders, and shout *"sleep!"*

NOTE TO HYPNOTIST: The word "sleep" must be shouted while the subject is in motion from your sudden pull forward, halfway between his original standing position and your shoulder, while his equilibrium is interfered with.

Start immediately to deepen the trance by rocking the subject from right to left. Do this by rocking your own body back and forth while his head rests on your shoulder.

The subject will go to sleep on the instant, and sometimes his legs will give way. If this happens, place your hands under his armpits and lower his gently to the floor. Should he not fall, you can push his head back from your shoulder and revolve his head around and around deepening the trance.

Chapter Twenty-Five
The "Pendulum Over Spiral" Method

This is a powerful way of hypnotising, as it is compounding in its effect. It makes use of both the swinging pendulum technique combined with the Hypnodisc. In operation, staring at the centre of the Hypnodisc starts the ideomotor response of the pendulum swinging around the spiral, which draws the subject into the spiral rapidly inducing hypnosis.

Cut out the Hypnodisc (accompanying this method) and mount it as required. Prepare a pendulum by tying a weight on the end of a length of string, and the method is ready to proceed.

Lay the Hypnodisc out flat on a table. Have the subject draw up a chair beside the table and hold the pendulum over the centre of the disc. Stand beside him and tell him how he is to direct his attention. Remove this page from book. Paste Spiral on cardboard making your Hypnodisc as used in this technique.

As he dangles the pendulum over the centre of the Hypnodisc tell him to relax and let his eyes revolve around the spiral and think, at the same time, of the pendulum beginning to swing around the spiral. Tell him to begin saying to himself the pendulum is swinging around and around and around the spiral, and to concentrate upon the movement.

In a few moments, you will notice that the pendulum, held in the subject's hand, will begin to revolve around above the surface of the spiral upon the table. As this occurs, tell him to continue letting his eyes follow the motion of the pendulum, as it goes around the spiral. As soon as you observe your subject is getting a good motion action of the pendulum, suggest: "The pendulum is swinging around and around and around now. Keep concentrating upon it. It is going around and around all by itself. You cannot stop it. The harder you try to stop it, the faster it goes around the spiral; your eyes are being drawn right into the spiral".

NOTE TO HYPNOTIST. The revolutions of the pendulum above the Hypnodisc will be found to be very compelling and hypnotic in effect.

145

The suggestions continue: "Your eyes are becoming fastened intently on the revolving pendulum as it goes around the spiral. It is fascinating you, and you cannot take your eyes off it. It is making your eyes become very heavy and sleepy. You want to close your eyes and go to sleep. Go ahead and close your eyes now and go to sleep."

The subject will shortly close his eyes, and you will note that the pendulum continues swinging around and around. Your suggestions continue: "Your eyes are closed now, so you can stop the pendulum from swinging. It is coming to a stop now. (The pendulum stops) You are becoming sleepy, very sleepy. Your arm is getting heavy holding the pendulum, and it is dropping from your fingers. (Pendulum drops) Your arm is falling to the table. (Arm falls to table surface) Now your head is dropping forward to the table, and you cradle it in your arm. (Subject's head falls to the table and he rests his head upon his arm) Breathe deeply and freely now and go sound asleep." Press upon the back of the subject head as he rests upon his arm. "Sleep. Sleep. Deep sleep now. Go sound asleep."

NOTE TO HYPNOTIST: This technique will be found excellent. It compels attention in combining the ideomotor action swinging of the pendulum with the spiral fixation. It is an absorbing process.

This method can also be used as a group induction for the committee on the stage during the show. Have enough spirals and pendulums so each person has one to work with. Each subject in the group places the mounted Hypnodisc on his or her lap and holds the pendulum above its centre. You stand before the line of subjects and give the directions.

Even while working with a group, you will find "The Pendulum Over Spiral Method" very individual, as the process occupies the full attention of each person participating. Watch your subjects and by the responses you can judge your best subjects for your hypnotic stage show presentations. As soon as a subject's eyes close, go to that person, push his head down into his lap, and forcefully suggest "sleep!" The order in which the subjects react to this hypnotic method makes it possible for you to accurately plan your show around the group.

Chapter Twenty-Six
The "Arm Levitation" Method

This method of induction was made popular by the late Milton Erickson. Erickson is one of the immortals of hypnotherapy, and this method has become a classic. Here it is designed as a stage demonstration.

Your subjects sit in a row on stage. You stand in front and address the committee. "The method we will use tonight, as you enter hypnosis, is the most popular employed in medical hypnotic practice by psychiatrists and doctors. You will find it a fascinating experience.

"Everyone now, altogether, I want you to sit comfortably in your chairs and relax. As you sit there, bring both hands palms down on your thighs, hands spread flat out palms down on your thighs. Now I want you to keep watching your hands and observe them very closely. Keep looking at your hands, as I explain to you.

"Just sit in your chair and relax and, as you do, you will notice certain things happening in the course of relaxing. These are things that have always happened, but possibly you have never noticed them so closely before. I am going to point them out to you. I'd like to have you concentrate on all sensations and feelings in your hands no matter what they may be. Perhaps you may feel the heaviness of your hands as they rest on your thighs, or you may possibly feel pressure. Perhaps you will feel the texture of your trousers or your dress as they press against the palms of your hands; or the warmth of your hands on your thighs. Perhaps you may feel tingling. No matter what sensations there are, I want you to observe them. Keep watching your hands, and you will notice how quiet they are, how them remain in one position. Yet actually there is motion there, but it is not yet noticeable. I want you to keep watching your hands. Your attention may wander from the hands but it will always return back to the hands, and you keep watching the hands and wondering when the motion that is there will show itself."

At this point, the subjects' attention is fixed on their hands. All are curious about what will happen and what sensations will be experienced. No attempt is being made to force any suggestions on the committee members, and, if they observe any sensations or feelings, each incorporates them as a product of his own experience. The object is to get the subjects eventually to respond to your suggestions as the hypnotist as if these too are part of his own experiences. A subtle attempt is being made to get each person in the group to associate their own sensations with the words spoken to them so that the words uttered by the hypnotist will evoke sensory or motor responses later on. Watch your subjects now and you will notice that some of them begin to show a slight motion or jerking in one or so of the fingers of their hands. As you observe this, mention it and remark that they can see such little nervous motions begin to develop in their fingers as they rest on their thighs and that such motions will probably increase. Watch your subjects and comment on whatever other objective reactions you observe, such as motion of the legs or deepening of the breathing. The result of this linking of the subjects' reactions with comments by the hypnotist is an association of the two in the subjects' minds.

"It will be interesting to see which one of your fingers will move first. It may be the middle finger, or the forefinger, or the ring finger, or the little finger, or the thumb. One of the fingers is going to jerk or move. You don't know exactly when or in which hand it will occur. Keep watching. There, the fingers jerk and move, just like that.

"As the movements in your fingers begin you will notice an interesting thing. Very slowly the spaces between your fingers will widen, the fingers will slowly move apart, and you'll notice that the space get wider and wider and wider. The fingers are spreading, wider and wider apart, just like that."

This is the first real suggestion to which the subjects are expected to respond. Watch your subjects and as it occurs you will know that they are reacting to suggestion. The hypnotist continues to talk as if the response is one that would have come about by itself in the natural course of events.

"As the fingers spread apart, you will notice that the fingers will soon want to arch up from your thighs, as if they wanted to lift, higher and higher. [Observe the subjects' fingers as they start moving upward slightly.] Notice how the index finger lifts. As it does the other fingers want to follow, up, up, slowly rising. [Observe the other fingers start lifting.]

"As the fingers lift you'll become aware of a lightness in the hand, a feeling of lightness, so much so that the fingers will arch up, and the whole hand will slowly lift and rise as if it feels like a feather, as if a balloon is lifting it up in the air, lifting, lifting, up, up, up, pulling up higher and higher and higher, as the hands become very light. [Observe the subjects' hands start rising.] As you watch your hands rise, you'll notice that the arms come up, up, up in the air, a little higher, and higher, and higher, and higher, up, up, up. [Observe the arms of many of your subjects will have lifted about five inches above their thighs and the subjects are gazing at their hands fixedly.]

"Keep watching your hands and arms as they rise straight up, and as they do you will soon become aware of how drowsy and tired your eyes become. As your arms continue to rise, you will get tired and relaxed and sleepy, very sleepy. Your eyes will get heavy and your lids may want to close. And as your arms rise higher and higher, you will want to feel more relaxed and sleepy, and you will want to enjoy the peaceful, relaxed feeling, letting your eyes close and being sleepy."

It will be noticed in this technique that as the subjects executes one suggestion, their positive responses are used to reinforce the next suggestion. For instance, as the arms rise, it is suggested in essence that they will get drowsy because their arms are rising.

"Your arms lift – up – up – up – and you are getting very drowsy; your eyelids get very heavy, your breathing gets slow and regular. Breathe deeply, in and out. [Observe your subjects. By this time many will have their arms stretched out directly in front of them, their eyes will be blinking and their breathing will be deep and regular.] As you keep watching your hands and arms and feeling more and more drowsy and relaxed, you will notice that the direction of the hand will change. The arm will bend, and the hands will move closer and closer to your face, up, up, up, and as they rise you will slowly but steadily go into a deep, deep sleep in which you relax deeply and to your satisfaction. The arms will continue to rise up, up, lifting, lifting, up in the air until it touches your face, and you will get sleepier and sleepier, but you must not go to sleep until your hands touch your face. When your hands touch your face you will be asleep, deeply asleep."

Your subjects are here requested to choose their own pace in falling asleep, so that when their hands touch their faces, each feels himself to be asleep to his own satisfaction. Hand levitation and sleepiness continue to reinforce each other. When the subjects finally do close their eyes, each will have entered a trance with his own participation.

"Your hands are now changing more and more their direction. They move up – up – up – up towards your face. Your eyelids are getting heavy. You are getting sleepier, and sleepier, and sleepier. [Observe that your subjects' hands are approaching their faces and all eyelids of the group are blinking more rapidly.] Your eyes get heavy, very heavy, and your hands move straight up towards your face. You get very tired and drowsy. Your eyes are closing, are closing. When your hands touch your face you'll be asleep, deeply asleep. You feel very drowsy. You feel drowsier and drowsier and drowsier, very sleepy, very tired. Your eyes are like lead, and your hands move up, up, up, right towards your face, and when they reach your face, you will be asleep. [Observe your subjects; hands touch their faces throughout the group; paces will vary a little; continue your suggestions until each subject's hands touch their respective face.] Go to sleep, go to sleep, fast asleep. And as you sleep you feel very tired and relaxed. I want you to concentrate on relaxation, a state of tensionless relaxation. Think of nothing else, but sleep, deep sleep."

And thus you have hypnotised your committee by this genteel and most impersonal of processes in which each subject becomes immersed in his own sensations and enters hypnosis at his own rate of response so gradually as to be scarcely aware of its occurrence. This will be found an excellent hypnotising method. It is applicable to almost all subjects, and may be used either solo or as a group induction.

Chapter Twenty-Seven
The "Candy Induction" Method

Hypnosis can be induced through any of the senses. This method employs the sense of taste, as the central point of concentration. I designed it especially for hypnotising children. However it works equally well with adults. People like it because it is tasty (a literal fact) as it uses a piece of candy to suck on during the process. The method can be used with either a solo subject or group.

Use a piece of hard candy which when sucked upon will fill the mouth with flavour. Lemon Drops and Peppermints work well. Use whatever sucking kind of candy you please.

Have the subject take a seat in a comfortable chair and relax back. Hand him a piece of candy. Tell him to place the candy in his mouth and suck on it. He is not to chew or swallow it but is to allow it to slowly dissolve in his mouth, filling his mouth with sweet taste. He is to keep his attention on the taste of the candy. Now have him close his eyes and you present these suggestions: "As you rest back in that comfortable chair and relax, think about how good the candy tastes in your mouth. Think of the taste so completely that it almost seems that your entire body is becoming the taste. And that good taste makes you feel so comfortable and relaxed. So relax now and just let yourself *go!*

"Now just let your mind drift, allowing whatever thoughts that come in to just pass through it, relaxing quietly, becoming completely quiescent in both mind and body. Now breathe deeply through your nose [inhale] Hold the breath, then exhale slowly [exhale slowly], and let your body relax with the breath; let everything *go!*

"Breathe in again [inhale]. Hold the breath. Visualise energy flowing into your body with the breath. Exhale now and, as you release your breath, visualise all negativity and tension going out of your body with the breath. Continue breathing in and out slowly and rhythmically … and with the breath going in and out of your body become aware of the energy, the vital energy of life moving into your body, energy that permeates every fibre of your being, and sends you down towards the realms of sleep.

"How good the candy tastes and how sleepy it is making you become. So just allow the taste of the candy to pervade your being and let it make your entire body relax. Relax. Relax. Relax. How good it feels to relax completely with that delightful taste of candy in your mouth.

"Let your thoughts of relaxation travel to every part of your body as the candy dissolves in your mouth, so you can relax now and let everything go, to go to sleep. Sleep. Sleep. Sleep. Go to sleep. Just drop off into hypnotic sleep, and all the while you are fully aware and your conscious mind moves to one side, and your subconscious mind opens wide and becomes receptive to all the suggestions presented to you. You will perform them all to absolute perfection. Chew up and swallow what remains of the candy now and as it goes down your throat you drop down, down deeply into hypnosis."

Chapter Twenty-Eight
The "Fatigue Out-of-Focus" Method

This method can be used with a solo subject or with a group on stage. Its operation is almost automatic in effectiveness.

Have the subject take a seat and extend his arms out straight in front of himself, at eye level. Have him grip his hands together and extend his thumbs upright from the clasped hands. Have the subject close his eyes and concentrate on his outstretched hands feeling fatigue "set in" as he continues to hold his hands out at arms' length before himself. Tell him to concentrate on the fatigue he will feel in holding his arms suspended, and to tell you when he feels they are so fatigued that he just cannot keep them outstretched any longer.

Having instructed the subject as to his positioning and concentrating on the fatigue he will soon experience, softly suggest in his ear how relaxed and sleepy he is becoming. Continue your whispered suggestions of his relaxing and how sleepy he is feeling except for his extended arms which are getting so fatigued he can scarcely hold them outstretched any longer. Mention this fact occasionally among the sleep suggestions, and tell him to be sure to let you know when his arms feel so tired that he must let them down. He will soon tell you.

As soon as the subject tells you, tell him to continue keeping his arms up, but to open his eyes now and gaze at his thumb nails held before him. Tell him to keep looking, looking, looking at the nails and that, as he does so, he will notice they go in and out of focus. Suggest: "Your thumb nails are going more and more out of focus as you stare at them, and when they are out of focus close your eyes and go to sleep." His eyes will soon close.

As soon as the eyes close, suggest: "Your eyes are closed now and you are going to sleep and, as you drop down into sleep, your fatigued arms will slowly drop down to your lap, and when they rest in your lap you will be asleep in great relief."

The arms will drop down to the lap, and the subject will drop into hypnotic sleep. You can then deepen the hypnosis by continuing with sleep formula for depth. This method of hypnotising works well because it takes full advantage of the physical situation you have placed the subject in which effects are amplified by the suggestions: the arms held outstretched with attention concentrated on how fatigued they are becoming very shortly demands that they be lowered to remove the fatigue, and the subject makes that request as instructed.

The eyes being then opened and focused on the thumb nails are bound to experience going out of focus, a physical reaction of the eyes which is likewise amplified by the suggestions. And with the going out of focus the command to close the unfocused eyes and drop into sleep is given combined with the removing of the natural fatigue the arms feel in being held outstretched overly long. The suggestions then continue that as the arms drop and rest in the subject's lap, sleep will ensue immediately.

NOTE TO HYPNOTIST: Observe this combining of dual physical reaction with the suggested (soft spoken) commands: the dropping down into sleep as the tired arms drop down to rest in the lap, which is culminated with a suggested "cue" that, when the fatigued arms rest in the lap, sleep will ensue immediately. Master this step-by-step hypnotic induction method and perform it smoothly. Step-by-step it leads the subject inescapably into hypnosis.

Chapter Twenty-Nine
The "Musical" Method

Mostly when music is used in conjunction with a method for inducing hypnosis it is kept softly in the background behind the voice of the hypnotist, so the verbalised suggestions stand out. This method reverses that process. In the Music Method, the music is predominant while the spoken suggestions are given softly as a background to the music. In other words, the concentration of the subject's listening attention is upon the music rather than upon the voice of the hypnotist.

The Music Method of Hypnotic Induction

Have the subject take a seat in a comfortable chair or lie upon a couch. Tell subject to close eyes and listen to the music will full attention, to concentrate upon the music. Play the music loudly so it overlays the voice of the hypnotist presenting the suggestions. While the music plays, whisper these suggestions: "Sit comfortably in your chair (or upon the couch, as the case may be) and pleasantly relax. Close your eyes and listen to the music as you relax. Concentrate upon the music. Give the music your full attention. It is such beautiful music it seems to flood your very Being with melodious harmony and rest. The music enters your very Being as you relax. It makes you feel so relaxed. Relax. Relax. Relax.

"Now, as you relax notice how sleepy you are beginning to feel. Experience the sleepiness. Your eyes are closed, your body is relaxed, and you are becoming so sleepy. So sleepy. Sleep. Let yourself go to sleep. It feels so good just to go to sleep.

"Breathe deeply now and go to sleep ... and every breath you take sends you down deeper and deeper to sleep. All you hear is just the beautiful music claiming your attention and lulling you to sleep. It is so soothing it makes you relax and go to sleep. To sleep in pleasant hypnosis. Drop down into pleasant hypnosis. You are breathing deep and full ... deep and full in the rhythm of sleep. Drop down now into deep hypnosis now as the music slowly fades away, and you will follow perfectly every suggestion I give you of interest to yourself."

Let the music slowly fade out now in this deepening process, and let your voice come in strong in full command of the situation. The hypnosis is complete.

NOTE TO HYPNOTIST: This is almost a subliminal method of hypnotising as the subject is concentrating on the music rather than upon the verbal suggestions, which allows the suggestions uncritically to slip into the subconscious inducing hypnosis.

Chapter Thirty
The "Outside/Inside" Method

This method of hypnotising was developed by Dwight Bale of Auburn, Washington. He developed it for use in his professional practice of hypnotherapy. It is an introvertive method productive of excellent results of quickly achieving hypnosis, as the subject does inside himself (or herself) what the hypnotist suggests outside.

Have the subject take a seat in a comfortable chair and close their eyes. The subject is instructed to begin by breathing in and out with the hypnotist: "Take a deep breath. Hold it. Now exhale slowly."

This deep breathing process is repeated six times, so the subject gets use to performing inside himself what the hypnotist instructs for him to do. Deep breathing also causes the brain to become somewhat "drugged" with the intake of excessive oxygen and the outflow of carbon dioxide, producing a condition similar to hyperventilation.

The subject is now told to relax his body as completely as he can and to say to himself (nonverbally inside his mind) the suggestions the operator gives him: "I am becoming very relaxed." Subject repeats this phrase to himself silently.

"My eyes are closed and I am becoming sleepy." Subject repeats this phrase to himself silently.

"My eyelids are so relaxed now that I cannot open them. I try but I cannot open my eyes, so I am drifting into hypnosis." Subject tries to open eyes but finds no response. The subject is drifting into hypnosis.

"I am drifting down, down into deep hypnosis. I am becoming so sleepy, so sleepy. I am drifting down into deep hypnosis where my subconscious mind will accept every suggestions and put it into action to perfection." Subject repeats these suggestions presented outside by the hypnotist to himself inside.

"I am so relaxed that my head is dropping forward onto my chest and I sink into deep hypnosis." Subject repeats suggestions to himself. As head falls forward he is hypnotised.

Hypnotist now moves from first to second person in presenting suggestions to the subject: "Good. You are going deeper and deeper into profound hypnosis now. You need not think for yourself now, as I will do the thinking for you. All you have to do is just relax and sink down deeper and deeper into hypnosis.

"Go deep to sleep now in hypnosis, and your subconscious will go into action and follow my every suggestion perfectly."

This method of hypnotising will be found very easy to use and readily induces hypnosis, as the subject voluntarily presents the hypnotist's suggestions to himself in an introverted direct repetition to himself, in accordance with the directions of the hypnotist. The method will be found usable both with solo subjects, and with groups.

Chapter Thirty-One
The Biofeedback Method

In this method, the hypnotist repeats back to the subject what reactions he observes occurring in the subject, as the result of bodily reactions his suggestions have produced in the individual. The result is a powerful compounding of the suggestions inducing hypnosis. The mind knows what reactions are occurring in the body, so when the suggestions presented by the hypnotist are in accordance, the results are magnified.

Commence by having the subject take a seat in a comfortable chair in preparation to being hypnotised. Stand before the person and have him (or her) stare upward into your eyes. Follow with this biofeedback presentation of suggestions: "You are seated in a comfortable chair staring upward into my eyes in preparation to being hypnotised. As you continue staring upward into my eyes notice how your eyes are becoming heavy and tired, and how your body is beginning to relax all over."

Now suggest back to the subject exactly what you observe occurring to his eyes and body, as he performs the process. Such as: "Your eyelids are commencing to droop from the tiredness of staring upward into my eyes. You feel them becoming so heavy and tired. Your eyelids flutter. They quiver. You want to close your eyes. Your eyes feel so tired and heavy now that you simply must close them. So go ahead and close them. [Subject closes eyes.] I see you have closed your eyes now. Good. They feel so much more relaxed now. And I see that your body is following exactly the relaxation your eyes are experiencing in equally relaxing itself. [Describe what you see the body doing.] Your shoulders are drooping. You are settling down in your chair more. Your arms are loose and free. [Pick up arms and drop them relaxed into lap.] I see your breathing deepening, as your chest rises and falls in the rhythm of going to sleep. Indeed you are dozing off to sleep. I see you as asleep. Good. You like that. Go ahead and sleep now. Fine. Sleep!"

Continue on with the biofeedback handling of the suggestions, describing to the subject what is occurring in himself. The method will quickly induce hypnosis. Once in trance, your suggestions to the subject can be altered into conventional direct approach handling.

Chapter Thirty-Two
The "Acupressure" Method

As a student of hypnotism, it is well that you learn this method. While it is hardly suitable for a stage demonstration, it assuredly is effective for solo subject use. The practice of the ancient Chinese Art of Acupuncture, using needles placed in various meridian centres of the body, has become very popular in the West. Acupressure produces similar effects without the need for puncturing. Pressure on the various meridian centres suffices for the purpose of this hypnotising method.

These centres are nerve-sensitive and when depressed automatically command attention and compound with the suggestions of the hypnotist to produce relaxation in the body leading directly to responsive hypnotic sleep. These meridian areas can be felt as little depressions in the body into which the fingertip can be inserted in maintaining pressure. Some areas are quite sensitive and pressure will produce slight pain sensations. This is beneficial to the process, so press in firmly and deeply. The method can be applied with the subject either in a seated position or lying down. The latter is recommended.

Begin by energising your hands. Shake your hands vigorously and clap them together several times. Feel them tingle. Then place palm to palm and slowly separate. Note the force (energy) that flows between them. Your "charged" hands are now ready to be applied to the meridian centres of the subject along with the presentation of your hypnotising suggestions. Deep hypnosis can be produced by this method. Perform the process in the following steps:

Step One
Have client remove any excess clothing and shoes and recline in a comfortable position with hands resting at sides and feet slightly apart. Client is to be absolutely comfortable. Explain that in this method of hypnotising you are going to apply pressure to various meridian centres of his body, using scientific acupressure; that the process will cause him to relax automatically and that he will very likely doze off to sleep. Tell him to just let himself go!

Step Two
Have client close eyes and take three deep breaths. Then touch centre of top of his head and instruct him to roll his eyes back under his closed lids

as though looking at the point inside his head. Tell him to keep looking at the inside point as you suggest "Eyelid Fixation". In this position, the client will find it physically impossible to open his eyes. This successful, tell him to relax his eyes downward now and drift off to sleep, as you stimulate the meridian centres of his body, starting at his feet and advancing to his head, each pressure point sending him down deeper and deeper into hypnosis.

Step Three
Locate point of left foot just behind ball of foot in line with middle toe. Press in deep. Hold for five seconds, while suggesting to client that he will notice how relaxed the pressure on this centre causes his foot to become. It feels numb. Do same on right foot.

Step Four
Locate point on left foot just below the bulge of inner ankle. Press in deep. Hold for five seconds. Continue suggestions of how relaxed the pressure is making his foot become. Do same on right foot.

Step Five
Move fingers up left leg about 3" above ankle and press on the inner rear edge of shin bone. Hold for five seconds. Suggest that the numbness and relaxation experienced in feet is now beginning to rise on up his legs. Do same on right leg.

Step Six
Locate point on left foot just below the outer bulge of outer left ankle. Press in. Hold for five seconds. Continue suggestions of feet relaxing. Do same on right leg.

Step Seven
Locate point on left leg just below level of knee cap. Press in at top of calf muscle. This is a tender spot. Suggest legs becoming relaxed and numb. Do same on right foot.

Step Eight
Locate point on front of body midway between pubic bone and navel. Press in firmly. Present suggestions: "Just let yourself go now and drift away to pleasant sleep." As the pressures on the meridians continue on up the body ...

Relax, then ...

Step Nine
Locate point on front of body just below end of breastbone. Press in firmly. Suggest: "Let yourself go completely now and just drift away into sleep."

Step Ten
Locate point on body three inches up from last point depressed, and press in thus upon centre of breastbone. Press in firmly. Suggest: "Sleep, go deeply to sleep now."

Step Eleven
Perform pressure together using both thumbs at points located in depression at the end of shoulder bones where arms and shoulders meet. Continue suggestions of: "Sleep. Deep sleep. Drift away into sleep, as you feel the pressures. The pressure will melt away as you drift away into sleep. Breathe deep and sleep."

Relax, then ...

Step Twelve
Locate point (called "Joy of Living" point) at inner crease of right elbow. Bend elbow and place tip of thumb in crease. Then unbend arm and press in. Press on relaxed tissue always. Suggest: "Sleep. Deep sleep." Perform same on left elbow.

Step Thirteen
Move hand down arm from point twelve, to point located two inches down arm on outside of right arm. Press in. Suggest: "Your arms are becoming numb and you are going to sleep. Sleep. Deep sleep." Perform same on left arm.

Relax, then ...

Step Fourteen
Move on down right arm further on outside to point two inches from wrist, in line with little finger. Press in. Suggest: "Sleep. Go to sleep. Deep sleep." Perform same on left arm.

Step Fifteen
Locate point on back of right hand between thumb and index finger. Press in deeply. Suggest: "Sleep. Deep sleep." Relax pressure. Press in deeply again and suggest: "Sleep. Deep sleep." Perform this relaxation and pressure on the point for five consecutive times. Perform same on lefthand.

163

Relax, then …

Step Sixteen
Locate point on crease inside of right wrist, in line with little finger. Press deeply. Suggest: "Sleep. Deep sleep. Breathe deeply now and go deep to sleep." Watch client's breathing in response to these suggestions. If it deepens, trance is ensuing.

Relax, then …

Step Seventeen
Locate point at top of each shoulder, midway between neck and top of shoulder. Press deeply with both hands together. Suggest: "Sound asleep now. Deep sound sleep now. Deep into hypnotic sleep now." Relax between allowing time for suggestions to sink home.

Step Eighteen
Locate point on face, press in on crevice between upper lip and tip of nose. Suggest: "Deep in hypnosis now. Sleep deep in hypnosis now."

Relax, then …

Step Nineteen
Press in on area between the eyes (third eye area). Skull bone structure does not allow depressing. On this point surface pressure will suffice. Maintain a steady pressure, as you suggest: "You are deep in hypnosis now and as you sleep your subconscious mind opens wide to receive the beneficial suggestions that will now be given it."

Relax, then …

Step Twenty
Press on top of head in small depression located there. Continue a steady pressure on top of head, as you suggest: "Sleep on deeply now completely undisturbed, but your subconscious mind is fully alert and is receptive to the beneficial suggestions which will now be presented to it. These suggestions are exactly what *you* want and will benefit you in every way. They will become your very own."

Relax a moment and remove pressure from top of head. Then press in again on the acupressure point, and present whatever positive suggestion formula is desired as requested by the client.

Repeat suggestion formula three times. Then suggest: "These suggestions go deep into your subconscious and become your habitual way of healthful behaviour for yourself. When they have become thus established as reality in your subconscious you will automatically arouse yourself from the hypnosis feeling wonderful and fine with a *knowing* that you have successfully accomplished what you desire."

Chapter Thirty-Three
The Marx Howell Nonverbal Hypnotic Induction

This is a pantomime method of hypnotising. It provides a technique for inducing deep hypnosis without the use of words, i.e. verbal communication. The technique was developed by police officer Marx Howell, forensic hypnotist with the Texas Department of Public Safety.

The Howell technique begins with acquainting the subject with nonverbal communication via an understanding of a few basic gestures. For example, when a minister holds out his hands and gestures upwards, what does it mean? Subject responds that it means for the congregation to rise.

What does it mean when a minister holds out his hands in a similar manner and gestures downward? Subject response is that it means congregation be seated.

What does it mean when you gesture towards yourself repeatedly? Subject response is that it means: "Come over to me."

What does it mean when forefinger is placed before lips? Subject response is that it means "Be quiet. Don't talk."

Having gone through this little introduction to nonverbal communication, it is concluded that subject has a basic understanding of the pantomime meaning of gestures. This initial procedure prepares subject for responding to this nonverbal hypnotic induction.

Ready for hypnosis, the subject is seated, and hypnotist stand before him or her, as the case may be. Hypnotist explains to subject that they will be hypnotised deeply by this silent method; that the eyes will be closed most of the time and that, when he gently pokes his forefinger into the side of the neck, the person will open eyes and immediately arouse from the hypnosis.

The process starts by hypnotist taking subject's right hand and turning it palm towards face, moving it slowly back and forth before subject's open eyes. Subject follows closely movement of the hand back and forth before the eyes.

When subject's attention becomes fixed, hypnotist makes a downward stroking gesture before eyes of subject, causing a response of eyes closing.

The left hand of subject is then taken and arm bent backward so hand can be placed behind neck; subject gripping back of neck with fingers of left hand in this position.

Subject's right arm is then lifted upward above head. Hypnotist strokes the upraised arm, pinches in at elbow, and pulling on it conveys the idea that it is becoming very stiff. Removing his hands, subject's arm remains outstretched above head.

Hypnotist then takes subject's upraised arm and gently lowers it towards lap, while stroking arm in a relaxed fashion, and shaking hand so it dangles limply. Complete relaxation is established in this pantomime manner. The right hand is then allowed to flop down loosely into subject's lap.

Now taking the backward-positioned left hand of subject gripping back of neck, hypnotist brings arms forward, grips wrist and shakes hand until it is entirely limp, and then allows it to flop down into subject's lap beside the right hand already there.

Hypnotist then grips subject's head between his thumb and forefinger, and in this grip presses in on temples. This pressure is maintained for a few moments and is then released.

Hypnotist next goes behind subject and placing one hand on each shoulder presses downward, causing subject to slump down more deeply into chair. Often the subject's head drops forward onto chest at this point. Downward pressure on shoulder is maintained for some moments.

Hypnotist moves hands upward from shoulders and grips subject's head on each side, and begins to revolve it around and around and around. These revolutions of head are continued until it is obvious that neck muscles are entirely loose. Head is then released and allowed to drop forward on chest, and hypnotist moves to front and again gently strokes down arm and exerts some pressure on backs of hands resting in subject's lap.

The subject's right arm is then again lifted and made stiff, outstretched above head. Catalepsy sets in very rapidly this time. Hypnotist may move arm in any position, and it remains as placed. Finally the arm, still rigid, is pushed downward under gentle pressure to subject's lap. Wrist of hand is then taken and hand shaken causing all stiffness to vanish. Complete relaxation has set in.

Both hands are then shaken and flopped about, then left limp in lap; subject's entire body has become flaccid, i.e. if a leg were to be lifted it would drop inert to the floor; the entire body of the subject has become mobile and may be easily rotated and moved in any direction. The pantomime demeanour of the subject presents clear evidence that hypnosis has been induced by this nonverbal process.

Now in hypnosis, whatever suggestions are desired for subconscious responsiveness may be presented to the subject in customary manner.

When the session is ready to be concluded, a gentle poke of hypnotist's finger into side of subject's neck will arouse the subject from the hypnosis; eyes open with a perfect return to normal wakefulness. The process is complete.

Chapter Thirty-Four
The Chakra Colours
Hypnotic Induction

This is a unique method of hypnotising that combines the modern science of brain waves with the ancient Oriental wisdom of chakra colour vibrations. Brain wave frequencies are divided into four classifications, given the Latin names of Beta, Alpha, Theta and Delta. The frequencies are dependent upon brain activity, and the borderlines between the states are not precise.

Brain Waves

Beta. The brain wave frequency spectrum present in waking consciousness, i.e. conscious objective behaviour.

Alpha. The brain wave frequency spectrum present in states of relaxation and reverie. It is the state of mind present in the suggestible state of hypnosis, i.e. subconscious subjective behaviour.

Theta. The brain wave frequency spectrum present in states of dreaming, such as in the borderlines between waking and sleeping.

Delta. The brain wave frequency spectrum present in the mental states of deep sleep, i.e. unconsciousness providing body rejuvenation.

Chakra Colours

In Oriental belief Man is regarded as having a psychic nervous system in addition to the visible physical nervous system. It is held that the spinal column provides an invisible channel in its centre called the sushumna. On either side of the sushumna flows a current of prana (vitality of life), of positive and negative types, the two currents passing through the substance of the spinal cord.

The two currents of prana which flow along the channel of the spinal cord have distinctive Hindu names: the current which flows on the right side

Illustration by Steve Chappell

being called pingula and this is the positive current. The current that flows on the left side is called Ida (pronounced "ee-daa") and is the negative current. Spaced along these psychic energy channels, in specific parts of the body, are special energy centres called chakras. The term "chakra" in definition means wheel, disc or whirling-around object, and this is stimulated into activity by rising psychic energy (termed "kundalini") ascending the channel of the sushumna. It is claimed that there are seven main chakra centres along the channel of the sushumna:

1. **The muladhara**, the lowest chakra located in the base of the spine.

2. **The svadhisthana**, the second chakra, in ascending order, located on the spinal column in the region of the reproductive organs.

3. **The manipura**, the third in ascending order, located on the spinal column in the region of the solar plexus.

4. **The anahata**, the fourth in ascending order, located in the spinal column in the region of the heart.

5. **The visuddha**, the fifth in ascending order, located on the spinal cord in the region of the throat.

6. **The ajana**, the sixth in ascending order, located on the spinal column in the regions of the pineal gland within the head (frequently referred to as "the third eye").

7. **The sahastrara**, the seventh in ascending order, located at the top of the head (the Hindus refer to this as "the thousand petalled lotus).

Each chakra centre is associated with a specific colour which when visualised within the mind is said to produce a vibratory frequency which stirs into activity the operation of the chakra associated with it. The Colours are:

*   **Red** – stimulating to the first chakra
*   **Orange** – stimulating to the second chakra
*   **Yellow** – stimulating to the third chakra
*   **Green** – stimulating to the fourth chakra
*   **Blue** – stimulating to the fifth chakra
*   **Violet** – stimulating to the sixth chakra
*   **White** – stimulating to the seventh chakra.

This colour is used to form **the white light of projection** about the subject.

When these colours are visualised within the mind in sequence they appear to alter the normal waking state of brain activity (*beta*) and transform *beta* into *alpha* (inclusive of even some *theta* activity) producing a state of mind which is exceedingly receptive to suggestions and amenable to hypnotic induction. Of such nature is this *ascending-colours hypnotic method*.

Hypnotic Method

Subject seated in comfortable chair with hands resting loosely in lap and feet flat on floor. Subject is told to close eyes, relax and take a deep breath. Hold the breath and exhale slowly. Do it again, this time while breathing in to visualise the WHITE caller of the Crown Chakra (Sahastrara) coming into nostrils and filling lungs with WHITE LIGHT, entering body and starting to spread throughout entire system. Just sit there breathing comfortably, feeling the WHITE LIGHT coming in and forming a protection of purity about SELF. Visualise it as a beautiful experience.

Now, tell the protected subject in this relaxed state: "I want you to now visualise within your mind the colour RED. Visualise RED in any way you please: a red rose, a red apple, anything that is RED! I want you to actually see this RED. The important thing is that you see the RED colour inside your head.

"Once you see it, then go down to the next colour which is ORANGE. Strongly visualise the caller orange in your mind, and actually see it there. See ORANGE anyway you please: a bowl of fresh oranges, a glass of orange juice, a Buddhist monk in an orange robe. Use whatever image you need to visualise the colour, but see the colour ORANGE in your mind's eye.

"When you have it, now go down to the next colour which is YELLOW. Visualise YELLOW ... actually see it inside your head. Picture it any way you please: say, picture the yellow yolk of an egg, the yellow centre of a daisy, a yellow sun blazing in a clear sky, whatever. I want you to actually see the colour YELLOW.

"When you have it, then go down to the next colour which is GREEN.

"Now, visualise the colour GREEN strongly in your mind's eye. Choose what you need to make it come into you: a green lawn, green leaves, a glowing green emerald. Whatever you need to see the colour GREEN inside your head.

"When you have it, now go down to the next colour, which is BLUE.

"Fill your mind with the colour BLUE. BLUE. BLUE. BLUE … possibly visualising a bright blue cloudless sky, a blue lake. Use whatever you need, but you must see the colour BLUE.

"When you have it, now go down to the last colour which you need to visualise, which is VIOLET. See VIOLET within your mind. Possibly visualise it as a bunch of violets, a violet light, entirely as you wish, just as long as you fill your mind with the colour VIOLET.

"Now, immerse yourself entirely within the colour VIOLET … let it be as a mist into which you drop yourself. Drop deep into the VIOLET, and as you drop into the violet you drop down deeper and deeper into hypnosis.

"And we are going to go down even deeper still, dropping down, down, down into deep hypnosis.

"You have reached the violet alpha level … now look in front of you, and you will see that you are standing at the end of a corridor which is made completely of white marble. The walls are marble, the floor is marble, the ceiling is marble. It is not a very long corridor, and there is a light at its end. Now, start walking down the corridor in the direction of the light.

"When you get to the light … *stop!*

"Now, in front of you, when you look down at your feet, you will see you are standing at the top of a spacious staircase. There are twenty-one steps to this staircase, and in a moment you are going to start going down … going all the way down the steps to the bottom, and each step you take in going down the staircase sends you down, down deeper and deeper into hypnosis … and by the time you reach the bottom of the staircase you will be completely entranced in profound hypnosis … deep in the realm of sleep in which you will vividly experience and react to each experience suggested to you.

"All ready now to start going down the stairs, step by step … and, as you do this, actually see your physical body going down the stairs. As you

175

commence walking down the stairs actually *feel* yourself descending deeper and deeper into hypnosis … into the realm of sleep.

"All ready, you are standing on the top step … the 21st step. Now step down to the 20th step. Good. Now down to the 19th step. Down to the 18th step, on down to the 17th step. You are getting deep into the alpha level … becoming more and more sleepy as you descend the stairs … dropping down, down into hypnosis … dropping down, down into the realm of sleep. Now step down to the 16th step. To the 15th, to the 14th, the 13th, the 12th, the 11th, the 10th. You are getting so sleepy you just drag your feet as you descend the stairs to the bottom. You are so sleepy … sleep … sleepy sleep. On down you go to the 9th step, the 8th, the 7th, the 6th. You are getting deeper and deeper way down into profound hypnosis. Way down deep asleep in profound hypnosis. Sleep. Sleep. Sleepy sleep. You step down to the 5th. You are almost there to the bottom of the staircase now. You are so glad because you are so sleepy, asleep in hypnosis you can just barely go on. But go on now and then you can drop away completely into a sound hypnotic sleep. On, on you go … to the 4th step, the 3rd, the 2nd, and, at last, the 1st. You have successfully reach the bottom of the staircase, and you are in profound hypnosis ready to follow and perform perfectly every suggestion that is given you."

The induction is complete and you have produced a deep level of hypnosis. You can proceed on to perform whatever you elect for the effective presentation of your hypnotism show. You will find this method works excellently with both solo subjects and with a group seated in a row upon the stage at the start of your show.

This method lends itself to a colourful (no joke intended!) presentation, especially of interest when you are performing before a New Age group, i.e. people who are interested in Oriental-type processes.

NOTE TO HYPNOTIST: Be flexible in your performing. Adapt your style of presentation and your program to fit the specific audience before which you are performing. Tailoring your show to suit your audience is the mark of a master showman.

Chapter Thirty-Five
Ormond McGill's "Guardian Angel" Stage Hypnotism Method

As far as I know, this method of inducing hypnosis is new. Hypnosis is a dissociation process, and this method causes a dissociation which relates the induction to the influence of an outside force. The method came to me one night in a dream and I have found it most effective with such a presentation to an adult audience of a serious nature. I regard it as a method to use on occasion with a specialised audience. When you come to the point in your show where you are going to invite volunteers onto the stage to experiment with hypnotism, make this announcement: "Ladies and gentlemen, in a few moments, we are going to invite a committee of volunteers on stage to experiment with the experiencing of hypnosis. For this purpose, I wish especially persons to come forward who feel they are in touch with their 'higher self'. I therefore ask you to answer the question which I will put to you now … How many of you in the audience have ever felt you have a guardian angel to whom you feel a closeness, as a guiding force in your life? If you have ever felt that you do indeed have a guardian angel, please raise your hand." You will often be very surprised at the response you get to this question. Many hands will go up, as many people feel they have such transcendental guidance in their life. Following this affirmative response, follow on to ask another question of the audience: "Those of you who have responded that you feel you have a guardian angel, are you by any chance familiar with the process of writing a personal letter to your angel with a request for a heartfelt wish? Have you written down what you requested, then burnt the paper on which the request was written, allowing the smoke of the smouldering paper to be concentrated upon, as it drifts upwards into space; feeling sincerely that your message has been directly received by your guardian angel? If you have heard of this process or possibly participated in such a sacred performance, lift your hand so I may know to whom I speak."

Not so many hands will be raised this time, but a number will, as many people have heard of it and some have used it – often with striking results in obtaining the materialised things and/or wish. The persons who give positive affirmation to this question you now invite to come forward as the committee of subjects you will use for your show on this particular occasion. You will have obtained a committee of serious-minded people, who will prove highly responsive to hypnosis. Now address the assembled committee of this evolved nature: "I will hand each of you a pad of paper and a pencil and ask you first of all to write a message to your special angel that I will dictate, affirming your expert mastery of your inner mind for the benefit of yourself in every way as we experiment with hypnosis on this stage together." Hand out pad and pencil to each persons on stage (or have your assistant do so). Then tell them to write this letter to their guardian angel:

DEAREST ANGEL

I AM ON STAGE BEFORE AN AUDIENCE OF PEOPLE FRIENDLY TO ME, AND I ASK THAT YOU GUIDE BOTH ME AND THE HYPNOTIST [mention your name] CONDUCTING THIS SESSION IN HYPNOSIS, AS I LEARN HOW BETTER TO USE MY SUBCONSCIOUS MIND TO CONTROL MY CONSCIOUS BEHAVIOUR. THANK YOU, DEAR ANGEL, FOR GRANTING THIS REQUEST. NOW IT IS TIME TO GO ON WITH THE SHOW. PLEASE STAY WITH ME AND HELP ME ENJOY THE PROFOUNDEST OF HYPNOTIC EXPERIENCES.

MY LOVE TO YOU

[Sign your name here]

Now, collect the letters, place the papers in a bowl resting on a little stand at centre front of stage before the committee. Set light to the letters and have the committee concentrate upon the rising smoke which the burning messages have produced (as the stage fixation object), while you proceed with your standard hypnotic trance induction formula. You will find this method of hypnotising fascinating, as it provides a committee of highly evolved subjects for you to work with, proves strong motivation to being hypnotised by those participating, while being of great interest for the spectators to witness. It is a method which will be found to build rapport between the audience and the volunteers on stage, as almost everyone, at one time or another, has related to their guardian angel.

Chapter Thirty-Six

A Condensation of 95 Methods of Hypnotising Gathered From Around the World

As this book is encyclopedic in scope, this condensation of a variety of methods of hypnotising is appropriate. It provides the student with a good coverage of successful techniques. All are based on the principle of the subject bringing the mind to one-pointedness of concentrated attention, causing the subject to subjectively respond to suggestions and thereby producing the state of mind of hypnosis.

These techniques follow a threefold pattern of hypnotic induction: 1. Fixation of Attention; 2. Eyelid Fixation (fixation = eyes stuck together so they will not open on conscious command); 3. Sleep suggestions following Eyelid Fixation. As "Eyelid Fixation" and "Sleep Formula" are inclusive to all of these techniques, the performance of these processes will first be given before proceeding to describe the method.

Method One – The "Eyelid Fixation" Process

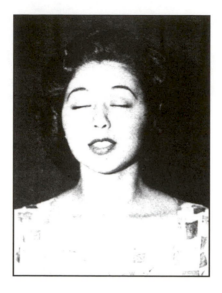

After the subject has gone through the initial process of hypnotic induction via whatever the method being used to concentrate attention and when the eyes are closed, say to him, or her, impressively: "Your eyes are becoming stuck together! The lids are stuck tight and you will find you cannot open your eyes. I will count from one to three, and by the time I reach the count of three you will find you cannot open your eyes try as hard as you will. Ready: one, two, *three*! Your eyes are fastened together so tightly you will find it absolutely impossible to open them now. Try! Try hard! You cannot open your eyes!"

The subject will find it impossible to open his eyes try as hard as he will. You can now immediately proceed to deepen the hypnosis by presenting the "Sleep Formula" presented in the following chapter.

If desired, you can increase the "eye-fixation experience" by having the subject roll back the eyes under the closed lids, looking upward and backward inside of head, as it were. This causes a muscular tension of the eye muscles making opening of the lids literally impossible, until the eyes are rolled downward. The hypnotist does well to take advantage of every expedient which increases the effectiveness of his work.

NOTE TO HYPNOTIST: In applying all of these hypnotic methods establish fixation of eyelids, and then proceed on to hypnotic sleep suggestions.

Method Two – The "Sleep Formula" For Deepening Developing Hypnosis

Immediately following the successful performance of "Eyelid Fixation" proceed on to presenting a Trance intensifying "Sleep Formula". The following is a generalised "Sleep Formula" that can be used in conjunction with each of the 100 methods of hypnotising here presented.

"Forget about your eyes being stuck together; just let them relax, and allow the relaxation from your eyes to flow down over your entire body, causing you to become relaxed all over. And as you relax all over, it makes you feel drowsy and sleepy. So just relax and drift away into the realm of sleep. "How sleepy you are becoming, so just drift away into sleep. Sleep. Sleep. Go to sleep. Things are all getting farther and farther away, and you are sinking down deeper and deeper to sleep."

NOTE TO HYPNOTIST: Lower your voice and speak softly as you present the suggestions of drifting away into the realm of sleep. Then gradually increase your tone as you continue the sleep-inducing formula:

"Breathe deeply and freely, and every breath you take sends you down deeper and deeper into hypnosis. [Watch the subject's breathing; as hypnosis develops, the respiration slows and intensifies.] You are in deep hypnosis now, and you feel wonderful all over. Being in hypnosis benefits you in every way. You are in neutral gear and you coast along in a state of absolute relaxation free of stress of every kind. You enjoy so much this peaceful state, so drop even deeper and deeper into it now. Go down into profound hypnosis."

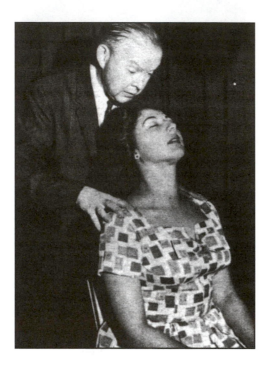

NOTE TO HYPNOTIST: Memorise both "The Eyelid Fixation" procedure and the "Sleep Formula" so that you can present them with confident ease. Their delivery should become as natural as is your breathing. That is the way to expertise.

Method Three

Have the subject take a seat in a comfortable chair. Rest feet flat on the floor with hands in lap or one on each knee. Take position in front of subject and hold a shiny ball before eyes. A shiny ball-bearing or clear glass marble works well for the purpose. This functions as "the fixation object" used in this method. Have the source of light come from behind the subject so that it will shine upon the ball producing a highlight. Ask the subject to keep his eyes focused forward and, without moving the head, to lift the eyes upward to stare at the ball which you hold in a position above the level of the eyes. This position is such that the subject has to strain to stare at it. It fatigues the eyes rapidly.

Allow the subject to stare in this manner for some moments. Then suggest: "As you stare up at the bright ball, concentrate your entire attention on it, and think of going to sleep. Think of how sleepy you are beginning to feel. How heavy and tired your eyes are becoming, and how drowsy and sleepy you are. Your eyes are becoming so tired it is difficult to keep them any longer. They are getting misty and tired; how they burn and smart. You want to close your eyes so much now. You want to close your eyes and go to sleep. All right, close your eyes and go to sleep."

Continue your suggestions in such vein for a few minutes. Soon your subject's eyes will assume a glassy look and will close. Forced now into "Eyelid Fixation", and having successfully performed that test, go directly into your "Sleep Formula", inducing a deep hypnotic trance.

Method Four

Place a lighted candle behind a bottle resting on table in front of subject. Have subject lean forward slightly and gaze on the spot where the light focuses on the opposite side. Proceed same as Method Three. When eyes close perform "Eyelid Fixation", and on into "Sleep Formula".

Method Five
Similar to Method Four. In this method, a lighted candle is placed directly before subject. This is used as "the fixation object" to be concentrated upon. Suggest eyes tiring in watching the flame. When eyes close, perform "Eyelid Fixation" testing and proceed into "Sleep Formula", inducing hypnosis.

Method Six
Have subject hold a hand mirror about ten inches before eyes, and look into the reflected pupils. Subject is to concentrate on the reflection in the mirror. Give eye closure suggestions and test for fixation. Then proceed with "Sleep Formula".

Method Seven
Strike a match and hold the flame about six inches in front of subject's eyes. Have subject stare at it until it is almost burnt out; then to close eyes until you strike another match. Subject is then told to open eyes again and stare at flame until it burns out. Repeat this with a third match, and suggest that with the lighting of the third match a condition of sleepiness will occur and to close eyes and keep them closed. Perform "Eyelid Fixation" and on to "Sleep Formula".

Method Eight

Have subject grip the end of a full length pencil between teeth, and allow gaze to run slowly up and down the polished surface of the pencil. Eyes quickly tire in doing this. Suggest eye-fatigue ... eye-closure ... test for "Eyelid Fixation" and on into "Sleep Formula" inducing hypnosis.

Method Nine
This is a variation of Method Eight. Have subject concentrate attention on the tip of nose. Then proceed same as in Method Eight to induce hypnosis.

Method Ten

Have subject hold hands, backs facing inwards, about seven inches in front of face. Commencing with the left little finger and working on towards the right, subject is to stare at each fingernail in turn. At each nail-gazing, subject is to slowly count from one to ten to self; then move on to the next nail in sequence. During this process, hypnotist softly suggests into subject's ear that the process is very tiring, that eyes are becoming heavy and want to close, to forget the whole thing and go to sleep. A responsive subject will rarely get beyond gazing at the fifth fingernail before the eyes will close. Test for "Eyelid Fixation" and into "Sleep Formula".

Method Eleven

Hand a photograph of some person unknown to the subject. Explain that it is a picture of a famous hypnotist and that by gazing into the eyes on the photo the hypnotist's influence will be experienced, and they will soon drop into sound sleep. As the subject stares at the photograph, following these instructions, proceed giving drowsy and sleep suggestions. When eyes close, test for fixation, and into "Sleep Formula".

Method Twelve

Extend your forefinger and move it slowly back and forth, about six inches in front of and a little above the eyes of subject. Request subject to follow unwaveringly the moving finger. Suggest eyes becoming very tired and closing. When eyes close, test for fixation and proceed into "Sleep Formula".

Method Thirteen

Hold the tips of your first and second fingers in front of subject's eyes, in position as in Method Twelve. Now separate the fingers slowly and then draw them together equally slowly. Have subject follow the movement with eyes. Suggest eye fatigue, closure, fixation and into "Sleep Formula".

Method Fourteen

Give subject a ring with a bright jewel in it. Instruct to hold it about six inches above head while gazing at it. Stand behind subject and suggest eyes becoming heavy and tired. Eyes will close, and suggest that when eyes close he will fall right over backward into your arms. You will catch him and, as he drops over backwards suggest that he will drop down into a deep hypnotic sleep. When eyes close and subject falls back, catch him and gently lower to floor while suggesting "Sleep Formula" close to subject's ear. Lower his body to floor.

Method Fifteen
Write the word "sleep" on a card, and tell subject to give full attention to that word and concentrate upon it, while repeating in mentally over and over. Suggest that the word is making him very sleepy ... to close eyes and drift off to sleep. When eyes close, test for fixation and into "Sleep Formula".

Method Sixteen

Have two subjects sit opposite each other. They grip each other's hands and look into each other's eyes. Tell them that what one does the other will do in like manner: that after staring at one another for a few minute their eyes will tire and they will put each other to sleep in hypnosis. If both parties are responsive subjects both will go to sleep. After eyes close, perform "Eyelid Fixation" on both subjects simultaneously: then into "Sleep Formula", for both to respond to.

Method Seventeen

Have subject close eyes and to clamp teeth tightly together. Then to relax the jaw, then to clamp the teeth together again, and so on. Have subject continue to do this clenching and relaxing of the jaw over and over, while you suggest it is becoming more and more difficult to do, so to go to sleep and forget about it. Subject will quickly enter hypnosis. Test for "Eyelid Fixation" and into "Sleep Formula".

Method Eighteen

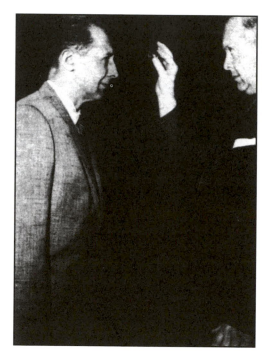

Have subject stand facing you. Hold a crystal marble about a foot in front of subject's eyes and have him stare at it. Then suggest that as you move it away from him (or her) he will feel compelled to follow it. Keep moving it away from subject slowly, and he will follow it. As he responds, suggest that he is starting to fall forward and, as he does, you will catch him, his eyes will close and he will go fast to sleep in profound hypnosis. When he falls catch him and gently lay him on the floor, while presenting "Sleep Formula". (This method will be observed to be a reverse handling of Method Fourteen.)

Method Nineteen

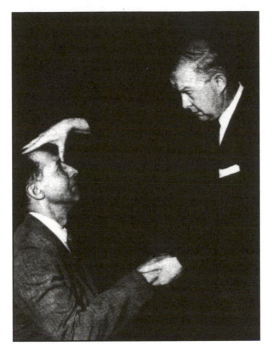

Have subject close eyes. Press firmly on top of head with your fingers and tell him to roll his eyes upwards and imagine he is looking through the top of his head. Let him do this for about three minutes, and then tell him his eyelids have become firmly stuck together, and he cannot open his eyes try as hard as he will. Place your right thumb at the root of subject's nose while resting fingers on top of head. Take the subject's right hand in your left as he tries vainly to open his eyes. This "Eyelid Fixation" test completed, put even more pressure on his head by squeezing your thumb and fingers on hand while you squeeze his right hand with your left. This adds emphasis to the power of your suggestions. Then go directly into "Sleep Formula".

Method Twenty

Draw a picture of a large eye on a card; hand it to the subject. Have him concentrate on the eye, as you give suggestions of the eye holding his attention and making his eyes very tired so they want to close. When eyes close test for fixation and go into "Sleep Formula". (Note that this method is a variation of Method Fifteen. It is well for the hypnotist to have a variety of methods at his command. This adds interest to his work.)

Method Twenty-One

Place a bottle of plain water on a table about two feet away from the seated subject. Tell the subject the bottle contains a powerful hypnotic drug and that, when the cork is removed the odour from it will put him to sleep. Explain that, while some like the odour, most people think it is rather obnoxious, so he will probably find it disagreeable. Then take the cork out and have him close his eyes. Tell him to inhale deeply the odour into his lungs. Wait a minute, and then suggest: "You have had time to smell it now, and from the expression on your face I judge you do not like it. Smell it now. It will put you sound to sleep. That's it, inhale the odour deeply and drop down deeply to sleep. You are going to sleep now. Your head is dropping forward on your chest. You dislike the odour but it is putting you fast to sleep." Proceed on into "Sleep Formula" inducing hypnosis.

Method Twenty-Two

Have subject seated while you stand in front. Firmly take hold of back of subject's neck with your left hand, and hold your right thumb in front of eyes, requesting that he concentrate full attention upon it. Then gradually bring your thumb in closer to his eyes. Do this very slowly and finally, when you have brought it right up to his eyes, tell him to close them. Then grasp his head between your hands and squeeze, while presenting "Sleep Formula".

Method Twenty-Three

Have subject stand before you. Firmly grasp his hands in yours. Have him look into your eyes for a few moments while you gaze intently at the root of his nose, between his eyes, while you tell him that the grip upon his hands is so firm that he cannot release himself from it no matter how hard he tries.

Continue these suggestions while squeezing more and more firmly your grip upon his hands. Then tell him to close his eyes and to pull against your hands with all his might, but he cannot get loose. After the subject has vainly tried for a few moments, tell him to relax now and go to sleep. Gradually relax your grip upon his hands, and go into "Sleep Formula".

Method Twenty-Four

Explain to subject that the centre controlling sleep is situated at the base of the brain, just above the spinal cord; and, that by riveting the attention upon that centre and willing it, sleep will come. Then request the subject to close eyes and concentrate on this centre. When subject has done this in silence for a few minutes, fasten eyelids together and go directly into "Sleep Formula".

Method Twenty-Five
Stand subject on his feet and have him close his eyes. You take position directly behind him, place your hand at the back of his neck and tell him to think of falling backwards and that you will catch him when he falls. Catch the subject when he falls and return him to upright position. Repeat the "Falling Backwards Test". The response positive, return subject to his feet and turn him around, and tell him to close his eyes tightly, as you press gently on his eyes telling him it is impossible for him to open them. While subject is trying to open eyes, clamp head between your hands, one hand over each ear with your thumbs resting over eyebrows, and go directly into "Sleep Formula".

Method Twenty-Six
Any one of the five senses (sight, hearing, feeling, taste and smell) can be used as the centre of concentration by the mind in inducing hypnosis. This method employs the sense of hearing. Have subject take a comfortable seat and close eyes. Tell the subject you are going to hypnotise him by giving attention to sound. Hold a watch close to his ear and have him give complete attention to the ticking: to concentrate so fully upon the ticking that it completely fills his mind. Now let him listen to the ticking for about three minutes while you remain silent. At the end of that time it will begin to seem that the ticking is becoming fainter and fainter and farther and farther away in the distance and as it recedes he is dropping down deeper and deeper to sleep in hypnosis. As you give these suggestions, gradually move the watch away from his ear, so the ticking becomes fainter and fainter. Finally suggest: "The ticking is all gone now and you are going fast asleep." Proceed directly into "Sleep Formula", inducing hypnosis.

Method Twenty-Seven
Hand subject a pen flashlight. This device has a plunger on the rear end which, upon being pressed, lights the light and on being released, out goes the light. These are obtainable at any hardware or variety store. Have the subject grip the light firmly and light the bulb. He is to stare at the light fixedly as he holds it before his eyes. As he gazes at it, suggest that his eyes will quickly become tired and as his eyes tire that his hand will relax and that finally, when the light goes out, he will close his eyes

and go sound to sleep. Then suggest that the hand holding the pen light is becoming heavy and is dropping to his lap; and when it hits his lap he will be asleep in hypnosis. As soon as hand drops to lap, go into "Sleep Formula", intensifying the hypnosis.

Method Twenty-Eight

This is an "afterimage" technique for producing hypnosis. To use it, have the subject close eyes and look at the bright spots which come and go behind the closed eyelids. These are "afterimages" of light stimulation of the optic nerve endings which continue on even when the eyes are closed. Anyone can see these if attention is directed to them. Tell the subject to concentrate attention on these flitting "spots of light", and suggest that while watching these internal spots his eyelids will become stuck fast together. Produce fixation of the eyelids and test. After the subject has failed to open his eyes, tell him to relax and go directly into "Sleep Formula". Hypnosis quickly ensues.

Method Twenty-Nine

Have the subject count his own pulse-beat in his wrist. After he has found it, tell him to close his eyes and count the beats to himself, at the same time willing his heart's action to grow slower and slower. Then suggest that the heart beat is slowing down in response to his thoughts, and that he is sinking down deeper and deeper to sleep, as a slowing of heart-beat is the pathway to sleep. Go directly into "Sleep Formula".

Method Thirty

Have subject seated while you kneel before him (or her). Have him centre his gaze upon your eyes and keep attention fixed. Then grip hands and press firmly your thumb nails on the centre of the nails of the middle finger of your subject. Make the pressure hard enough to be almost painful. Suggest that the sensation of the pressure on the nails will extend up arms and, as this occurs, eyes will close. Give suggestions for eye closure. Perform "Eyelid Fixation" and on into "Sleep Formula".

Method Thirty-One

Have subject close eyes and place hands over eyes, so that the hollow of the palm of each hand covers an eye. Have subject sit thus for five minutes. The process remarkably relaxes the eyes. Then suggest that he cannot open his eyes as they have become so relaxed. Perform "Eyelid Fixation". Now suggest that hands will drop down from closed eyes to lap; and when hands drop to lap that he will go immediately to sleep. As the hands fall, go directly into "Sleep Formula".

Method Thirty-Two
Have subject close eyes, cross arms and place the middle finger of each hand on either elbow tip. Tell subject this will so affect the "magnetic currents" of the body as to produce sleep in a few minutes. Further suggest that, in all probability, the currents will be felt rising up the arms as the pressure on the elbow tips is continued, and that his closed eyes will become firmly fastened together so he cannot open them. Perform "Eyelid Fixation" and on into "Sleep Formula".

Method Thirty-Three
Hand subject a watch and ask him to follow the second hand closely, for about thirty seconds, at the end of which time he is to close his eyes for another thirty seconds. He is then to open them and repeat the operation until his eyes refuse to open. Keep suggesting that each time he will find his eyelids becoming increasingly difficult to open, and finally that he will not be able to open them at all. When they finally remain shut, go into "Sleep Formula".

Method Thirty-Four
Seat subject in a comfortable chair. Have him make himself absolutely comfortable and relax completely while thinking of how very comfortable he is. Now, tell him he is so comfortable and relaxed that he feels just like drifting off to sleep, and that he will yawn. Tell him to think of yawning and to try to yawn. As soon as he yawns, tell him that his eyes are now stuck shut and he cannot open them. Test for "Eyelid Fixation" and go into "Sleep Formula".

Method Thirty-Five
Tell subject to close eyes and to cross the first and second fingers of right hand. Have him then put the crossed fingers in mouth and touch his tongue: first with the tip of one crossed finger and then the other. Tell him that, as he continues to do this, touching with fingertips back and forth, soon he will not be able to tell which fingertip is touching the tip of the tongue; that shortly he will lose all inclination to touch the tongue and he will finally cease to touch it at all, and will go fast to sleep. Continue suggestions that he is getting sleepy. Finally tell him to drop his hand from

mouth into lap and go into deep hypnosis. Proceed directly into "Sleep Formula".

Method Thirty-Six
Have subject press thumb and first finger firmly together with the head of a pin between them as he extends his arm out before himself. Have him close his eyes and tell him that the pressure on the pin will gradually lessen as he becomes tired and sleepy, and that finally the pin will drop from his grasp. Continue your suggestions of how sleepy he is becoming and of the pin dropping. When the pin finally slips from between his fingers tell him to drop his extended arm to his side and go fast to sleep. Proceed directly into "Sleep Formula".

Method Thirty-Seven
Have the subject take a comfortable seat or lie outstretched on a bed, if convenient. Have subject close his eyes, and pretend to sleep by snoring slightly. Allow the snores to proceed in and out with the breath while suggesting how sleepy he is becoming. It is surprising how quickly this encourages sleep to incur. Test for "Eyelid Fixation" at the end of three minutes of this "snoring", and proceed into "Sleep Formula".

Method Thirty-Eight
Ask subject to name his or her favourite colour; then to close eyes and imagine nothing can be seen but this colour in front of eyes beneath the closed lids. As the colour is visualised, suggest eyelids are becoming stuck so tightly together they will not open, so the colour continues to persist beneath the stuck eyelids. Proceed into "Sleep Formula", associating it with the sleep, producing colour, inducing hypnosis.

Method Thirty-Nine
Have subject close eyes and imagine that he is counting the number of bricks appearing on the corner of a high building. He should commence at the bottom and count up. If he reaches the top before dropping off into hypnosis, he should count them again, starting this time at the top and working downward. As he does this, suggest that he is getting very tired of the chore and is becoming so sleepy that he must doze off and forget about counting the bricks altogether. Test for "Eyelid Fixation" and proceed on with "Sleep Formula".

Method Forty

Have seated subject close his eyes; hand him a book and have him turn the pages over very slowly by the sense of touch alone. As he does this tell him to see in his "mind's eye" the word "sleep", written in large black letters, on every page as he turns them. As he does this, continue suggestions of how drowsy he is becoming; how he is becoming more and more sluggish, and is dropping off to sleep. If he does not "drop off", wait until he has turned about a hundred pages in the book and then test for "Eyelid Fixation", and proceed directly into "Sleep Formula".

Method Forty-One

Have subject close his eyes and imagine he is stretching out to arm's length a heavy rubber band. Imagine the band to be about two inches in size at first. Have him go through the actual movement of stretching it out further and further, until he has stretched as far as him arms will reach. Just before he stretches his arms out to full length, grasp his head between your hands and press in firmly on temples while presenting forcefully the "Sleep Formula".

Method Forty-Two

Have the subject stand before you and close his eyes. Then place your hands directly over his ears. Press in on the ears, shutting out sound. Allow subject to experience this "silence" for about five minutes. Then suddenly take your hand away, and place one hand on top of his head; press down firmly and forcefully suggest that his eyes are stuck shut and he cannot open them. Test for "Eyelid Fixation" and proceed with "Sleep Formula".

Method Forty-Three

Place a cork between subject's teeth. Tell him to close his eyes and to bite firmly into the cork with all his might. This quickly tires the jaw part of the head, and when one part becomes tired the tiredness is transferred to all parts of the body emphasising your suggestions of how tired he is becoming. How very much he wants to drop off into slumber. Proceed with "Sleep Formula".

Method Forty-Four

Have subject sit with eyes closed, and imagine the juice of a lemon is being dripped into mouth, and to notice how this thought causes the flow of saliva in mouth to increase. It actually occurs, and as he feels it suggest how very sleepy he is becoming. The saliva response combined with the sleep suggestion produces a powerful hypnotic effect. Proceed with "Sleep Formula" inducing hypnosis.

Method Forty-Five

Place a few drops of a strong perfume upon a handkerchief. Have subject close eyes and place near nose so the smell is intense. Tell him or her that while it will not produce sleep in itself, yet it will cause drowsiness and will fasten his eyes together so he cannot open them. Perform "Eyelid Fixation". Proceed into "Sleep Formula".

Method Forty-Six

Have subject close eyes and imagine he or she is looking at the ceiling of the room. Tell him to imagine that he is looking into the corners of the ceiling, one after the other in order around the room. He is to continue in imagination to go around and around the room from corner to corner. Then suggest how this is making him very sleepy and he wants to stop and go to sleep. Tell him to relax, let the imaging go, and just drop off to sleep. Proceed directly into "Sleep Formula" inducing deep hypnosis.

Method Forty-Seven

Have subject take a comfortable seat and close his eyes. Stand beside him and lightly touch the top of his head with the tips of your fingers, at intervals of about two seconds per tap. Do this head tapping for about two minutes as you suggest: "Sleep. Sleep, Sleep! Go to sleep!" in rhythm with the tapping. Fasten eyelids together and proceed into "Sleep Formula".

Method Forty-Eight
Have your subject close his eyes and roll his tongue back in his mouth as far as he can. Tell him to hold the tongue in that position steadily by pressing it against his palate. Go into your suggestions of how tired and sleepy this is making him become. Perform "Eyelid Fixation" and go directly into "Sleep Formula".

Method Forty-Nine
Put a little Vaseline on your subject's eyelids. Have subject close eyes and then place a strip of adhesive tape over each eye. Tell the subject now to try to open eyes. Of course he cannot, but tell him to continue trying until he gets a conception of what it is like to have his eyelids stuck tight like that, so he cannot open them. Let him try to fight against the tape to open his eyes, as you suggest that his efforts are becoming less and less as he becomes more and more sleepy. Do this for about three minutes, and then remove the tapes while commanding him to keep his eyes still tightly closed. Then ask him to sit still for a moment while holding in mind that his eyelids are stuck tightly together and will not open, just as they were when taped. Perform "Eyelid Fixation" and go into "Sleep Formula". Hypnosis is quickly induced.

Method Fifty
Have subject close eyes and hand him a small rubber ball with the instructions that he is to roll it around and around in his hands. Tell him as he rolls it to imagine he can see it rolling. Have him keep rolling it between his hands for a minute. Then present suggestions of how tired and sleepy this rolling of the rubber ball is making him become; fasten his eyelids together, and go directly into "Sleep Formula".

Method Fifty-One

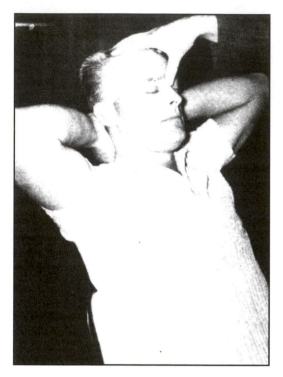

Have subject close eyes and lock his fingers together behind his neck. Stand in front of subject and rest the fingers of your right hand on top of his head and thumb on root of nose. Suggest that he is getting drowsy and his eyes are tired and are becoming locked together just like his hands behind his neck. After a minute or so of such suggestions, test for "Eyelid Fixation". Following this, tell your subject that his hands are locked together likewise and he cannot get them apart from behind his neck either, try as hard as he will. After he fails to get them apart, tell him that his hands are now pulling forward forcing his head down upon his chest and that he is going to sleep. Relax his hands; put them in his lap; proceed into "Sleep Formula".

Method Fifty-Two

Have subject close eyes and instruct that he is to breathe deeply and rapidly sixty-nine times; that he is to keep track of the count as he breathes, and is to stop the deep breaths when he reaches that number. Explain to him that this deep repeated breathing will put him to sleep. Have him commence the breathing, and you count with him. Many subjects will go to sleep long before they reach sixty-nine. You can tell when sleep occurs by the change in the subject's respiration. Should he reach sixty-nine, immediately fasten his eyelids together and go directly into your "Sleep Formula".

Method Fifty-Three

Have subject close eyes and, picking up a tuft of hair on top of head pull it gently, yet hard enough to produce a definite sensation. Tell subject to give complete attention to hair being pulled. As you do this, present suggestions to concentrate on the sensations which are causing drowsiness producing sleep. After three minutes of such suggestions, let go of hair and grasp head between hands pressing in on the ears. Fasten eyelids together and go directly into "Sleep Formula".

Method Fifty-Four

Have subject close his eyes and have him drop his head forward on his chest. Then instruct him to imagine he is looking through his body to the base of his spine. Let him continue with this imagined experience for about two minutes. Then slowly commence your suggestions of how sleepy this is making him become. He is getting so drowsy and sleepy. Fasten his eyelids together and go directly into "Sleep Formula".

Method Fifty-Five

Have subject close eyes and tie a length of string around head and across forehead. Then tie another length of string around each of middle fingers, just below last joint, as hands rest in lap. Have subject sit in silence for two minutes after doing this, and then directly fasten eyelids together by the command they are stuck tight and will not open. Proceed on into "Sleep Formula".

Method Fifty-Six

Wrap the end of a length of soft copper wire around subject's head. Extend it out and wrap the other end of the wire around your own head. Explain to subject you are going to transmit thoughts of sleep along the wire which will cause the eyes to become firmly fastened together so it will be impossible to open them. State that your thoughts will travel along the wire causing drowsiness and sleep to occur. Have subject stare steadily into your eyes for a full minute, while concentrating in silence. Then command: "Close your eyes!" Wait a further two minutes in silence, and fasten eyelids together; go directly into "Sleep Formula" producing hypnosis.

Method Fifty-Seven

Take a glass of water and tell subject you will show how water can produce sleep when it is concentrated upon. Hand glass of water to subject. Have subject close eyes and instruct to take a sip at a time until it is all gone and, in swallowing each mouthful to repeat to self. "This is putting me to sleep!" Subject should take a short pause between each sip. When subject has drunk the entire glassful, take glass from subject and suggest "Eyelid Fixation" and "Sleep Formula". Hypnosis is induced.

Method Fifty-Eight

Have subject close his eyes and raise his arms above his head. Have him hold this position for a few moments and then lower his arms very slowly to sides, keeping them stiffly extended throughout. Subject is then to raise his arms again above head and repeat the raising and lowering process six times. As he does this, keep giving suggestions of how tired, drowsy and sleepy this process is causing him to feel. As he lowers his arms for the sixth time, fasten his eyelids together, then go directly into "Sleep Formula".

Method Fifty-Nine
Tell subject you will drop a powerful hypnotic solution into his eyes and that this solution, though harmless and pleasant, will fasten his eyelids so tightly together that he will be unable to open them. Then, with an eye dropper containing soothing eye-drops, drop a little into each eye. Immediately request subject to close eyes tight while you suggest that his eyes are becoming stuckfast together by the solution. Continue thus for a few minutes. Test for "Eyelid Fixation" and then go directly into "Sleep Formula".

Method Sixty

Take two metal plates to which wires have been attached. The wires lead outside the room apparently to an electrical source. Actually they are unattached, but this is unknown to the subject. Place one of the metal plates beneath the subject's feet and the other plate is held against top of head. Have subject close eyes. Explain there will be a mild electric current passing through body by this arrangement which will produce relaxation of all body muscles causing his eyelids to become fastened together, and inducing hypnosis. After about three minutes of silence, during which you request the subject to experience the passing of the electrical current through body, test for "Eyelid Fixation" and go into "Sleep Formula."

Method Sixty-One

This is a variation of the foregoing method. For this use smaller sized metal plates attached to the wires, and have subject close eyes and hold one plate gently over each eye, as you explain that the mild electric current passing through the plates will cause the eyes to become fastened together so they will not open. Suggest that the continuing current through the eyes will produce sleep. After about three minutes, remove the plates from eyes, push subject's hands down to sides. Test for "Eyelid Fixation" and proceed to "Sleep Formula".

Method Sixty-Two

Hand subject a pencil and a pad of paper, and have him write the word "sleep" very slowly forty times, and to close his eyes for a moment between each writing of the word. After he has written it for the fortieth time he is to sit with his eyes closed. As soon as you see he has finished the writing and his eyes remain closed, perform "Eyelid Fixation" and go directly into "Sleep Formula".

Method Sixty-Three

Have subject hold his nose tightly between thumb and forefingers and breathe deeply through his mouth while holding the thought of sleep in his mind all the while. Then close eyes and perform "Eyelid Fixation" and into "Sleep Formula".

Method Sixty-Four

Make a cone out of a sheet of paper and have subject place the large end of cone against his face and look through the small opening at the opposite end towards a small light, such as a candle flame. After he has done this for about three minutes, tell him to close his eyes and imagine that he still sees the light. Suggest that things are beginning to fade away, and he is falling to sleep. Fasten his eyelids together and proceed directly into "Sleep Formula".

Method Sixty-Five
Have your subject close his eyes for half a minute. He is then to open the right eye and say the word "sleep" to himself. He is then to close his right eye and is to open the left, saying the word "sleep" again. He is to keep this process up for about two minutes, alternatively opening and closing one eye and then the other about every second of time. At the end of two minutes, close both his eyes with gentle pressure of your thumbs; press gently on the lids for about fifteen seconds while giving suggestions of fastening the eyelids together. Test for fixation and go directly into "Sleep Formula" producing hypnosis.

Method Sixty-Six

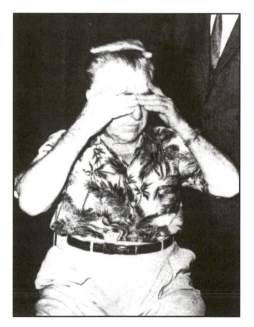

Have the subject sit with the thumbs of each of his hands closing his ears and his fingers closing his eyes. While he is doing this, stand beside him with your hand resting lightly on his head. At the end of a few minutes take down his hands from ears and eyes, and rest them in his lap. Fasten his eyelids together and go directly into "Sleep Formula".

Method Sixty-Seven

Have subject look you steadily in the eyes for about half a minute, then close eyes. Next, grasp subject firmly by back of neck with your left hand. Then, place your right hand on forehead and begin revolving head around and around slowly in a circle. Continue these head revolutions while you give suggestions of ensuing drowsiness and sleep; then test for "Eyelid Fixation" and proceed with "Sleep Formula".

Method Sixty-Eight

Have subject close his eyes. Now dip your forefinger in cold water and, beginning at the centre of his forehead draw your cold finger down to the tip of his nose. Again dip your finger in the cold water and draw it over the subject's left eyebrow; then from the centre of the forehead down each cheek to the chin; then from the back of his neck up over the head to the centre of the forehead again. Keep dipping your finger in the cold water after completing each pass. Then touch him on the tip of each ear with the cold finger and also in the centre of the palm of each hand. Have the subject now clasp his hands together, interlocking the fingers, and press them tightly together. Have him hold this position for two minutes and then tell him he cannot unfasten his hands no matter how hard he tries. This test successful, then fasten his eyelids together and go directly into "Sleep Formula".

Method Sixty-Nine

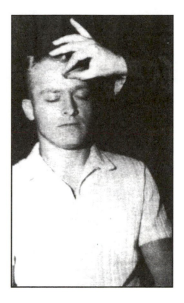

Have your subject close his eyes and press a penny against his forehead. Dampen one side of the penny with a little saliva before pressing it on his forehead, and it will stick there. Tell the subject you are going to press it on his forehead so firmly that he will be unable to shake it loose no matter how hard he tries. Have the subject close his eyes and press the coin firmly against his forehead for a few moments; then secretly remove it in your fingers, as you take your hand away. However, the impressions to the subject will continue to be that the coin is stuck to his forehead. Ask the subject to shake his head and wrinkle the skin of his forehead to shake it loose. He will try, but of course he cannot. As he does this, you keep repeating the suggestions: "It is there; it is stuck so tightly on your forehead that you cannot shake it loose no matter how hard you try." Hold your subject's hands as he continues shaking trying to get it off. Then suggest that the coin is starting to become hot on his forehead, and he will increase the vigour of his shaking. Tell him to relax now and remain quiet for a minute. Then perform "Eyelid Fixation" and go into "Sleep Formula".

Method Seventy
Give your subject a marble to hold in each hand. Tell him to grip them tightly and then place the closed fists gently over eyes. Have the subject continue squeezing the marbles, as you suggest the eyelids are becoming tightly stuck together ("Eyelid Fixation"). Having successfully performed this, then proceed directly into "Sleep Formula".

Method Seventy-One
Have subject close eyes and ask the person to follow you through an imaginary trip around the country. By your verbal suggestions take the subject to the seaside, on a picnic to a park, to various places, etc. The more vividly you can describe the different imaginary scenes the subject is to visualise, the more effective you will find this method of hypnotising. After about four minute of this mental wandering (reverie) go directly into "Eyelid Fixation" followed by "Sleep Formula".

Method Seventy-Two

Sit opposite the subject and have the person stare into your eyes while doing everything (action) you do for a few minutes. For example, place your forefinger on nose, take hold of your ear, touch your chin, wink, cough, open your mouth, etc. Do all manner of things which the subject repeats in like manner. Finally close your eyes as you suggest: "My eyes are closed now just as yours are, and they are becoming fastened together so I cannot open them no matter how hard I try. See, they are fastened together; try hard to open your eyes, but you cannot for they are stuck tightly together just like mine." Having succeeded in thus fastening the subject's eyelids together, you can now go into "Sleep Formula" putting the subject to sleep in hypnosis.

Method Seventy-Three

Have your subject seated, close his eyes, and tell him to take a deep breath, and then sustain a low pitched tone in his throat as long as he can, as he exhales. Perform this process a dozen times. Then tell him to relax and go to sleep. Give relaxation suggestions; perform "Eyelid Fixation" and go directly into "Sleep Formula".

Method Seventy-Four

Have subject seated in a chair beside a table on which is a bowl of warm water. Tell subject to close eyes and place a hand in the bowl of water. At the same time place a damp cold sponge on top of forehead. Suggest that this will draw the blood away from head in order to produce sleep, as during sleep the blood tends to leave the brain. Keep suggesting how sleepy the process is making the subject become. After about five minutes of this procedure, fasten eyelids together and go directly into "Sleep Formula".

Method Seventy-Five

Take hold of both of your subject's hands and grip them firmly. Have him look you squarely in the eyes, as you tell him he will soon feel a tingling, like an electrical current, pass into his hands from yours. Keep suggesting he is feeling this and ask him, from time to time, if he feels it; to be sure to tell you the moment he feels it. When he says he does feel the electric-like current in his hands, tell him to close his eyes. Now grip his hands even more firmly in yours while stating positively that his eyes are fastened and they will not open. This test accomplished successfully, tell him that the current sensation will begin to pass over his entire body, relaxing him and putting him to sleep. Proceed into "Sleep Formula".

Method Seventy-Six

Have subject stand before you and give him a couple of small coins to hold. Have him hold one in each of his fists. Now have him rest his hands on his hips and close his eyes. Now suggest that the coins are beginning to grow warm! They are becoming warmer and warmer in his hands. Continue suggestions: "The coins are now becoming *hot!*" Continue the suggestions: "The coins are *hot, hot, hot!*" Tell him he wants to drop the coins but he cannot let go of them, as his fingers are stuck tightly around the coins. Then, tell him to forget about the coins completely as now his eyes are stuck together and he cannot open them. From "Fixated Eyelids" proceed into "Sleep Formula" inducing hypnosis.

Method Seventy-Seven

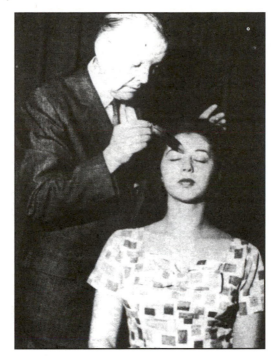

Have subject close eyes, and with a soft feather draw it gently and slowly down over the subject's face. First draw it over each eye a few times, and then continue to stroke the face with it for about three minutes. Then, take a firm hold of subject's head with one hand while continuing to stroke the feather over the eyes with your other hand. Then suggest "Eyelid Fixation", following which you can go directly into your "Sleep Formula".

Method Seventy-Eight

Have subject close eyes, and picking up left hand apply a firm and steady pressure on back of the hand. Suggest that the pressure sensation will soon become a pain; that it will extend up the arm gradually, and to tell you the moment it extends above the wrist. When subject does, place your other hand firmly on top of head and press down. Perform "Eyelid Fixation" at this time and proceed directly into "Sleep Formula".

Method Seventy-Nine

Sit opposite your subject, grip hands and stare into each other's eyes while straining the eyes as widely as possible. After a minute in silence with this open-eyed staring, suggest subject's eyes will stay open. Suggest the feeling that they must stay open and they will not close. Hold your own eyes wide open simultaneously to emphasise the suggestion. Increase your grip on subject's hands declaring it is impossible for subject now to close eyes, and defy subject to do so. After subject struggles for a moment, command now to instantly relax, close eyes and go to sleep. Proceed immediately into "Sleep Formula".

Method Eighty

Have your subject stand before you. Ask him to breathe deeply in time with your own breathing, as you set the rhythm by stating: "Breathe in with me now, one, two, three, IN. Hold the breath. Now breathe out with me, one, two, three, *out*." Repeat this over and over establishing the mutual rhythm of your breathing. Continue the rhythmical breathing thus between you, as you suggest: "Look into my eyes now as you breath *in* and *out*, in this rhythm, and, when you see my eyes converge and appear as *one big eye*, then close your eyes, but do not do it until you see *one big eye*." As soon as the subject closes his eyes, proceed with "Eyelid Fixation" and go directly into "Sleep Formula".

Method Eighty-One

Have subject stand before you, and grip a stick tightly in both hands. You likewise grip the stick between subject's hands. Have subject concentrate on your eyes, and suggest the grip on the stick is becoming tighter and tighter. Keep subject's attention firmly on you at all times, and suggest positively subject's hands are so firmly fastened to the stick that it is impossible to let go. Then state that since the stick cannot be released it must be followed however you pull it. Pull on the stick causing subject to follow you wherever you lead. Lead the subject around a little, then command eyes to close and perform "Eyelid Fixation". Go into "Sleep Formula" while subject is still grasping the stick and is standing before you. Hypnosis is quickly induced.

Method Eighty-Two

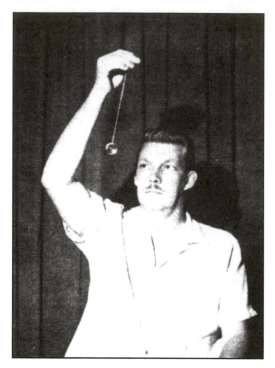

Have subject take a seat in a comfortable chair and dangle a pendulum before his eyes. Have him hold it up high so he has to strain his eyes to look at it. Tell him to fasten his attention upon a highlight on the pendulum and, as he watches it, it will soon begin to swing back and forth before him. Tell him as soon as it starts swinging he will begin feeling very sleepy and will close his eyes. When his eyes close, then suggest that his upraised hand holding the pendulum is becoming very heavy and is dropping down to his lap, and that as his hand hits his lap he will go promptly to sleep in hypnosis. When this occurs, proceed into "Eyelid Fixation" and "Sleep Formula".

Method Eighty-Three

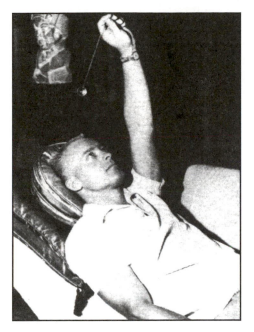

This is another hypnotic induction method using a pendulum. Have subject lie outstretched on couch and dangle a pendulum before his eyes, as he holds it aloft. A crystal pendulum or one with a shiny surface is best to use, so that it will catch a highlight for the subject to concentrate upon while thinking of the pendulum beginning to swing back and forth. As the pendulum begins to swing, have subject follow the movement with his eyes, and suggest his eyes are becoming tired, will close, and he will go to sleep while lying outstretched on the couch. As soon as eyes close, perform "Eyelid Fixation" and go into "Sleep Formula".

Method Eighty-Four
Have subject draw up a chair in front of a table and, placing his arms upon it, cradle his head on his arms and close his eyes. Tell subject to begin rocking his head back and forth on his cradled arms, as you go into "Sleep Formula". Then proceed into "Eyelid Fixation" and continue on with "Sleep Formula" until hypnosis is induced.

Method Eighty-Five
Have subject take a seated position and hold his left hand, with palm facing inwards, six inches in front of his eyes. Tell him to concentrate his gaze upon the very centre of the palm of his hand, as he holds it up before himself. Suggest that his vision will soon blur as he gazes steadily at the palm of his upraised hand; that his eyes will become tired and he will close his eyes. Then suggest that the fingers of the hand he is holding before his face are beginning to slowly separate, i.e. they are moving apart from each other until fully extended. Continue suggestions of finger separation until this occurs. Once the fingers have separated in response to the suggestion, suggest the upraised arm is becoming so heavy it is dropping down to this lap and, when it falls to his lap, he will drop right along with it into deep hypnosis. Emphasise when the arms drop to lap the subject will drop into profound hypnosis.

Method Eighty-Six
Have subject lie on a couch on his stomach and cradle his head on his arms. Have him close his eyes and relax completely as you begin scratching his back below the shoulder blades. As you do this, go into suggestions of how good it feel to stretch out like this and have his back massaged. Tell him it is making him very sleepy and to go to sleep. Proceed on into "Eyelid Fixation" and "Sleep Formula".

Method Eighty-Seven

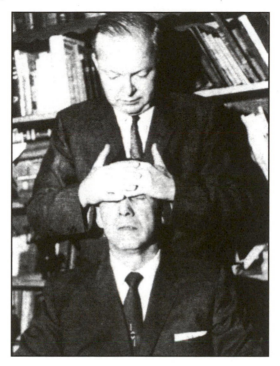

Have your subject take a seat in a chair. You take a position standing behind him. Interlock the tips of your fingers and place them against his forehead. Ask him to close his eyes now and you then exert pressure against the sides of his head as you squeeze your palms inward forcing his head against your chest. Give suggestions of how the pressure on his head is making him sleepy. Proceed on into "Eyelid Fixation" and "Sleep Formula".

Method Eighty-Eight

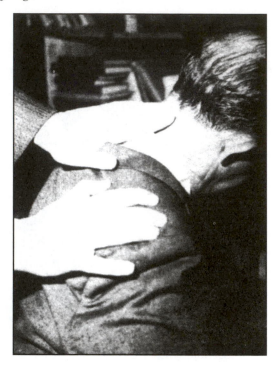

Have your subject seated, close his eyes and tilt his head forward upon his chest. Stand behind him and begin making downward strokes between the cords at the back of his head working from base of brain to top of spinal cord on the trigeminal nerves. Continue this stroking pressure between the neck cords as you continue to suggest how sleepy the stroking is making him become. Proceed to "Eyelid Fixation" and "Sleep Formula".

Method Eighty-Nine

Have subject lie on his back on a bed. Standing near the end of the bed, bend over subject bringing your face almost in contact with his eyes, with your eyes wide open staring into eyes of subject lying prone. Place one of your hands on the pit of subject's stomach while making passes across subject's forehead with your other hand. As your face is so close to the subject in this method whisper your suggestions of "sleep" very softly. When subject's eyes close blow gently on eyes and proceed directly into "Eyelid Fixation" followed by "Sleep Formula".

Method Ninety

Have subject stand erect and you stand by his side. Hold a small stick in front of his eyes, and tell him to stare at its tip. Tell him to follow the tip with his eyes no matter how much you move it. Now, hold the stick pointing directly at him, about eight inches in front of his face on a level with his eyes, while gripping the back of his head firmly with your free hand. Commence moving the stick up and down in a slow arc before him. Since you are holding his head solidly he cannot do other than move his eyes. When they reach the highest point they will automatically blink shut. Perform this action six times; then after the sixth time, when the eyes blink shut, tell him to keep them closed and place the side of the stick against the top of his skull and press downward at the same time performing "Eyelid Fixation". Then go directly into "Sleep Formula".

Method Ninety-One

Have your subject seated in a chair and tell him to close his eyes. Then explain that you are going to pass an open bottle of ammonia beneath his nose and that as he smells it to stop his breathing for a moment until the bottle has passed his nose. Then he can breathe again until he again smells the odour. In this manner, he will continue on holding his breath and breathing, in sequence, as you pass the bottle of ammonia back and forth under his nose. Perform the process slowly while you tell the subject: "Here comes the ammonia now ... hold your breath ... now it is past and you can breathe ... here it comes again ..." etc.

Then gradually, in the same rhythm, begin giving suggestions of how sleepy he is becoming, how his eyes are stuck together, how the odour of the ammonia is fading away, and as it fades away, he is dropping down, down deeper and deeper asleep in hypnosis. (As you give these suggestions of the odour of the ammonia fading away, actually move the bottle farther and farther away from the subject.) Proceed on with "Sleep Formula".

Method Ninety-Two

Have subject take a seat in a comfortable chair and relax. Hand subject a piece of hard candy. Tell him to place the candy in his mouth and suck on it. He is not to chew or swallow it, but is to allow it to slowly dissolve in his mouth filling his mouth with sweet taste. Tell subject he is now to close his eyes and to keep his attention on the sweet taste.

Present these suggestions: "Concentrate on the sweet taste of the candy in your mouth, and as it slowly dissolves, it will send you down into a pleasant sleep. It will be a sweet sleep just like the sweetness of the candy. As the candy dissolves in your mouth you dissolve into sleep. You dissolve into hypnosis." Continue on into "Sleep Formula".

Method Ninety-Three

Have subject extend both hands out in front, with palms facing each other, about twelve inches apart. Have subject concentrate his attention on the extended hands and imagine they are magnetically attracted to

218

each other. Suggest they are slowly moving in toward each other until they touch, and when they touch palm the magnetic attraction will be so strong he will find he cannot pull them apart.

Continue these suggestions until the hands are so attracted together palm to palm. Then suggest: "Close your eyes now, and you will find the lids are stuck together just as the palms of your hands are." (Eyelid Fixation.) Push the hands down forcefully into lap simultaneously exclaiming "*Sleep!*" Then proceed into deepening "Sleep Formula".

Method Ninety-Four
Have the subject lie comfortably on a couch or bed. Tell him to relax and close his eyes. Then instruct him to raise his arms and legs up twelve inches from the surface of the bed. Tell him to hold them in that position at a 45-degree angle and resist lowering them even when you suggest they are lowering.

Continue: "But you can't resist lowering your legs because they are becoming so tired they just have to drop down again to the surface of the bed. Even when you try to resist lowering them, down, down go your legs to relax on the bed. It feels so good not to resist any longer and let your legs relax completely and sink down toward rest and sleep.

"Now your arms, also, are getting so heavy you simply cannot hold them up any longer. Your arms are dropping down, down to your sides, and as they drop down you drop deeper and deeper into hypnosis."

When both arms and legs are completely relaxed and resting comfortably on the bed, state: "You are relaxed all over now, so drop down into a sleep. Drop down into profound hypnosis." Proceed on into deepening suggestions, as desired.

Method Ninety-Five
This is the Hyperventilation Method of hypnotising. Tell the subject to turn his eyes inwards and gaze upon his nose, as best he can. This is a strained position for the eyes and they will quickly tire. Things will begin to blur to his eyes. When you notice eye fatigue setting in, tell him to close his eyes.

When eyes are closed, instruct subject to commence breathing faster and faster through his nose. Tell him to take deeper and deeper breaths as he breathes faster and faster and faster.

Tell him: "You can feel your head begin to swim. You feel almost as though you are going to faint. You feel yourself dropping down into the blackness of an abyss. Drop down into profound hypnosis".

The effect of this faster and faster breathing causes a hyperventilation overloading the brain with oxygen producing an intoxicating effect which renders the subject highly responsive to suggestion. Proceed on with "Sleep Formula".

NOTE TO HYPNOTIST: You have a wealth of hypnotic induction methods now in your possession. Take your choice and use of them what you wish. You can combine various processes together, as you develop your own method and/or methods of hypnotising. Above all, be original.

Chapter Thirty-Seven
Instantaneous Method of Hypnotising

Rapid methods of hypnotising would probably be more accurate than instantaneous. However, the mind can work with such computer-like swiftness that to witnesses they appear almost instantaneous. Methods of this type work most effectively when the subject has been "keyed up" and expects to be hypnotised in such instances as participating in a hypnotism show.

The Posthypnotic Method

Possibly the surest way to obtain instantaneous hypnosis is to give the hypnotised subject a posthypnotic suggestion that when you do such and such he will immediately become hypnotised.

The "such and such" can be any cue desired. A simple one would be to suggest: "When I look into your eyes and tell you to 'Go to sleep', you will instantly become hypnotised."

The subject is then awakened. You can then test the response. Passing by the subject, suddenly turn and look in his eyes and forcefully state: "Go to sleep!" Immediately, hypnosis is induced.

In my show I frequently employ a posthypnotic instantaneous method and give it an Oriental touch by suggesting: "When I touch you in the centre of your forehead ... between your eyebrows ... in what is known as 'the third eye', which they call in India 'the Eye of Shiva', you will immediately return to sleep in profound hypnosis."

The subject is then awakened. When you wish to demonstrate, a mere touch in the centre of the forehead of the post hypnotically conditioned subject returns the person to trance.

The Expectancy Method

Expectancy to being hypnotised is a great factor in being hypnotised, instantly! That is why subjects watching others being hypnotised become excessively responsive themselves. By way of example:

A person is sitting beside a subject being hypnotised on stage. They see him "go to sleep" on your command. If you suddenly turn your attention to that person, look him squarely in the eyes and shout: "*Sleep!*" Down he goes!

It takes experience to use effectively "The Expectancy Method". The hypnotist has to learn to recognise the symptoms of readiness in the potential subject, i.e. intensity of interest, a focusing of the eyes, even an increasing of breathing rate. The skill of successful instantaneous hypnotising comes through an instinctive recognition of anticipation plus forceful boldness!

The Sudden-Jerk Method

Hypnotist Jim Hoke used this method of instantaneously hypnotising with great skill. Whilst passing through the audience, when he notices a spectator showing symptoms of susceptibility to hypnosis, he will suddenly reach out, grip the person's hand, and give a forceful jerking forward causing the person's head to flop down to their lap. At that very instant he will command: "Go to sleep this very moment!" Immediately he will then place his free hand on the back of the party's head and press down, while rapidly continuing the suggestions: "Melt down, melt down into deep hypnosis now." "Melt down" is an effective suggestion.

From experience the hypnotist can become expert in seizing the "moments of anticipation" of members of his audience resulting in instantaneous hypnosis. It looks miraculous. Hoke will pass through an audience snapping person after person into hypnosis by this method. The effect is compounding on the spectators: seeing it work on another excites expectation that it will work on oneself.

The Toothache Method

With experience you can catch the hypnotic anticipation look in a subject's eyes. Pass down your group and when you see the "look" suddenly turn upon the subject and capture immediate eye-to-eye contact. At this moment, place your right forefinger firmly against the side of his jaw and start tapping steadily in a continuous vibration movement, without lifting the finger from the jaw. Make the vibratory tapping forceful so it even hurts a little, as you exclaim: "You have a toothache. It hurts! It hurts! Say '*Ouch!*'"

If the subject says "Ouch!" stop the tapping and suggest: "Close your eyes now and the pain will all go away. Your teeth feel all fine and healthy now so you can go to sleep. *Sleep!* Go sound asleep!" Hypnosis has been induced on the moment.

The Head-Rap Method

A sudden pain response will often snap the subject into hypnosis. This method is related to the foregoing. Passing by a subject, suddenly catch his eye. You can tell when this occurs as his eyes set upon yourself on the instant, with something of a surprised, bewildered blank look in their focus. Having captured such attention, suddenly snap the knuckles of right hand with a rap (not too gentle) on the top of his head. At the moment of contact with the skull, shout, "*Sleep!*" The subject will instantly snap into hypnosis. You can then soften things by suggesting: "The pain from the rap is all gone now for you are in hypnosis. You feel all comfortable now. Go deep to sleep now in profound hypnosis."

The Release-From-Tension Method

You and your subject sit opposite each other. Have him place the palm of his left hand against the palm of your left hand. Tell him to press hard against the palm of your hand as you press hard against his. You have developed a state of tension between you. Now tell him to look into your eyes and think of sleep as he continues to press hard against your hand. Let the tension mount, and when it has reached a peak suddenly withdraw your hand. The result will plunge the subject forward in his seat. At this psychological moment exclaim: "*Sleep! Go to sleep this very moment, now!*" Push the subject's head down in your lap. A few more suggestions of "Sleep, deep sleep …" etc., and the hypnosis is complete.

From Waking Hypnosis Into Profound Hypnosis On The Instant!

The tests of Fastening the Subject's Eyelids Together, The Posture Sway Experiment of Falling Backwards, and Locking the Hands together can be used to initiate instantaneous hypnosis.

Instantaneous Hypnosis Following Eyelid Fixation

In this handling, seat the subject and suggest: "Close your eyes. Squeeze them tight together. Squeeze them so tightly together that you find they are stuck so tightly together that you cannot open your eyes try as hard as you will."

When the subject tries and fails, continue right on with your suggestions: "Forget about your eyes now. They are closed so you can go to sleep. Go right ahead and go to sleep."

As these suggestions are given, the operator presses between the eyes of the subject with his thumb and slowly tilts the subject's head back. He then tilts it forward so chin rests on chest. The process of pressing between the subject's eyes and tilting the head backward and forwards, along with the verbal suggestions, occupies the subject's attention to quickly induce hypnosis, immediately following the "eyelid-fixation" experience.

Instantaneous Hypnosis Following the Falling-Backwards Test

In this handling, hypnotist and subject stand facing each other. The operator says: "Stand erect. Place your feet together. Relax your body. I will step behind you and, when I do, you will feel yourself swaying right over backwards toward me. I will catch you as you fall. Close your eyes now as I step behind you."

In this moment, before the hypnotist steps behind the subject, he can decide whether or not the time is right for using the test as a hypnotic induction. If he notices an increase in taking in breath or a fluttering of the eyelids, he knows the subject is ready and he presents his suggestions in this manner: "You feel yourself falling backward. You are swaying right over backwards into my arms." Subject responds. As the operator catches subject in his arms, he continues: "I have caught you so you are all safe and fine, so go to sleep now, as I place you gently on the floor. Sleep. Go deeply to sleep."

Gently lower the subject to the floor. He will lie outstretched; hypnosis has been induced.

Instantaneous Hypnosis Following the Hand-Locking Experiment

This handling can be performed with the subject either seated or standing. The hypnotist instructs: "Look directly into my eyes. Stretch out your arms and lock your hands together. Now turn the palms outwards away from your body. Make the muscles of your hands and arms tight. Squeeze your hands together tightly. Tighter. Keep your eyes on mine. Squeeze your hands together even more tightly and you will find your hands have become so tightly locked together that you cannot separate them no matter how hard you try. Try. Try hard ... but you cannot unlock your hands."

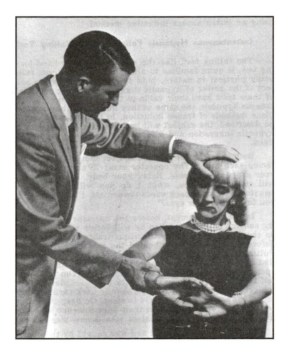

Keep your subject's gaze firmly fixed on yours the entire time and, when he fails to unlock his hands, follow right on with these suggestions: "Now close your eyes so that you can go to sleep. Your arms are relaxing now, and your hands are coming apart as you relax. You relax so completely that you are going to sleep. Go to sleep now as I place your unlocked hands gently into your lap. (Place hands upon lap.) Sleep deeply now and enjoy and sleep." Hypnosis is on its way.

Two "Sleeper" Methods of Instant Hypnotism

Who invented these two methods is unknown. They are powerful physical methods that render the subject unconscious in the appearance of instant hypnosis. *They can be dangerous, so their use is not recommended.* However, for the sake of completion in this Encyclopedia of Stage Hypnotism they are included, as many stage performers have used them in the past, especially when dealing with an annoying subject who persistently challenges the performer to hypnotise them. They work very rapidly but I repeat: *they are dangerous and not recommended.*

The Chest-Squeezing Method

Stand behind the subject you intend to put to sleep. Wrap your arms around his chest and entwine your hands and place them just on the lower part of subject's ribs in front. Grasp your hands firmly.

Now tell the subject to take three deep breaths and to hold the third breath in his lungs, and not release it.

As he starts the breathing processes as directed, you begin whispering suggestions of his going to sleep in deep hypnosis into his ear. When he has taken the third breath and is holding it in his lungs start squeezing his chest, exerting a firm pressure. Squeeze! Squeeze! Squeeze strongly! Within thirty seconds you will notice a slight contraction and releasing of breath by the subject. Continue right on squeezing for a few more seconds, and suddenly he will go limp and relaxed and loose in your arms. He will be asleep (unconscious). When this happens, release your squeezing grip around his chest and lower him gently to the floor. Leave him lying there.

You can complete the test by bending over and telling him to "wake up". He will "come to" right away. The experience to the subject is a "swimming sensation", and he feels himself "blacking out". The effect is caused by the squeezing of the chest while holding the breath producing an upsetting of the respiratory system. When the pressure is released, immediately the blood carrying oxygen again flows freely to the brain, and consciousness returns.

In using this as an hypnotic method, throughout the entire process, keep a barrage of suggestions that he is going into hypnosis as you squeeze his chest. Just as soon as he gasps, release the pressure and shout: *"Sleep!"* in his ear. If you release the pressure at this moment he will enter hypnosis. If you continue the pressure he will drop into unconsciousness.

The Carotid-Artery-Pressure Method

This is the famous (or infamous depending upon your point of view) "Bulldog Method" which has been used by stage hypnotists in past times to apparently hypnotise those who challenged them. It is even more dangerous than is the foregoing. Have the challenger take a seat in the centre of the stage. Stand directly in front of the subject with your back to the audience so they cannot see exactly what you are doing.

Start by giving the usual process of hypnotising moving into sleep suggestions. Ask the subject to close his eyes and relax comfortably, etc. In the course of this, lean forward and gently place your thumbs against the sides of his neck where you can feel the pulse of the blood moving to the brain. Then close your fingers against the sides of the neck, but do not exert any pressure with the fingers. All the pressure is applied by the thumb pressing straight forward upon the arteries. Apply no pressure against the wind pipe or you will strangle the subject.

NOTE TO HYPNOTIST: All pressure is on the carotid artery which causes unconsciousness through cutting off the blood supply to the brain. These two points on the throat are located one on each side of the Adam's apple, about half an inch higher, and exactly in a vertical line with the eyes. You can feel a pulsing against your fingers as you press in at these points. A firm pressure on these two points will, in addition to stopping the flow of blood to the brain, affect the puemogastric nerve and a nerve that goes to one of the vertebrae. Pressure for a few second will cause a subject to tremble, then relax and finally to drop into unconsciousness.

Continue the sleep suggestions and keep the pressure firmly forward on the pressure points until you see the subject relax and slump in unconsciousness. Immediately release the pressure and step back so the audience can see the subject apparently hypnotised. After the a few moments say "Wake Up!" and the subject will "come to". If you catch the subject at just the moment when he starts to plunge into unconsciousness and command him to sleep, it is possible to obtain genuine hypnosis by this method.

Do not perform either of the "Sleeper Methods" on older persons or persons with a heart condition. Probably the best advice of all is not to use them. Just consider them as educational knowledge relative to stage hypnotism.

The "Hypnoheat" Method

This method of rapid hypnotisation employs a trick which comes as such a surprise to the subject that it bypasses consciousness and opens the subconscious to instant realisation of hypnosis.

This method uses a trick called "Hypnoheat", which can be purchased at various stores specialising in magical supplies. The effect is for the performer to tear off a bit of tinfoil from a cigarette package, roll it into a small ball and have a person grip it firmly in his hand. Right in the subject's hand it commences to become so hot the person has to drop it. That's the trick which is a real surprise! I have found this "surprise" to provide an excellent instantaneous hypnotic method.

The secret of the effect is the use of mercuric chloride. The chemical may be obtained from chemical supply houses. However, it must be warned that it is a deadly poison and, while it will not cause harm used on the fingers in performing the effect, it must under no circumstances be placed in the mouth, such as absentmindedly placing the fingers to the lips. After use make sure that you wash it thoroughly from your hands.

In performing, the chemical is in a small container in your pocket, so when required you can get a bit of it on your right fore-fingertip. Only a very small amount is needed. To make it operate, tear off a small tab of tinfoil from a cigarette package, rub the chemical on the foil as you roll it up into a tiny ball and quickly place it in the hand of the subject who is told to grip it tightly. The foil under reaction of the chemical will heat up quickly and will become so HOT the person has no recourse but to drop it from his hand.

"Hypnoheat" as an Instantaneous Hypnosis-Induction Method

Tell the subject you will demonstrate how powerful suggestion can be in influencing the body. Be serious in your explanation. Tear off a tab of tin foil, secretly apply the chemical, roll it into a ball and have him grip it tightly in his hand. Command that he look into your eyes and firmly suggest: "Think! Think of heat! Think of how hot that tinfoil is becoming in your hand. You can feel it becoming hotter and hotter in your hand as you look into my eyes and concentrate upon the suggestion of it getting hotter and hotter. You can feel it! Experience it! It is becoming so hot you have to drop it, and when you drop it your eyes will close and you will drop instantly into hypnosis."

NOTE TO HYPNOTIST: Keep your flow of suggestions of heat, "hot, hotter, hotter", going in a continuous barrage until the subject throws the ball of foil from his hand. At that very moment shout: "Sleep!", stroke his head as it rests on your shoulder while you continue to whisper suggestions of sleep into his ear. You will have induced hypnosis on the spot. This is an excellent rapid method, but remember mercuric chloride is a poison so handle with care. The secret of successful Instantaneous Hypnosis lies in being bold and forceful. Be willing to take a gamble on it working. Most important of all, know within yourself that it will work. In other words, expect it to work and it will.

Chapter Thirty-Eight
Techniques for Deepening Hypnosis

The stage hypnotist naturally wishes to induce as deep a level of hypnosis as possible so that the subjects in his show will exhibit striking and startling responses. This technique will help increase trance depth.

The Staircase Technique

Hypnosis having been induced, suggest to the subject that he will now go into greater depths of hypnosis by visualising in his mind's eye seeing himself standing at the head of a great staircase that descends before him into the depths below. He is to start at the top and is to visualise himself walking down the staircase, step by step, and each step he takes will send him deeper and deeper into hypnosis.

The Elevator Technique

This is a self-visualising technique similar to the foregoing. In this instance, the subject is to see himself entering an elevator on the top floor of a tall building. He starts the elevator and observes its descent floor after floor ... going down, down, down into the very basement of the building ... the basement of the mind in the deepest level of hypnosis.

Hypnotic Physical Movement Responses that Increase Depth of Hypnosis

The Hand Revolution Technique

Take the hypnotised subject's hand and revolve it around in a circle while suggesting that the revolutions will continue unabated. As the hand whirls around the suggestions are given that every revolution of the hand will increase the depth level of the hypnosis.

The Revolving Head Technique

The hypnotised subject's head is revolved around and around accompanied by the suggestion that every revolution of the head emphasises of going deeper and deeper into hypnosis.

The Revolving Torso Technique

When the hypnotised subject is seated in a chair, move behind the person and grip the shoulders; move the torso of the body from waist upward associating the movements of the body with suggestions of deepening hypnosis.

The Head-Tapping Technique

It is suggested that every tap on the top of the head will increase the depth of hypnosis. The operator commences a series of regular tapping upon the top of subject's head. The subjective effect of the method being that each tap is recognised by the subconscious as meaning: "You are going down deeper and deeper into hypnosis." It is an effective technique for deepening hypnosis.

The Breathing Technique

In this process, the breathing of the subject is associated with the deepening of the hypnosis, suggest: "With every breath you take you will go deeper and deeper into hypnosis." This method tends to retain the depth level of hypnosis along with deepening it, as breathing being a continuous process, the hypnosis is continued in like manner.

Fractional Hypnotism Technique

As a process for deepening hypnosis, the operator will find this method very effective. The method increases the depth level of hypnosis in the subject(s) by a series of rapid consecutive rehypnotisations. The method can be effectively employed with the group on stage, each short hypnotisation tending to make the subjects more responsive. It favours the deepening of the hypnosis on each successive trial.

In professional use, the subjects are first hypnotised in conventional manner. It is then suggested: "In a moment, I will tell you to awaken and when I do you will wake up but you will immediately begin to feel very sleepy again. You will find it difficult to keep your eyes open and stay awake. And, as you look at me, your eyes will gradually close again, and you will return to a deep hypnotic sleep, deeper than ever before. All ready now, at the count of 'three' you will wake up. One, two, *three*! Awaken!"

Your subjects on stage will awaken from the first induction. Then, as they look at you and you continue your suggestions, they will close their eyes and re-enter hypnosis. Give some further deepening of trance suggestions and then again repeat this awakening and immediate returning to hypnosis process.

Perform the procedure three or four times in succession on the group. By this means it will be found that an intense deepening of hypnosis is accomplished. This process of hypnotising, awakening, rehypnotising, awakening, rehypnotising on occasion is an excellent method for the stage hypnotist to employ. The method is known as "Pyramid Hypnosis".

How Properly to Use Suggestion on the Hypnotised Subject to Increase Depth of Trance

The principle of having the performance of one hypnotically suggested effect lead to the successful performance of subsequent suggested effect is an important technique for deepening hypnosis. For example, the hypnotised subject is told that his arm is still and he cannot move it. He tries and finds it rigid. It is then suggested that, when you say "Drop", his arm will immediately drop to his lap, and when it hits his lap he will drop down yet deeper into hypnosis. The suggested response occurs, and the trance level is increased.

Another process for the development of deep hypnosis is to allow the subjects sufficient time to orient themselves to both the induction of the hypnosis as well as to respond to the suggestion given in the hypnotic state. This is especially true when the suggestions are of a complex nature; the subject must not be pressed to produce the desired phenomenon too rapidly. Complex phenomena occur best when brought about gradually.

Time for performance is not the only factor in orientating the subject; sometimes the situation itself must be manipulated. The stage hypnotist must recognise the fact that when two or more suggestions conflict, the one which was given first, in the greatest depth of hypnosis, is the one most likely to be responded to. In this regard the stage hypnotist must always remember the importance of removing the operation of each suggestion fully before going on to a new suggestive response. Failure to do this can give rise to psychological difficulties to the subject as well as to the smooth running of the stage show. Especially in relation to subject well-being is it important.

The stage hypnotist should always integrate the subject's needs into the suggestions being given, as the more a suggestion satisfies such needs the better it will be acted upon. This associating suggestions of possible benefits being reaped as the result of the response to the suggestion(s) is of great value in intensifying the phenomena. A practical application of this principle is to associate in the subject's mind a benefit he will obtain by following the suggestion. For example by giving a suggestion of this nature: "If you are able to achieve this hypnotic test of reducing your body sensation in going down into deep hypnosis, you will, at the same time, develop the ability to remove pain sensations from your teeth the next time you go to the dentist."

This providing of a beneficial result occurring if the suggestion is followed goes a long way in motivating towards depth of hypnosis. In this regard, the stage hypnotist can assist the subject adapt to the suggestion by associating suggestions of familiar experiences of situations, so that the suggestions to be realised fall on familiar ground. In practice, suggestions such as "what you have done repeatedly all your life" or "you are having fun like being at a party performing such and such" are examples of this handling.

Further deepening of hypnosis occurs when the hypnotist allows the subject and/or subjects complete opportunity to respond to the suggestion fully (to its greatest potential) before proceeding on to another experiment. In this way, the hypnotised person is "trained" to react with maximum effectiveness rather than to slur over from one response to another, as in the case when the suggestions are given too rapidly to allow sufficient time for each to perform fully.

NOTE TO HYPNOTIST: As previously commented upon, it must be recognised that there is actually very little stability to the depth of hypnosis and that, even when a subject has entered deep trance, he will often tend to drift away from it, generally into the lighter stages, sometimes to the degree of arousal. To maintain trance depth requires maintaining attention to the hypnotised individual. For this reason the stage hypnotist does well to return to all subjects occasionally, during a performance, to present reinforcing suggestions thus maintaining depth of trance level.

More on Somnambulism

Dictionary Definition: Sleepwalking and talking during sleep. Somnambulism is a rare stage of mind that can be of natural occurrence. When induced as an hypnotic phenomenon it is referred to as "artificial somnambulism". In relation to hypnosis, it is a profound state.

Dave Elman presents this method for producing somnambulism in the hypnotised subject: It is suggested to the hypnotised person that, on command, he (or she) will begin to count out loud from 100 backwards, and that gradually the numbers will disappear until they are all gone (no further numbers can be recalled.) On command start counting: "100, 99, 98 …' etc. Often the numbers disappear this early in the count. If desired, you can increase the influence by suggesting, as the person counts: "The numbers are fading away, and you cannot recall any more numbers at all. They are gone!"

NOTE TO HYPNOTIST: It cannot be overly emphasised that hypnosis is productive of a hyper-suggestible state of mind. Suggestion in definition is a subconscious realisation of ideas. As a stage hypnotist, if you want something to happen in your show, do not hesitate to ask for its occurrence, i.e. if you want amnesia to follow hypnotic experiences on stage during the show, as the subjects leave the stage suggest: "As you leave the stage, you will forget entirely everything you did, and, when your friends tell you what you did, you will think they are only trying to kid you." Sometimes the amnesia effect of somnambulism is automatic. However, if you wish it to be an effect in fact, suggest it!

Rounding Out
Your Hypnotic Knowledge

Chapter Thirty-Nine
Hypnotising Children

Children love a hypnotism show and swarm upon the stage to volunteer. The stage hypnotist has to be careful about this, as adults feel self-conscious on stage seated amongst a bunch of children. Unless the show is presented especially for a young audience it is best not to allow them to volunteer. You can handle the matter diplomatically by stating something like this, in your opening remarks: "In so far as the experiments in hypnotism that you will witness at this performance require adult concentration, I cannot invite children upon the stage. However, if you are in high school or of college age upwards, you are cordially invited to participate."

This handles the matter for you nicely, and high school students are most welcome. They make excellent subjects, and you can be sure they do not consider themselves children. With this age requirement made clear, should any children come up on stage, you can dismiss them with a smile.

NOTE TO HYPNOTIST: This matter of age selection is important to the stage hypnotist, as adults do not like to respond before an audience to tests to which children respond.

Children in general are excellent hypnotic subjects, but to effectively hypnotise them you must place your suggestions on the child's level. To instruct a child to relax his eye muscles, for instance, means little; you must speak his language.

In working with children, hypnosis can be most readily produced by playing the "let's-pretend-to-play act". Children are always pretending they are cowboys and Indians, or cops and robbers etc., so, if you ask a child to pretend, he instantly knows just what you mean him to do. You can use this approach for producing hypnosis quickly in children.

Ask the child if he likes to play games. If the answer is in the affirmative, say: "All right, I have a game to play with you and, if you learn to play it really well, it becomes a 'Magic Game', and the nicest things can happen to you. Would you like to know how to play it?" Child responds.

"All right, it's a game of pretend. You've played pretend, haven't you? Pretending you're a cowboy, or maybe cops and robbers. You've played that game, haven't you? All right, I'll show you how to play this pretend game, and you do just as I tell you.

"Just open your eyes really wide, and I'll close them with my thumb and middle finger, as I draw my fingers down over your forehead and eyes. Now, just pretend that you can't open them. Pretend just as hard as you can. Are you pretending just as hard as you can? All right, I'll just snap my fingers and make it come true." Snap your fingers.

"Now, even though you try to open your eyes, they won't open, as long as you keep pretending. Try it and see, and the more you try, the less they will open. Now, just keep on pretending and some really nice things will happen to you."

The child is in hypnosis, as quickly as that. Now is the time to give him suggestions for improvement of his conduct, his manners, for getting better results in school or anything that will be of help to him for on the stage he will perform all sorts of interesting tests if you explain such simply as a game he is taking part in.

To the child it seems that he is playing pretend, yet actually he is being hypnotised and is responsive to your suggestions. Children respond very quickly to hypnosis and do not generally need deepening techniques. As soon as they start pretending, their sense of judgement is bypassed and they are ready for suggestions. You can try this experiment: "Johnny (or whatever the child's name is), when I tell you to open your eyes you will open them wide, and an odd thing is going to happen. You will find that, when you try to walk away, you will not be able to lift your feet from the spot you are now on. You will try very hard to walk away but the more you try the more your feet will be stuck to the floor, until I snap my fingers and then they will come free right away. Now, that would be a funny thing to have happen, wouldn't it? So open your eyes now. How do you feel?"

Child answers, "Okay."

"That's fine. Now, Johnny, will you please bring me that dish from the table there."

The child tries to move, but cannot lift his feet to take a step. When ready to cancel the suggestion, just snap your fingers, and say: "Now, you can get the dish and bring it to me."

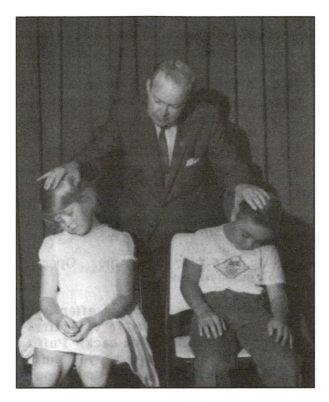

Hypnotising children
Children make excellent hypnotic subjects, but keep them in their place.

Child brings you the dish and again takes his seat. Again, you drag your thumb and middle finger down over his eyes closing them and tell the child to again pretend they are stuck and that he cannot open them. Child will be unable to do so.

Now suggest: "Johnny, when I have you open your eyes next time, an odd thing will happen in this game we are playing. Every time you see me comb my hair, you will have a tickle on your back and you will rub it, and the more you rub it the more it will tickle; it will make you laugh because it is so funny. When I clap my hands, the tickle will stop. That's okay with you, isn't it?" Child responds.

"All ready? Let's play the game. Open your eyes!"

Comb your hair after you have the child's attention. He will begin to tickle, laugh and rub his back. Comb your hair again, and the tickle will get more pronounced until you cancel the suggestion by clapping your hands.

You can remove the child from the hypnosis by merely saying: "All right, the pretending game is over now. I will count to three, and at the count of 'three' you will open your eyes and be your bright, happy self and feeling just fine."

Children will always respond to hypnosis if your suggestions are presented correctly. If you will make your suggestions something that will be fun for the child (or children you are performing with) there is no limit to the fascinating stunts you can present.

Chapter Forty
Hypnotism and the Sense of Time

When it's time to go to bed for the night's sleep, there is a mental ability that some people have of being able to set their mental "alarm clock" to awaken at a specific time in the morning. They awaken on the dot.

It appears that the mind has a sense of time. Very likely it is a learned pattern which has become instilled in the subconscious so that it functions as a habit through long association with clocks.Whatever the mechanism, it is an operation the stage hypnotist can use to advantage for some effective demonstrations. Here are some tests that can be tried:

Tell the hypnotic that in three minutes his shoes will pinch and he will take them off.

Tell the hypnotic that in five minutes the seat of his chair will get hot and he will leap up from it.

Tell the hypnotic that in exactly eight and a half minutes he will turn to the person seated on his right, place his hand on their head and find it stuck there.

Experiments with "the sense of time" can likewise be used posthypnotically, as these examples:

Tell the hypnotic that ten minutes after you awaken him he will fall asleep again.

Tell the hypnotic that at exactly fourteen and one-quarter minutes after you awaken him he will suddenly shout: "Hooray for the Irish!"

It is obvious that the performer can include "sense of time" suggestions in almost any experiment he pleases. It is quite dramatic to have the spectators take out their watches and time the subject(s). When the action occurs on the minute it is impressive.

NOTE TO HYPNOTIST: You will find that some subjects relate to the sense of time better than others.

There is another phenomenon relative to hypnotism and the sense of time known as "time distortion". Doctors Linn F. Cooper and Milton H. Erickson have done excellent research in this regard.

In brief, through time distortion in hypnosis it is possible for the hypnotic to experience mentally, in complete detail, and seemingly in normal time, an activity that would actually take (by way of example) ten minutes to realise in ten seconds.

The significance of the phenomenon is obvious as, to quote Cooper and Erickson: "With marked alteration in time perception accelerated mental activity appears possible."

Many experiments in this regard can be tried, such as a subject in one minute flat seeing himself:

• Walking for ten minutes.
• Cutting down a tree with an axe for five minutes.
• Listening to music for fifteen minutes.
• Studying a lesson for half an hour.
• Talking with friends for an hour, etc.

The human mind functions much like a computer. It can transcend time with a flash of thought.

NOTE TO HYPNOTIST: For further study of the matter, the book Time Distortion in Hypnosis: An Experimental and Clinical Investigation, by Linn F. Cooper MD and Milton Erickson MD is recommended, published by Irvington Publishers, New York, 1982.

Chapter Forty-One
Woman's Place in Hypnotism

Women have successfully entered almost every field that men have opened up, and there is no reason in the world why they cannot be eminently successful in that of stage hypnotism. Indeed they are!

Way back in the Victorian 1890s, Marina Flint, daughter of the famous hypnotist of that era Herbert Flint, pioneered the field. She was featured in the show. In contemporary times, Joan Brandon started the trend to be followed eminently by Pat Collins, Ginger Court and others.

Marina Flint (1890), daughter of the famous hypnotist Dr Herbert Flint. On Stage.

Hypnotist Ginger Court uses this interesting copy in her advertisements:

> She uses none of the hocus-pocus often associated with hypnotism. Her volunteers sit in a row on a brightly lit stage. As she guides them, they rapidly glide from their everyday world into the fantasy world of their subconscious. She gives them suggestions that lead them into pleasant and fascinating circumstances providing entertainment for all. She proves that hypnosis is loads of fun for everyone.

Basically there are two kinds of hypnotist:

1. The *Mother Type*, who comforts the subjects and plays upon the innate desire of individuals to retreat to a childhood behaviour response of being protected, and thus doing what the mother instructs.
2. The *Father Type*, who dictates to the subject and tells them what to do! This plays upon an innate desire which some people have to retreat to a childhood behaviour response of accepting authority as the safest course to follow.

As to which of these hypnotic approaches is best it is difficult to say. Both have their place. Actually, it depends upon the personality of the subject and some hypnotists are sensitive enough to size up the individual and apply either a persuasive or a dominating approach, as seems better suited to the particular individual.

Some subjects respond best to "the mother approach" while others to the father role. The most successful hypnotist is he or she who can correctly judge their subjects. Striking results are then achieved. Hypnotist Arnold Furst points this out in stating that in his opinion there is no such thing as a good or bad subject, there are only good and bad hypnotists.

On first consideration it might seem that women would naturally fall into the mother type approach while men would assume the father role. In professional practice, however, such is frequently not the case. A woman hypnotist, because of her sex, can often get away with a bossy, almost intimidating approach that would be next to impossible for a man who must on occasion resort to a persuasive, almost humble role to adapt to the personality of his subject.

Stage hypnotism is an art, and true art conceals art and calls for sensitivity of expression. Of such nature is the work of a great artist. Women often have this sensitivity in their nature. They make good hypnotists.

Woman's place in hypnotism is assured!

Chapter Forty-Two
The Extraordinary Phenomena of Hypnotism

The remarkable hypnotic phenomena here considered are of special interest as they appear mysterious. While these supernormal mental powers are rather too experimental to be used during a general hypnotism stage show they are excellent for entertaining social groups who enjoy participating in exploring the wonders of the mind.

Mesmerism versus Hypnotism

Basically there are two ways of hypnotising: the bio-energy method of Mesmerism (animal magnetism) and the psychological method of Hypnotism (suggestion). For those seeking to experiment with the extraordinary phenomena of hypnotism, the Mesmeric Method seems the more effective. Why? Because the production of the extraordinary phenomena requires energy, and in the Mesmeric Method the operator adds his energy to that of the subject, which is compounding in effect, thus producing a quantum leap in awareness. It is then that extraordinary things happen. The following two techniques work well.

The Magnetic/Mesmeric Method

Have the subject take a seat opposite you. You face each other. Take his or her right hand in your left and his left hand in your right. Then firmly grip hands allowing the balls of thumbs to meet. Lean forward in your chair until your knees touch, and your face is about twelve inches from the subject's.

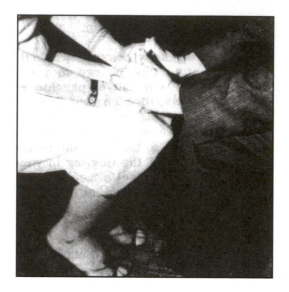

Tell the subject to gaze steadily into your eyes as you gaze back in turn. You will experience an electric-like sensation passing between your hands. Then explain: "You will soon feel a tingling in your hands as I hold them. This tingling sensation will gradually extend up your arms to the shoulders, and a sort of numbness will creep over your body. Do not be uneasy at any sensations which may occur, and do not allow yourself to wonder at anything that may happen. Just make yourself receptive to the psychic influence that I shall project into your mind and body. As the numbness proceeds and you find you can no longer bear to keep your eyes open and fastened upon mine, close them, and they will not come open again. You will then pass into a profound sleep, your whole body will feel warm, and you will feel a gentle current, which will seem to you like a surge of body electricity, and the pulse in your thumbs will throb."

As you give these suggestions, *think* them as occurring to the subject. Continue: "When your eyes are closed, I will make passes over you which will fill you with bio-energy, animal magnetism, which will feel like a warmth coming into your body, and you will drop down deep into Mesmeric Sleep."

Stand now before the subject and make long sweeping passes in front of the body of the person. The purpose is to increase the magnetic influence and distribute it evenly throughout the body of the subject.

The Magnetic/Mesmeric Method of hypnotising employs a minimum of verbal suggestions. Let your mind give the suggestions not your voice, for the most part. Think how relaxed the subject is becoming in the chair. How comfortable. How pleasantly warm. How heavy and tired the eyes are becoming. How sleepy. Think close your eyes and sleep. Think the subject to sleep.

Continue your passes down over the subject's body in a slow sweep, terminating at the knees. At the end of the pass, throw your hands outward and shake them. Turn your hands palms inward again and continue the passes. Repeat this process for ten minutes all the while concentrating on the flow of "psychic force". Your purpose is to entrance the subject in a way in which the individual becomes "charged" with vital energy. Such seems needed for ESP experimentation.

Observe the subject as you make the passes, and you will note the respiration become deep, sometimes even spasmodic. You may stop the passes now, and you are ready for experimenting with the extraordinary phenomena of the mind.

When you conclude your experimenting, awaken the subject by a reversal of the downward pass process. Make the passes upwards and throw off the energy. Think awaken. Blow on the subject's forehead, and the arousal will be complete.

The Blue-Light Method

This method of hypnotising with the energies is likewise good for developing the extraordinary phenomena of hypnotism. Arrange a blue light so that it shines down on the forehead of the subject as he lies prone upon a couch. Take your seat beside him, and have him gaze upward into your eyes as he relaxes.

Like the Magnetic/Mesmeric Method this method keeps verbal suggestions to a minimum and emphasises mental commands. Begin by making gentle passes towards the subject's face, and very softly suggest that his eyes are becoming heavy and are closing. When his eyes are closed, make passes over his face, while thinking of him going down into a deep trance.

Next, stand beside the subject and, leaning over him, make long passes starting at his head and going over the entire body. As you make the passes, extend your fingers tensely outstretched while visualising a "magnetic current" passing out of them into the subject. As the process proceeds, you will sense a magnetic tingling sensation in your fingertips in making the passes.

Next make short circular passes around the closed eyes of the subject. As you make these passes, concentrate on your mental suggestion of him going to sleep in profound hypnosis. Then bring your hands slowly down his body in straight passes, stopping at the heart. Over the heart make further circular passes. Make these circular passes without contact, about six inches above the surface of the body. Then continue the long passes down to the feet.

When you reach the feet, having completed the long passes down the entire length of the subject's body, violently give your hands a flipping motion as though you were throwing off from the fingers a sticky substance, turn your palms outward and again approach subject's head, turn hands palm inward over the forehead and repeat the process of long passes over the length of his outstretched body.

Continue these "magnetic passes" for ten minutes, and when you feel your subject has reached sufficient depth test for ESP talents. Awaken the subject from this induced Mesmeric trance by making passes in reverse along the body, starting at the feet and ending at the head.

Supernormal Phenomena

Hyperaesthesia of the Senses
With the Sense of Feeling

Try this test: hypnotise a sensitive subject and blindfold him or her. Now hold your hand near any part of the subject's body or head, without contact, and that part will slowly move in the direction in which the fingers are drawn. A horseshoe magnet used in the same manner as the hand produces a similar result. Some subjects appear to be so sensitive to emanations of a magnet, even when unaware that a magnet is in the room, that they complain of unpleasant sensations when the magnet is held near the back of the head.

Bramwell says on this point: "The enigmatic reports of the effect of magnets, even if due, as many contend, to unintentional suggestion on the operator's part, certainly involve hyper-aestheric perception by the hypnotised person; for the operator seeks as well as possible to conceal the moment when the magnet is brought into play, and the subject finds it out that moment."

Hollander states: "There is not doubt in my mind but that a magnet gives some force which can be felt by a hypnotised subject, and that our body, particularly in the fingertips, exerts a similar influence. I became convinced of this by placing a hypnotised person in a completely darkened room, then letting him open his eyes and describe what he saw. I held a magnet suspended in my hand, at the poles of which he perceived a luminous glowing. He was able to locate the magnet in the dark by reaching out towards "the magnetic light". He described similar luminous emanations proceeding from my fingertips.

"In order to see the "magnetic light", not only must the subject be sensitive, but the darkness must be absolute, and, if not at once successful, the subject should remain in darkness for an hour. Not the smallest gleam of light must be allowed to enter the darkened room. None of the audience should go out or come in during the experiment for if the door is opened even for an instant the admission of bright light may spoil the performance."

It is not unlikely that the human organism is surrounded by what some refer to as an "aura", some sort of an electromagnetic field which extends from the body for a distance and then gradually fades away. The aura from each person seems to be individualised and distinguishes the person. You can make this group experiment: hypnotise a person, blindfold him and have him sit in a chair. You tell the subject to recognise the feeling (emanation) from your hand. Hold your hand close and let him become familiar with it. Then tell him various persons are going to place their hand near the nape of his neck, and that when yours comes close to him he will advise you of it immediately.

Have the experimenters line up behind the subject and each in turn, including yourself, hold their hand near the subject. When your hand approaches, it will be recognised. Try the test a number of times, and each time your hand comes around it will be identified.

With the Sense of Sight

This is a fascinating hypnotic demonstration you can present of hyperaesthesia, showing super-sight. Take a deck of playing cards and have a card selected. Its name is noted. Then hand the card to the hypnotised subject, back upward, and tell him that it is a picture of his mother and that he will be able to recognise and locate that picture under any conditions.

Then mix the card in the pack and hand the entire pack, backs uppermost, to the subject. One by one he will run through the cards looking at the backs of each in turn until finally, stopping at one card, he will declare it to be the photo of his mother. On turning the card over, it will be found to be the correct one.

The explanation for this surprising demonstration is that every card, no matter how new or seemingly unmarked, has on it some minute difference which sets it apart from its neighbours. In this experiment, in the course of the illusion of seeing the suggested picture, the subject interprets into the illusion these minute differences, and through hypnotically induced hyperaesthesia is able to distinguish that card by its back alone from amongst all the others. Thus the card is located. It is an amazing experiment.

ESP Experiments in Hypnosis

Telepathy

There are many interesting experiments in extrasensory perception (ESP) you can try with the hypnotised subject. Begin by suggesting to the hypnotic that he will feel an electric-like tingling sensation from your fingers as you pass them down his arm without contact, and, as he senses it, that his arm will slowly rise up from his lap. This phase of the experiment is similar to the sensing of your hand from others in the hyperaesthesia feeling test. It is used as a start to sensitise the subject for subsequent ESP performance. Continue the practice of making passes down his right arm from the elbow to the fingers, and slowly the arm will raise. Repeat the experiment with the subject's left arm.

Now explain to the hypnotic that you are not going to tell him over which arm you will make the passes but that as he feels the tingling he is to raise that hand accordingly. Experiment with this test a few times to determine the subject's sensitivity.

Then suggest that he will feel the same sensation when you merely think of which arm he is to raise – he is to raise the hand in which he feels the tingles.

Now experiment with ESP by concentrating on his lifting either his right or left hand, as desired. In transmitting a telepathic impulse, such as lifting a hand, just visualise in your mind an image of the subject lifting up a specific hand. Experiment.

You can now advance your experiment with telepathy to complete body movement. Have the hypnotised subject stand with feet together, explaining that he will feel an impulse to take a step forward or a step backward, as the case may be, when he senses an impulse to move in that direction. Then flip a coin. If it comes up "heads" think him stepping forwards if "tails" think him stepping backwards. Keep track of the results.

Take two subjects, hypnotise them and suggest they are in rapport; that one is the "transmitter" and tell him to concentrate on the other subject lifting the corresponding hand. Then the "receiver" is told to lift up the hand he feels a mental impulse to lift. Keep track of the results.

Clairvoyance

This is another ESP talent you can test for in hypnosis. Clairvoyance means "clear seeing". It is psychic visioning. To experiment with it, place your subject in profound hypnosis, then take your watch and swirl the hands, so that you will have no knowledge of the time at which they are set. Without looking at the face, hold the watch face inward to the subject's forehead. Tell him you want him to tell you what time it is set; that he will see the face of the watch within his mind clearly. Demand that he sees it. If he says he cannot, ask him what you can do to make it easy for him to see. Do exactly whatever he tells you to do. If the subject still does not tell you what to do, make passes over his forehead and insist that he tell the time at which the watch is set. Force him to see.

Another experiment in clairvoyance you can try is to write various numbers on different cards. Turn them face down and mix the cards so you have no idea of which is which. Without looking at it, pick up a card and hold it to the subject's forehead. Ask him to tell you the number on it. Experiment.

Astral Projection

Hypnotise the subject by the Mesmeric Method, and while entranced tell him he can leave his body and astrally project to any place you name. Have him go to somewhere that you know, and have him describe what he sees. You can check what he reports to you.

NOTE TO HYPNOTIST: Performing ESP experiments under hypnosis provides fascinating entertainment, but do not expect to succeed with every test you try. You are dealing with "the wild talents of the mind". They are unpredictable. You must develop your subjects for such tests. The extraordinary phenomena of hypnotism are like a game you play. Sometimes you win and sometimes you lose. The human mind is the storehouse of miracles. When you practise stage hypnotism you become a practitioner of miracles.

Chapter Forty-Three
Hypnotic Tips and Bits

This chapter will provide a résumé of hypnotic knowledge to give you expertise in the art, fill you with vitality, provide additional instructions and function as a transition featuring entertainment with hypnotism plus a bibliography. All the material is important to your developing professional status as a hypnotist.

Use Preliminary Experiments

Generally speaking, in working with a group, before you try for trance phenomena, it is well to commence with some of the waking suggestion experiments you have learned such as drawing the subject backwards, locking hands together, etc. In doing so, explain that before you hypnotise anyone you wish to ascertain which of the subjects can concentrate best, and work with as many subjects as possible in these preliminary tests before you attempt to induce hypnosis. This is expert handling and provides you with an opportunity to locate who among the group are the most susceptible subjects. Use these subjects for your first experiments in hypnosis as leaders of the group. There is good psychology here as your success in hypnotising your first subjects will bring you success with the others as well.

Establish Confidence

Whenever it is possible, let a new subject see you hypnotise someone whom you have hypnotised previously before you try to influence him. This immediately develops the potential subject's confidence in your ability to hypnotise and gives him an appreciation of the art. Success begets success!

Do Not Boast

Nobody likes an egotist. Always approach your work as a hypnotist in a modest, confident manner. To boast of your ability is to develop a challenging attitude in your subjects and can undermine the success of your performance. Adopt the manner of the successful physician.

Keep Your Promises

Never have your subject(s) do anything you promised they would not do. Some persons will request that, if they are hypnotised you will not make them do embarrassing acts. When you promise to follow their wishes, always honour that trust.

Use Deepening Techniques

Refer to Chapter Thirty-Four for deepening techniques. Processes such as Revolving the Head, Compounding of Suggestions, Fractional Hypnotism etc. are valuable. Incorporate such processes into the methods of hypnotising you elect to use.

Gradation of Responses

It is easier to deceive the sense of taste than it is the senses of sight and hearing. A suggestion that the subject will experience a bitter taste in his mouth is much more certain to work than one that he will see a landscape unfolding before him when he opens his eyes. This principle of progressively arranging the hallucinations from the simpler to the more complex is important in developing a new subject.

Illusions versus Hallucinations

It is easier to make a subject believe that one object is another object (as an illusion) than it is to make him believe that an object exists in empty space (as an hallucination). For example, you can make him see a blue carpet as a pool of water more easily than you can an elephant in an empty room. Use this device of utilising a stimulating object resembling the suggested illusion when first creating optical deceptions.

Producing Anaesthesia

If you prick your subject with a pin he will feel and react to it unless you suggest that a certain area of his skin is immune to all pain. Run your fingers over an area of his arm as you suggest: "All sensation is leaving your arm. It is numb and cold. You will feel nothing in it whatsoever." Then prick it with a sharp sterile needle, and the puncture will be completely ignored if your subject is deeply hypnotised. Refer to Sensational Hypnotic Feats.

Complete Body Catalepsy

Large groups of muscles can be made cataleptic as well as smaller muscle groups. For such a demonstration, after you have placed the subject in hypnosis, have him stand up straight and tell him that the muscles of his entire body are becoming stiff and rigid, so stiff and rigid that they will not bend. As you give these suggestions, make passes over his body, pressing in here and there on the muscles of his arms, legs and chest as though to tighten them, and say: "You are absolutely rigid." Then suggest emphatically: "Rigid!" Your subject will become stiff like a pole and be unable to bend in any direction. You have produced a condition of complete body catalepsy.

When you are ready to remove the cataleptic state, tell him that his muscles are now beginning to loosen and relax and are becoming flexible and normal in every way. When his muscles are again relaxed, awaken him, and the experiment is complete. Refer to Volume Two, Chapter Eighteen for presentational details of this feat.

Pressing Upon the Eyelid to Induce Hypnosis

When the eyes of the subject are closed, steady pressure applied at the corners of the eyes, near the root of the nose, will often assist in bringing about hypnosis.

Using a Combination of Methods to Induce Hypnosis

Hypnosis may be induced by suggestion, bright objects, passes, etc. A combination of processes will usually hypnotise more persons than any single device. Refer to Chapter Thirty-Six for ninety-five techniques.

Keeping Others from Influencing Your Subjects

If you do not wish anyone else to hypnotise your subject, simply put him into a deep sleep and tell him that he cannot be hypnotised by anyone but you, unless he first says the words, "*Zam, zam, zam*" (or any word cue combination desired). This serves as a cue that the subject unconsciously waits for as the opening door to entering hypnosis. Never tell a subject just outright that he cannot be hypnotised again, as such might render him insusceptible to all future experiments. If he thinks he is too susceptible, you might tell him that he cannot be hypnotised unless he, himself, expresses a wish to be.

Preventing Others from Hypnotising You

If you are ever in a situation where someone tries to hypnotise you, and you wish to prevent influence completely, do this: roll up your tongue and press it firmly against the roof of your mouth. Keep your attention on the tongue, and all hypnotic effects will bypass you completely.

How to Transfer Hypnotic Control

You can transfer the hypnotic control of the subject from yourself to another person if you wish. To do this, after the subject is in hypnosis, suggest: "You will now follow the suggestions that Mr So-and-so (person's name) gives you, and will respond to his suggestions just as you have to mine."

As you present these "transfer of control suggestions" to the subject have the person to whom the transfer is being made place his hand on the forehead of the subject; this identifies the person and increases the strength of the transfer control.

Subtle Symptoms of Hypnosis

There are subtle observations you can make that indicate the ensuing hypnotic trance. Watch your subject closely. Often when hypnosis sets-in there will be noted a sort of dropping of the corners of the mouth. This is often coupled with a little intake gasp of breath. Breathing will deepen as hypnosis develops. In lifting up the closed eyelid of a hypnotised person, the eyeballs will frequently be found rolled upwards. This process often deepens the level of hypnosis.

After you have placed your subject deeply in hypnosis, tell him very positively that at some definite time he will do some particular thing. For example, you may suggest: "At one o'clock in the afternoon you will feel a desire to change your shoes for another pair that you believe will be more comfortable. You will not remember that I gave you this suggestion, but at precisely that time you will change the pair of shoes you have been wearing for another pair. And if anyone asks you why you did this, you will simply say: 'Because the new pair is more comfortable.'"

On the stroke of one, the subject will develop the impulse and will change his shoes and if asked about the matter will rationalise his actions, as you have suggested. An experiment such as this shows the spontaneous nature of responses to posthypnotic suggestions.

In giving posthypnotic suggestions, be sure they are clear, positive and emphatic. While not always necessary, it is good practice to repeat such suggestions a few times to be sure they are well understood by the hypnotic. Then awaken the subject and, at the appointed time, he will perform as you have hypnotically instructed.

Use caution as to the character of the posthypnotic suggestions which you give the subject, being sure that they are not too difficult or precarious for him to perform. The whole secret of this hypnotic influence consists in telling the subject, while he is in hypnosis, the thing you wish him to do when he awakens. As mentioned, it is well to repeat your posthypnotic suggestions several times so that they are strongly emphasised. If he should fail to carry out the suggestions, you may be sure that the failure is due either to lack of conviction in the way you presented the suggestion, or that the subject was not in a sufficient depth of trance to experience successfully posthypnotic effects.

Increasing Hypnotic Responsiveness via Posthypnosis

Before awakening your subject, give him suggestions to the effect that the next time you attempt to hypnotise him he will go immediately into hypnosis; that as he gazes into your eyes, he will enter the hypnotic trance immediately. Such hypnotic suggestions will increase your ease in hypnotising the subject at a later period.

Hypnotising by Telephone

Use a subject whom you have previously hypnotised and have him place the receiver to his ear. Have him seated so he can pass into the trance in comfort. Then suggest: "In half a minute you will be sound asleep. Already your head feels heavy. You are getting tired, so tired. Your eyelids are heavy, they are closing. You cannot stay awake, you are going sound asleep. Now you are sound asleep. Sleepy, sleep, sleep." By this time, the subject usually will be deeply sleeping. In this test, give your first suggestion very firmly and positively: "In half a minute you will be sound asleep!"

Hypnotising by Mail

Select a subject who is very responsive to your influence. Then write on a slip of paper in large letter: "In a few seconds after reading this you will be sound asleep. You can already feel yourself getting sleepy. You cannot stay awake. You are going fast to sleep. Go to sleep now." Then sign your name in big letters. When your subject opens and reads such a letter from you he will drop into a deep trance. Needless to say, if, when you previously hypnotised him you had given him a posthypnotic suggestion to the effect that when he received such a hypnotic letter from you, that it would send him immediately down into trance, it will increase the effectiveness of the test a hundredfold.

The Crystal Ball Method of Hypnotising

This is an interesting method of hypnotising for social entertainment with people who are interested in ESP. Select a subject who shows such interest and tell him that the crystal ball is used by mystics for scrying, and how many people believe it exerts a subtle influence which develops psychic powers.

Next explain to the subject how he is to use the crystal ball for this purpose, i.e.: he is to place it on a table in front of himself, sit back comfortably in a chair and centre his eyes on the crystal ball.

The subject is to gaze directly at the ball, on past the reflections on its surface and into its very depths. Explain that if he is doing the experiment correctly the crystal will gradually appear to become darker and a sort of milky mist will form in front of his eyes. The mist will seem to grow and expand. He is then to allow his mind to float out in to this mist, until blackness envelopes him. And with the blackness will come hypnosis.

When all is understood and your subject is in an eager mood to try the experiment of entrancing himself by using a crystal ball, have him enter alone a semi-darkened room and close the door. In silence and alone he performs the experiment.

After a period of about twenty minutes you enter the room quietly, and in many instances you will find the subject seated in the chair with his eyes closed, or else staring blankly into space, entranced. Speak to him quietly and, if he answers without being disturbed, you can swiftly bring him under hypnotic control.

Hypnotising a Group of Subjects Simultaneously on Stage

Have your subjects sit in a semicircle while you take a position standing in front of the group so that everyone can see you clearly. Tell the subjects to look directly at you. Pass your eyes around the semicircle so that each person feels you are looking directly at him/her.

As you do this, allow your eyes to focus on a point about a foot above the head of the central subject and give your suggestions forcefully towards this space. You then proceed to hypnotise the entire group exactly as you would in hypnotising a solo subject. Many of the methods described in this text work perfectly for the stage show.

Causing the Subject to Blush

Get him into a deep trance and present the suggestions that he will blush, that his face will become red, etc. Then repeat some incident of embarrassment that will make him blush and describe that the conditions around him are such as to make him blush. Such physiological experiments are very strong tests with which to convince a sceptical audience of the reality of your phenomena.

Hypnotising in Natural Sleep

It is possible to turn natural sleep into hypnosis by this process. Go quietly to the sleeping person and speak gently, in a whisper, saying: "You are sleeping soundly. Sleep. You are sleeping soundly. You are sound asleep and nothing will disturb you. You will not wake up as I talk to you, for you are going down deeper and deeper asleep. Sleep. Sleep deeply."

Repeat these suggestions of sleep several times. If you notice any signs of the sleeper awakening, immediately desist; otherwise keep the suggestions up for three or four minutes. Then put your hand on the sleeper's head, and say to him: "You hear no sound except my voice for you are fast asleep."

Now ask him some simple questions, such as: "How do you feel?" or tell him that he smells a rose and ask if he smells its beautiful fragrance? Insist on a reply to your question until he answers it. When he does so without awakening you may be assured that he is in the hypnotic state. You have converted natural sleep into hypnosis.

You can now proceed to present whatever suggestions you feel are worthwhile to the subject. Usually suggestions benefiting the subject's well-being are given during the night. As you conclude the session, tell the subject to return to his normal, healthy sleep, that he will not have been disturbed in any way, and will not remember the transfer from sleep to hypnosis. When he awakens the next morning he will have no memory of the experience. This is a good technique to know, especially for parents who wish to give helpful suggestions to their children.

On the Use of Passes

Passes made in a downward direction are used to induce the trance, while passes made upward are used to remove it. Passes can thus be used to assist in the gently awakening process in bringing the subject out of hypnosis. The procedure is to turn the palms upward and, starting about level with the subject's stomach, move them upwards past his face. Repeat these upward passes several times in conjunction with the giving of your awakening suggestions. Blowing gently on the closed eyelids is also useful in awakening the subject.

Supplementing the Effect of Suggestions

Any physical means to increase suggestive influence are useful to the hypnotist. Devices such as those described help on occasion and pressing heavily upon the arms when suggestions are given that the arms are becoming heavy increase effects, or, for example, when suggesting to a subject that things are becoming dark, by placing your hands over the eyes of the person intensifies the suggestions of darkness.

On Awakening Difficult Subjects

Only rarely will you experience any difficulty in awakening a subject, but in such a case say to him: "All right now, I want you to wake up. I know you are sleepy and tired, but you *must* wake up now. You have slept long enough. Tell you what I will do. I will count very slowly from one to ten, and when I reach the count of 'ten' you wake up. Fair enough? Will you awaken at the count of ten?" If the subject does not answer, persevere until he does, and make him promise that he will wake up when you reach the count of "ten". Then continue: "All right then, here we go. One, two, three, four, five, six, seven, eight, nine, *ten!*" Just as you say "ten" clap your hands loudly together (in the case of a subject of this nature you need not worry about noise shocking his nervous system as he is the lethargic type) and say: "Wake up! Wake up! All right, wide awake now!" Keep striking your hands together, make upward passes and give awakening suggestions until the subject is fully awake. This process will awaken the most difficult subject.

Awaken Subjects with Confidence

There are two main reasons why a subject will not awaken readily from hypnosis (1) because of enjoying the hypnotic state so thoroughly that he hates to come out of it and (2) because he has lost confidence in the operator. A hypnotised person is often very sleepy; to ask him to come immediately out of the trance sometimes seems just too much trouble, and hence the subject makes no immediate attempt to follow your command. But never for a moment lose confidence in your ability to awaken the subject. Remember, a hypnotised person is highly suggestible, and a betrayal of nervousness on your part over concern about awakening him can be interpreted as a suggestion that he is difficult to awaken, and such a suggestion is reacted to accordingly. Always in performing all aspects of your hypnotic work be calm and collected, and keep in mind that a lack of confidence is as unfavourable to success in removing the trance as it is in producing it.

Awakening a Subject Someone Else has Hypnotised

Occasionally you may be called upon to dehypnotise a subject whom some inexperienced operator has hypnotised. The method is to proceed to gain rapport with the subject by the process of hypnotising him personally even though he is already in hypnosis. To do this, place you hand on his head, repeat a "sleep formula" to him and then test him for response to your suggestions. After he has responded to a few tests, say very decidedly to him: "Now when I tell you to do anything you will do it at once." Then give him a suggestion producing physical movement of some kind. After this response, apply the technique previously explained for awakening difficult subjects, and he will awaken readily to your command.

Self-induced Hysteria

There is a factor in relation to hypnotic awakening that you should understand. This is self-induced hysteria. We are all familiar with how teenagers at a rock-and-roll concert will sometimes work themselves up into such a frenzy that they will literally pass out. In such an instance the hypnotist has little rapport with his subject, as the rapport has become self-centred. In other words, the subject has induced his own condition. Sometimes the "mental set" is so strong the person refuses to come out of it when told to. If a subject acts in this fashion, immediately remove attention from him by stating: "Okay, go ahead and do whatever you wish. No one will pay any attention to you." You will be surprised how often this simple handling will quickly bring the subject out of his self-induced condition.

Vitality Hypnosis

This is a method of hypnotising which is directed towards increasing the vitality (personal energy) of the subject. Proceed as follows:

Preliminary

Wherever you are, be it in a private room or in the midst of a crowd, you can hypnotise with this method. You can even present this method for an entire audience to try together. It will prove of benefit to everyone. It is filled with electrifying force, for the method stirs up vitality.

The Method

Have the subject, subjects, group or audience seated before you. Give these instructions: "Relax now and become silent. Close your eyes and allow yourself to drift down into the privacy of your inner self. This is your personal space. Allow your mind to enter this space and become silent for some moments. For some moments become quiet and enter the silence of your inner self. Silence. Silence. Silence."

Have a quiet piece of music which has a rhythmical beat ready to play on your tape recorder. After about three minutes of the silence, softly start the music and let it become a background to your voice. Continue: "Now into this inner silence allow this gentle music to flow in. Listen with attention to its beat, as it cascades up and down. Up and down the rhythm goes. As you listen, allow your breathing to take on the same rhythm; inhale on the upbeat and exhale on the down beat … breathing in and out, in and out, in and out with the rhythm. Establish this rhythm to your breathing so that it becomes the automatic rhythm of your respiration, and you will find it begins to make you drowsy and very sleepy, and you commence to enter a pleasant day-dreaming state of reverie. Hmmmmmmmmmmmmmm … how good it feels.

"How nice and peaceful you begin to feel … and the musical rhythm fades into the background. [Fade music to background.] But it is always there leading the rhythm of your breathing in and out and out and in as you relax deeper and deeper into a state of mental reverie.

"Now turn your attention to yourself and think of how absolutely relaxed and free of all tension in every way you are becoming. And as your body enters this super state of relaxation your mind equally enters the state … and as your mind becomes more and more relaxed so equally does your body. You have started a circle of sweeping relaxation which takes you down deeper and ever deeper into the realm of hypnotic sleep … and all the while in the background the rhythm of the music maintains your breathing at its beat … down and down you go into the lassitude of hypnosis. So now relax, relax, relax, in complete freedom of yourself. So now commence to go over each part of your body, in this order …

"Think of your feet relaxing. [Pause.] Think of your ankles relaxing. [Pause.] Think of the calves of your leg relaxing. [Pause.] Think of your knees relaxing. [Pause.] Think of your thighs relaxing. [Pause.] On up and up your body, step by step, you move your thoughts of your body relaxing. On up to your torso you go ... Think of all your torso muscles relaxing. [Pause.]

"All the muscles of your stomach and chest relaxing. The entire central part of your body is relaxing. Relaxing. Relaxing. [Pause.]

"Move up your body further and think now of your shoulders relaxing. [Pause.]

"And now your sweeping relaxation flows down your arms to your hands. Relax your arms and hands. [Pause.]

"Now think of your face ... think of all the muscles of your face relaxing. [Pause.] Relax the muscles of your jaws ... and the muscles of your closed eyes relax ... all the muscles of your entire face relax. Relax. Relax. Relax. How good it feels. [Pause.]

"Now let your thoughts wander on to the top of your head, as you think of the muscles of your scalp relaxing. [Pause.] Your entire body ... from the tips of your toes to the top of your head ... totally relaxed. *Totally let go!* Let go. Let go. Let go. How good it feels to just let go! [Pause.]

"And all the while you are breathing in and out as the cadence of the music you so softly hear maintains the rhythm of your breathing. How drowsy and sleepy you are becoming. How good it feels to just gently drift away. Just rest and drift and dreamily move along. [Pause.]

"Now slowly lift up your hands and place your opened palms along each side of your face, and gently stroke your face. How good it feels ... and ever deeper becomes the relaxation of both your mind and body deepen and ensue. [Pause.]

"Now place the palms of your hands with one palm over each of your closed eyes. Hold them there in silence for some moments and feel the warmth that enters, relaxing your eyes even more. How good it feels! [Pause.]

"Now move your hands down from your eyes and stroke the muscles of your under jaw and massage your neck. How good it feels! [Pause.]

"Down, down on to your shoulders now move your hands … first one and then the other, stroking pleasantly over your shoulders and down your arms. First your right hand strokes your left arm right down to the hand. And then your left hand strokes your right arm right down to the other hand. How good it feels. Pause a moment and just experience how good it feels. Indeed, *how good you feel!*

"Now rest one hand on each side of your body upon your breastbone where your rib cage starts … spread apart your fingers until they mesh with the spaces between your ribs, and then gently stroke them outward toward the sides of your body. Over and over do this stroking. How good it feels! [Pause.]

"Now rest your two hands upon your solar plexus and, in the deep relaxation you have established in yourself, think of a flow of energy from your hands entering that section of your body. Think it and you will experience it. You will sense a most pleasant warm flow of energy from your hands entering into your solar plexus … and in that flow of force which enters into your Being ever more and more you relax and enter the realm of sleep in hypnosis in which the tide of your subconscious rises to receptivity to arouse vitality within yourself.

"But first just rest some moments and enter yet ever deeper into the quiescence of yourself. Silence. Silence. Silence. Let the silence ever mount within the very *centre* of your being, and your subconscious phase of mind becomes receptive to the instructions you will now present to it, as a treasure of great value. [Music gradually fades out completely.]

"As you rest thus quietly in this deep reverie … with your hands pressed flat against your solar plexus with their energy entering this important *centre of your self*, turn your attention to visualising in your mind's eye a mass of energy the size of a glowing light bulb forming in the base of your spine. Imagine it as a glowing ball of light. See it glowing bright in your mind. Now feel it also, as that area of your body becomes warm from the glowing light you visualise. [Pause.]

"Feel the glowing light strongly. Experience it fully. It brings life-giving vitality into your being. Now you are ready to move the light throughout your body, from organ to organ, bringing you wonderful health, strength, and well-being. All ready, let us start. One, two, three …

"Now visualise the energy moving up your spine to the top of your head. Experience it![Pause.]

"Now take a deep breath and draw the light into your nose. [Pause.] Visualise it going down into your throat and into your lungs. [Pause.] Strongly with your mind see your lungs as alive with light. Experience it. [Pause.]

"Imagine the energy of the light permeating your lungs ... filling all the space between your armpits. Your lungs are alive with light. Your lungs are alive with vitality. Experience it. [Pause.]

"Now with your mind move the vitality of the light from your armpits down your arms to your thumbs. Feel your thumbs become warm and commence to throb. Then, from your thumbs visualise the energy in your thumbs sparking across to your forefingers, as a living electric current, until your hands become charged with electric-like energy. Experience the tingling in your hands. [Pause.]

"Now move the energy from your hands back up your arms to your shoulders. [Pause.] Then move across your shoulders to your neck to the points where your jaw meets your cheeks. Feel your cheeks flush and glow with warmth. Experience it.

"Now move the energy of the vitality of the light from your face down the front of your body to your navel ... to a point in the area of your appendix just to the right of your navel. Experience it. [Pause.]

"Now move the energy up the right side of your abdomen, and move it into the colon ... bathing the colon with the light. [Pause.]

"Now move the energy from your colon on out of the rectum. [Pause.]

"Now imagine the warm tingling energy flowing over your sex organs causing teasing sexual sensations. Experience it. [Pause.]

"Now from your sex organs move the energy straight up the front of your body, up and up until it covers your chin. Now let it divide and move over each cheek just below your closed eyes. Experience it. [Pause.]

Now from your cheeks visualise the energy flowing down your cheeks over the sides of your jaws, and again descending clear down to your stomach. Bathe your stomach in the energy of the light, aiding every digestive and assimilation process. Feel your stomach glow ... filling the entire centre of your being with vitality and radiant well-being. Experience it. [Pause.]

"Now move the energy down either side of your abdomen and on across your groin … continue on and move it on down the front of your legs allowing it to find its way, flowing to your feet, centring the energy in your big toes. [Pause.]

"Now let the energy move across to the second toe of each foot. [Pause.] Now let the energy leap from toe to toe until your toes are tingling with energy. Take your time; there is no hurry. Experience it fully. Think it and you will feel it. You will feel a throbbing in your feet. [Pause.]

"Now move up the inside of your feet to your ankles, and on up the inside of each leg. Experience it. [Pause.]

"Now let the energy move into the inside of your thighs. [Pause.]

"Now move the light energy again into your groin, and then divide it so that it passes up each side of the centre of your body, moving up to reach each armpit. Experience it. [Pause.]

"Now let the energy move to the area of your pancreas which is located on the left side of your abdomen just below the bottom of the rib cage. Feel this entire area become warm and aglow with light. Experience it. [Pause.]

"Now let the energy, which is your life-force, move to the centre of your body and on to your heart. Feel your heart become filled with light … healing the heart in every way and opening it to loving emotions for everyone and everything. Let the energy bathe your heart. Experience it. [Pause.]

"Now move the energy again back into your armpits … then move it on down the inside of each arm … and on across the palms of each hand to the fingers. Feel your fingers tingle. [Pause.]

"Now move the energy up the back of your arms … to the outside of your elbows … and again on up to the armpits, and on across your shoulders. Experience it. [Pause.]

"Now move the energy from your shoulders on up and across your jawbone, and bury it in either cheek. [Pause.] Now imagine the energy manifesting itself deep in the centre of each ear. Experience it as a tickling in each ear. [Pause.]

"Now move the energy to your 'third eye centre' at a point between the eyebrows. Imagine a glowing in this centre like the bursting of a star! Let the glow from that centre move on to the top of your head, and let your entire head become hot with the force. [Pause.] Then see it in your mind's eye as sending the light as a searchlight of energy from the top of your head far out into the space of the Universe itself. Your entire head is aglow with energy. Your brain is filled with energy ... the energy brings in a KNOWING of your true nature, the truth of your Divine Being and knowing who you are. It activates your powers of ESP and intuition. Experience it well! [Pause.]

"Now you know you have benefited your body in every way. You have filled it with vitality, and have become master of your *self*. Experience it deeply and feel your entire being aglow with light. [Pause.] ... [Slowly and very softly, gradually being in the beat of the music again.]

"Now rest ... resting in the deepest of relaxation so very close to sleep ... and experience your entire body being alive with vitality; aglow with energy. Breathe deeply and fully and just relax, as the vital energy of life surges through you from head to toes. [Pause.]

"Gradually, gradually, very gradually now allow the energy within yourself to subside and sink down into even deeper rest, from which you will return to full alertness, the master of your life. [Music becomes louder and louder.]

"The process is complete. How wonderful and filled with vitality you feel. How wonderfully alive you feel! And so just rest on a few moments longer. And as it is your wish come back to full awareness in the here and now. Rise and shine, vital being that you are!"

And now, practise, practise, and practise!

You now have the knowhow to make you an expert hypnotist, but the skill with which you apply that knowledge is entirely up to you. Hypnotism is like any other performing art: it is how you interpret and present it that counts. As those in the theatre would say: "It's not what you do, it's how you do it!"

So ...

Practise diligently. With practice comes perfection. Practise with single subjects. Practise with groups. Practise in private. Practise in public.

Learn your hypnotic methods so thoroughly that they become second nature to you. Make your techniques as much a part of yourself as are your most familiar actions, so that they occur with smoothness and ease. Know exactly what you are going to do when you do it. It is by knowing hypnosis well that you can then concentrate your attention on the showmanship and entertainment values of stage hypnotism. Remember always that, in show business, *entertainment is the thing*!

Now, read, read, and read!

This cannot be recommended too highly. Read everything you can get your hands on about hypnotism. The mastery of hypnotism is a perpetual learning process. For your convenience in continuing study, excellent books are listed in the bibliography at the back of this book.

Part Two

Entertaining
with Hypnotism

THE PROF. & MRS. KNOWLES HYPNOTISM SHOW 1901

Entertaining with hypnotism then and now. After the death of Charcot and the decline of the Nancy School, it was the stage hypnotist alone who kept hypnotism alive in public interest.

THE ORMOND McGILL "CONCERT OF HYPNOTISM" SHOW 1991

*Preliminaries to
the Hypnotism Show*

Chapter Forty-Four
An Introduction to Entertaining With Hypnotism by Gil Boyne

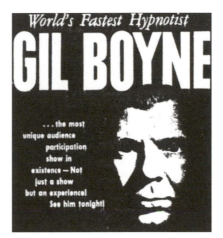

For many years, Gil Boyne performed as a stage hypnotist. He was billed as "The World's Fastest Hypnotist". He presents this introduction to this section of the *Encyclopedia*. (The complete Gil Boyne Hypnotism Show will be found in the appendix of this book.)

"People are interested in people, thus entertainment that conveys 'human interest' provides superlative entertainment close to the interest of everyone. Stage hypnotism is based on human interest entertainment.

"The term Stage Hypnotism, in this text, is used synonymously with Demonstrational Hypnosis, i.e. hypnosis related to performing situations such as social gatherings, club groups, lectures, stage shows, etc. This text trains you in the art of stage hypnotism. By following the sequence of first considering yourself as the performer and, then revealing the secrets of professional mastery for successfully presenting the hypnotism show for both scientific and human interest entertainment.

"You learn how to open the show, how to get the best subjects on stage as your committee, how to hypnotise the committee, how to programme the show and how to climax the performance.

"You are given a complete hypnotism show, including presentational ideas from the programmes of famous stage hypnotists. You study hypnotism stagecraft along with dozens of professional routines you can use to assist you to develop your own, including Sensational Feats and Hypnotrix to make you a master showman. Originality is stressed as your key to success.

"Associated features to stage hypnotism are presented: the field of hypnotism in the night club, routines, presentation, showmanship, production, staging the hypnotism show, and so on.

"I have always considered stage hypnotism and/or demonstrational hypnotism to be of great value in advancing the entire profession of hypnotism, especially in relating to valuable work in hypnotherapy. The stage hypnotist has an opportunity to show what can be done. What can be accomplished through hypnosis is truly remarkable, as the human mind is the most priceless possession of Mankind. To that end, as a professional in the field, I have always maintained a certain dignity should be afforded to all hypnotic demonstrations on stage.

"Genuinely humorous situations are entirely permissible to stage demonstrations of hypnotism, as entertainment is a major prerogative. However, lewd exhibitions have no place in the art. Such are both degrading to the subjects and hypnosis itself. Stage hypnotism should be presented with class. Ormond McGill brings that class to all his demonstrations. You do the same. It is a professional obligation.

"Also, in this volume the business side of stage hypnotism is considered, i.e. advertising the show, legal protocol, publicity features, etc.

"Finally, you are instructed in how to present an after-the-show diplay of Oriental hypnotism (*yoga nidra*), which can become an outstanding attraction in your programme.

"In this *New Encyclopedia of Stage Hypnotism*, Ormond McGill has left no stone unturned to assist you to become a master of the art."

Chapter Forty-Five
First Understanding

Properly presented stage hypnotism provides quality entertainment which emphasises the work done in medical and academic fields.

Few forms of entertaining are more intimately appealing than hypnotic exhibitions, as the show is devoted entirely to audience participation revealing uninhibited aspects of human behaviour. The show is exceedingly interesting to watch, and every show is different since the cast on stage is different.

There is something so warmly human, while, at the same time, verging on the magical, that hypnotism stands unique on the entertainment spectrum. An audience will be literally convulsed with laughter in watching the fun-filled antics of hypnotised persons on stage; a few minutes later, that same audience will lean forward in their seats staring in wonder at the mental phenomena unfolding before their eyes.

The hypnotism show is an action show based on the greatest wonder and mystery of all, the human mind. Hypnotism demonstrates the magic of the mind.

In this book, the performer will find a wealth of information for successfully presenting stage hypnotism. The non-performer will find a wealth of knowledge about the psychology of hypnotism and its practical application. Stage hypnotism provides an opportunity to acquaint thousands of people with the science/art through the medium of entertainment. Making knowledge entertaining is the best way to learn.

Most importantly, hypnotism must never be regarded as a toy one plays with. The human mind is a delicate instrument which must be handled with great care. The hypnotist has a legal and moral obligation to approach the performance of hypnotism in a completely ethical manner, and appreciate that the most important person, in his (or her) presentation are those who volunteer as subjects, and not himself.

Chapter Forty-Six
You as a Stage Hypnotist

When one thinks about stepping out on stage expecting to entertain an audience for a period of thirty minutes to a full evening with nothing for support but a group of empty chairs, it is an undertaking to make the stoutest showman pause and reflect. Indeed, it is the real skill it takes to handle well such a presentation that makes stage demonstrations of hypnotism become an art.

Qualifications of the Hypnotic Entertainer

The qualifications of the successful stage hypnotist rate amongst the top in the entertainment profession, for stage hypnotism is one of the most complex of all forms of entertainment, as it entails two shows being given simultaneously (one for the subjects on stage and one for the audience), while, at the same time, having to meet and master the uncertainties of precisely knowing just what is going to happen in audience participation situations.

Unlike other entertainers such as singers, dancers, magicians, etc., who have their respective act entirely under control, the hypnotist's show is one on which he relies upon the conduct of unknown volunteers invited up from the audience itself. If the persons who come up on to his stage respond and perform well to his hypnotic efforts, he succeeds in producing superlative entertainment, and his show is a success. Conversely, if his subjects do not perform well (and in a hypnotism show the subjects are really the show), his entertainment is a failure.

It is not uncommon for a performer to feel that relying upon the responses of volunteers to put a show over is too great a risk to take. However, it can be done with one hundred percent success.

Through your study of the earlier material, you have learned how to hypnotise and manipulate the state. You will now be shown how to make the stage presentation of hypnotism successful, and reduce to the minimum the possibility of failure. For in truth, while hypnosis must always deal with the human equation, the "cards can be stacked" in your favour to a sufficient extent that success can be largely certain.

Hypnotism as entertainment has everything: comedy, mystery, drama, coupled with educational and thought provoking phenomena, and every show is different! So complete is the appeal of the hypnotism show that, when properly handled, scarcely any other form of entertainment is capable of creating more spontaneous interest and enthusiasm.

The successful presentation of the hypnotism show calls for both a thorough knowledge of hypnotism and an understanding of showmanship. This latter is most important as a major purpose of the show is to entertain.

Three Basics for Successful Stage Hypnotism

1. You must be thoroughly acquainted with hypnotic induction methods and know how to produce all manner of hypnotic phenomena through to expertly presenting suggestions for the production of waking hypnosis experiments and trance phenomena.

2. You must be a showman. By a showman is meant a qualified entertainer. Showmanship is the ability to present to an audience whatever is shown in a manner to produce its maximum entertainment appeal.

3. The hypnotism show must be precisely routined. The stage hypnotist must know exactly what he is going to do. The show proceeds through a basic pattern, from start to finish with precision.

The hypnotism show is similar to a stage play: it has an opening, a body, a climax and a conclusion. The exact drama of your particular show is in accordance with how you wish to stage it. However its presentation must be completely mastered and become as second nature to yourself.

Advantages of the Hypnotism Show

There are many advantages to the hypnotism show as it is based on human interest, and human interest is the paramount form of entertainment. Also the fact that it is an art form raises its prestige and entertainment appeal. Such a show is spectacular and full stage size in scope; and yet you need carry no equipment, as the audience itself provides the apparatus. However you can elaborate upon that factor and turn it into as large a full stage spectacular as you wish. After all you have a big cast working with you.

Your Appearance as a Hypnotist

The way you look, the way you dress, the way you speak and act all contribute to your appearance as a hypnotist. The way you appear to an audience depends upon how well you conduct yourself on stage. In such regard, the successful hypnotist does not boast or challenge. He adopts the manner of the successful physician: being quiet, reserved, dignified and confident in knowing his work. And above all do not make your show a personal ego trip. It is the purpose of your show to advance the art of hypnotism and entertain the audience, not to flatter yourself.

The profession of stage hypnotism carries a charisma of its own. The performer is an artist who deftly plays upon the most wonderful of instruments, the human mind. It carries an obligation to be immaculate in every way.

In regard to speech, speak clearly and well, and always with flawless language. Know your hypnotism show so perfectly that every word is spoken with perfection. In addressing your audience your comments should be professional and good natured, much in the manner of an authoritative lecturer. To your subjects your speech must be positive and direct. In this regard, while your delivery of suggestions is quiet in tone, let there be no doubt as to the authority expressed, i.e. obedience is expected!

Performing Attitude

The matter of performing attitude is extremely important to successful stage hypnotism. There is a tendency for the hypnotism show to inflate the importance of the performer and belittle the subjects. In other words, the performer becomes dominant and the subjects submissive. Such an attitude can be very harmful to the entertainment values of the show and must be carefully countered.

Remember, always, the audience tends to psychologically identify with the subjects; thus, to ridicule the subjects is to ridicule the audience. Guard against this carefully by placing the subjects, in every instance possible, upon the pinnacle of audience acceptance. Follow these five directives in this regard:

1. Whenever applause is indicated, direct the applause toward the subject(s) who performed the demonstration rather than towards the performer who causes the demonstration.

2. Explain that all hypnotic efforts are the result of the excellent concentration of the subjects rather than the unique virtues of the hypnotist.

3. Explain in any experiment that might seem too ridiculous the underlying significance of what it illustrates in an entertaining manner.

4. Stress the true dynamics of the hypnotic situation, which is one of cooperation and trust between hypnotist and subject, in which each has their respective role to perform, in order to achieve hypnosis.

5. Do not upstage your subjects, literally meaning *do not stand in front of your subjects while you are wroking with them on stage*. It is all too common in a hypnotism show to see the performer with his back turned to the audience with the subject half hidden by his body.

NOTE TO HYPNOTIST: Always bear in mind your stage positioning so that the subjects are properly visible to the audience.

Audience Acceptance

Possibly no aspect of showmanship is as important to successful stage hypnotism as that of audience acceptance. The hypnotist must do everything in his power to make his show a winner in the eyes of the audience.

Hypnotically speaking, the more the audience is in favour of the show being presented, the better hypnotic results will be obtained upon the stage. The committee of volunteers likes to feel they are participating in a successful show and responds accordingly. Conversely, they do not like to feel they are participating in an unsuccessful one.

The principle of audience acceptance cannot be emphasised too strongly, for it is not in the number of subjects you secure to work with on stage, or whether you have persons who are especially suggestible that counts, so much as it is that the volunteers want to be part of the show and want to accept your suggestions. Actually, the more naturally suggestible a subject is, the worse he will respond to adverse audience reaction.

By the same token, just the reverse is true when the audience is in favour of the show. Then the volunteers can't respond quickly enough to both please you and the audience.

Psychologist, R.W. White suggests this theory: "As a first step, it is proposed that hypnotic behaviour be regarded as meaningful, goal-directed striving, its most general goal being to behave like a hypnotised person as this is continuously defined by the operator and understood by the subject. The subject, it is held, is ruled by a wish to behave like a hypnotised person, his motive is submission to the operator's demands. He understands at all times what the operator intends, and his behaviour is a striving to put these intentions into execution."

The above is essentially true, but in the hypnotic stage situation the subject's drive is directed not only to please the hypnotist but even more to please the audience.

> NOTE TO HYPNOTIST: It is well to appreciate fully the audience-pleasing factor in relation to stage hypnosis. It is the audience that greatly influences the subjects, which is very likely a reason why more startling hypnotic phenomena are seen upon the stage than in other more closely controlled situations. There is a "mass psychology" at work in audience acceptance and audience pleasing that is intensely hypnotic in effect.

The stage hypnotist should always make his audience respond and show their appreciation of the subjects. When a subject or group of subjects have performed especially well, actually lead the audience in applause by stating, such as: "The members of the committee have performed such an excellent job of concentration so let us give them a rousing round of applause to show our appreciation." An audience can be trained to applaud. Especially get them to respond to the subjects. Remember a huge audience reaction makes for a huge hypnotic reaction from the subjects on stage.

> NOTE TO HYPNOTIST: Making his show a winner is important to both subject and audience pleasing. In such regard hypnotic procedures should be gentle and gracious. Rough tactics such as pushing subjects should be consistently avoided. Avoid undue physical handling as much as possible. After all, hypnosis is a mental phenomenon, so keep it mental. And above all keep alert so that no subject gets hurt from suggestion-action on the stage. It is ever your promise to all volunteers that they will leave your stage feeling better than when they came upon it.

Subject Welfare

Of paramount importance to the hypnotism show is subject welfare (subject well-being). This is the first obligation of the stage hypnotist. The subjects are volunteers who place themselves in your hands in good faith, and you must honour that trust and not harm them either psychologically or physically. The psychological care is obvious to the hypnotist, but the physical may be overlooked.

The physical aspect of subject welfare is very important as the hypnotism show can, on occasion, become a real "rough house" free-for-all. Sometimes subjects can be seem scrambling over each other, hands being stepped on, bodies falling out of chairs, heads being bumped, all manner of bruising situations occurring. As a stage hypnotist you cannot be too careful to guard against physical injury and to protect subject welfare.

Chapter Forty-Seven
Secrets of Successful Stage Hypnotism

The principles here considered are basic to the entire field of hypnotism. As a hypnotist, you may have learned them already. Learn them again.

Expectancy

One of the great secrets of Stage Hypnotism is the expectancy of the subjects to be hypnotised by you. If the subjects expect to be hypnotised they are two-thirds into hypnosis before the show even starts. Accordingly, every stimuli you present must be aimed to arouse to greater and greater heights that expectancy.

The process starts with the show's advertising. It continues with attending the show. It builds through your opening lecture and in volunteering to come on stage. It develops further as each test proceeds, and climaxes in being hypnotised. Appreciate that all these factors of expectancy are in your favour and are under your control.

The Stage Situation

There is an advantage the stage hypnotist enjoys over any other type of hypnotist and that is that there is an atmosphere about the stage which is conducive to successful demonstrating of hypnotism. The stage is a place for demonstrating, and everyone who attends the show knows it instinctively. For the moment that stage is your domain. It is your home. You are the host and the subjects are your guests. You have a right to direct your guests.

The lights, the music, the curtains, the audience out in front all are factors productive of hypnosis in the stage situation. It is because of this "stage situation" that hypnosis can more generally be induced with greater speed than in any other situation.

The Importance of Importance

The more important you make your work appear the greater will be your success. In this regard observe these rules:

(a) Make the state of mind produced by hypnotism important.

(b) Make the audience respect your performance of hypnotism. It is important. Make the spectators realise they are witnessing mental miracles, which is important.

(c) Make your subjects feel that being hypnotised is important. Let everyone realise the importance of the mental skill they have learned.

Social Approval

The more you convince the audience of the value of hypnosis the more of a superior light you will shine upon your subjects. They become adventurers exploring the realm of the subconscious mind. Aim all your work towards building both social approval of hypnosis and of the subjects entering hypnosis.

Group Size, Age, and Sex

For most hypnotic shows do not use less than ten chairs or more than twenty-five. For a large stage, an average of twenty is ideal. The night club situation can use less depending upon space available.

Keep the age level of the volunteers as even as you can. No children please. The majority of your committee will be composed of young adults. They make a splendid group to work with.High school and college students are excellent.

Regarding sex, let that be a matter of who volunteers. A mixture of half and half is ideal. Sometimes you will have an over-abundance of volunteers, and all seats are taken; you can have the overflow stand behind the chairs of the seated subjects. Explain that you want all to have an equal chance to participate, but obviously there are more persons on stage than you can work with. You propose a group test that all can try. The ones who respond well you retain; the ones who do not do so well you dismiss with a smile. Soon you will have all the chairs filled with excellent subjects.

Judging Your Committee

Observation is the best teacher in spotting your best subjects; it's a knack that comes with experience. Generally speaking, your best subjects are persons who are serious and possibly a bit nervous, have a self-conscious demeanour, and sit with both feet on the floor. Usually you can notice a certain "anticipation" look about them.

Subjects you should avoid and dismiss, as promptly as is diplomatic, are ones who sit with crossed legs or a "you show me" air. Likewise subjects who insist on talking to each other, chew gum, smoke, or smell of alcohol should be dismissed. And beware of the subject with the perpetual grin. He may not mean harm but his smirk can harm the show.

The ability to spot and judge at a glance "good" and "bad" subjects is one of the first things the stage hypnotist must learn for the smooth staging of the show.

Assembling the Committee

If it is convenient, you can have a few persons seated in the audience who have expressed interest to volunteering. When you make the call, have them come right up. It starts the parade.

You can almost tell by the way the subjects volunteer how your show is going to go. If they swarm up it will be a bang-up show. If they come up slowly it will be more difficult. This factor of reticence on the part of subjects, on occasion, to come forward willingly is important to the showman. It is never good to have to beg for volunteers.

An enthusiastic bunch of volunteers who come up promptly gets the show off to a good start. Everyone then knows the show has social approval. A useful tip in assembling your committee is to separate people who come up together. Seat them next to strangers on stage; this avoids conversation and other distractions.

Group Hypnotism

Group hypnosis is important to the stage hypnotist, for the percentage factor in a group of persons promptly locates the most responsive subjects. Actually it is often easier to hypnotise a group of subjects than it is only one. A group seems to develop a mutual spirit of cooperation that carries from one subject to the next until all are performing in unison.

Progressive Selling

Although it is rarely expressed in such terms, Stage Hypnotism is pretty much a selling job. Your whole approach is to arrange the show so that each test sells the subjects on responding to the next. A chain reaction is created which flows throughout the entire show. In such regard, generally speaking, progressing your show from the less complex to the more complex is a logical sequence to follow. "Progressive Selling" is the answer to the successful hypnotism show.

The High Pressure of Stage Hypnotism

The term "high pressure" is aptly used in describing the techniques of the stage hypnotist. Every device the performer can muster is thrown in a continuous barrage at the subjects to induce the proper conditions for hypnosis. The "high pressure" must be artfully applied however, as the more completely it is disguised the more effective the technique.

Repetition and Clearness of Suggestions

In order for the mind in the hypnotic state to properly assimilate suggestions they must be clearly given. To that end repeat suggestive ideas. It is not a bad idea to make it your habit to repeat, at least twice, suggestions given, so that there may be no confusion as to what is wanted to be accomplished.

One Thing at a Time

Remember, a basic rule in the presentation of suggestions is to give one idea, or suggestion series, at a time. The mind works best that way. Also, be sure to remove the influence of a suggestion before another is advanced. This is important not only to the smooth running of your performance but for subject well-being as well.

Don't Expect Too Much

In presenting suggestions for your subjects to react to, don't give them things too foreign to their natures. Gauge the tests you try with each subject as being within his capacity to perform. If you adhere to this rule your work will prove more universally successful in producing striking phenomena.

Use Your Best Subjects

As your show progresses, you can invariably spot your best subjects. Your audience will too. Use these best subjects in your most important tests. The audience will be glad you did, as they are the most interesting to watch.

Trance Depth in Stage Hypnosis

Although naturally it varies with individuals, in general the depth of trance produced via the rapidity of the stage situation is not as deep as in using more methodical methods when more time for induction is allowed.

Trance depth is not overly important to the stage hypnotist, other than it must be considered in handling the subjects. Generally, on stage make your tests as easy for your subject(s) to perform as possible.

From the audience's viewpoint the tests performed in light trance (including waking hypnosis) are as impressive as more advanced experiments. So until you are certain of your subject's trance depth don't over extend his capacities as a subject.

Keeping the Subjects Entranced

As stage methods of hypnotising are so rapid in nature they sometime tend to be unstable, so, unless pressure is maintained, some subjects slip out of trance if left too long unoccupied. To keep them entranced keep them busy doing something. In other words, give them attention. For the most part keep your subjects active and busy responding to a flow of suggestions. Unless there is some reason not to, it is often well to awaken subjects between tests.

It is important also to give "sleep" reinforcing suggestions at intervals, such as: "You will continue to go on down deeper and deeper into hypnosis right along with every breath you take." They have to breath, so this proves a good reinforcing suggestions. Or you can suggest: "No one can disturb or awaken you except myself." Such suggestions tend to keep the trance in force.

Simulation

When working with a large group of subjects on stage it is not uncommon to find some simulating being hypnotised rather than actually being entranced.

This simulation is not necessarily voluntary deception, but is frequently born of a genuine desire to cooperate with the performer and help the show. In other words, not being able to enter true somnambulism, the subject does his best to imitate the condition.

This factor is important for the performer to recognise, and it can increase the number of entertaining subjects he has to work with on stage. However, he should be able to pick the genuine from the false in order to properly select subjects for his more profound tests. This takes a practised eye and means you must pay close attention to what you are doing throughout the show. Actually you need not be too concerned if the simulation is good, as the precise mental condition of the subject is not as important as is his outer appearance in a show. On the stage the show is the thing and, as long as the audience is satisfied you can afford to be. But recognise that the audience is composed of intelligent people, and they can spot simulation too, as genuine hypnotic phenomena has a certain intensity to it that simulation lacks.

However what begins as simulation can frequently transform into hypnosis. Just be alert to what is happening throughout your show. Then you will be in control.

Deliberate Faking

It is a far cry from a subject simulating to help the show to the subject who deliberately pretends to be hypnotised just to fool you. This latter kind of person is dangerous, as he will try to make a fool of you.

Always keep a wary eye out for such pranksters as they can harm your show. Such subjects have a habit of pretending to be asleep while you are watching them and, when your back is turned, open their eyes and poke fun at you; then appear to return to sleep before you can spot them.

Whenever a laugh comes in your show for no apparent reason, be on your guard that someone is faking, and spot the troublemaker(s) as soon as possible and dismiss them from the stage immediately. Make no bones about it – of they go! The audience will admire you for your perception and command.

A way to catch these fakes is to unexpectedly turn around, or have some-one stationed in the wings who watches the subjects constantly and, if he sees that a subject is faking, holds up the number of fingers representing the chair number in which the subject is seated. It is in giving attention to these details that the Hypnotism Show advances from being mediocre to being great!

Making Your Show Personal

When it is possible, greet your subjects when they come on stage. Sometimes you can even go to a chair and shake hands. Be friendly. When possible learn the names of your subjects (first name is sufficient) and call them by name when you perform a test and give suggestions to the person. A device that can be used on stage is to pass name tags to all committee members. They write their name of these and fasten to coat or dress. A personal approach in working with subjects frequently increases personal response to the induction of hypnosis.

Be Alert on Stage – Always

Never perform on automatic. Stay alert at all times and continually watch your subjects. Then you can recognise the space they are in and tend to their needs. Then you can plan your show, as it goes along, in deciding which persons you will use in such and such tests, etc. The more fully conscious you are during your performance, the better show you will present.

Chapter Forty-Eight
Hypnotism as Entertainment

The idea behind the old-time hypnotism show was to establish the performer as a sort of mastermind who dominates the wills of his subjects. His subjects were regarded as sort of "victims" he masters with his hypnotic powers. Such old fashioned shows of hypnotism often included experiments which made the subjects look ridiculous under the supposition that it was ludicrous and heaped glory on the hypnotist in his apparent mastery of humanity.

The new hypnotism show is just the opposite of the old. Instead of attempting to heap glory on the hypnotist it heaps glory on the phenomenon of hypnotism and the skill of the subjects at being able to master the art. By the same token, such does not remove the audience's respect for your "hypnotic powers" (skill as a hypnotist), and it assuredly does ensure that they accord you as an individual far more respect.

In the contemporary hypnotism show, the hypnotist assumes the role of guide. There is sound psychology in this approach that revolutionises the hypnotic show from its antiquated predecessors, modernises it in accordance to its stature as a science of the mind, and lifts it to the height of artistry.

The Presentation of Modern Stage Hypnotism

Every performer has his own style of working. Some will hypnotise with persuasive methods while others will utilise more aggressive means. And the routines, too, and the variety of effects presented will vary with different hypnotists but, underlying the entire structure of the hypnotic show, always incorporate these six presentational rules:

Rule 1: Never clown

Hypnotism from the viewpoint of the performer must be essentially a serious business. This does not mean you are to be glum in your presentation. Indeed, be lively and dynamic. But deliberately trying to be funny has no place in the presentation of stage hypnotism. Let all humour come from the subject matter itself.

Rule 2: Never ridicule your subjects

Bear in mind that your committee is composed of volunteers from the audience and to ridicule them is the same as ridiculing the audience ... which is entertainment suicide. Always treat your subjects with the utmost courtesy and respect. While some of your tests may be extremely funny, always make them serve the end of illustrating some hypnotic principle; never to make the subjects appear ridiculous.

Rule 3: Incorporate science into your presentation

Just how much scientific explanation about hypnotism you can incorporate into your shows depends upon your personality as an entertainer and the type of audiences to which you play. But always, to some extent, retain a background of scientific experimentation to your work.

Rule 4: Take your audience into your confidence

Hypnotism has long enough been shrouded in mystery. There is no need for you to prolong the mystery. You will find that a frank explanation of hypnotic phenomena, as you demonstrate, serves only to increase the marvel of hypnosis. The human mind is the greatest wonder of all.

Don't be afraid to admit that you have no special powers over the minds of your subjects. Don't be afraid to explain that the underlying principles of hypnotism are the workings of psychological laws without a vestige of the supernatural. You will find that your frankness, far from destroying your prestige in the eyes of the audience, will actually increase it. We live in an age which appreciates explanations.

The public nowadays like to consider themselves intellectual enough to consider scientific problems, and facts that relate to how their mind operates hold real fascination for everyone. As far as reducing mystery goes, one might ask if you reduce the mystery of electricity by explaining some of the things it can do? Actually, the more you explain, the more you increase its wonders. Hypnotism is of similar ilk.

Rule 5: Interest your committee

As a hypnotist all your really important props are human. You must, therefore, hold the interest of those "props" with full attention. To such an end, the presentation of your show must encompass your committee of subjects equally as your audience of spectators.

Rule 6: Always entertain

Always remember your foremost purpose as a stage performer is to entertain. It is so easy to become wrapped up in the phenomena of hypnotism that you tend to entertain yourself and forget your audience. In other words, you get caught up in doing things you personally find interesting but are not necessarily of interest to the audience.

Make everything you do in the hypnotism show convey a message and have a purpose. Make every effect you show have entertainment value. No matter how intellectual your hypnotic show may be, its paramount value diminishes unless it is also entertaining.

Make Your Hypnotic Phenomena Visual

No matter how profound the hypnosis you induce, there is little entertainment value unless you make it visual to those who witness it. For example, you suggest an hallucination to a subject that when he opens his eyes he will see a cat on the floor. The subject may see the cat but the audience is not entertained. To make the hallucination visual how much more effective it is to suggest: "When you open your eyes you will see a big, black cat on the floor. It will rub itself against your leg, and you will bend down and pat it. You will love the cat; you will pick it up and play with it. Then it will suddenly get angry and try to scratch you, and you will toss it away."

You have created a scene, you have made the phenomena visual to the audience by the subject's reaction to the suggestions. They are entertained. Use this principle in all you do on stage.

> NOTE TO HYPNOTIST: Make it your rule to establish, in all your hypnotic tests, an action response so that the audience can visually follow the experiment and be entertained by its effect.

Emphasise your Hypnotic Effects

You can increase the entertainment value of your effects if you will amplify the subject's reactions by your showmanship in exhibiting the reactions. By way of illustration:

Suppose you have suggested to a subject that when he awakens from the trance that he cannot see, he will grope his way about the stage as though blind until you tell him that his sight has returned to normal. Observe how you can easily emphasise such an effect by having members of the audience wave their hands in front of the "blinded" eyes, or by having him stare wide-eyed looking out at the audience. You then light a match and pass the flame before his eyes causing the audience to gasp at the unwavering stare. Of such devices is the showmanship of hypnotism made.

Speed and Timing in the Hypnotism Show

Every device you can muster to add to the pace of your show will add to its entertainment value. To such ends, use the principle of post-hypnosis to increase the speed with which you can hypnotise on stage.

And give consideration to the length of your performance. The Hypnotism Show offers such a gamut of emotions it can literally exhaust an audience if it is too lengthy. While shows of two hour length have been successfully presented, in general a show of one hour length is quite sufficient. Make it your rule to always leave your audience wanting more rather than to over-saturate them. Conversely don't be too stingy with your programme either. At least a half an hour will be needed.

The Skeleton of the Hypnotism Show

Regardless of its length or what you do, its pattern will follow along this general line of construction. Use this skeleton in developing your own programme:

INTRODUCTION
OPENING LECTURE
COMMITTEE INVITATION
SUBJECTS COME UP ON STAGE
FIRST DEMONSTRATION WITH THE GROUP
(which may be an induction)
EXPERIMENTS IN WAKING HYPNOSIS (if you elect to use such)
INDIVIDUAL EXAMPLES OF HYPNOTISM
GROUP HYPNOTISM (unless used at the beginning)
EXPERIMENTS IN HYPNOTIC SUGGESTION
POSTHYPNOTIC PHENOMENA
COMMITTEE DISMISSAL
CONCLUSION OF THE SHOW

NOTE TO HYPNOTIST: Entertaining With Hypnotism is essentially a show that reveals the magic of the mind through graphic demonstrations, humorous incidents, scientific explanations and thought provoking phenomena.

Chapter Forty-Nine
Five Important Extra Tips

In this chapter, you are given five additional tips, which will increase the effectiveness of your hypnotism show. Give them attention.

Tip 1: The Subject is Listening

Remember, hypnosis produces a hypersuggestible state of mind and accents the senses. The subject is listening to you at all times during the show, even when not directly spoken to. So what you say even to others has an indirect influence on the behaviour of the subject.

When spoken to directly, you can even increase the attention simply by suggesting: "Listen to what I tell you now with complete attention." Conversely, you can stop the listening, by suggesting: "Stop listening to me now and pay no attention to what I say." Should you give a suggestion, be sure to cancel it out before performing other demonstrations with that person or the inattention may persist. To amplify the importance of this tip consider the next tip with care; it is directly related.

Tip 2: Subject Double-talk

The hypnotism show is really two shows going on simultaneously, each interwoven into the texture of the other. One show is to the spectators seated in the audience, and the other show is to the subjects seated on the stage. Appreciating this fact, suggestion double-talk can be used effectively.

As an example of this handling, when you tell the audience that you are going to perform such-and-such a demonstration with a subject, although you are speaking to the audience and telling them what is going to occur, at one and the same time you are presenting a suggestion to the subject to perform what is being explained. This is a point of performing mastery the stage hypnotist must both appreciate and utilise to full advantage.

Tip 3: Hypnotised Subject's Agreement

As a prelude to each experiment, the hypnotised subject can be told what is going to be performed and requested to nod his head if such is agreeable (acceptable). Invariably a "nod of agreement" will be achieved, as amenity to pleasing the hypnotist is innate to hypnosis. Further:

This requesting of permission from the hypnotised person goes a long way in eliciting maximum performance of the test suggested. The "agreement nod" can be obtained from a group of subjects as well as from a solo subject. It provides both an artistic way of demonstrating hypnosis as well as producing striking effects. It is democratic, and is appreciated by the spectators. (See Jerry Valley Show, Chapter Sixty.)

NOTE TO HYPNOTIST: Hypnotist Jerry Valley uses the "agreement response" with almost every test he presents. He explains to the hypnotics what is going to happen, and then requests a nod of the head if they understand. Following such, the test is performed to maximum effectiveness. Subconscious agreement to understanding what is expected produces responsiveness to perform what is expected in direct ratio to the agreement existing between subject and hypnotist.

Tip 4: Involve Yourself in the Action

The hypnotism show frequently involves the subject in the performance of various dramatised scenes. These are entertaining, and, the more you involve yourself as an actor in the scenes the subjects are performing, the more unified the dramatics become and entertainment value is increased.

As an example, you hypnotically suggest to the subjects that they are going back in time to when they were children of eight to nine in school. It is an interesting age regression experience in an imaginary sense which you amplify by further suggesting that they have a stern teacher they dislike, and that with every opportunity they get they will cause annoyance. Then suggest: "I am that stern teacher and when I turn my back make the worst face you can at me, but if I turn around wipe it off quickly or you'll be in trouble."

In such handling, you have set up a dramatic situation for the hypnotics to act and react in. Now allow yourself to enter into the action by assuming the role of the stern teacher who is trying his best to keep the class under control but getting more and exasperated by the antics of the incorrigible students.

In other words you act out the part and, the more dramatic the skill you do this with, the better. Not only does this handling increase the entertainment value of the scene, it likewise increases the subjects' responses to the suggested scene. In a nutshell, it increases entertainment for the audience.

Tip 5: The Suggestive Value of Pantomime

Directly related to the foregoing, the use of pantomime to convey the suggested ideas can be effective. I sometimes have used the principle dramatically in enacting the scene of Dr Jekyll & Mr Hyde. In the demonstration, it is explained (remember the subjects are listening even when you speak to the audience) that you have developed a powerful chemical elixir such as Robert Louis Stevenson told about in his famous story. Show the elixir in a bottle (it is only coloured water) and offer to demonstrate how it will change a gentle person, such as Dr Jekyll, into the horrible Mr Hyde. Then drink the contents and go into the pantomime dramatics of changing (à la John Barrymore) from yourself to Mr Hyde. Hunch yourself, grimace your face, claw your hands. The better show you can make of it the greater the impact, as your pantomime functions as suggestion to the hypnotic.

Turn to a subject and state: "I will give you a drink of this now, and it will turn you into Mr Hyde." (This can be presented as a group test also; in which case you give a glass of the liquid to each subject.) Hand the elixir to the subject. Tell him to drink it. He does, and you have Mr Hyde on stage. Your previous pantomime has suggested to the subject how he will react. As an hypnotic response, he will very likely perform an even better dramatisation than you did. On occasion this test can be presented as part of a "screen test" to determine the subject's dramatic talent for a film. When you wish to conclude the test, simply suggest the effects of the elixir has worn off, and he is now to return gradually to his own good-natured self.

Chapter Fifty
Hypnotic Show Programming

Current pace of entertainment has initiated the practice of beginning The Hypnotism Show by a direct mass hypnotic induction of the committee to get things off to a rapid start. This is fine if the hypnotist has a reputation or is playing an extended engagement. However in cases of isolated performances, more certain results can be obtained by applying slower initiation of the committee members to the phenomena of hypnosis by conditioning via waking hypnosis tests first, in other words, demonstrating waking hypnosis prior to going into trance induction.

I have found waking hypnosis tests to have entertainment value in themselves and to assist in ultimate induction. The hypnotist must pretty much use his own judgement in such programming matters. Use what works for you. Actually, it largely depends upon the time allotted to the hypnotic show, the pace required and the performing situation being faced.

By way of illustrating hypnotic programming for an entire evening's show, here are two examples: my personal "concert of hypnotism" and Prof. George Singer's "hypnotic marvels" programme. As the show has an intermission, an effective posthypnotic method is employed to have the subjects return to stage ready to continue the performance, as described.

It will be noted in this programme that the show is arranged in two acts. Act One specifies "Experiments in Waking Suggestion and Hypnosis", and Act Two, following the intermission, "Advanced Experiments in Hypnotism".

The first act of the show features various waking suggestion tests, then proceeds into an hypnotic induction with the committee climaxing with a group hand-raising test, and ending with a posthypnotic suggestion to the effect that when a certain piece of music is played all of the subjects, following the intermission, will automatically march back up on to the stage, resume their seats, and will return again to the hypnotic condition – fast asleep. The music is then played so that all may hear it, and the suggestions emphasised. The hypnotics are then awakened and dismissed, and it is intermission time.

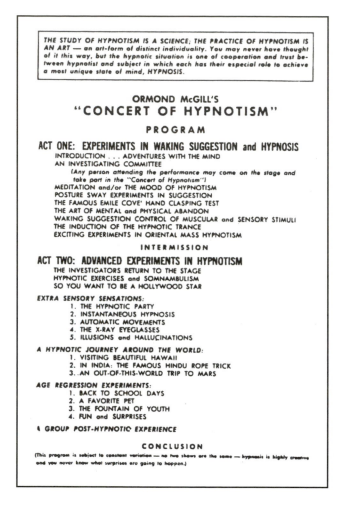

THE STUDY OF HYPNOTISM IS A SCIENCE; THE PRACTICE OF HYPNOTISM IS
AN ART — an art-form of distinct individuality. You may never have thought
of it this way, but the hypnotic situation is one of cooperation and trust between hypnotist and subject in which each has their especial role to achieve
a most unique state of mind, HYPNOSIS.

ORMOND McGILL'S
"CONCERT OF HYPNOTISM"
PROGRAM

ACT ONE: EXPERIMENTS IN WAKING SUGGESTION and HYPNOSIS
INTRODUCTION . . . ADVENTURES WITH THE MIND
AN INVESTIGATING COMMITTEE
 (Any person attending the performance may come on the stage and
 take part in the "Concert of Hypnotism")
MEDITATION and/or THE MOOD OF HYPNOTISM
POSTURE SWAY EXPERIMENTS IN SUGGESTION
THE FAMOUS EMILE COVE' HAND CLASPING TEST
THE ART OF MENTAL and PHYSICAL ABANDON
WAKING SUGGESTION CONTROL OF MUSCULAR and SENSORY STIMULI
THE INDUCTION OF THE HYPNOTIC TRANCE
EXCITING EXPERIMENTS IN ORIENTAL MASS HYPNOTISM

INTERMISSION

ACT TWO: ADVANCED EXPERIMENTS IN HYPNOTISM
THE INVESTIGATORS RETURN TO THE STAGE
HYPNOTIC EXERCISES and SOMNAMBULISM
SO YOU WANT TO BE A HOLLYWOOD STAR

EXTRA SENSORY SENSATIONS:
 1. THE HYPNOTIC PARTY
 2. INSTANTANEOUS HYPNOSIS
 3. AUTOMATIC MOVEMENTS
 4. THE X-RAY EYEGLASSES
 5. ILLUSIONS and HALLUCINATIONS

A HYPNOTIC JOURNEY AROUND THE WORLD:
 1. VISITING BEAUTIFUL HAWAII
 2. IN INDIA: THE FAMOUS HINDU ROPE TRICK
 3. .AN OUT-OF-THIS-WORLD TRIP TO MARS

AGE REGRESSION EXPERIMENTS:
 1. BACK TO SCHOOL DAYS
 2. A FAVORITE PET
 3. THE FOUNTAIN OF YOUTH
 4. FUN and SURPRISES

A GROUP POST-HYPNOTIC EXPERIENCE

CONCLUSION
(This program is subject to constant variation — no two shows are the same — hypnosis is highly creative
and you never know what surprises are going to happen.)

The English hypnotist Peter Casson is credited with developing this intermission posthypnotic feat of having the subjects return to the stage "on cue" when a certain piece of music is played as a device to span the intermission gap. Franquin of Australia also makes use of it. It is a very interesting stunt as, not only does it serve the function of bringing the subjects back on to the stage to continue on with the show, but it also gives the spectators something to look forward to, to see what is going to happen when the show resumes.

Just before the intermission is over, the overture for the second act is played to get the audience back to their seats, following which the posthypnotic "cue" music is played, and the subjects march up from various parts of the auditorium or theatre onto the stage and drop off into hypnosis ready for the start of Act Two, and the show is ready to roll again.

Act Two: "Advanced Experiments in Hypnotism" features many hypnotic routines, some of which are my own originations. These will be found detailed in chapters describing routines.

In summation, hypnotism show programming follows the principles of solid theatrical production. In other words, the show opens with an attention capturing beginning, goes into the body of the show, providing dramatic balance in having more serious episodes interspersed with comedy, and then gradually advances to a climactic conclusion. The field of entertaining with hypnotism is so broad that there is practically no end to the many effects the performer can design to produce an original and distinctive show, remembering always that it is not what you do but how you do it that is the key to master showmanship.

Here is the programme of Prof. George Singer, the well-known New York hypnotist. It illustrates effective handling of theatrical programming.

PROGRAMME: "HYPNOTIC MARVELS"

ACT I

SCENE 1. "The ABCs of Hypnotism"
The Professor in an interesting, entertaining and informative way explains briefly the history, background and possibilities of hypnotism.

SCENE 2. "Everybody Gets Into the Act"
A thrilling demonstration of relaxation through positive hypnosis using the entire audience.

SCENE 3. "Count No Sheep. Just Sleep, Sleep, Sleep!"
Chosen subjects brought onto the stage are effortlessly put into a deep hypnotic trance.

SCENE 4. "Dig That Crazy Hot Seat"
A subject is placed in an ordinary chair which is not wired electrically. Not treated with heat radiation of any form, yet at the sound of a specified word spoken by the Professor the subject is forced to rise from his seat.

SCENE 5. "Kiddin' on the Keys"
A suggestion given by the hypnotist causes the subject to imagine himself a piano virtuoso, and he performs as a great concert pianist.

SCENE 6. "Put Your Foot In It:
In this laugh-provoking demonstration, it becomes impossible for a hypnotised subject to keep her shoes on her feet, except when they are reversed, with the right shoe on the left foot and vice versa.

SCENE 7. "Saturday, The Knight of the Bath"
Under hypnosis a subject believes himself under the shower and makes the motions of adjusting hot and cold water, using the soap and then the towel.

SCENE 8. "It's a Date"
The subjects become the Professor's guests, and in his luxurious automobile he takes them on a most eventful trip. Then they join him at the local movie theatre where they see a double feature.

ACT II

SCENE 1. "On Your Marks. Get Set. Go!"
The subjects take part in a race to the finish to establish a record time for finishing an ice cream cone, without biting or chewing.

SCENE 2. "How Strong Is a Strong Man?"
An individual who is obviously strong, after receiving a suggestion from the Professor, cannot lift a chair or pick up a cigarette.

SCENE 3. "Sweet As Sugar"
Subject eats lemon, believes it is a sweet fruit.

SCENE 4. "In the Long, Long Ago"
Experiment into age regression as used in the famed "Bridey Murphy Case".

SCENE 5. "The Human Bridge"
Baffling demonstration of catalepsy. A subject under hypnosis has his body made rigid and is suspended between two chairs. While in this position he is able to support more than two hundred pounds of weight on his abdomen.

SCENE 6. "The Finale Fun Feast"
Subjects are eliminated from stage, each with individual suggestions, to which they react *after* they have returned to their seats in the audience.

(PROGRAMME SUBJECT TO CHANGE IF EXPEDIENT)

NOTE TO HYPNOTIST: It will be recognised in Prof. Singer's programme various of the tests outlined in the chapters dealing with routines. This programming provides an opportunity to observe how these are combined to form a complete and entertaining stage show. It will be noted that in this text I have repeatedly stressed that each performer be as original as possible, so that one hypnotism show does not become too much a copy of another hypnotism show. Not only is this important to the performer, it is also important to the enjoyment of the show by the spectators, as people in general do not care to see the same show over and over, no matter how clever it is. Too much repetition of the same thing loses entertainment sparkle. Originality gains entertainment sparkle.

The Hypnotism Show

In this section, you are given two introductions to the show (the Ormond McGill Introduction and the Pat Collins Introduction). You are taught how to get the best subjects on stage, how to hypnotise the committee, present a complete hypnotism show, and climax the show.

Chapter Fifty-One
Opening the Hypnotism Show

Overture. House lights out. Footlights on. Curtain opening on a stage flooded with blue and red lights (border and foots) revealing a row of waiting chairs. White spot on stage right to catch performer's entrance from right wing. Follow with spot to stage centre for opening introduction to show.

Modern show business has pace and gets things going without delay. Performer enters, acknowledges greeting applause. Goes to mike stage centre. A pause for a moment of eye-to-eye contact with spectators, then into introduction.

The Ormond McGill Introduction

"Good evening Ladies and Gentlemen. In just a few moments we are going to invite volunteers from the audience to come on stage and occupy these chairs. [Indicate chairs.] Anyone in this theatre tonight is cordially invited to become members of an investigating committee to experiment with what has been called The Magic of the Mind – The Science of Hypnotism. But first a few words about hypnotism.

"Hypnotism is no longer regarded as just a show upon the stage. It is today recognised by the American Medical Association as a valuable form of therapy, and is being used by many doctors, dentists and psychologists.

"According to psychologists, hypnotism is based upon the power of suggestion, and suggestion by definition is the subconscious behaviour rather than the normal conscious behaviour, which is what makes it so fascinating to observe.

"I will give you an example of how an idea subconsciously realised can affect the body physically. It is a simple experiment that we can all try together.

"I have here a lemon and a knife. [Show lemon and knife.] This lemon gives you a suggestion of something sour. Think about it; about how very sour it is. Now watch …

"I take this knife and cut the rind off the lemon and squeeze it … and let that sour lemon juice trickle down to the stage. I will now suck that sour, bitter lemon."

Place lemon to lips and suck it. Make a show of it by audibly sucking and puckering up your lips. Let your actions with sucking the lemon emphasise your suggestions of how sour it is. Your audience will enjoy the obvious reaction of sucking a sour lemon.

"And as I suck the lemon notice how our mouths fill with saliva. It is a subconscious process. It is the subconscious realisation of an idea that you experience. Notice how your mouth fills with saliva as I suck the sour lemon."

Everyone in the audience will experience the effect of the sour lemon suggestion and will react accordingly.

"And in that simple experiment, ladies and gentlemen, you have the basis of hypnotism, and the more you concentrate on the suggestions given the more profound will be the hypnosis you will experience.

"In so far as these experiments are based on mature concentration I will not invite children upon the stage at this time, but if you are of high school, college age or upwards then you are most cordially invited to join our committee on stage tonight and experiment with the wonderful phenomena of hypnotism.

"I ask only two things of you if you elect to come up on stage, and that is that you be serious about experimenting with hypnotism and be willing to concentrate upon the suggestions which will be given you.

"So come right on up and occupy these chairs. You will have a wonderful time, and I guarantee you will feel better when you leave the stage than when you came up. Come right on up. Happy to have each and every one of you."

If you are using background music to your show, this is a good time to play a lively march as the volunteers march up upon the stage and fill the chairs.

Some performers like to include an additional experiment or two that the entire audience can try before volunteers come on stage. These assist in obtaining the best subjects for the show. The following chapter gives you a number of such that you can use.

Your introductory lecture to the show is important to its success: it sells you as a personality; it sells your audience on the current importance of hypnotism; it explains how hypnotism operates through the power of suggestion via an actual experiment that everyone experiences; it secures volunteers to come on stage to experiment with hypnosis. Your introduction to the show has an important selling job to do. Deliver it well!

The average audience the hypnotist appears before is generally composed of three types of spectators: 1. the sceptics who tend not to believe in hypnotism; 2. the credulous who respect hypnosis as an awesome phenomenon; 3. the show-goers who hope the show will be amusing.

The introduction to the hypnotism show has the responsibility of evening out these three types of spectators and setting them on common ground: convincing the sceptics that hypnotism is real; fascinating even more the believers; arousing the interest of the show-goers to witness sparkling entertainment. This introduction does the job. Present it to the audience with a confident air and a friendly smile.

> NOTE TO HYPNOTIST: You can almost tell by the way your opening introduction goes over how your show is going to go. If the response results in a flood of volunteers rapidly coming on stage and filling the waiting chairs you will have an easy show to do that rolls along. Then you can work rapidly in your initial induction of the committee and dismiss those who do not respond readily. On the other hand, if you have a limited group then you must use a more cautious and thorough approach to this initial hypnotisation of the committee, as you will wish to retain and influence as many of the volunteers as possible. Now study the Pat Collins Introduction, the gist of which is given here. My approach is more formal while her approach is more informal. Both do the job.

The Pat Collins Introduction

"Welcome, gang. It's show time, so get ready for a hypnotic pyjama party. For those who have not seen the show before I am going to give a very fast and very brief run-down on what is about to happen.

"In a few minutes we are going to invite five or six persons on stage to be hypnotised. Now, this is for real, and if you come up you will be hypnotised, but actually I do not hypnotise you at all ... you hypnotise yourself. You do this by concentrating on and accepting my suggestions. The whole thing, gang, is what you do, not what I do ... all I do is present the proper words in the proper place at the proper time, and if you are willing and will concentrate you will go under.

"When you are hypnotised the only thing you will feel is complete relaxation. The point I am trying to make is that when you are hypnotised you will not be unconscious. You will be entirely aware of everything that is going on. You will see everything; you will hear everything. In fact you will not even miss the show. In fact you may enjoy the show even more because you will be sleeping with me.

"So get ready to just have a good time, and if you are shy don't worry about it. If you are shy, stay shy. If you are an extrovert, be an extrovert. Just be your natural self and you'll be fine. If you go under you'll feel great, but if you want to know what the greatest bonus of all will be, it will be that while you are up here from 45 minutes to an hour or so, in that short time, when you return to your seat, you will have as much benefit as having the equivalent of eight to ten hours of wonderful sleep. So it'll be a nice way to spend the night and enjoy yourself.

"On the serious side of hypnosis, if you do go under and I can help you in some way ... when the show is over and in private I will help you in any way that I can with suggestions. So don't hesitate to ask, as I love to help people. It's my way of saying 'Thank you.'

"For example, let's say that your name is Casey. After the show you would like me to help you stop smoking. I can suggest to Casey that cigarettes taste bad, and if he accepts it will work. On the other hand, it will not work if he doesn't accept the suggestion. So I don't want to mislead anybody. I don't care how deeply you go into hypnosis; you have to accept the suggestion and want it to work for it to work.

"So, when the show is over just let me know and I'll be glad to help you, if you go under. On the stage we're going to hypnotise you; but, I repeat, gang, it's up to you, not me, but if you want to give it a try you're more than welcome. So now that you understand come on up, gang, and be hypnotised."

The gang flocks up on the stage, and Pat performs an induction on the group. The show starts rollin' bang, bang, bang. Its emphasis is on entertainment.

NOTE TO HYPNOTIST: It is well to study the construction of Pat Collins' introduction to her show. It is modern and cleverly designed, in four divisions:

1. It is informal as befits the night club setting in which it is presented. The audience is referred to as a "gang". This is appropriate to a young adult audience.

2. It tells exactly what is going to occur and a disclaimer is made of any personal power, and the ability to be hypnotised is placed entirely in the laps of the volunteers depending on how well they concentrate and accept the suggestions. All the hypnotist claims is to present the proper suggestions which, if concentrated upon, will produce hypnosis.

3. The sensations of being hypnotised are related to being completely relaxed and continual awareness as to what is going on. Relaxation is pleasant to everyone, and fear of losing consciousness is removed. Removing the fear that some people have of becoming unconscious actually minimises resistance to being hypnotised. Further, it is suggested that when hypnotised you will enjoy the show even more! And everyone is encouraged to just be themselves. Each person is unique as an individual, which makes each show unique in revolving around the particular subjects participating.

4. Finally a "carrot" is dangled before the volunteers that, if they come on stage and are successfully hypnotised, after the show the hypnotist will give them personal attention and assist in their problems. It is a great incentive to come on stage and be hypnotised. The invitation is then given to come on stage, be hypnotised, and the show gets under way.

In relation to the hypnotism show, let the two introductions outlined here serve to assist you to create your own. Never be a copycat. What fits one person does not necessarily fit another. Be original!

Chapter Fifty-Two
The Invitation to Come on Stage

It is well for the stage hypnotist to have some understanding of the intro-spective motivation of the people which draws them forward to be hyp-notised on the stage. Other than one of challenge – in which a person tries to outwit the hypnotist (concerning which type of volunteer is quickly eliminated) – there are four main motivations:

Motivation 1: Thrill of a New Experience

One of the main purposes of show business is to provide thrills for the audience, to take them away from humdrum everyday existence into a world of fantasy. That's entertainment! The hypnotism show does that wonderfully. Many subjects are motivated for this very reason. They come on stage for the thrill of a new experience that they feel hypnotism can provide. And thrill it can ... the mere suggestion of a "thrill", can send goosebumps up one's back.

Motivation 2: To Adventure into the Unknown

The labyrinth of the human mind is the most unexplored of areas. Delving into its depths is an adventure par excellence. Hypnotism pro-vides just such an opportunity to probe into areas of the unknown. Many people find this fascinating, and they come on stage to be hypnotised seeking to learn more by first hand experience of mental mysteries which have been shrouded in darkness.

Motivation 3: To Find Serenity

Life in the world has so many tensions. So much is unpeaceful. Coming onto the stage of the hypnotist offers an opportunity to get away from the outside world for a time, and enter the state of peacefulness of being which everyone instinctively knows is at their "centre". It takes vitality to live in the world. Hypnosis can give that vitality. It takes the need to relax to live in the world. Hypnosis can give that relaxation. It takes a mind in control of itself to live in the world. Hypnosis shows the way it can be disciplined. A disciplined mind can be at peace with itself, and so many join the group on stage to find that peace.

Motivation 4: Just For the Fun of It

Life is meant to be a playground not a battleground. The stage of the hypnotist is a playground. It is a place to have fun in. So many come up just for the fun of it; to let go! to laugh and perform with free abandon and just not give a darn. Such abandon the hypnotism show provides.

The stage hypnotist can further advance the fun aspect of his show in his opening remarks. The famous Australian hypnotist, Martin St James, uses this approach, telling the audience that the show he presents is packed with fun, thrills and excitement for the enjoyment of everyone. That the audience will enjoy every moment of it, and the volunteers who come on the stage will enjoy it even more. Everyone will have a good time! As a stage hypnotist you know the value of direct suggestion. If you want something to be, tell it as you want it to be.

In this chapter, you have been given four motivations of why people come on stage, often with a rush of enthusiasm, to be hypnotised. All of these motivations, the hypnotist can expressly mention when he invites the committee on the stage: "I invite all who wish to come up on the stage this very evening to have a wonderful and glorious time, giving you thrills you will enjoy, adventuring deep within the abyss of the human mind, experiencing the peace of serenity of yourself, as you come to realise that you are the real master of your mind and your mind not the master of you. Come on up and join me now. We'll have a lot of fun!"

Chapter Fifty-Three
Getting the Best Subjects on Stage

Everyone can be hypnotised to some extent, but some persons are more responsive than others. For the purpose of an hypnotism stage show you want the most responsive subjects possible, subjects who will drop quickly into a somnambulistic state. About 20 per cent of the population have this natural ability, so that gives you plenty of excellent potential subjects in each audience to work with. You want to get them on the stage. The methods given in this chapter will help.

To get your best subjects on the stage your introduction is important as it explains what they are going to experience and invites persons to come up as the committee. A demonstration, such as the "lemon test" given earlier, ties in perfectly to the introduction, captures audience interest and graphically explains how suggestions operate in relation to hypnotic phenomena. I have used this "lemon test" in my own shows for years, and it has always proved effective in showing the audience, in a demonstrational form, how suggestion automatically affects their responses. The following six audience preliminary tests, before the committee comes on stage, are likewise effective.

Hand-placement Deception

1. Tell the spectators to do what you do and following instructions exactly:

2. Form right hand into a fist. Spectators do the same.

3. Make an imaginary "pistol" of your hand by lifting thumb upwards and point forefinger out, forming the barrel. Then cock the thumb in imitation of getting pistol ready to fire. Point it about in different directions in pretence of shooting while saying "Bang! Bang!" Spectators do it. Lots of fun.

4. Now form your right thumb and forefinger into a circle by placing tips together. You demonstrate and spectators do the same. Now tell them

to place the finger-circle they have made upon their chin. As you say this, place your finger-circle against your right cheek.

The majority of the audience will follow your example. Automatically and without even thinking they will place their finger-circle against their cheek – missing entirely your instructions to place it on their chin.

There will be a moment of silence followed by laughter as they wake up to the realisation of how suggestion influenced them. It is a good demonstration of the power of suggestion in operation.

The "Can't Drop a Pencil" Method

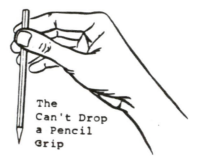

The
Can't Drop
a Pencil
Grip

The entire audience can try this test, and it comes as a bit of a surprise to find they cannot do what they thought they could. Have each person take a pencil and hold it out in front of their lap, gripping the top end of the pencil between thumb and forefinger, as shown in the drawing.

While pencils are being universally suspended amongst the crowd, you comment that the voluntary action of dropping the pencil would seem to be easy to perform. You explain that you will show them how the power of suggestion can inhibit deliberate doing of that which would normally be easy; making it almost impossible to do. Tell the spectators to make up their mind to do exactly as instructed that they may appreciate the experiment.

Have the spectators hold the pencil in its suspended position in front of themselves for a minute while staring at the point of the pencil; to keep their eyes fixed on the point, and, as much as possible, to refrain from blinking.

Now tell them to think to themselves: "I can drop it. I can drop it." Tell them to think these words over and over without interruption, and while doing this they are to try to drop the pencil, but that they will find they cannot. Suggest: "In fact, the harder you try to drop the pencil the tighter your fingers will hang on to the pencil. You will find it is impossible for you to drop the pencil until I give you the command when to drop it."

Continue: "Try, try hard to drop it, but you cannot. But when I say 'three' it will drop from your fingers to your lap immediately. One, two, three! Now drop the pencil!"

Immediately the pencil will drop from everyone's fingers to their lap. Continue with your comments.

You will find this an interesting experiment to perform for what you wish to happen will not happen when you are thinking exclusively of one idea; even when the idea is an act that you wish to perform.

Persons who successfully perform this test show that they can carefully follow directions and, as such, can be considered good potential subjects for your hypnotic tests on stage. On concluding the test, you can follow it up with an invitation to come on stage:

"If you found this test worked for you successfully, it indicates that you can follow instructions and concentrate well, so those who succeeded and would like to learn more about how the mind operates I invite to come forward, to come on stage as members of the committee and take part in the wonders of hypnosis."

The "Imaginary Rubber Band" Technique

This experiment provides another method to test suggestive response by members of the audience and gives you a means to select the best subjects for your stage demonstrations. Tell the audience to hold their left hand about a foot in front of their eyes, turning the hand upwards at the wrist so that the eyes are focused on the fingers and back of the hand. Tell them to keep their eyes fixed on the back on the hand and imagine that a rubber band has been placed around their fingers.

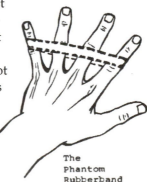

The Phantom Rubberband

(You can demonstrate this by actually placing a rubber band around your own fingers, as you explain what they are to imagine.) Now, while imaging the rubber band is around their fingers they are to strain against it and force their fingers as far apart as they possibly can, as shown in the drawing.

As they do this, keep suggesting that this imaginary rubber band is small in diameter and very thick and that their fingers have been inserted through it, and they can feel it continually pulling against their fingers as they stretch them out. Suggest: "Think to yourself that the harder you try to keep your fingers from drawing together the more they tend to do so. See this happening in your mind. Now close your eyes and imagine it happening. The rubber band is drawing your fingers together. Imagine that you are trying very hard not to have this happen, but to no avail. The rubber band is so strong it is impossible not to have it pull your fingers together. And once they touch you will find it is impossible to move them apart, as the rubber band keeps them tightly clasped together and you cannot separate your clamped fingers no matter how hard you try. Try, try, but you cannot.

"But now imagine that the rubber band has been removed from your fingers, it is *gone*! Open your eyes and see there is no rubber band; it has all been imaginary all the time, and now you can separate your fingers easily. (The fingers of all trying the experiment now come easily apart.) You have demonstrated the wonderful power of imagination. Imagination is the creative power of the mind. If you succeeded well in this test, come up on stage and learn more about the magic of the mind."

Handlocking on the Entire Audience

This test was used by the celebrated German hypnotist, Konrad Leitner, to obtain the most responsive subjects for his stage show. He presented it for the entire audience to try.

Request the audience to stand. When all are standing, say slowly: "Stand erect and relax. Now everybody inhale deeply. Hold your breath. Now exhale slowly."

You breathe in and out right along with those in the audience. Get your audience to follow your breathing rhythm and instructions. Perform the process of deep breathing three times. Your instructions continue: "Now harmonise your breathing with the movement of your arms. As you inhale, stretch your arms out in front of yourself. Hold them thus a moment while you hold your breath. Now as you exhale lower your arms again to your sides. Ready, let's start."

Demonstrate with your own arms as you give the instructions. The breathing must be in harmony with the arm movement. Perform this exercise three times in unison with the audience.

"Now everyone stretch out your arms and turn your palms to face each other. Spread your fingers wide apart. Now bring them together and interlock your fingers. Keep breathing deeply as you do this. Now with your fingers interlocked lift your arms straight up above your head turning the palms of the hands upwards toward the ceiling of the auditorium." See drawings.

THE
LEITNER
METHOD

Demonstrate with your own interlocked hands how they are to be turned upwards and stretched upward above the head. Continue the suggestions: "That's it. Turn your palms upward and stretch out your arms straight above you head. Squeeze your fingers tightly together. Very tight. Keep your attention concentrated on me. Your arms are becoming stiff. Push them up stiff! Stiff! Your arms are becoming stiff and tense, and your hands are becoming tightly locked together. They are stuck tight together. Stuck so tightly they simply will not come apart no matter how you try. They are stuck tight! Keep pushing your arms up stiff, so very stiff. Your fingers are locked together. Your hands are glued together, and you cannot get them apart no matter how hard you try. Try to pull with all your might, but you cannot get them apart! You cannot! They are stuck!"

Watch your audience and observe their reactions. Some will take their hands apart when you say: "Try to pull them apart." Others will find their hands stuck firmly, so firmly that they only come apart after considerable effort. Still others will have their hands locked together so tightly that all their efforts fail to separate them. These people you address:

"Those with their hands locked above their heads have learned how to use the power of suggestion effectively for themselves. Come forward to the front of the stage with me, and I will unlock your hands."

Down the aisles they come with hands locked over their heads. They stand in front of the stage. You gaze in to the eyes of each of them, and with a firm command state: "The influence is all gone now. Relax your arms. Unlock your hands. You can separate them now. Your hands are free!"

One by one their locked hands will come free, but you do not let them go back to their seats. Rather with a gesture you request them to go up on stage and occupy the chairs.

Just released from the "Hand-Locking Test" and now up front most will comply so you will shortly have your chairs on stage filled with responsive subjects. Should anyone express a wish not to come up on stage, just smile and let them return to their seat in the audience.

Always give freedom of choice. It is an invitation to come on stage, not a command. The audience respects this. It shows you are considerate of personal wishes. It is the democratic way.

The test here describe works splendidly, incorporating breathing with the hand-locking suggestions, plus the fact of the fingers being so interlocked with the palms turned upward, above the head. As long as the arms are held stiff and straight up, it becomes almost a physical responsibility to release the hands. The stage hypnotist takes advantage of every expedient to ensure the success of his show.

The "Flame Under Water" Visualisation Method

This unique method of preliminary testing of audience response to suggestion influence was designed by hypnotist/scientist Gerhard Wolter. It is an inner visualisation method to test suggestibility. It uses a clear glass of water and a burning candle. Face your audience with candle held in right hand and glass of water in left. Comment: "We are going to try an experiment to see how well everyone in the audience can visualise. That is, who can best see imagined mental pictures in their mind vividly. Try this: I have here a glass of water and a burning candle. Is there any way we can make the candle burn inside the glass of water? Your conscious mind will say it is impossible, but to your subconscious mind nothing is impossible. You can do it and clearly see it happen.

"To start I place the burning candle behind the glass of water, so that you can see it burning clearly through the water … Look at it carefully and get that image firmly in your mind." Demonstrate by holding the burning candle behind the glass of water.

"Now when you have that image firmly in your mind, close your eyes and see in your mind's eye the candle burning inside the glass of water. Imagine it! Imagine it! When you can clearly see the candle burning inside the glass of water raise your hand so I will know you can see it in your mind's eye." Many hands will go up.

"Good. You have demonstrated that you have the power of visualisation of an image in the mind. Everyone open your eyes now and, while the image is gone, you will still remember you saw it."

The audience responds: open eyes and lower hands. You continue: "Those who have the power of visualisation can use the power of the subconscious mind to do wonderful things. If you saw the image of the candle burning under water clearly in your mind's eye, come up on stage and learn how to perform more magic with the mind."

Many who saw the image will come forward to fill the chairs on the stage, and you will have a select group of persons responsive to suggestion. These initial experiments in suggestion form a dual purpose: (1) they bring the most responsive subjects on to the stage to take part in your hypnotism show; (2) the tests are very interesting to the audience, and give the entire audience a chance to try some experiments in suggestion for themselves, even if they do not elect to come on stage.

Unexpected Mass Hypnosis

This is a good experiment for the entire audience to try, following one of the foregoing preliminary suggestions tests. As it emphasises only relaxation with no mention of hypnosis or going to sleep, many who try it will be caught unaware and will unexpectedly become hypnotised. It conditions the best subjects to come up on stage as members of your committee. Tell the audience you want them to sit comfortably in their seats, with legs straight out in front and hands resting in lap.

State: "Now close your eyes and relax comfortably in your seats. Think of nothing in particular ... just listen to my voice and do what I tell you. All comfortable! All eyes closed! Fine! Now I want you to keep your eyelids tightly closed and roll your eyeballs up just as though you are looking right into the top of your head. Right inside your brain. All eyes closed, looking right inside your head. Relax, comfortably relaxed and thinking of nothing but what I tell you.

"I am going to count to 'six', and while I am counting you will find it impossible to open your eyes. You are all relaxed, with your eyes closed, looking right up inside your heads. Eyes tightly closed.

"One ... you cannot open your eyes because the more you try the tighter they keep shut.

"Two ... your eyes are so tightly shut, looking up into your head, that try as you will you cannot open them. Try, try hard, but you cannot do it, because they are tightly shut.

"Three ... you cannot open your eyes. They are glued shut. All relaxed and comfortable. Hearing nothing but my voice. Thinking of nothing but what I tell you. Eyes tightly closed.

"Four ... you still cannot open your eyes, and you do not want to now, for it is so comfortable sitting there, comfortable and relaxed, with your eyes shut, hearing nothing, thinking of nothing but my voice. Eyes shut, shut tightly, relaxed and comfortable.

"Five ... you cannot open your eyes because you are sinking into a comfortable, pleasant deep, deep sleep. So nice and relaxed, sleeping deeper and deeper. Thinking nothing, hearing nothing but my voice. All comfortable and relaxed. Sleeping, sleeping, deeper and deeper to sleep.

"Six … now you are all in a deep, deep sleep. So comfortable in a deep, deep sleep. Your eyes are shut and you like them shut; you like to sleep because it is so comfortable and relaxing. Go deeper and deeper to sleep.

"I will bring you back out of the sleep now so that those who very much enjoyed the sleep can come on stage when I invite you. You will come right up on the stage and take a seat and be prepared to have a wonderful time.

"All right, begin to come back now … you are stirring in your seats. You are waking up. Wake up everyone. You enjoyed the rest and sleep of these moments very much. It was so restful … and now in just a moment you can come up on the stage and enjoy taking part in the show, as you learn about the wonders of hypnotism."

This handling has a surprising effect on the audience as they take part in it thinking they are participating in an experiment in "relaxation" until they wake up and find they have been hypnotised.

It will be found that quite a fair number of the audience will have unexpectedly entered the realm of hypnosis, and they have thus been "conditioned" to come on the stage and try further experiments in hypnotism. It is an excellent way to get the best subjects on stage.

Chapter Fifty-Four
The Committee on the Stage

When you invite the volunteers to come on stage, it is often good practice to keep a running line of suggestions going, such as: "That's it, come right on up. Let's fill all the chairs quickly. You will have a wonderful time on stage. There is plenty of room for all. Come right on up. And if we need more room we'll make more room. Come right on up. Happy to have each and every one of you!" Then start some lively marching music.

Such a barrage of "come forward" suggestions along with the music tends to get volunteers flowing upon the stage. Also, it draws the so-called "suggestibles" in the audience, as your constant repetition of the suggestion: "Come right on up" is compelling to many people.

Occasionally, as the volunteers come on stage and get seated, you can fill the interval with some comments about hypnosis, viz.: "People often ask the question: 'What does it feel like to be hypnotised? Well, being hypnotised is very much like having a dream experience. You know how dreams are: some dreams are vivid and they stay with us for a while. Other dreams are elusive and they vanish quickly from our consciousness. But all dreams are interesting. They are a subconscious experience. Hypnosis is likewise a subconscious experience, and, like dreams, you will enjoy the experience."

This association of hypnosis with dreams is sound psychology. While you are speaking to the audience, if you have an assistant working with you, he (or she) can usher participants to the chairs.

Sometimes your hypnotic call for volunteers will fill the chairs and have an overflow. In such an instance, you can form a second line of subjects standing behind those who are seated. In that case, you can frankly state you will test them all and will retain on stage those persons who prove most responsive to hypnosis.

NOTE TO HYPNOTIST: This matter of properly inviting subjects up on to the stage calls for finesse. From experience you will learn to judge your audience correctly. If they are obviously eager to come on stage and take part in the show, they you can be as demanding as you wish in whom you retain on stage. Conversely, if your audience is timid and seem reluctant to come forward, then, as a showman, you must adapt to the situation and be more gracious in your invitation to the volunteers, for it is essential that you get a good group of subjects to form the committee.

For members of your committee the best age group for effective hypnotic experiments are the young adults of high school and college age. Not only are such young adults responsive but they make a good appearance on the stage.

In stage hypnotism the show's the thing, and, since your subjects function as a major part of the show, the more impressive the committee the more impressive the show. So, as you can, arrange and form the committee of good appearing subjects. *It's good theatre!*

Your hypnotism stage show is about to begin, and, as you stand before your seated committee, smile and make eye-to-eye contact with each one. Now is your opportunity to arrange the volunteers to your liking, i.e., if any come up together have them exchange seats with someone else; the same if any two are talking. When you can, alternate the men and women as they form the row. Remember, you are the host on the stage, and they are your guests. You have the right to arrange things as you wish. Further, you are developing subject responsiveness here as, in following your suggestions for rearrangement of the seating, they are starting to automatically accept what will be your subsequent hypnotic suggestions. All set. The show is ready to roll with the initial hypnotising of the committee.

Chapter Fifty-Five
Initial Hypnotising of the Committee

The "Mood of Meditation" Induction Method

I have used this method of initial hypnotising of the committee in many of my shows. To some being hypnotised can be scary, so I call it meditation. No one is scared of meditation, and actually hypnosis and meditation are very closely allied. It could almost be said that meditation is the Eastern form of the state while hypnosis is the Western state. I present the "Mood of Meditation" in this manner:

Addressing the committee: "I thank you for being my guests on the stage tonight. The first experiment we will try together will not be hypnotism: it will be meditation. As you know, meditation is a pleasant way of relaxing the body and entering the inner realm of mind. Meditation originated in India, and has become very popular in Western countries. Classes in meditation are even taught in colleges and universities.

"To meditate, begin by sitting comfortably in your chairs, place your feet upon the floor, and rest your hands in your lap so your fingers do not touch. In showing you how to meditate I will use a crystal ball as it is used for meditation in India."

Pick up crystal ball and exhibit it to subjects and audience. Continue: "The crystal ball is used by the Yogis as the object upon which they concentrate in meditation. We will use it that way."

Face the committee while standing in centre of stage before the line of subjects, and say: "I will hold the crystal up before you and will move it from one end of the line to the other, so everyone can see it clearly. Direct your attention upon it as it moves before you, and watch the changing lights within the crystal."

Move crystal slowly from one end of the line to the other and back again. Continue: "As the crystal moves before you concentrate on relaxing your body step by step in this manner:

335

"We will go over the body in a progressive manner of relaxation, and, when I tell you to close your eyes, close your eyes and go deep inside yourself. That is meditation. So start now by thinking of relaxing the muscles of your scalp. Relax the muscles of your head and face. Now let your thoughts move on down and relax the muscles of your shoulders, and allow the relaxation to flow down your arms to your hands as they rest in your lap. Relax completely.

"Now relax your chest and torso muscles. Go on down your body further in your mind, as you watch the crystal move before you, and relax your thighs, your knees, your calves right on down to your feet. Your entire body has become relaxed.

"Now close your eyes and relax completely. Just let yourself go! Drop deep inside your self. It makes you feel peaceful and drowsy all over. And your head drops slowly down upon your chest as you begin to feel so sleepy."

Starting at one end of the line go to each person in turn and gently push their head forward so it rests upon their chest. As you move from person to person down the line gives these suggestions: "You all feel so relaxed and good. And on this stage tonight you will find that you can concentrate better than you ever have before. And you will be able to control your body through your subconscious mind. Let's test that power even now."

By this time you will have reached the opposite end of the line of subjects from where you started. All rest relaxed with heads resting on their chests. To the audience they all appear asleep. Continue: "Your eyes are closed now and are becoming stuck tightly together. They are stuck so tightly together you will find that you cannot open them try as hard as you will. Try. Try but you will find you cannot open your eyes."

This is the "eyelid-fixation test" introduced here. Watch your subjects. Most eyes will remain closed. If any do not, you can go to those persons and quietly dismiss them from the stage. In this very beginning you are weeding out unresponsive subjects, although in most instances you will have none to dismiss. Continue: "Forget about your eyes now and just go deeper into relaxation. You will find that you will be able to concentrate wonderfully and master the effects of every experiment we perform together. I will bring you back out of meditation now, and when you come back you will feel splendid and filled with energy. And then I will show you how to perform some experiments using the power of suggestion. Get ready to come back out of the inner recesses of your mind. Back out of meditation. I will count slowly from one to five, and by the count of five you will be fully alert, filled with vitality and ready to experiment with the magic of the mind of hypnotism."

Count slowly from one to five and the subjects will awaken. Continue:

"Your eyes all open now and you are fully alert and awake. And notice how filled with vitality you feel. And now we will experiment with waking suggestion."

The "Mood of Meditation" has accomplished your initial hypnotising of the committee in this subtle manner, and your show is ready to proceed.

NOTE TO HYPNOTIST: This initial experiment has "conditioned" your subjects to respond to future experiments. During the process, suggestions have been given for that very purpose. And the entire procedure has been accomplished by directing attention to meditation rather than to hypnotism in this first experience. This moving from a less resistant area subtly into a more resistant area is useful to your presentation of stage hypnotism.

A Rapid-Fire Method to Initially Hypnotise the Committee

This method has been used successfully in television presentations. Have the subjects stand up in front of their respective chairs in a row upon the stage. Tell them to look upwards towards the border lights above their heads and to place their hands alongside their head and press in upon the temples. Suggest: "As you look at the bright lights above you, you will find your eyes very quickly becoming tired, and you will want to close them. So I will count from one to three, and at the count of three close your eyes.

"One, two, *three*! Close your eyes. Now underneath your closed eyelids roll your eyes upwards as though you were trying to look inside your head. And now you will find your eyes have become so tightly fastened together you cannot open them try as hard as you will."

The subjects will find it impossible to open their eyes, for, as you know, as long as the eyes are rolled upwards under the closed lids it is physically impossible to open them. Continue your suggestions: "Now that your eyes are closed and will not open, it is time to go to sleep. You will find that you have become so relaxed that you want to fall back into your chair and go to sleep. You will be lowered gently into your chair behind you, and when you are in your seat go to sleep! Your hands will drop down from your head to your lap, and you will be in deep hypnosis."

Starting at one end of the row push the subject gently in the centre of his forehead, so he starts to fall backwards. As you do this, have your assistant, standing behind the subject, grip him and lower the person down into their chair. Seated, the subject's hands will drop down from the sides of his head to lap, and you will have induced hypnosis.

Proceed thus down the entire row of standing subjects. By this rapid method the committee can be initially hypnotised in record time.

> NOTE TO HYPNOTIST: It will be observed that this eye rolling upwards is related to the similar process used in the "Unexpected Hypnosis Upon the Audience" described in the foregoing chapter. The technique will be found productive of hypnosis.

The Nonverbal Method of Initial Induction

I have found this method to be quite dramatic and to work well as an initial process for hypnotising the committee in a novel way. Explain to the group that you are going to hypnotise them by a silent method. You will manipulate their hands in certain ways which will put them to sleep, in an hypnotic trance. This explaining to the committee of what you are going to do in the building up of expectation to be hypnotised is important to the success of the method.

Explain that, since this is a nonverbal method of hypnotising, it is a method frequently used when hypnotising deaf people. Accordingly, since the ears will not be used, each person is given a set of ear plugs to insert in their ears. (Subjects do this.)

Then have some soft music start which is pleasant for the audience to listen to, as you go to each subject in turn, starting at one end of the row and proceeding to the other, and in complete silence do the following: in a gentle, graceful manner sweep your hand across the open eyes of the subject, indicating they are to close them. The eyes closed, you gently stroke them downward. Then lift the subject's arm upward; straight up into the air above head. Do the same with each subject in turn down the row.

Having completed the eye-closure and arm raising, via gesturing, return to the first subject in the row and begin to slowly manipulate the fingers of the person in various ways: for instance, separate the fingers of each hand; turn hand about in various directions; move thumb to a different angle. Do whatever you wish with the lifted hands. What you do is not important; what is important is that you are silently doing something to the hands in a way that is experienced by the silent subject. Having completed whatever hand manipulation you elect with the first subject, then move on down the group and do the same with the others in turn. Put some variety in to whatever you do. You must make it interesting to the audience when you use this method of induction. Even a bit mysterious. Work precisely and deliberately, as though there is special purpose in what you do.

Having completed the finger manipulation on the hands of each subject, then return to the first and push raised hands down into lap and head onto chest. Remove the ear plugs. Do same with each subject. They will be in trance. You can now very softly begin to present your suggestions verbally: "You are resting and sleeping so quietly now. It has been a wonderful experience for you to have been hypnotised in silence like this. So pleasant and restful. Now that your ears are free of the plugs you can hear everything sharply and clearly, and you will follow my every suggestion with perfection." Stop the music. The induction is complete.

This nonverbal method will be found an excellent way to start your show. Present it in an almost dance like way. Make your movements rhythmical. Dim the stage lights, if you like. Sometimes you can flood the stage in green. Remember, always, the secret of good stage hypnotism is to make it good theatre.

NOTE TO HYPNOTIST: Other methods for initially hypnotising the committee will be found in subsequent chapters of this book. Study them all and use whatever appeals to you most. Very possibly you will have preference for an induction method of your own creation.

339

Chapter Fifty-Six
A Complete Hypnotism Show

This is a hypnotism show I have used internationally. It illustrates how many of the waking hypnosis and hypnotising techniques you have learned are applied in stage presentation. The show is given you in complete detail, from beginning to end, including patter and operational procedures to instruct you in exactly how a hypnotism show is designed.

On With the Show

With your volunteers seated before you in a semicircle on stage, address the group as follows: "On behalf of the entire audience, I wish to thank you, ladies and gentlemen, for so kindly volunteering. I will do my very best to make your stay here on stage interesting to both you and the audience, and, above all useful to you, for you are going to learn how to become masters of an ancient and wonderful art, the magic of the mind: *hypnotism*.

Turn then and address the audience: "And ladies and gentlemen in the audience, kindly pardon my back as I must turn from time to time to address the committee during the hypnotic experiments you are about to witness. And, please, at the beginning of these experiments, kindly be as quiet as possible as this will assist these people on the stage in their efforts to concentrate properly. Later you may respond as you wish, but at first quietness will be a help and you will be extending to these friends upon the stage the same courtesy that you, yourself, would desire were you up here in their places."

First Group Experiment: The "Hypnotic Mood" Test

Turn sidewise to the audience and address the committee: "In our first experiment together, we shall produce what is called the hypnotic mood. It is a mood of rest, calmness and relaxation. First, everyone sit back comfortably in your chair, place your feet flat on the floor, and rest your hands in your lap, each hand resting separately on each knee.

"That's fine. Just adjust yourselves in your chairs so you will be perfectly comfortable. Now, everyone direct your complete attention towards me and pay close attention to every suggestion and idea which I will give you.

"Entering hypnosis is a skill. One might almost say it is a talent to be developed. The ability to enter hypnosis you can master with practice, and it is our purpose to practise together the development of this skill."

Watch your subjects carefully, and make certain that everyone gives you his (or her) undivided attention. This is most important: be sure you have the complete attention of everyone in the committee exactly as you wish it before you proceed any further. The subjects must be serious and absorbed in performing the hypnotic experiments together.

Then continue: "In order to be hypnotised, you must be able to relax while at the same time you are concentrating intently, so we shall relax progressively, step by step. As I give you these thoughts to think about, concentrate like this: for example, if I should say that your arms are becoming heavy and that your hands are pressing down into your lap, think to yourself that your arms are getting heavy and that your hands are pressing down into your lap … and, as you do so, you will find that your arms and hands actually do feel heavier just as is being suggested.

"All right then, everyone think first of relaxing the muscles of your head, the scalp muscles. As you concentrate on relaxing these muscles, you will begin to feel a tingling sensation coming over your scalp. Now let your thoughts wander down over your face and relax the muscles of your face. Relax the muscles of your mouth. Relax completely. Now relax the muscles of your neck and shoulders, down through to your chest. Relax every muscle of your body, right down through your thighs, your legs, down to your feet. It feels so good to so perfectly relax your body. And, as you relax your body, your mind, too, begins to become relaxed and calm, and your eyes feel heavy. Your eyelids feel tired and heavy. Your eyes want to close. I will count now from one to three, and at the count of 'three' everyone close your eyes and relax completely. All ready! One ... two ... three. Close your eyes. That's it, everyone close their eyes down tightly."

Observe the subjects closely and, if anyone does not close their eyes, point at them directly and say: "Close your eyes. Close them right down tightly." Make sure all eyes of everyone in the committee are closed before you continue.

Then say: "Now with your eyelids closed tight, roll your eyes back upward under the closed lids. Look upwards toward the very centre of your head. Roll your eyes back, and keep staring into your very brain. Your eyes are becoming stuck together, stuck so tightly together that they simply will not open, try as hard as you will. Keep looking back into your brain and try to open your eyes. Your eyes are stuck tightly closed, and you cannot open them, try as hard as you will." Here you are applying the "eyelid fastening test" which you have learned so well.

Your subjects will try in vain to open their tightly closed eyes. This is important as it convinces the group that some subtle influence is in operation over them. Continue on: "Forget about your eyes now, just rest quietly in blackness, and let that relaxation seep through every fibre of your being. It feels so good, so calming, so restful. And now you are becoming so sleepy and drowsy. I will count slowly from one to ten. With every count you will become drowsier and drowsier, and sleepier and sleepier. Let yourself go, let yourself just drift, drifting down to pleasant rest. One ... two ... you are getting so sleepy and drowsy. Three ... you are becoming so relaxed. Let your head fall forward if you wish. Let every muscle of your body relax completely. Four ... five ... six. You are getting so calm and relaxed. So drowsy and sleepy. Let yourself just drift down to sleep, pleasant rest and sleep. Seven ... eight ... nine. Let yourself just drift down towards sleep and rest. Every muscle of your being is relaxed. Ten!

"Now pay close attention to every suggestion that I give you. As you rest there all calm and quiet, your mental processes are becoming intensified, becoming acute, so that you will find that you can concentrate easily and powerfully upon every suggestion I will give you. You will find that you can easily accomplish every demonstration, and follow perfectly every suggestion that I give you. You are resting calmly and quietly. Nothing will disturb or bother you, and you will find that you can concentrate intently upon every suggestion that I give you, and respond to every one."

Throughout all of your demonstrations on the stage, make generous use of your hands as you talk, performing graceful, rhythmic passes out from the sides of your head in gently sweeping motions towards your committee. These tend to hold the attention of both the subjects and the audience upon you.

"All right now, I shall count slowly from one to five. With every count you will begin to arouse yourself and, by the time I reach the count of five, you will be again all awake and alert. Ready, one, two, three ... that's it, open your eyes now ... four ... all active and alert and ready to proceed to more advanced experiments. Five! Open your eyes everyone."

This first experiment performed upon the committee is most important to the success of your entire hypnotism show. To the audience, it appears merely as an interesting beginning demonstration of relaxing the subjects and influencing them lightly. But actually you are accomplishing far more than this.

Notice that, in presenting this beginning test, you do not mention that you intend to hypnotise, but rather that you will show the committee how to experience the hypnotic mood of relaxing while concentrating. Thus you avoid any possible challenge from any of the subjects resisting, and if one or two do not respond it makes little difference. But even though you are not deliberately hypnotising, still every suggestion is designed to lead your subjects progressively into a light hypnotic state (such conditions are know as hypnoidal states), first through relaxing of the body, then the eyelid closures and fastening, and finally through suggestions of drowsiness and sleep.

As you perform this test, you can determine which of your subjects are the most responsive; likewise you can see which are the most resistant and, knowing the hypnotic effects you plan to present in the programme, you can almost tell at this point which subjects will be best to use in the various tests as you have routined them.

Further, this initial test will have relaxed and calmed the group down from any tendencies of boisterousness, and you have set in their minds suggestions leading to the ready acceptance and the following of every suggestion which you will give them to respond to each experiment perfectly.

As a performer, you can see how very vital this first experiment is, so take your time with it and get the group thoroughly relaxed and drowsy. Although some spectators in your audience seeing the subjects with their eyes closed and slumped down in their seats so relaxed will think that you have hypnotised the entire group, actually very few will have gone into complete hypnosis up to this point, but such is unimportant. The important thing is that you have increased the suggestibility responses of the committee members.

Your hypnotism show is but beginning, yet through this very first step you have "stacked the cards" in your favour for the total success of your entire performance. Now address the audience: "We are now ready for some psychological experiments demonstrating the power of suggestion in the waking state ... first, affecting the sense of balance. Who would like to be the first subject for this experiment?" (You have learned how to perform experiments in waking suggestion in early chapters of this book. These tests are now being used in relation to stage show handling.)

First Individual Experiment: The "Posture Swaying" Tests

The "Falling Backwards" Test

Turn and look over the committee, select a subject who followed your suggestions well in the first group experiment so you can feel certain he will respond positively to this test. This is your first individual demonstration of hypnotic effect, and it is important to your performing prestige that it succeeds.

Always select a responsive subject for this test. Have him step forward and ask him in a friendly fashion if he is willing to try an experiment in suggestion. When he agrees, follow on with your presentation: "All right then. Stand facing me here in the centre of the stage with your feet side by side together. That is fine. Now in this experiment we are going to demonstrate how thoughts can actually influence the sense of balance as you concentrate. In a moment, I will stand behind you, and you will feel an impulse to fall right over backwards. Now, have no fear of falling, as I will be right behind you and will catch you. All ready?"

As you give these directions, look him steadily in the eye and in a soft confidential manner request him to keep his mind intent on the ideas you will give him. When his eyes become fixed and steady on yours, compliment him by saying: "Fine, you concentrate splendidly." Now tell him to close his eyes and relax his body. Place your hand on his shoulder moving him backward and forward a bit to make certain that he is properly relaxed; tell him to imagine himself as a plank of wood hinged to the floor, and that he can sway easily in either direction backward or

345

forwards, then say: "All right now, I will step behind you, and you will feel an impulse pulling you right over backwards toward me. Have no fear of falling; I will catch you. All ready now, eyes closed, relax and concentrate."

Then softly, to the subject confidentially, say: "Let yourself go and don't resist. Let yourself come right back towards me as you concentrate on the influence which will pull you right over backwards."

These intimate "asides" spoken quietly and personally to the subject are important to your stage handling of the hypnotism entertainment. The audience hears only the major portions of your comments which describe and explain each experiment, but the subject receives full benefit of your confidence which makes him feel responsible to concentrate well and respond successfully to each test. Further, such handling increases the direct influence of your suggestions. This is a professional stage hypnotism technique that is frequently employed in diversified ways.

Now step behind your subject, touch him lightly on the back of his head so he will know that you are standing behind him, and begin suggesting: "You will feel an impulse pulling you right over backwards. Concentrate your thoughts on falling over backwards. Falling backwards. You are falling back, back, right over backwards. Have no fear of falling, I will catch you."

As you give these suggestions, draw your hands back from his body. To the spectators, it appears exactly as if some mysterious "force" from your hands were pulling him right over backwards. Soon the subject will fall directly backward into your arms. You catch him and at once assist him to regain his balance.

Here is an important piece of business in handling this test. If you were to stand behind your subject and begin at once your drawing passes, and if he did not fall, then you are "on the spot" as having failed in your very first individual test. This seldom happens but it is not impossible, and a failure at this, the starting point in your show is very bad indeed. To safeguard the operation, as you begin your suggestions of falling backwards, do not stay directly behind the subject but rather step to his side momentarily, cross your arms unconcernedly. Then, as he starts to fall in response to the suggestions, step behind him and commence your mysterious pulling passes, catching him as he falls.

It is the little things like this that make the stage hypnotist the master of each situation, as observed in this subtlety: from the audience's point-of-view you have not even started your experiment until such time as you step behind the subject and begin the passes that appear to draw him over backward. Also, it gives you a chance to judge the responses of your subject. Should it appear that he is not relaxing sufficiently or is resisting your suggestions, you can stop the process before going any further and explain to him the importance of his concentrating, not resisting, and letting himself respond freely. Or, should he by some chance absolutely refuse to respond (this is very rarely the case since you had a good opportunity to select a suitable subject from the group) you can even send him back to his seat and select another subject for the experiment.

This principle of basically conducting two shows at the same time, one for the audience and the other for the subject or subjects is an important factor to keep in mind in relation to your successful staging of the hypnotism show. I have gone into this matter at some length in connection with this test as I want you to have these insights of expert performance.

Your first individual subject having fallen backwards and again returned to his seat, you can say to him: "It felt just like a force of some kind pulling you right over backward, didn't it?" The subject will confirm. Here you have further established the audience's impression that you actually drew the subject over through the application of some special "force", and have also prepared the other subjects in the group to respond accordingly. Throughout the hypnotism show, it is well to maintain this pattern, letting each successful experiment lead directly on to other successful experiments.

Now select another, responsive subject and repeat the "Falling Backward" test. Next perform it with a young woman. The use of a young woman adds variety and charm to the repeated tests.

Next take another subject and draw him over backwards. After he responds, apparently as an afterthought hold on to him and keep him beside you as you explain to the audience: "Occasionally I have heard the comment from people witnessing these experiments that a person tends naturally to fall over backwards. Such is not true and, to prove it, let us reverse the experiment and try it, this time falling forwards. You see, the influence operates in any direction, backward, forward, or to the sides."

The "Falling Forwards" Test

Using the same subject who has been standing beside you, perform this experiment. Have him take a position before you with his feet together, tell him to keep his eyes open this time and stare directly into your right eye, while you, in turn, gaze into his. Then lift your hands to position on opposite sides of his head, and suggest: "You will begin to feel an impulse this time to fall forward … you are swaying forwards right over towards me. Let yourself come. I will catch you. You are falling forwards, forward. Right over forward!"

As you give these suggestions, draw your hands in passes away from him, and slowly move your body backward and downward. The subject will follow your eyes and, as you draw back, will sway forward and topple right over in your arms. Catch him, and help him to regain his balance.

The Sitting Test

Since the subject you have been using has proved himself responsive to your suggestions, retain him for the performance of this experiment which immediately follows the foregoing. Have a chair brought centre stage and request the subject to be seated. Then address both the subject and the entire committee: "Rather than performing these, what psychologists call posture sway experiments upon each of you individually, we will try an experiment all together. So watch this next test very closely; then, in a moment, we will all perform it together."

Turn to the seated subject and ask that he rise and stand directly in front of his chair with his feet together, and explain: "In this experiment, you will feel an impulse not only pulling you over backwards, but your knees will come forward, and you will sit right back down in that chair."

Then ask the subject to close his eyes, and start making passes, pushing out from the sides of your face in towards him, as you suggest: "Already you begin to feel an impulse pulling you over backward. You are going to fall right back, your knees are bending, and you are going to sit right back down in that chair. Sit down in the chair. Sit down. You are swaying backwards, sitting down. Sit down. Sit down. Sit down!" Bend in close to the subject as you give these suggestions. He will shortly sway backwards and suddenly sit down in the chair with a thump! Thank him for his fine concentration, and allow him to return to the group.

Second Group Experiment: The "Committee Sitting" Test

Turn and address the committee: "All right, now, let us all try that experiment together as a group. Everyone stand up right in front of their chair. That's fine. Place your feet together, and let your hands relax at your sides. Now, one thing is very important. Be sure your chair is right behind you.

"All right, everyone, stand relaxed and directly in front of your chairs. Now there is a large group performing this experiment, so obviously I cannot work individually with each of you, but you can work individually with me. So forget all about the others near you. Forget all about the audience. Consider this an experiment just between you and me. All right now, close your eyes."

In performing this test, your back is towards the audience and you are facing the committee. Commence making passes out from the sides of your head in large sweeping motions pushing towards the group, and suggest: "In a moment, you will begin to feel a swaying impulse to fall right over backward and sit down in your chairs. All ready, you begin to feel that swaying sensation. You are going over backwards, losing your balance, you are falling back, back, backwards. Let yourself go right along with it. You are swaying back, back, backwards. Your knees are coming forward, you are falling backwards, and sitting right down in your chairs. Sit down. Sit down in your chair. Sit down!"

By this time many of the committee will have started to sway, and as you continue your suggestions some one or two persons will suddenly fall back in their seat with a thump. And this "thump" of the first subjects falling will start the others ... and down they go, falling back with thuds into their seats, until almost everyone in the group finds himself seated. Possibly one or two subjects will still be left standing. If so, merely request them to open their eyes and have a seat, as you graciously gesture and explain that next time you hope they will be able to concentrate better. They take their seat, feeling a little foolish at finding themselves the only ones standing while all the rest are seated. You immediately turn to the audience and comment: "Ladies and gentlemen, you see here an interesting example of personal variability in response to suggestion. Some of the subjects felt the effects almost immediately, others not quite so rapidly, and some few not at all. Why is this? The reason lies mainly in the degree of the concentration on the suggestions by the individual person."

Turn now so you are facing halfway towards your subjects so they can get the full benefit of your next remarks: "You see, a person must concentrate to their very utmost if they are to acquire this skill of mastering their body with their mind." In this forceful statement, you have again hammered home the necessity of full attention and concentration, and motivated the subjects yet further to try even harder in the experiments yet to follow.

You have made a big production out of this series of posture swaying experiments as a sensational opening for your show, and this group sitting test last performed is exceedingly important for observing the reactions of your subjects. Note in what order they fall back in their chairs. The ones who first respond (and respond the best) are the subjects you are going to especially select for the next effective tests.

Second Individual Experiment: "Muscular Catalepsy"

The "Hand-Locking" Test

This classic experiment in suggestion is used in this manner as a stage demonstration. It is a transitional demonstration to more advanced experiments yet to come.

Address the audience: "We will try some more advanced experiments in the power of suggestion, this time influencing the muscles of the body."

Turn to your committee, and point to the person in the group who fell back into his chair the most rapidly in the preceding test, and ask: "Will you kindly assist me?"

The subject comes forward and takes a position near the front of the stage. He stands sideways to the audience facing you, as you state: "We are now going to lock your hands together by the power of suggestion so firmly that they will not come apart no matter how hard you try to separate them."

Then say to the committee: "Everyone please watch this experiment carefully as, in just a few moments, we will all try this test together at the same time."

As I have previously commented, you will notice how the routining of these tests are psychologically handled, so that one demonstration sells the one following next. In this instance, your subject here feels that he is setting an example for the group, and hence feels responsible that he must do a good job in performing the experiment. The group, on the other hand, become expectant of shortly trying the test themselves and look forward to it, and when they see its success on the one subject, they are set to expect it to work upon themselves.

Tell your subject out in front to look directly into your right eye, as you gaze back into his. Watch his eyes closely. If they wander in the slightest, command him to keep them firmly fixed on yours, and when they become set, compliment him softly: "Splendid, you concentrate excellently."

Now suggest loudly: "All right, raise up your hands, hold your arms straight out towards me and interlock your fingers in this manner." Illustrate the procedure by interlocking your own fingers and holding your hands outstretched in front of yourself.

Continue illustrating the process by pressing your hands tightly together right along with the subject. Then, as you proceed, separate your hands and make gentle passes down his arms from the elbows to the hands. Squeeze his arm muscles here and there, as you suggest: "Your hands are tense and tight. All your muscles are tense and tight." Take his hands in yours and press them tighter together as you say: "Your hands are becoming locked together so tightly that they simply will not come apart, no matter how hard you try. I will count from one to three, and at the count of 'three', you will find that you cannot pull your hands apart no matter how hard you try. Your hands are locked tight, tight together."

Keep your subject's eyes firmly fixed upon your own as you slowly back away from him, as you count:"One ... two ... three!" Then increase the force and tempo of your suggestions, saying very positively: Your hands are locked fast together. They won't come apart no matter how hard you pull on them. Pull on them! Pull on them with all your might, but they won't come apart! They are stuck! They won't come apart no matter how hard you try! Pull! Pull! Pull with all your might!"

The subject will pull and struggle to separate his locked hands, but they resist all his efforts. Some subjects will try to pull their hands apart so violently they will actually become red in the face. Keep your eyes intently on the subject as he starts to pull on his hands, but, after you see that they are powerfully locked together, you can turn your gaze away and leave him entirely on his own. It is a very effective test.

After the subject has struggled for a time, approach him and say: "All right now. When I snap my fingers beside your ear, your hands will instantly come right apart. All ready now." Snap your fingers, and his hands instantly separate. Thank the subject, and have him return to his seat as you address the group.

Third Group Experiment
The "Hand-Locking" Test on Committee

"Everyone in the committee, now give me your complete attention. We are all going to try together the hand locking experiment you have just witnessed. This test is an achievement in concentration; the more powerfully you can concentrate, the better it will succeed … so let's all try hard for one hundred percent results.

"Everyone ready? Good. Sit back in your chairs and place your hands in your lap, and look directly at me. Now everyone push your arms out towards me and make them stiff and rigid. That's fine. Now interlock your fingers in this manner."

Demonstrate by interlocking your own fingers to show them how to do it. Continue: "Very good. Keep pushing your arms right out straight in front of you, and squeeze your hands tightly together. Keep your eyes fixed on mine and concentrate on your arms and hands becoming stiff and rigid with your fingers locked together."

Run your eyes rapidly from one end of the committee to the other, then, as you start your actual suggestions, focus your gaze at a point about a foot above the head of the central subject in the group and direct your suggestions forcefully towards that spot. This bit of technique, as was previously mentioned, seems to produce an effect of abstraction that holds the attention of the entire group more firmly than if you shift your gaze constantly about from one person to another. Having the attention of all the subjects on you, start your "hand locking suggestions" (use the same suggestion formula for this in working with the group as you did in working with the solo subject), becoming more and more forceful as you proceed, and climaxing your suggestions with: "I will count now from one to three, and at the count of 'three' your hands will be locked so firmly together they won't come apart no matter how hard you try! One ... two ... *three*! Your hands are locked tight. They won't come apart. Pull on them with all your might! They won't come apart, they are locked tightly together, tight, tight together! Pull on them. *Pull! Pull! Pull!*"

As you give these suggestions in group experience, use the familiar sweeping passes out from the sides of your head in towards the committee as you have in all the group tests; these passes assist greatly in holding the attention of everyone riveted towards you.

The subjects will find their hands locked together in response to your suggestions. Struggle as they will, they cannot separate their hands. You quickly pass around the committee of subjects and, one by one, release their hands with a snapping of your fingers, and the suggestion: "All right, all right. It's all gone now. Relax and take your hands apart."

I always regard the completion of this group "hand locking test" as a sort of milestone in the hypnotism show. Your subjects in responding to it will have made themselves responsive to further experiments in suggestion. Also by keeping tabs on the various subjects in the group you can accurately select those best for subsequent tests. Concentrate your attention now on this next experiment with the committee members.

Fourth Group Experiment

The "Fingertip Sticking" and "Fingertip Missing" Tests

This experiment with the group follows naturally the foregoing one. Your show is beginning to take on tempo and speed, so keep the pace going. Ask the committee to raise up their hands in front of themselves and place the tips of their forefingers together. Tell them to centre their eyes on their touching fingertips, and to press them firmly together.

Suggest: "Concentrate on your touching fingertips. Your fingertips are becoming stuck tightly together just like your hands were before. They are stuck tight together; they are glued to each other. They are glued tight together, and you cannot get them apart. Try hard to pull them apart, but they will not separate no matter how hard you pull." Give your suggestion for this test in a rapid, forceful manner. It is amazing to the spectators to see the subjects unable to unlock their hands, but this test making it impossible to pull their fingertips apart is positively astonishing!

After the members of the committee have struggled to separate their fingertips for a few moments, say: "All right, everyone look at me. Forget about your fingers. They will come apart now." Clap your hands, and everyone's fingertips separate.

You will find, as you get your performance rolling and your subjects under control, that you can increase the speed of performing each test. Less and less "suggestive formula" need be employed, and you can become more and more commanding in the giving of your suggestions. Proceed immediately from the foregoing test into this one: "Now everyone hold your fingertips about six inches apart. Those fingers are getting so nervous that you simply cannot make them meet. No matter how hard you try, you cannot make them meet. Those fingertips simply will not meet. Try to bring the tips together. See how they miss touching each other every time. See how they miss, how nervous they are. They simply will not meet. Try to touch them together but it is impossible. They miss every time. Try hard. It is impossible to make them touch!"

As you give these suggestions, emphasise the action by holding your own fingertips apart and making them miss every time you approach the tips together. When the whole committee is excitedly striving in vain to make their fingertips touch, suddenly clap your hands and say: "All right. All right. It's all gone. Your fingertips will meet now!"

Further Waking-Hypnosis Experiments with Individual Subjects

You can now perform some sensational tests in waking suggestion using your best subject in the group.

Heavy Water – Shaky Pouring – Bitter Water – The Mouse on the Floor

This experiment makes use of "the confusion technique" which was previously discussed. Each suggestion is heaped upon the subject in rapid succession. Each test leads directly from one to the other with scarcely a pause between them. Your manner is aggressive, and the subject is given little time to think as you forcefully pile suggestion upon suggestion and the experienced responses lead to increased suggestibility. This test (or combination of tests) is a masterpiece and was used by the famous Danish hypnotist De Waldoza as a climax to his programme.

For this experiment, bring forward a subject who has proved responsive to your suggestions. Have him sit in a chair near the centre of the stage as your gaze into his eyes and suggest that he will respond positively to every suggestion you give him. When his eyes take on that intense fascinated look which you will have come to associate with experiments in waking suggestion, tell him to go over to the side of the stage to a table on which is a glass and pitcher of water. Ask him to lift up the glass in one hand and the pitcher in the other.

The subject does this, and you tell him to replace the glass and pitcher on the table. Request him to retain his grip tightly upon these objects and to concentrate on your suggestions as you say: "Now that glass and pitcher of water are becoming very heavy, so very heavy that they are stuck to the table. You cannot lift them no matter how hard you try. Try hard to lift them, but you cannot!"

The subject struggles to lift the objects from the table but is unable to do so. While he is tugging, you approach him and without a pause continue right on with further suggestions: "All right now, you can lift the pitcher and the glass. Lift them right up, and pour the water from the pitcher into the glass."

The subject does as you directed, and you continue: "Say, look at your hands ... look at your hands, they are getting shaky. Your hands are beginning to shake ... your hands are getting nervous. You are shaking so much that the water is spilling about all over the place."

As you present these suggestions, stand in close beside your subject, and make your own motions jerky and nervous, shaking your hands spasmodically. And continue to give your suggestion in this test in a short, jerky manner in keeping with your gestures of nervous shaking.

The subject will follow right along with you; his hands will begin to shake, and the more he shakes the more he will soon be spilling water every which way. Your suggestions at this point are directed not so much at him apparently as at the offending objects themselves, as you continue: "Why are you so nervous? What is the matter with those objects? Why can't you control them? What is the matter? You are spilling water all over yourself."

After the subject has spilled a good portion of the water in his pouring efforts, calm him with: "All right now. You're all calm now. Take the pitcher and fill the glass of water. That's it. See, it's easy now. Take the glass of water back to your chair, and have a seat."

You move with your subject and stand in front of him at his chair. Stand a bit to the right side so as not to mask the view of the audience from the action. Tell the subject to take a sip of the water, and ask him how it tastes? He will say okay. Then catch his eye and suggest forcefully: "That water no longer tastes good. It is old and stagnant. It is putrid water ... the kind with the green scum on top. It reeks and smells. How awful it tastes. You hate it! Take a sip of that vile, scummy water. Just a little sip, for it will taste so bitter you will spit it out right away!"

Force the subject to take a sip of the water, and instantly suggest: "How awful it tastes. It is so bitter. Spit out that water. Spit it out!" The subject will wrinkle up his nose, go through a wonderful pantomime of disgust and end up by violently spitting out the water, much to the delight of the audience.

Immediately catch his eye again, and tell him: "All right now, that bad taste is all gone. It's all gone. The taste is now all sweet and good."

Note how you are piling suggestions upon suggestions, each response leading to a further response as one test in suggestion dovetails into the next in this confusion technique. The mind of the subject is not allowed time to analyse things or be critical. The suggestions are positive and must be accepted.

Take the glass from the subject, point to an imaginary spot in the air, and continue right on: "Look up there. See that bright light ... way out there. See it! Look at it!"

The subject stares and you continue: "Say that light is beginning to grow larger. It is getting closer to us." Gesture with your hands as though something were passing through the air and coming right up onto the stage. Then point to the floor at the subject's feet, as you say: "Here it is on the floor. Look, it isn't a light at all, *it's a mouse*! It's running all about."

Make your suggestions with mounting excitement, as you say: "It's a mouse, and it's running up your leg! Get it out! Get it out!" Suddenly bend over, move your fingers rapidly in a zigzag low to the stage as though you were following the running course of the mouse, and plunge your right hand up the cuff of his trouser leg as you say excitedly: "Get it out! Get it out! Get it out!"

The subject will jump about, shaking his leg trying to rid himself of the imaginary mouse. You bring a chair forward, tell him to get up on it to get away from the mouse. And when the action is at its pitch, clap your hands and suggest: "All right. Everything is all right now. It's all gone." You thus end the experiment rapidly right at its climax. The subject will shake his head in bewilderment. You thank him, and he returns to his seat in the committee.

You have observed in this progressive experiment in waking suggestion a very significant type of hypnotic phenomena, for you have produced an hallucination in the waking state. It is little wonder that some psychologists refer to such experiments as waking hypnosis. Indeed, as you progress upwards towards more advanced demonstrations in waking suggestion, an overlapping seems to occur and what began as waking suggestions (in normal consciousness) becomes hypnosis (altered consciousness).

You are now ready to present the induction of hypnosis upon the stage. Turn and address the audience: "Thus far, ladies and gentlemen, you have witnessed demonstrations in suggestion in what is called the wakeful state of mind. Let us now experiment with the actual induction of hypnosis. Who would like to volunteer to be the first subject?"

Individual Hypnotic Induction on Stage

Point to someone in the committee that you feel would respond well to hypnosis; if you wish, choose a subject who, while responsive, has been somewhat sluggish in reacting to waking tests. In every committee you are bound to note such persons who are on the lethargic side and this is a good chance to put one to work. Bring the subject forward and have him sit in a chair, centre stage, with his right side towards the spectators. You take a position in front of the subject, ready to hypnotise. Begin by asking the subject a few questions: "Have you ever been hypnotised? Are you perfectly willing to be hypnotised?" Get his answers, and then explain: "Now, hypnosis is a condition very closely resembling sleep. The major difference is this however: if I were to approach you while you slept and were to speak to you, you would be disturbed and might awaken. Right? However, when you are hypnotised, I can talk to you all that time and you will not be disturbed, but will go right on sleeping in hypnosis. You see, your mental state in hypnosis is almost exactly the same thing as when a person walks in their sleep. See what I mean?"

Turn to the committee and say: "Now everyone please observe very closely this experiment, for just soon as it is completed, we will all try hypnotism together." You are establishing prehypnotic suggestions which will later assist in hypnotising the entire group.

Directly facing your subject, bend towards him slightly and hypnotise him. I use my "progressive method", which you have learned. On the stage you can usually condense it and proceed quite rapidly, as you say: "Look at me directly in the eye, the right one. Keep your gaze fixed upon my eye. Your eyes are becoming riveted to mine, and already your eyelids are beginning to get heavy. Your eyes are beginning to burn. You want to close them. But you cannot close them yet, for they are fastened intently upon my eyes. But now I will count slowly from one to ten, and with every count your eyes will become heavier and heavier, until by the time I reach ten, before, you will close those tired eyes. Ready, one ... two. Your eyes are so tired. So tired. Three ... Four ... Close those tired eyes. Get that pleasant relief. Five ... six ... seven. That's it, close those tired eyes. How good it does feel to close those tired eyes. Close them tight. Tight.Eight. Eyes all closed. Nine ... *ten*. Now your eyes are becoming stuck tightly together."

At this point in the induction, you lean forward and make contact passes gently over his eyes, rubbing outward from the root of the nose toward the temples, and suggest: "Your eyes are stuck so tightly together now that they simply will not open. See how they stick together!" The subject struggles to open his eyes, but fails. You follow right on: "All right, forget all about your eyes now, and go sound to sleep. Go deep asleep. Deep, deep asleep."

Step to rear of subject, stroke his forehead a few times and then the back of his head, from crown down to the nape of his neck. Continue to suggest: "You are going down, deep, deep asleep. Go sound to sleep!"

Watch the subject's breathing and, as it deepens, suggest: "Your breaths are coming in deeper and deeper. Breathe deep and free, and every breath you take is sending you down deeper and deeper to sleep." Then place your left hand on subject's left shoulder and press downward firmly so his body tends to slump down in the chair. At the same time tilt his head forward with your right hand, so it rests on his chest.

Continue: "Everything is becoming far, far away from you. You are going deep, deep to sleep."

Then step to the front of your subject and, as you suggest that every muscle in his entire body is relaxed and that he is asleep, pick up one of his hands and let it drop limply to his side. Let his other hand drop likewise. Put your hand on the back of his neck and push his head down so it rests on his knees.

Again pick up the subject's dangling arms and let them drop rag-like to his sides. Then flop his arms about loosely. This always causes a reaction from the audience, as you address them: "You will note, ladies and gentlemen, that perfect relaxation. And right here you are observing an important aspect of hypnosis – the complete relaxation it produces. Indeed, some say that the relaxation produced in hypnosis is so great that in ten minutes of the hypnotic trance a person can obtain as much rest as the average person does in a full night's sleep. And yet, a mere suggestion and that relaxation can instantly change to catalepsy."

Pick up the subject's right hand and stretch it out straight from his shoulder as you suggest to the hypnotic: "Your arm and hand are becoming stiff, *stiff*! Hold it out straight and stiff." You will feel the muscles of the subject's arm contract. You can let go of his hand, and the arm remains outstretched in the air, as you suggest: "That arm is becoming so stiff and rigid that you cannot bend it no matter how hard you try. Try to bend it, but you cannot!"

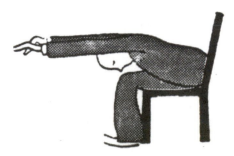

The subject will try to bend the arm, but it resists all his efforts and remains rigid. Then pick up his left arm and make it rigid also. Hold it outstretched alongside the other arm, and say loudly: "*Stiff!*" That arm also becomes rigid. Both of the subject's arms are now outstretched and appear immobile. Again speak to the audience: "Now watch the instant return to complete relaxation."

Again address the subject: "The moment I reach the count of 'three' your arms will instantly relax and will fall limply to your sides, and the moment they hit your sides they will send you down deeper and deeper into the very deepest sleep. (Note compounding of hypnotic suggestions again.) All ready, when I reach the count of three, your arms will instantly relax and fall like rags to your sides."

Gently touch the sides of the subject's thighs as you give the above suggestions, then count slowly: "One ... two ... *three.*" Instantly his arms will collapse and drop limply to his sides. Again flop his arms about illustrating the complete relaxation produced in hypnosis, then address the audience: "Ladies and gentlemen, this hypnotised man could sleep, just as you see him here, in the hypnotic trance for a number of hours, but time passes rapidly, so let's remove the state at once. Now, the one thing most people seem to fear about hypnotism appears to be the removal of the trance. It is a fear without basis in fact however, and there is no danger whatsoever if it is handled correctly. Note how gently and easily the subject awakens."

Now address the subject: "You have been having a most pleasant sleep in hypnosis, and it has done you a great deal of good, but now the time is coming to awaken. So get ready to wake up. I will count slowly from one to five. With every count you will gradually awaken, and by the time I reach 'five' be wide, wide awake and feeling fine. All ready. One ... two ... three ... four ... *five.* That's it. Wake up ... wide awake and just feeling fine."

The subject awakens, looks about and stretches. You thank him and invite the audience to give him a round of applause, and he returns to his seat in the committee.

In performing on the stage, always hypnotise as rapidly as you can. A long, drawn-out technique of hypnotising is not very entertaining to the audience. Fortunately, the stage situation makes it possible to often hypnotise in a matter of seconds. Some subjects will go into hypnosis almost instantly the moment they close their eyes, and you have but to command: "Sleep!" and proceed directly into the arm relaxation and catalepsy test. This rapidity of trance induction in stage entertainments of hypnotism is one of the marvels that thrills the audience.

Fifth Group Experiment

Mass Hypnotising of the Committee

Face your committee and say: "All right, everyone, let's all try the experiment of entering hypnosis together. You have come on stage for the purpose of being hypnotised, so here is your chance to enter this very interesting state. You will find it most pleasant, so everyone give it your undivided attention and concentrate to the utmost, and I will likewise do my very best to help you.

"All ready, seat yourselves back comfortably in your chairs, place your feet on the floor and let your hands rest in your lap. That's right, let one hand rest on each knee, so your fingers do not touch. Now each of you direct your gaze fixedly towards me and, all together, when I say inhale, inhale a deep breath. Hold it, and then exhale as I direct. Everyone now, inhale."

Gesture towards the committee as you give the suggestions to the group by making hypnotic passes with your hands outstretched above your head and move them downward towards your sides as you inhale along with the subjects, and then move them upwards as you exhale. Continue: "Hold it … hold that breath. Hold it and now exhale slowly. Good. Now once again … Inhale … hold it … and exhale. And for a third and last time. Inhale deeply … hold the breath … now exhale.

"How pleasant and relaxed that makes you feel and, as you look directly at me, already you begin to feel a calmness creeping over you. A pleasant sensation of warmth is growing all about you, and your eyes begin to feel heavy and tired. They want to close. All right, I will count slowly from one to ten, and with every count they will slowly close more and more, so by the time I reach 'ten' or before, close your eyelids right down tight together and shut out the light. Ready. One ... two ... three ... four ... eyes closing all down tight. Five ... six ... seven. Close those tired eyes and let them rest. Eight ... nine ... *ten*. Eyes all close together shutting out the light. Eyes all closed tight!"

Glance over the entire committee: All subjects' eyes should be closed. If any are not, point to such persons and request them to close their eyes, then continue: "It feels so good to close those tired eyes. So good, and they are so tightly closed that they are getting all stuck together, and you cannot open them. The eyes are stuck and they will not open. See how they stick."

In working with the entire committee, don't make an issue of this, but rather continue immediately on: "Forget all about your eyes now and go to sleep. Go sound to sleep. Sleep. Sleepy sleep. You are going down deep, deep asleep. Go sound to sleep."

By now many subjects will be nodding and breathing deeply so, starting at the left end of the group, go to each in turn and make a few contact passes on their foreheads out from the root of the nose towards the temples as you pass along, and suggest directly into the ear of each: "That's right ... go to sleep now. You are concentrating splendidly. Go sound to sleep. Nothing will bother you. Just go sound, sound to sleep." And push each subject's head forward onto their chest on through the entire group. Work rapidly, then return to stage centre and suggest: "Nothing will bother you at all. You are all sleeping pleasantly and deeply. Go deeper and deeper to sleep. You are breathing deep and freely, deep and freely, and every breath you take is sending you on down deeper and deeper to sleep. (Note once again how in this deep breathing suggestion you are compounding suggestions in which the response tone suggestion increases the force of another: it is a professional technique for inducing hypnosis.) Go deep, deep asleep. Sound asleep."

Look your committee of subjects carefully over at this point, for here is an opportunity to diplomatically get rid of those persons who are not responding as they should, and you do not wish to retain on the stage. If any subjects are proving undesirable, quietly approach them and, with your finger to your lips, whisper: "Thank you very much for volunteering but since you find it difficult to concentrate from the stage I believe you will enjoy the show more from the audience. Please walk down very quietly so as not to disturb any of the subjects concentrating in hypnosis."

There is good psychology in this handling as it removes unwanted subjects at a time in the show when the audience's attention is centred on watching the subjects who are responding. Also your words in dismissing unwanted subjects are picked up inconspicuously by those who are concentrating correctly and motivate them to yet more effective efforts. Dismissal of unwanted subjects at this time is very logical, as it is obvious that you would not wish to retain any wakeful persons who might possibly disturb the hypnotised subjects.

Group Hand-Raising Test

Continue on with your suggestions: "Now in a moment you will begin to feel a sort of tingling sensation coming into your fingertips. It will be a pleasant tingle, and you can feel it passing up your arms. It makes your hands restless in your lap. Your hands are getting lighter and lighter; they are beginning to rise up from your lap. Your hands are rising up, *up*! Hold them outstretched directly out in front of yourself."

Observe your committee closely. Hands will begin to slowly lift up from the laps of subjects throughout the group. Some will respond more rapidly than others. As long as you have a good showing there is no need to make every subject respond. A good two-thirds of the committee with their hands up in the air is sufficient.

Spot the five subjects who raised their hands up first in the group. Walk over to the one nearest you, touch him lightly on the head and command: "Rise up out of your chair and walk!" Take him by the hand and get him started. As soon as he is on his feet and walking, pass on to each of the remaining selected subjects and repeat the test. The effect of the five subjects slowly walking across the stage, zombie fashion, with their arms stretched out in front of them, is weird and startling.

Keep your eyes on the subjects so that none of them get too close to the edge of the stage during their "sleep walking". Then go to each in turn and say sharply: "Stop! Every muscle of your body is frozen in that position. You cannot move!" The subjects stand like statues in whatever position they happened to be when you gave them the command.

> NOTE TO HYPNOTIST: Sometimes you can increase the rapidity of response in this test by directly telling the hypnotised subjects: "Lift your hands six inches up from your lap into the air. [Directions followed.] Now become conscious of the air around your hands. Now become conscious of your hands becoming lighter and lighter and floating up in the air, up, up until they are extended straight out from your shoulders." Then go into arm immobility part of test.

Return to the seated group of entranced subjects, rapidly walk to each, touch him or her on the hand and say: "Follow every suggestion that I give you." This serves to focus their attention strongly as you suggest: "There are two things I want you to remember: when I reach the count of 'five' you will be wide awake and feeling fine, but also you will find that you cannot lower your arms no matter how hard you try even when you are awake. You will not be able to lower your arms until I snap my fingers by your ear ... then, and only then, will your arms lower. Remember, when I reach the count of 'five' you will be wide awake, but you will be totally unable to lower your arms until I snap my fingers beside your ear. And secondly, remember this, the moment I point my finger directly at your forehead you will instantly go to sleep no matter what you may be doing. Remember, the moment I point my fingers at your forehead you will go instantly asleep. All ready now, get set to wake with your arms frozen out straight in front in you. One ... two ... three ... four ... *five!*"

The subjects awaken in various stages of surprise at finding themselves unable to lower their arms. Their arms still seem "asleep", but otherwise they are fully awake. The five standing subjects also awaken with their arms cataleptic.

Carefully observe the variety of reactions to this group test as it is important. Here is your opportunity to spot the somnambulistic subjects you will wish to use in the advanced hypnotic tests shortly to come in your show.

If a subject responds forcefully to this posthypnotic suggestion, then you know he is one of those you will use. The ability to judge your subjects well and to use them correctly in the performance of the various tests of which they are capable is the mark of an expert hypnotist.

When this test of "the frozen arms" has proceeded long enough to prove its full effect, rapidly release each person by snapping your fingers beside his ear. Also request the standing subjects, as they are released, to return to their seats. You are now ready for the next experiment.

The Cigarette Test

Turn and directly address the audience: "Amazing as some of these experiments seem upon the stage, ladies and gentlemen, the real wonders of hypnotism come from its clinical value, for example, in the way it can be employed to correct habits such as smoking and drinking. Let me illustrate its power by removing the cigarette habit from someone. Turn towards the committee and ask: "Who among you smokes cigarettes?"

Select from among your responsive subjects someone who smokes. Have him step forward and take a seat centre stage. Next, conduct a little quiz, asking him how long he has smoked, how many cigarettes he smokes each day, if by way of an experiment he would be willing to overcome the habit, etc. Finally, have him light a cigarette and ask him how it tastes? He'll say: "Fine", and smile in satisfaction. Then request him to look directly into your eyes, to think of himself as floating far, far away, floating into a deep hypnotic sleep ... and then, point your finger directly at his forehead. Instantly the posthypnotic suggestion you have given goes into action, and he drops over his chair sound asleep in hypnosis. The audience will gasp at this demonstration of instantaneous hypnosis!

Then suggest to the hypnotic: "Now we are together going to master a habit that you have had for a long time, the habit of smoking. You will find that the next time you smoke you will no longer like the cigarette. It will taste dry and parched in your mouth. It will taste like soggy old straw. You won't care for cigarettes any more. In fact you will hate cigarettes: they taste so bad. They make your mouth all dry and parched. You will throw them away in disgust. And they make you choke and cough. Even the smoke makes you choke and cough. You dislike even the smell of smoke."

As you give the above suggestions commenting on disliking the smoke, hold the smoking cigarette directly under the subject's nose, and continue to suggest: "You hate the smell of even the cigarette smoke. You want to get away from it. Turn your head away from that smoke." Almost immediately the subject will cough and sneeze, a disgusted curl come on his lips, and he will turn his head away from the smoke. This occurrence is your cue to climax your suggestions with: "All right now, when I say 'three' you will open your eyes and you will find that you positively hate cigarettes: they make you sneeze and cough. You cannot smoke them any more. You will throw the cigarette away in disgust. All right. One . . two ... *three*. Open your eyes and try the cigarette and see what you think of it now!"

You will note that you have not entirely awakened the subject in this test, but merely suggested that he open his eyes for its performance. The test would very probably work equally well posthypnotically, but for the purpose of this stage demonstration let him remain in a sort of half trance. Proceed right on:

"Here, try the cigarette." Force it between the subject's lips, and say: "Take a good puff of the cigarette. How you hate it. You hate that cigarette. Throw it away in disgust!" The subject will take a drag, cough, splutter and throw the cigarette from him with a vengeance.

You turn and address the audience: "You see here an example of how a habit can be rapidly removed through hypnosis. This subject has admitted that he has smoked cigarettes for a number of years and yet, in less than two minutes, he now finds himself utterly unable to smoke. Let us check this with a different brand of cigarettes. Will someone lend me a cigarette please." Someone either from the committee or the audience obliges.

You hand the cigarette to the subject, place it to his lips and light it for him, as you say: "You will find this one will taste ten times as bad as the other one. Oh, how you hate cigarettes."

The subject will again cough and splutter, much to the amusement of the spectators who thoroughly enjoy this human interest sort of thing, and will throw the cigarette far from him. Now suggest: "Let's bring the old good taste back again, shall we? Look me in the eyes. Your eyes are growing heavy already. Close them and go to sleep!" Your subject already in half trance will respond immediately. You carry on with the suggestions: "In a moment, I will count from one to five. At the count of 'five' you will be wide awake and feeling fine. At the count of 'five' you will be wide awake and feeling fine. And you will find that cigarettes taste all good and sweet again, just as they always have. All ready now, I will count from one to five, and at the count of 'five' you will be wide awake, and you will enjoy smoking just like you always have. One ... two ... three ... four ... *five*." The subject awakens and you offer him a cigarette which he now smokes with obvious enjoyment. An effect of this nature is important to the stature of your show; it impresses the spectators with the clinical and practical value of hypnotism.

As he has proved a good subject, there is no need to dismiss this man you have just used in the cigarette test, as he can take part in the next one also. And select six or seven other subjects from the committee as well. Select subjects you have previously noted as being responsive to posthypnotic suggestions. Ask them to move their chairs forward and form a line near the centre of the stage. Have everyone take a seat.

Sixth Group Experiment

Group Hypnotising from Audience

You are now going to introduce a sensational test in your show. Also it is one that closely identified you with the spectators, as you are going to hypnotise from in their midst. You address the audience: "Ladies and gentlemen, I will now show a type of hypnotic demonstration that is very rarely performed, the hypnotising of a group of persons all at the same time, from the rear of the audience."

Then to the front row of expectant subjects explain: "I am going right down into the audience, and from that distance hypnotise you. So pay very close attention to me, and concentrate with all of your ability."

And to the audience again say: "And you in the audience can assist me a great deal in this difficult experiment, if you, too, will hold in your minds the idea of these subjects, here on the stage, going down deep into the hypnotic trance." It is this intimate interplay between stage and audience that makes the hypnotism show different from any other. It is great entertainment.

Then, just before you leave the stage, turn towards the committee and add: "Now primarily I am going to concentrate on these subjects here in the front row but, if there are others in the back group who also wish to participate in this experiment, feel free to do so, and concentrate right along with them. All right everyone, sit back in your chairs, feet together, hands in your lap, and all ready for this experiment in hypnotism from the rear of the audience."

You have arranged your presentation psychologically so your conditions for this dramatic test are pretty well set for its success even before you start. The row of eight subjects in front represents some of the most responsive hypnotics in the group, so they are persons who are almost certain to go readily into hypnosis. Some of the remaining committee members are also good subjects, and you have paved the way for them likewise to enter hypnosis if they choose to follow. Frequently many do, as subjects come to enjoy being hypnotised. Those who do enter trance in the course of the experiment you can then bring forward to join the front group of selected subjects. The subjects who do not respond are all seated to the back of the stage anyway, and are not bothersome. Just let them sit there as observers of the action, and their merriment at the hypnotics' reactions will only add to the general enjoyment of the audience. You are now ready to perform this feat.

Go down into the audience, walk well into the midst of the spectators and stand on an aisle seat near the back row in the auditorium. Call out to your subjects on stage to look directly at you at the back of the audience.

You suggest: "As you all look out here at me in the audience and concentrate your attention towards my eyes, already even over this great distance you begin to feel the hypnotic effects of sleep coming upon you, each and everyone. You are becoming sleepy and the hypnotic trance is coming over you. Your eyes are getting heavy, and the lids want to close. Close those tired eyes and sleep."

From your stance at the rear of the audience, dramatically point your right forefingers out towards the subjects on the distant stage in a sweeping arc so it covers each of them. That pointing forefinger conveys a posthypnotic cue to reenter hypnosis, and almost at once the subjects on stage will close their eyes, start to nod, and go to sleep. You will amaze even yourself at how rapidly the hypnotics will respond at this point in your show, and to the spectators it is positively astonishing!

You now begin your "sleep formula" to the subjects, stating: "You are all going to sleep, deep, deep asleep, etc." as you walk up the aisle back onto the stage from the rear of the audience. Stand behind the subject on the right end of the front group first. Stroke his forehead a few times, press on his shoulders so that he slumps in his chair, and push his hands off his lap so that they dangle limply at his sides, as you continue to suggest: "Nothing will bother you in the slightest. You are sleeping deeply in perfect peace. Keep on going down deeper and deeper to sleep."

Then go to the subject next in line sleeping beside him and repeat the process. Just before you pass on to the next subject in the row, push the heads of the first and second subject together so they support each other while they sleep. This is a whimsical bit of business.

Experiments for the Front Group Of Subjects

The "Revolving Arms" Test

When all the front row of subjects are sleeping peacefully, look at your back group, and if others are entranced, go to them and push their heads down onto their chests, as you instruct them to go deeper into hypnosis.

Then return to the first subject in the front row, lift up his hands, turn them parallel to each other, and start them rotating rapidly around and around each other, as you say to him: "Keep your hands revolving. They will not stop. The more you try to stop them the faster they go. Try to stop them. You cannot! They are revolving faster and faster." Work rapidly down the row until all the subjects are rapidly revolving their arms.

Then say to the group: "Your hands are revolving around faster and faster. You cannot stop them. But when I say 'three' they will instantly stop, and freeze in that position, and you will find you cannot move them try as hard as you will. When I say 'three' your revolving hands will instantly stop and freeze dead still in the air. One … two … *three!*"

Instantly the revolving arms freeze still in the air. The subjects can't move them try as hard as they will. Then suggest: "When I say 'go,' around and around your hands will revolve again." Suddenly shout: "*Go!*" Immediately, the hands begin to revolve in a frenzy as you suggest: "Around and around they go, faster and faster and faster!"

While all the subjects' arms are revolving at a pitch, step quietly behind the first subject in the row, make a few hypnotic passes without contact in front of his face, and softly suggest directly into his ear: "It is all going away. You are going back to sleep. Your arms are dropping to your lap. You are going fast to sleep."

The visible transformation of moods that flit across the subject's face as he slips from violent motion into peaceful slumber is fascinating to behold. Push his hands off his lap so that they dangle at his sides, and leave him sleeping as you pass from one subject to the next, leaving each sleeping in turn, until the entire front row of subjects are all again sleeping soundly.

The Canary Test

Then address the front group: "At the count of 'three' you will all open your eyes, and you will see perched on the fingers of your left hand the cutest little canary you ever saw. You will love this little bird and will have a wonderful time playing with it.

"All ready now, get ready to play with the little bird. Sit back in your chair and hold out your left hand, so you can look at the little bird." The subjects will respond, adjusting themselves in their chairs and holding out their left hands perch-like, as you repeat the suggestions: "Remember, at the count of 'three' you will open your eyes and look directly at your left hand, and perched on it you will see the cutest, little, yellow canary you ever saw. And as you look at it, and play with it, it will send you down deeper and deeper into hypnosis all the time. Get ready now to look at that little yellow bird in your left hand. One ... two ... *three!*"

The subjects open their eyes, stare at their left fingers, as you continue: "Pat that little bird. Isn't it cute? Hold it gently. Let it hop onto your lap if it wants to." The subjects will begin going through a variety of pantomimes of patting and playing with the little bird.

Advance to one of the subjects who is responding well, place your finger in his left palm and them waft it in the air, as you say: "There goes the little bird flying about. Catch it! Catch it!" The subject will grab air trying to catch it. Then tell him to chase it, and he will leave his seat, chasing the imaginary canary about the stage.

Make "the little bird" fly about from the hands of a few other subjects until you have plenty of action going on stage. Be sure to keep a careful eye on the subjects as they move about the stage to make sure no one gets too close to the footlights. Forewarned is forearmed; always safeguard your subjects.

In this regard, always keep in mind this important rule of hypnotic show-manship: the hypnotic can become so fully absorbed in the performance of your suggestions that he will fail to look out for himself, so it becomes your duty to watch out for his welfare during your show.

Then go to each subject who is trying to catch the imaginary bird and say: "Here it is, here is the little bird," as you pretend to catch it. Hand it to him, and add: "Hold it gently but don't let it get away." The subject will at once cup his hands carefully, and you suggest: "Take it and go back to your seat."

When all of the subjects are again in their seats patting "the bird", step behind the subject seated at the end of the row, make a few passes in front of his face and suggest: "You are getting sleepy again. The little bird is all gone now. Forget all about the little bird and go sound, sound to sleep." As the subject slumps over in trance, whisper directly into his ear so that only he can hear the posthypnotic suggestion here repeated: "Remember, the moment I point my finger at your forehead you will go instantly asleep."

Going to each of the subjects in turn you place them again in trance, quietly repeating to each the posthypnotic suggestion: "Remember, the moment I point my finger at your forehead you will go instantly asleep." In this subtle handling, you have prepared your subjects for the test in instantaneous hypnotism which is to follow.

To conclude the canary test, save the subject who is showing the most reaction to the "canary" for the last, and when all the others are sleeping peacefully with the exception of him, walk over to his side and say: "Let me show you a magic trick. I call it the vanishing canary bird trick. Hold the little bird perched right on your fingers directly before your eyes. That's it.

Fine. Now watch very closely, for I am going to count very slowly from one to three, and at the count of 'three' that canary will disappear right before your eyes, and you won't know where it goes, and you will look all around trying to find the vanished canary. Here we go, watch closely! One ... two ... three ... the bird has gone!"

The subject will stare is stark amazement as the bird disappears right before his eyes, and will begin searching all about the stage trying to discover where it went, to the delight of the audience. After the fun has proceeded long enough, quickly return the subject to a deep sleep among the committee.

The "Instantaneous Hypnotism" Test

Turn and speak direct to the audience: "Ladies and gentlemen, you are about to witness what has been called the fastest demonstration of hypnotism on the stage today. Instantaneous Hypnosis. It is something you will remember as long as you live."

Go to one of the subjects in the row. Have him stand up and move about. Ask him if he is sure that he is wide awake and feels perfectly normal. When he assures you that he does, have him move his chair a little forward from the group and take his seat. Then, suddenly point your finger directly at him, and exclaim: "Sleep!" Instantly the subjects drops over in a trance. It is a very impressive demonstration.

Then suggest to the subject: "When you wake up again at the count of 'five' you will feel perfectly normal in all ways, but you will find that you are stuck to the seat of your chair. You cannot get out of that chair, pull as hard as you will, for you are glued tight to the seat. You cannot get out of your seat until I clap my hands. Then you will come instantly free! All ready, at the count of 'five' you will again be wide awake. One ... two ... three ... four ... *five.*"

The subject awakens. You ask him to try to rise from his chair; but he is stuck tight. He tugs and struggles but cannot get free. Right while he is in the middle of a violent tug, suddenly clap your hands, and he will leap from his seat! Thank the subject, and have him return his chair to the row and be seated.

Then quietly walk past the row of subjects, turn suddenly on a subject, catch his eye, point your finger directly at this forehead and say: "Sleep!" Instantly he is hypnotised. Then hypnotise two other subjects in the same manner. The way the hypnotics, one moment wide awake and then suddenly with a little gasp are slumped over instantly into hypnosis, is uncanny. The test builds amazement upon amazement and is something the spectators will never forget. It looks like a miracle.

The Amnesia Test

Three subjects are now deeply entranced, as you address the audience: "You have all heard tales of missing persons who show up strangely in different cities who when questioned by the police seem utterly unable to remember their names, where they are from or anything about themselves. Such persons are called amnesia victims, amnesia being a peculiar mental condition characterised by loss of memory.

"Now, this state of amnesia can be experimentally demonstrated through hypnosis. Let us attempt such an experiment." Turn towards your three sleeping subjects and say: "In a moment, I am going to awaken you, and when you wake up a strange thing will have happened. You will feel fine in every way and be perfectly normal, except that you will find you cannot remember your name when you try to do so. Also, you will not have the slightest idea of where you are, how you got here or anything about yourself. Your minds will be a complete blank. You won't remember your own names where you are or anything about yourself ... until I snap my fingers beside your ear when everything will come back to you instantly. Remember now, after you awaken you will feel fine in every way, but you will not be able to recall your own name, who you are or anything about yourself ... until I snap my fingers beside your ear, then everything will come back to you in a flash.

Ready now. At the count of 'five' you will be wide awake and feeling fine. One ... two ... three ... four ... *five!*"

The subjects awaken with a sort of blank look on their faces. You bring one of them forward to the front of the stage and ask a few questions, just as a police sergeant would do, as: "How do you feel?" The subject answers: "Fine." "Would you like to tell the audience your name?" The subject looks blank and appears uncomfortable. "Well, what is your name?" No response. "Well, if you can't remember who you are, then tell us where you are?" The subject thinks hard and shakes his head in bewilderment. "Alright now, keep thinking hard and see what happens." You suddenly snap your fingers beside his ear. Immediately the blank look vanishes from his face and the subject smiles and is relieved as you again ask: "Can you tell us your name now?" The subject answers: "Of course" and states his name. You thank him and he resumes his seat.

Call the second subject forward. Let us say you use a girl this time for variety, and you repeat the test. She is totally unable to give her name or tell anything about herself until you snap your fingers by her ear. It is extremely interesting to observe the variety of responses the subjects will go through as they react to such an experience. Some will tend to get panicky while others will take it all with stoic calmness. When the test is complete, thank the young lady, gesture her to her seat and explain to the audience: "You have seen here, ladies and gentlemen, some examples of experimentally produced amnesia. In normal life, the amnesia is usually produced through a mental conflict within the individual from which the person tries to hide by retreating into this condition. Basically, from a psychological standpoint, there is very little difference between spontaneously produced amnesia and that induced through hypnotism. Let us test this last subject."

You bring the subject forward and proceed with the test by asking him various questions about himself that he seems utterly unable to answer. His amnesia is complete. You ask him what he intends to do about it to get out of his predicament? Some subjects get quite concerned about the matter. Then, to climax the experiment you borrow a small hand mirror and hold it up directly in front of the subject's face, as you ask:

"Whom do you see in the mirror?" The subject usually will say: "A face." "Is it a nice face?" you ask. "Do you like it?" The subject shakes his head. "All right now, watch that face closely in the mirror and see what happens. Suddenly snap your fingers; the subject starts, smiles and sheepishly admits that it is the face he sees every day in the mirror. Modern audiences very much appreciate a scientific test of this nature. It gives credence to the hypnotism show.

There is a climax to the amnesia test that I sometimes include following the point where the subject is unable to recognise herself in the mirror. Suggest: "Not only do you not know who you are, you don't even know any person with whom you are acquainted. Close your eyes now and rest a moment."

Advance to front of stage and address the audience: "This young woman does not seem to know who she is or where she lives. Is there any person in the audience who knows her?"

When someone responds (usually it is a party who has come to the show with the subject), invite the person to step up on stage and see if they can help identify the young lady.

As the friend advances, tell the subject to open her eyes and she will see someone who knows her who will try to help her identify herself. The subject opens her eyes, and the party calls her by name, tries to tell her where she lives, etc. To all such, the subject remains oblivious of any recognition. It is a dramatic situation.

Finally suggest: "The moment I snap my fingers by your ear your memory will completely come back to you in a flash and you will know who you are, where you live, and you will be surprised at seeing your friend standing here on the stage before you."

Snap your fingers and the resultant flood of memory and recognition is remarkable entertainment providing a very effective climax to this test.

NOTE TO HYPNOTIST: Do not perform any amnesia hypnotic experiments on persons who show unstable symptoms of behaviour.

Seventh Group Experiment

The "Motion Picture" Test on Committee

You are now going to perform one of the most entertaining of all stage hypnotism demonstrations. A test that literally convulses the audience. Stand in front of your row of subjects, ask them to look at you, and hypnotise the entire group very quickly with a few suggestions of sleep while making use of the posthypnotic cue of pointing your finger directly towards them, as you sweep it slowly from one end of the line to the other. When the members of the committee are all in deep hypnosis, go rapidly to each and push them farther down in their chair, as you repeat to each individual quickly: "Sleep, sleep deep." Then address the committee as a body:

"In a moment, you will all open your eyes and you will see before you a motion picture screen, and on it is playing a very exciting Western movie. You are going to have a wonderful time watching this picture. You will see the hero and the heroine. You will see the villain and the comic, and you will have the time of your life watching this motion picture unreel before your eyes.

"Get ready, everybody, to watch this motion picture. Sit up straight in your chair and at the count of 'three' open your eyes and watch the movie. All ready, one ... two ... *three*! Open your eyes and watch the movie."

The subjects all open their eyes and, staring out excitedly in front of themselves lean forward in their chairs, as you suggest: "Now the picture is getting very exciting. You're having a wonderful time. You are getting so excited watching that picture. And here comes the comedian. Say, isn't he the funny fellow! You never saw anyone so funny. You just want to laugh and laugh and laugh. Go ahead, laugh and laugh."

Give your suggestions in this test with the enthusiasm of a sports announcer, and as you narrate the happenings in the imaginary motion picture interpret it in your voice. Your interpretation of mood functions as much in the way of suggestions to which hypnotics respond as to your words. When you say, for example: "Laugh", really laugh. And how the subjects will respond. They will be literally convulsed with laughter. Laughter is contagious, and the audience will be laughing right along with the subjects.

And right when the laughter is at its peak, suddenly change the mood and suggest: "Say, the picture is not funny any more, the movie is getting sad. Look there is a poor little old lady out in the snow freezing to death, and her tiny grandchildren are in the log cabin starving to death. Oh, it is so sad. You feel so sad. You've never felt more sad at any movie. It makes you want to cry."

The quick transformation of moods is astonishing as the subjects immediately shift from gales of laughter to sadness, and begin to cry. Then suddenly suggest: "Look everything is alright now. The old lady is back in her warm cabin and there is plenty of food on the table to feed the children. And, look, the motion picture is getting funny again. You want to laugh at it. Go ahead and laugh and laugh!"

Get all the subjects laughing once more, then step behind each in turn, pass your hand slowly in front of each person's face and the hypnotic goes to sleep. It's laughter to sleep. It's amazing. You simply suggest to each subject: "The picture is fading away now. It is all gone. You are going down sound to sleep." And down they go, one by one, until all are sleeping soundly, and you are ready to perform your concluding test.

Eighth Group Test

Posthypnotic Climax to the Show

Turn and address the audience: "Ladies and gentlemen, to conclude the programme I will show you now a demonstration in mass posthypnotic suggestion. I believe you will find it highly thought-provoking. As you witness these demonstrations in hypnotism unquestionably you will find many of them amusing, for entertainment is our purpose. But look beyond the humour and appreciate the remarkable qualities of mental control these show. These volunteers have learned, in this short time, how to control their subconscious mind. They can use the ability to take away pain in having a tooth filled at the dentist. They can use it to overcome unwanted habits. They can use it to increase their memory, develop self-confidence, and use the power invested in hypnosis in many useful ways for better living. It is a wonderful mental skill.

"And now I am going to awaken the entire group. And when they wake up everyone will feel just wonderful and fine, and good all over. Notice how pleasant, gradual, and gentle the awakening from hypnosis is, and everyone will awaken just feeling fine. And watch, also, mass posthypnosis.

Turn and address your sleeping hypnotics: "You have all had a wonderful time at the show, and you can use the hypnotic skill you have learned in many ways to help yourselves. It can bring you confidence and success. And you have had a wonderful sleep and relaxing experience. When you wake up in just a moment, you will feel refreshed and fine. *But* here is a strange thing, when you awaken and try to leave the stage, you will discover that your left foot is stuck to the floor. And pull and tug as hard as you can, you will not be able to free your left foot … until I snap my fingers by your ear … then your left foot will come free, but your right foot will then get stuck to the stage.

"All right, I will now count slowly from one to five. With every count you will gradually wake up, and by the time I reach 'five' be wide, wide awake. *But* you will find you cannot leave the stage because your left foot will be glued, stuck to the floor … and it will not come free, but your right foot will then become stuck … until I snap my fingers again when your right foot will come free but your left foot will get stuck to the floor all over again. And so it will go, back and forth … first one foot stuck to the floor and then the other every time I snap my fingers, until I clap my hands loudly beside you and say it is all gone.

"All ready now. I will count from one to five, and by the time I reach 'five' you will be wide awake and feeling fine, *but* you cannot leave this stage because your left foot is glued and stuck to the floor. Ready, one … two … three … four … and *five*. Everyone wide awake and feeling fine!"

Addressing the now awake committee members, you say: "Allow me, at this time, to thank each and every one of you for your splendid cooperation and fine powers of concentration, and now if you will try to return to your seats, please."

The subjects start to leave the stage and pandemonium ensues, as everyone finds to his or her amazement that their left foot is stuck to the floor. Confusion reigns supreme as they pull and tug trying to free their foot. You pass to each and snap your fingers by their ear; their left foot comes free, but the right is now stuck fast to the stage. More finger snapping, and the right is now stuck fast to the stage. More finger snapping, and first one foot and then the other gets stuck. Finally, you slap your hands loudly beside one subject as you say: "All right, it's all gone. You are free to leave the stage," and he gingerly picks up his feet, looks at his soles and marches off the stage. As the subject leaves encourage the audience to give him a nice round of applause. Do this for each subject as he or she is dismissed from the stage so each person may receive recognition for their hypnotic performance during the show.

Free another subject, and then another. They march off the stage and return to their seats in the audience. The next person you release you walk over with to the side of the stage as though to escort him to the steps and, just when you get to the side pillar, you suddenly place his hand flat against the wall, and say: "Your hand is stuck there. You cannot pull it free." Heightened suggestibility remains with the subject for a time after coming out of hypnosis; he will still be in a responsive mood, and his hand will instantly become stuck to the post. Leave him there tugging while you release another subject or so. Then walk to the front of the stage and, just as one of your subjects is in the aisle returning to his seat, ask him to turn about and look at you, and as he does so hold out your right forefinger and say: "Your eyes are fixed to the tip of my finger. See, you sway about as it sways. Your eyes are closing. You are sinking, sinking. Your knees are sagging. Knees sagging. Dropping right down to the floor in the aisle." The subject still in a hypnotic mood will instantly respond; he begins to sway and sags down to the floor. It is an impressive demonstration of hypnotism. This test performed right in their midst, as it were, is very dramatic and brings the power of hypnotism forcefully home to every spectator. End the test by quickly clapping your hands, and say: "All right, the influence is all gone now. You are wide awake, and you feel just fine."

Then dash quickly about the stage, release the subject stuck to the side post and all the rest of the subjects except one, whom you apparently overlooked in your feverish activities of freeing all of the subjects. Thus the stage is clear with the exception of this last subject still valiantly tugging at his stuck foot. You continue to apparently absent-mindedly overlook him as you advance to the front of the stage to give your closing remarks to the audience.

"And so, ladies and gentlemen, you have witnessed a gamut of demonstrations of some of the interesting and unusual aspects of the science of hypnotism. On behalf of the volunteers and myself, let me thank you for your most courteous attention, and may I bid you a pleasant, good evening."

All during these salutatory remarks, various members of the audience will be calling up trying to remind you that you have overlooked one subject who is still stuck on stage. You appear oblivious to this. Suddenly you seem to catch on, turn and spot the subject and, with a tongue-in-cheek apology, dash to him, clap your hands and release him. Walk with this last subject to the side of the stage, shake him by the hand, thank him for volunteering and let him return to his seat. Take your final bow, ending the show, and exit.

This entire last sequence should be performed with as much dash and verve as you can manage to put into it. Heap action upon action. Lift your audience up to a fever pitch of laughter and excitement, and then the last humorous bit of seemingly overlooking the remaining subject provides a marvellous concluding tag. In show business, it's a topper! Of such nature is the designing of the hypnotism show.

Chapter Fifty-Seven
Climaxing the Hypnotism Show

Effective climax routines are important to the show, as you want to end on a high note. Posthypnotic effects work well for climactic purpose, which can be handled in this manner: several of the best and most active subjects are brought forward forming a line near the front of the stage. The subjects are quickly hypnotised and given a suggestion that they will do such and such on "cue" (the "cue" can be simply pointing at them by the performer) after they return to their seats.

All the other subjects on stage are thanked for their participation and dismissed. The standing line of subjects are then awakened and told to return to their seats in the audience. As you point to each in turn they perform their posthypnotic stunt. Ending the show on posthypnotic reactions is hilarious.

The Tex Morton Posthypnotic Climax

The late Tex Morton hailed from Australia. He became particularly well known in the western hemisphere through his transcontinental tours playing the largest cities in Canada. He used the posthypnotic climax to his show by telling one subject that he would return to his seat in the audience, but that on "cue" he would return to the stage and ask for a cigarette. When he tries to light the cigarette his hands will shake so much he cannot light it, to his great annoyance until you remove the suggestions.

Another hypnotic is told that on "cue" he will return to his seat in the audience and look all around to find his overcoat which he believes is lost. He will even accuse some people around him of having taken it. He finds the imaginary coat and puts it on and, on the suggestion being removed, is surprised to find he wears no coat at all.

A woman subject is told that on "cue" she will go into the audience and kiss three baldheaded men on the top of their head, and after she will return to her seat and go fast to sleep. All happens and the hypnotist goes into the audience to awaken the girl right at her seat.

Another subject is told that on "cue" he will note there is a fire on stage and will go out to fetch a glass of water to put it out.

Another Tex Morton posthypnotic climax is to tell the subject that when he is dismissed from the stage his shoes pinch and he has to take them off and carry them. He leaves the stage in his stockinged feet.

Of such nature, were the homey comedy posthypnotic stunts Tex Morton used to climax his show. Being a rodeo star as well as a hypnotist his shows carried a somewhat rural flavour.

The Michael Dean Posthypnotic Climax

The hypnotist Dr Michael Dean uses a sophisticated ending to his show, as his work is in night clubs. He tells a woman subject that on "cue" she will return to the stage and perform a strip tease when the appropriate music starts. "Just in time" the act is concluded. Yet another Dean posthypnotic climax is for the subject to return to the stage and tell the performer he (or she) is a great singer, and request permission to sing a song for the audience. Permission is granted.

Another Michael Dean climax to his show is to tell the women they will go into the audience and find their husband or boy friend and give him a passionate kiss. The men are told they will kiss the wife or girl friend. It is lots of fun and a great climax, as all the world loves a lover.

Dr Dean uses another interesting slant to end his show by telling the subjects (as a posthypnotic suggestion) that they will gather at the bar following the show and he will then remove all hypnotic influence from them.

There is good psychological handling in this careful removing of all residual suggestions by this after-the-show attention. Also, it is good showmanship as it continues audience interest in hypnotism, as many come to watch subjects at the bar. Needless to mention, it is also good for bar business!

The Pat Collins Posthypnotic Climax

Pat Collins frequently ends her show by telling each subject, in turn, as a posthypnotic suggestion that, they will return to their seats in the audience and go back to sleep. Each is instructed to walk off stage in a different way:

One subject walks off as a Western film star, à la John Wayne. Another walks off as a muscle man displaying his muscles macho style: Another walks off (if a woman subject) as a fashion model displaying her gown. Another walks off as though he were drunk. A woman subject walks off as a socialite with great pomp and dignity. Another walks off stage as a small child having difficulty finding where his seat is in the audience.

It provides a lot of entertainment seeing the subjects return to their seats in different ways. The acting of hypnotised persons is often superb. Returning to their respective seats each subject goes back to sleep. Pat comes to each in turn and awakens them right in the audience. The Pat Collins handling provides an intimate performer/audience relationship that is very effective.

The Dance Contest Climax

A dance contest provides an excellent climax to a hypnotism show. Suggest to the subjects they are expert dancers and have come to compete for the prize money. They are to dance their very best when all is ready for the contest to begin. The audience is told they are the judges and are to decide who is the best dancer who will win the contest. This involves the audience in the action. Then have the hypnotised subjects stand and get ready to dance. When the rock and roll music starts they are to dance their wildest steps. When the music stops they will freeze in whatever position they happen to be in at that time. When the music starts again they will go on with their dancing, accordingly dancing and stopping as the music plays and stops.

Contest ready. The music starts and pandemonium ensues on stage. You shout: "Stop!" and the music stops on cue. The subjects "freeze" in immobile positions. Hilarious fun! More music, more dancing. Stop music, more freezing. Stop and go, the contest proceeds, finally ending on a freeze, as you tell the audience that they all danced so well, let's say they are all winners, and give them a rousing ovation of applause. It is a great climax!

385

NOTE TO HYPNOTIST: Keep up to date on the music played for the dance contest, and suggest the subjects do the latest dance craze. And a tip: your assistant backstage will probably be starting and stopping the music. There can be such a din with the subjects dancing and the audience laughing that a verbal cue is difficult to hear. Have a whistle handy, and you can blow shrilly to cue the off-stage music player.

Turn of the Century Hypnotism Stage Show
There is little that is new under the sun: A 1901 dance contest climaxes the show just as it now often does in current times.

Hypnotism Show Routines

In this section, you are given a compilation of successful hypnotic routines: for example, Further Ormond McGill Routines; The Great Hollywood Motion Pictures Screen Test; Ideas from the Jerry Valley Show; Ideas from the Pat Collins Show; Ideas from the Martin St James Show; Dr Flint's Routines Modernised; Successful Hypnotic Routines From Around the World; A Selection of Sensational Hypnotic Feats.

Chapter Fifty-Eight
Further Ormond McGill Routines

As a professional hypnotist, you will most likely establish your more or less standard show, however there will be times you will wish to vary it by changing the programme to some extent. The routines detailed in this chapter are those I have originated to change my programme on occasion. I have used them all, and all have proved effective. These routines will serve as examples to illustrate how you may create your own routines based on interesting and dramatic situations. Some of these will be described, in part, in the first person.

The Hypnotic Exercisers

I use this routine at the start of the second act of my show (following the return of the subjects to the stage posthypnotically after the intermission) as an opening test in my "Concert of Hypnotism". The subjects are seen sleeping in their respective chairs on stage, I advance, acknowledge the audience, and then go to each subject in turn to start them on a variety of physical exercises.

The first subject is told to stand up from his chair, then to sit down, rise up, sit down, and is to continue this motion over and over taking his exercise. Going to another subject the process is continued. And then on to several others.

Additional exercises are also introduced: one subject extending his arms out and in front of chest over and over, another bending up and down at the hips, others trotting their legs up and down.

Any desired physical exercise may be introduced until the entire group is vigorously performing. I help each subject to get them started and then leave them to carry on by themselves.

Just keep the exercises going for a short time as it is strenuous. Suddenly I say: "Stop, be seated and sleep." The action is instantly ended.

This is an exceedingly effective test, as it is very funny to the audience to see the hypnotics taking their exercises. It has proved an excellent opening test for Act Two of the show as it has action and is entirely visual. It quickly captures audience attention, gets the subjects responding again after the intermission, and the show ready to roll again.

The Boxing Test

Occasionally, I use this test in combination with the hypnotic exercisers described above. A subject is marched forward almost to the footlights and is told that he is a champion prizefighter shadow boxing in the gym. The ensuing fracas is a riot as he ducks, punches, lunges and boxes his shadow.

I end the test by suggesting: "Hold it, hold it right there. Stop boxing now, lower your hands, close your eyes and sleep." I then lead the subject back to his chair and let him sleep.

Just a word of warning. Stay out of the way of the subject's punches when you get near him or you may end up with a "black eye". I always approach him carefully from the rear, as I give suggestions ending the stunt.

The Rowing Test

Another stunt I sometimes include with the hypnotic exercisers is to take a subject over to the side of the stage opposite the "boxer" and have him sit in a chair right at the footlights. It is then suggested that he is in an exercise rowing machine. The fun begins as he rows and rows and rows.

Along the line of exercising machines, one of the funniest stunts I ever devised was to suggest that the subject was belted in a mechanical vibrator to take off weight. The effect can be imagined as the subject shakes, shakes and shakes.

I repeat, be careful not to continue these physical action tests too long as they are strenuous, and the subjects often engage in them with great vigour.

The "Elixir of Youth and Old Age" Test

This has long been one of my favourite hypnotic routines as it is both visual and very thought provoking. It illustrates how very much youth and old age are elements of belief in the mind of every person. It is suggested to the subject that two amazing elixirs have been found, one that will produce youth and the other old age.

The assistant enters carrying a tray on which is one glass of red liquid and one glass of blue liquid (water coloured with fruit dyes is used). It is explained that when the "Red Elixir of Youth" is drunk it will cause a person to go back through the years becoming younger and younger and younger. And that when the "Blue Elixir of Old Age" is drunk it will cause the person to become older and older and older.

Having established the effects of the Elixirs, the subject is given the red one to drink. When it is consumed, continue with suggestions describing the effects the subject will experience: "As you drink this 'Elixir of Youth' you will feel it coursing through your being and you are beginning to feel and become younger and younger and younger. You are becoming a little boy again."

Continue your suggestions describing exactly how the subject is to react and watch the performance. When it has gone on long enough, suggest: "Now the Elixir is making you still younger, and you are becoming a little baby again and are crawling about on all fours."

As has been mentioned previously in this course, be sure to have a rug on the floor in working such a stunt as this or the subject may ruin his clothes. A rug will soften many a bump and save many a suit or dress.

And now comes the most amazing part of the routine. I suggest: "You are becoming yet still younger: you are going back in youth so far that you are actually the embryo inside your mother's womb." The way the subject curls up in the foetal position is astounding.

When this action has gone on long enough, I pick up the blue glass of liquid and suggest: "I am going to give you the 'Elixir of Old Age' now. It will make you become gradually older again." Bend over and force some of the liquid into the mouth of the subject, as the suggestions continue expressing exactly what is expected to happen.

"It is beginning to take effect now ... you are gradually becoming older again. You are a baby again ... now a small boy ... now a young man ... now you are back to your original age."

Under these suggestions the "foetus" uncurls, the subject crawls about again on all fours as a baby, then gradually stands up and becomes himself again. The suggestions continue: "But now the effects of the 'Elixir of Old Age' are advancing on past your current age and you are becoming older, older, older. It is turning you into an old, old man."

The response to these suggestions is as astonishing in this direction as are the ones of youth in the other. Finally, have your assistant come in with a cane which you hand to the subject, and he totters about on the stage.

Keep the flow of suggestions going describing to the subject exactly the effect he will experience and you will get precisely the performance you desire. This giving of continual descriptive suggestions of the reactions the subject is expected to experience is an important principle of successful stage hypnotism, and is one I have stressed before. Its importance cannot be over emphasised. Subjects will improvise upon your suggestions, but don't expect them to do too much. Your flow of descriptive suggestions constantly assists them in the development of their responses, and you can thus direct them to perform exactly in the direction you wish.

To end this test, I state: "I am mixing the two elixirs together now; youth is blending with old age and old age is blending with youth." Proceed to mix the two elixirs together before the audience and have the subject drink it, as you suggest: "This blending of the elixirs is making your age exactly right now. You are becoming younger and are returning to exactly your own correct age. When I count 'three' and you wake up, you will be entirely yourself again at exactly your right age." The subject is then awakened.

This experiment has proved a most dramatic way to present the well-known age-regression and age-advancement experiment so popular in hypnotism. As it is entirely an imaginary experience, it is completely harmless to the subject. Likewise the test introduces an innovation in the using of "props" which are suggestively given credit for the "causation" of the phenomena to be experienced, as in the case in this instance of the red and blue elixirs. This principle may be used in many ways in routines you can develop.

The Rain Storm

I frequently use this test in conjunction with the "Hot and Cold" test. After the group of subjects have responded to hot and cold sensations, it is suggested that a rain storm has suddenly come up and that it is pouring.

The way the subjects scramble about and try to find cover is most exciting. Finally the test is ended with the suggestions: "The rain storm has died down and the sun has come out. It is pleasantly warm, and you are dry and comfortable now." A wonderful effect in stage drama is achieved by tying in these hypnotic experiences of hot, cold and rain into an imaginary situation in which the subjects all find themselves out in the country. First, the sun comes out and makes them hot; then the sun goes behind the clouds and a chilling wind comes up that makes them cold, and finally it rains and rains. Hypnotic experiments are much more entertainingly established into dramatised situations this way than they are as just isolated sensation experiments.

Asleep in the Audience

This is a test I frequently use when ending the awakening of a group of subjects. One by one I go down the line awakening each in turn until only one sleeping subject is left. This person's head I then start revolving around and around with the suggestions: "Your head is beginning to go around, and around, and around and you cannot stop it," as I gently move the head around and around in a circle.

Stepping back from the subject, I allow the head to continue its revolutions for a few moments, finally suggesting: "Your head is becoming heavy now. It is stopping revolving and is coming to rest on your chest. It is resting on your chest and you are fast asleep."

I then suggest: "Now, in just a moment, I am going to awaken you ... and when you wake up you will leap from your chair and will go directly down from this stage back to your seat in the audience, and will return at once back fast, fast to sleep right in your seat in the middle of the audience."

Awaken the subject. At once he bounds out of his chair, marches off the stage to his seat in the audience. Watch the subject. If he doesn't at once return to sleep, I point my finger at him to attract his attention and say the one word: "Sleep." The response is instant. I then address the audience: "The subject is sleeping so soundly that nothing can awaken or disturb him. I want two gentlemen seated nearby to pick him up and bring the body back on the stage."

Get two gentlemen to do this. "That's it, one of you pick him up under the arms and the other take the feet, and bring the body right up here on the stage and place it in this chair." Emphasise this "body" line; as the subject dangles limply between the two men as they bring him back to the stage, literally "dead to the world", it is always good for a laugh. Finally the subject is deposited in the chair on stage, you thank the two men and they return to their seats, as the suggestions continue: "You have been through quite an experience, yet when you wake up you will have no memory of ever having left this chair here on the stage in the first place. It will seem to you that you simply dozed off and woke from your sleep right here in this chair where you were all along."

Awaken the subject and end the test. This is a good opportunity to explain to the audience that the experiment clearly shows how truly deep and intense the hypnotic trance is, as not even this complicated handling disturbs the "sleeper".

The Frankenstein Monster

Audiences like routines, such as the one previously described, that tie themselves in naturally as an experiment leading from one hypnotic feat to another. In this regard my "Frankenstein Monster" test has the same appeal. While the subject is sleeping on stage, I ask if there is any friend of this person in the audience, and for them to come forward and stand at the side of the stage. It is then suggested to the hypnotic: "When you open your eyes and look over to the left side of the stage, you will see standing there the original Frankenstein monster and, as it comes towards you, you had better hide and get away."

Have the subject open his eyes and look over at the "monster". His reactions provide great fun for spectators as they know that the monster he sees is actually his friend. Tell the person from the audience to walk slowly towards the subject, and watch the subject scamper and hide. Play the stunt for tongue-in-cheek fun, not for horror. Finally tell the subject not to be scared now for it is only a fellow in make-up portraying the Frankenstein monster. Have the subject advance towards the "monster" and run his fingers lightly over the person's face to examine the make-up. Then suggest: "When I snap my fingers you will instantly wake up and will you be surprised at seeing your friend standing before you."

Snap your fingers and conclude the test. This will be noted as a variant of the amnesia test climax, as previously outlined in this chapter.

The Invisible Hypnotist

This is my handling of the "Hypnotic Negative Hallucination" experiment. It is suggested that when the subjects open his eyes he will be able to feel and hear the hypnotist clearly, but that he cannot see him no matter how hard he tries. The hypnotist will be completely invisible. The subject then opens his eyes and the action ensues.

The operator stands at one side of the subject and speaks to him, claps his hands, and in every way tries to attract the subject's attention. The subject hears the voice and turns in that direction but is unable to see the hypnotist. The operator moves to the other side and repeats the actions. The subject's puzzlement is obvious.

The operator strokes the subject's hair much to his amazement. Then a handkerchief is tossed into the subject's lap. Just as he goes to pick it up, it is grabbed and tossed to the floor. Then the operator moves it about in front of the subject. To the subject it appears to be dancing in the air by itself. The operator move his hands quickly in front of the subject's face and eyes; there is no response. The hypnotist is absolutely invisible.

Then the voice of the hypnotist suggests: "When I snap my fingers by your ear I will be instantly visible to you." A snap of the fingers and the hypnotist appears. The reaction of the subject is most striking.

This effect of hypnotic negative hallucination will be found absolutely fascinating to the audience, and clearly shows the power of hypnotism.

The Seasick Test

While performing in Tahiti and throughout the islands of French Polynesia, my interpreter, Louis Aitami, suggested the test of having a group of subjects take an ocean voyage from island to island and become seasick. The effect was terrific. The subjects lolled about in the imaginary ship and rolled from side to side as the waves tossed the boat. Then it was finally suggested that the boat was sinking and that the subjects must swim for it to reach the Island beach.

The effect was all that could possibly be asked for in the way of hilarious entertainment. Needless to repeat, there must be a rug on the stage to conduct any such tests safely. All such routines must be handled in a light, good humoured manner by the performer. Subjects have a way of unconsciously sensing the performer's mood and, if it is in fun, they respond to the test in like manner. It would hardly be enjoyable theatre to actually see persons suffering the pangs of shipwreck and drowning, but it is fun to see them react to such a situation as "imaginary play".

Going for a Swim

It is suggested to the subjects that you will clap your hands three times. On the first clap they will see a beautiful lake before them. On the second clap they will feel an urge to go swimming in the lake. On the third clap they will start undressing to take a swim.

You clap your hands and they open their eyes and see the lake. You clap your hands a second time and they express a desire to go swimming. On the third clap they start undressing for the swim. You stop them just in time!

The Barbershop Quartet

Four male subjects are stood in a line and are told they are a popular Barbershop Quartet, and when the music starts they will start moving their mouths as though singing, but they will not utter a sound. Then start music of a popular quartet group, and the subjects "mouth" the words of the song. It's entertainment!

Money, Money On the Floor

This is a routine I sometimes use as a follow-up to the "Dance Contest". It is suggested that the hypnotics have danced so well that each person won the contest and deserves some prize money. I then explain that I am sprinkling hundred dollar bills all over the floor and that when I say "three" everyone will open their eyes and see the money on the floor; the boys will scramble forward and pick up the money and fill their pockets with the wealth. The girls are to remain in their seats and watch the collection, but not to worry as the boys will share the money they collect with them.

The signal is given and there is a mad scramble to collect the money. The effect can be imagined. It is a terrific situation. In the test it is extremely important to remember this suggestion that the girls will remain in their seats and only the boys will scramble for the money. Otherwise the women could be easily hurt in the ensuing fracas!

When enough money has been collected, I suggest: "Return to your seats now and give half of the money to the girl seated on your right." Following which I suggest a return to sleep.

This principle of combining one routine with another so they blend and flow together as a unit is important to the hypnotic showman. It can be used in many ways to build drama into the hypnotic experiments. Smooth combo-routining can lend infinite variety to the hypnotic show.

The Aeroplane Trip

The hypnotics enter the plane, fasten their seat belts, experience the take off, look out of the plane's windows at the landscape below, and when they hit an "air pocket" – watch out – it's "oops, up and down we go!" The plane lands, and all get out for some further interesting hypnotic adventures. The showman can appreciate the many ways he can develop original routines that glide along smoothly from sequence to sequence by such staging.

The Flying Saucer and a Trip to Mars

I always try to insert some material into my show that is right up-to-date. Few things express the *now* more than outer space. These routines have proved most interesting, and I feature them constantly in my "Concert of Hypnotism."

I tell the group of hypnotics to watch carefully and be alert, for a Flying Saucer will soon be coming in for a landing. Then I take one particularly responsive subject forwards and let him act as the leader of the group. I point to the back of the theatre and suggest (I direct my suggestions towards the one subject but make certain that it is clear that the other subjects in the background are to respond also. It lends dramatic emphasis to the proceedings to thus have one subject reacting out in front while the others shadow his actions behind): "Look way back there. [Point to the back of the theatre.] In the air is a flashing silver spot. It is coming closer now. Look, look it is a flying saucer. A flying saucer coming in from outer space. Follow it. It is a getting closer and closer. Swoosh, here it comes in for a landing. Back up, back up. Get out of its way for the landing." As I give these suggestions, I jump back myself out of the way of the imaginary landing of the flying saucer. Such lends emphasis to the suggestions and the subjects react accordingly. The subject out in front jumps aside, and the other subjects in the background respond as well; it makes a most dramatic tableau.

"Look, the saucer has landed now. A door in its side is beginning to open, and look what's coming out. Why, they are little green women! Aren't they cute? Look, they are marching towards you. [The other subjects on stage are included in the suggestions along with the subject out in front.] They want you to pick them up. [The subjects pick the "little green women" up and hold them in their hands.] See, I pick one up, too. [Pretend to pick a little woman up.] She is talking to us. Hold her by your ear and listen to what she has to say. She invites us all to take a trip in the 'flying saucer' back to her home planet of Mars. Wonderful! We all want to go on a trip to Mars. 'Close your eyes a moment,' she says [subjects do so], and when you open them you will all be inside the 'flying saucer' and ready for the journey into outer space. All right, open your eyes now, and what a strange and interesting place it is inside the 'flying saucer.' [The reactions of the various subjects are fascinating as they seem to observe the marvels of the spacecraft.]

"Ready, now, we are taking off ... leaving Earth, going up, up, up through the atmosphere into outer space. Feel that acceleration as it pushes you down deep into your chairs. [The reactions of the subjects are astonishing to behold as their bodies assume the effects of acceleration.] We are out of Earth's gravity now, the acceleration pressure is gone, and we all feel comfortable in our seats.

"What tremendous speed we are making. There, you can all see Mars through the front spaceship window. Look, it is getting larger and larger, and we are coming in for a landing. Better fasten your safety belts. [The subjects all fasten the imaginary belts.] And we have landed at the spaceport. We are on Mars. They are opening the door of the ship. Unfasten your safety belts, and let us all go outside on the planet. We can breath fine; the air is fresh and fine. But, say, watch out, the gravity is weak here. Everyone stand up, step out and try it. Test that weak gravity; it feels just as though you are walking on a cloud, as you sort of bounce and float on the fluffy stuff. [The reaction of the subjects to this 'low-gravity suggestion' is amazing: they literally seem to be moving in slow motion.] And say, what did you do with the 'little green woman' you each were holding? There, you have her. Perch her on your fingers now. She says

'Watch!' And when I snap my fingers she will instantly disappear and you won't know where she has gone. You'll look all about trying to find her as you love her very much, but you can't find her. The subjects react accordingly. Well, never mind, she is gone and we are told to return to our seats in the 'flying saucer'. Sit down, sit down, close your eyes, close your eyes. We are travelling back through space via the fourth dimension. Open your eyes, we are back home again on Earth, and our trip to Mars was a complete success."

This is a brilliant experience, and it shows the handling of how subjects may be taken through any variety of scenes in routines that unfold the happenings before them. Another example of this handling I have made use of is the following.

The Hindu Rope Trick

It is suggested to the group of hypnotics: "We are going to India now and there the great Hindu magician, Rhan Rahid, will show you the famous 'Hindu Rope Trick'. This is something you have always wanted to see, and at last you are going to have your wish granted. Close your eyes everyone and open them when I tell you to, and we'll all be in India.

"Open your eyes, everyone. We are in India and are going to see the 'Hindu Rope Trick' performed by the great magician. Watch closely. Here comes the magician. He bows before us. Look, he has a large coil of rope in his hand which he tosses up into the air; it unwinds as he throws it upwards and remains hanging in the air ... ascending from earth to the sky. It is amazing. [Pantomime the performing of the trick as you tell about it. These are suggestions that the hypnotic will follow. They see exactly in hallucination form what you describe, and their reactions are clearly noted by the audience who enjoy the trick through the subject's eyes.]

"Now the magician invites a little Hindu boy forward. The boy grips the rope and starts to climb, up, up, up. Now he is at the very top of the rope. Look! It's amazing! The boy disappears into thin air!

"The magician calls to the boy to come back, to reappear and come back. But there is no boy. The boy is gone. The magician is becoming angry. He picks up a sword. He is climbing up the rope to try to find the boy. Look, the magician has vanished from the very top of the rope. There is the noise of a fight in the air. Look – parts of the boy's body are falling to the ground. There's an arm, there's a leg, there's his head. If it is too gruesome to watch, perhaps you had better turn your head or hide your eyes."

At this point in the routine, I bring one girl forward and state: "There's the boy's head on the ground. Kick it with your foot to get it out of the way. [The subject's reaction can be imagined.] You'd better go back and join the crowd now. And here's the magician sliding down the rope. Look, he is gathering up the parts of the boy and is placing them in a large basket. He covers the basket with a colourful cloth, he removes it, and there is the boy once again alive and all together.

"It was a wonderful trick. How we all enjoyed it. Let's give the magician a big hand! [And the subjects applaud enthusiastically.]"

This presentation of the "Hindu Rope Trick" has proved a popular feature in my show. Audiences thoroughly enjoy it. The reactions of the subjects as they hypnotically witness the famous spectacle is most entertaining.

School Days

This is a favourite routine that has long been associated with my show. I have used it internationally. It is entertaining and demonstrates hypnotic age regression in a simple manner familiar to everyone. The test provides a good example of how the hypnotist can involve himself in the action of the suggested situation (see Chapter Four). The tableau is presented against the background music of "School Days":

To the hypnotics, in a group, it is suggested: "When you open your eyes, we will have gone back in time and you are all children again in school; all children of the age eight to nine. And you have a teacher you just can't stand. Every time he turns his back, you will make the worst face you can at him, but when he turns around you'd better wipe it off quick or you'll get into trouble. All right, open your eyes … we are at school."

As the subjects open their eyes, you assume the role of an old-time school master and instruct: "Attention class. Students pick up your books by your side, and turn to your lesson for today on page fifty-three."

The subjects will follow right along with your instructions, act exactly like school children, pick up their books and turn the pages. It is very amusing.

"All right. Now, class, pay close attention, and I will put the assignment on the blackboard."

Turn your back on the subjects and while facing towards the audience pretend to write the assignment on the school blackboard. Act the part of the stern schoolmaster. Immediately your back is turned the fracas will start. The subjects will make all manner of funny faces and gestures of derision towards you as the hated schoolmaster. By your pantomime, show puzzlement and turn around sharply asking: "What is going on here?" Instantly the "students" will quiet down and look very innocent. The situation is a riot. Pretend not to know what was the cause, and announce that you will continue to put the lesson on the board.

As soon as you turn your back, the fracas starts again. When you quickly turn around to the students they wipe off the "faces" instantly, and assume the most innocent expressions possible.

Laughs build on laughs, and you can work this routine several times for increasing merriment. When you've played it long enough, suddenly turn around and catch the students making the faces. Look extremely annoyed and put the class back to sleep, and you can then end the test by returning everyone to their normal age and awakening them.

Developing Routines For Your Own Show

These routines I have created for my shows will serve as examples to point the way so you can develop your own routines. Be original, as then your show will be novel and different. The surface for developing effective hypnotic routines has not even been scratched. All around us are constant happenings, situations, news events, occurrences of interest that can be used by the hypnotist. *Think creative!*

The X-ray Glasses

The hypnotic is hallucinated that these glasses give him X-ray vision like Superman. In looking out into the audience through the glasses, he is requested to point out things he sees that strike him as especially funny. Laughter begets laughter. Played tongue-in-cheek the test is loads of fun for everyone. The famous hypnotist, the late Franz Polgar also featured this test in his show.

403

Ormond McGill demonstrating his X-ray-vision glasses

Chapter Fifty-Nine
The Great Hollywood Motion Picture Screen Test

In relation to hypnotic routines, using the principle of "important premise" as the basis upon which your suggestions of various actions are to be performed increases the intensity of responses in stage hypnotism demonstrations. The "Great Motion Picture Screen Test" provides an example of this handling.

Tell the group of hypnotised subjects on stage that they are in Hollywood having a screen test of their acting ability and, if they do well they will get an important part in a movie. Most people would like to star in a motion picture, so this provides strong basic motivation to act out with enthusiasm the various situations suggested.

Impersonation of Favourite Movie and TV Stars

Tell the subjects that when you tell them to start acting for this movie test they are each to impersonate their favourite movie or TV actor. The girls are to impersonate a female star of their choice and the boys a male star. Say in a commanding voice: "Ready ... lights ... cameras ... action, now!" and the test starts. Each subject goes into their respective acting bit. The test fills the stage with action, and in some cases the impersonations are remarkably good. Tell them they are doing really well. Hypnotics are in a highly suggestible mood, and they like to be complimented. To end the group test, shout: "*Sleep!*" and the hypnotics immediately stop all action and return to trance.

Being Great Movie Lovers

There is romance in the soul of Man. Audiences love this test. The screen test continues: Tell the subjects that when you say "*Go!*" they are to act out the role of being the most romantic lover they have ever seen upon the screen. You will find that, as the action starts on stage with the group, one suggestion of a situation will suffice for its performance, and some subjects will even strive to outdo the others on stage. Say: "*Go!*" and the romance starts. Say: "Back to sleep!" and it stops on the instant.

To end the test, suggest that they rest now, and that when you place the mike before their mouth they will express out loud what the word "love" means to them. Go to each subject down the row, and ask each in turn, to say what love means. The responses will be many and varied, depending on the personality of the subject, from straight-out sex to romantic rapture, and some into even spiritual interpretation. This inner searching of the inner meaning of love to the various participants is fascinating to the audience.

Impersonation of Their Personal Jobs

The movie test continues. Subjects are told that they are next to pantomime the actions of the jobs they work at in their daily activity, whatever such may be. They are to act it out so effectively that the director can guess what the job is. Ready, set go ... the action starts. All manner of things take place on stage as the subjects pantomime their respective line of work. The audience has a lot of fun trying to guess what such may be. To end the test, go to each in turn with mike and have them tell what their job is. This handling increases audience appreciation of the skills the subjects are demonstrating.

Then it is back to sleep.

Impersonation of Various Things in Operation

Finally, as a studio test, the subjects are to impersonate the operation of various gadgets, such as a washing machine, typewriter, egg beater, jackhammer, computer, etc. All manner of things can be suggested. Then do down the line and tell each subject, in turn, what object they are to impersonate when you say: "Start theopera". Say it and the fun begins. Telling the subjects that they are things could be belittling, but as an impersonation it becomes clever. The "Great Movie Screen Test" is sensational entertainment. It was designed by the famous Australian hypnotist, Martin St James, and is packed with sparkling show-business. To end the test, have all subjects return to sleep and state that they all did excellently. The producer is well satisfied with their talents, and they will be notified when the screening is to start. Then tell them to forget all about the screen test they have taken and to just sleep on peacefully ready to carry on with the show.

Chapter Sixty
Ideas From the
Jerry Valley Show

NOTE TO HYPNOTIST: This and the following two chapters present a brief résumé of the work of three successful stage hypnotists. This is valuable study as it brings to mind the adage of show-business: "It is not what you do that is important: it is how you do it." In this consideration of the work of Jerry Valley, Pat Collins and Martin St James, the great flexibility of hypnotic presentation stands out. Each of these performers is outstandingly successful in his or her work, and yet each works in a very different presentational style. The important point is that each is an original. An original has great value while a copy has little. As an example, consider an original work of art. An original Van Gogh sells for several million dollars while a copy (even if expertly done) would be luck if it sold for fifty. Take this fact to heart if you would be outstanding in your work. Be an original.

Jerry Valley is one of the busiest hypnotists in the business. Billed as "America's Most Captivating Hypnotist", he is a performer of high charisma. He works throughout the continental United States and on the High Seas on luxury cruise ships. In addition to his stage work, he conducts a Clinic of Hypnotherapy at his office suite in Methuen, Massachusetts.

As a stage hypnotist, Jerry Valley has three completely different full evening shows. The variety of entertaining material the stage hypnotist has at his or her command is great, as every aspect of human interest can be utilised.

Jerry Valley works full stage with enough chairs to accommodate from twelve to twenty subjects, depending on the situation. Following a brief introduction about hypnotism, the committee of volunteers is invited on the stage. This performer wastes little time on preliminaries and performs an immediate induction on the volunteers using a method such as this:

The Rhythmic-Breathing Hypnotising Method

The row of seated subjects are requested to relax and to breathe deeply in unison, as indicated by the performer. Standing before the group, the hypnotist extends his arms out with the palms of his hands turned upwards. As he raises his extended arms upward the subjects are to inhale; as he lowers his arms they are to exhale. Thus the breathing is controlled by the hypnotist in a rhythm he establishes. As background to the breathing, music is played which has a distinct up-and-down rhythmic pattern. Accordingly, the performer can gauge his gestures of inhaling and exhaling to match the rhythm of the music. The effect is powerful.

The directing of the group's breathing is continued up to a dozen times, causing an over-oxygenation of the subjects which produces a dizzying state. The group is then told to close their eyes and to continue breathing in the same rhythm (the music in the background ensures that this is maintained).

It is now suggested that as they continue breathing with their eyes closed each person will pass down into a deep hypnotic state. The hypnosis is then deepened by the operator, stating: "When I tap you on the top of your head you will go limp and relaxed in your chair, and will go sound to sleep." The performer then goes down the line tapping each head in turn, resulting in a general slumping in the chairs. Any subjects who prove resistant are quietly requested to leave the stage. Further deepening suggestions of: "Sleep, deep sleep. You are going sound to sleep ..." etc. are then given completing the stage induction.

Some Jerry Valley Hypnotism Show Routines

The Funny TV Show

Following the induction, Jerry Valley starts his show on a full stage action test productive of much laughter. Laughter is entertainment. Laughter is enjoyed by everyone. It is suggested that when each hypnotised person on stage is tapped on the shoulder they will open their eyes and will be watching the funniest TV show they have ever seen. They will be convulsed with laughter at the funny antics on the screen. "Are you agreeable to this? If so, nod your head." Jerry asks the hypnotics. The subjects nod their heads, and the test is ready to proceed with perfect response, as it has been subconsciously agreed to so respond before the actual test is demonstrated.

One by one the subjects are touched, open their eyes, and the action begins. This handling approaching each subject in turn to elicit a respons works well; and as the test proceeds the laughter mounts until the entire stage is filled with laughing subjects. To end this opening group demonstration, returning to sleep is suggested: the subjects close their eyes and return to a quiescent state.

> NOTE TO HYPNOTIST: This "Laughing at a TV Show" hypnotic demonstration is a good one to begin the show with, as it is entertaining to the audience and gets the subjects started to action. Basically it is productive of an hallucination which leads to an emotional response (laughter). This is productive of somnambulism. And laughter is contagious: the more the subjects laugh the more the audience laughs, and the more the audience laughs the more the subjects laugh. It is a circling of behaviour. Hypnotised persons, as stars of the show, instinctively like to please the audience before whom they are performing.

The "Pinching Butt" Test

This is a funny stunt, but it must be performed with tongue in cheek as good natured fun so as not to prove offensive. In presenting a demonstration of this kind, much depends on the place and situation in which it is shown. The posthypnotic suggestion is given that when the subjects hear the performer say the word "radio" they will experience the sensation that someone seated next to them has pinched their butt. It will be explained that while they will not get angry they will be annoyed, as they do not appreciate this intimacy.

The subjects are then aroused from the hypnosis. The performer turns to the audience and mentions that he heard a most interesting news commentary on his radio (emphasise the word radio) last night. Immediately a squirming and annoyed reaction will occur among the subjects seated in a row on the stage. On asking what is the matter it is explained that they got pinched. Shrugging it off, again the performer mentions the word radio to the audience, and again the pinching reaction occurs amongst the group. Play the situation up for laughs but do not overdo it. Finally, the test is ended by returning the subjects to trance by the command "Sleep!" and a sweeping gesture of the hand encompassing the group.

The "Seat With No Bottom" Test

This is a ludicrous test that can be performed with one subject or a group. The subject is told that when he tries to sit down he will find that he has no bottom to sit upon. It is a bewildering situation. A chair is placed centre stage if working with a solo subject, or the group of subject can be requested to stand and, following the suggestion of "having no bottom to sit upon", they attempt to reseat themselves. It is a dilemma to be solved, and the individual way the subjects attempt to solve this paradox provides hilarious entertainment. Keep the test playful. Ending the test, the subject is entranced again, told that he has a bottom to sit upon okay. On being aroused,he returns to his seat in the group and sits without difficulty.

A tag to the performing may be added, if desired, by suggesting to the responsive subject, just as he goes to take his seat that his knees will not bend and that he cannot sit down try hard as he will. It is a humorous situation. The test is ended by the removal of the suggestion, and the subject taking his seat.

The "Lie Detector" Test

This is a Jerry Valley specialty. It is an astonishing hypnotic demonstration as it illustrates how subconscious (ideomotor) response signals operate to reveal whether a person is telling the truth or is lying in answering questions. It makes a splendid group test with several subjects standing in a row centre stage.

Tell the group of hypnotised subjects, with their eyes closed, that they will be asked, each in turn by a touch upon the head, various questions to which they know the answers. They may answer these questions either truthfully or untruthfully, as they wish. Then explain that if they tell the truth they will remain peaceful and quiet, but if they tell a lie their right ear will itch so irritably they will have to scratch it, as the itching is irresistible.

Then ask each subject, in turn, various personal questions to which they know the answer, such as what is the colour of their car; what is their telephone number; in which city were they born; how old are they, etc. If they tell the truth they will remain quiet, but if they lie they will be compelled to scratch their ear.

Go down the group asking each to answer a question, either lying or telling the truth. Any questions desired may be asked, and the subconscious ideomotor reaction will reveal whether it is true or not via the response suggested.

The test can be varied with the subjects as desired, by having the girls lift the forefinger of the right hand if they tell a lie, while the boys start to squirm in their seats when a lie is told. Design the truth or untruth response signals any way you find most entertaining. The test is both a riot and immensely thought- provoking at one and the same time. Psychology in action.

Two Novelty Items Used by Jerry Valley

Finished files are the result of years of scientific study combined with the experience of many years.

(Read the above sentence and count the Fs).

How many "Fs" can you count in this sentence?

Tonight we take you into the Amazing World of Hypnosis with

Jerry Valley

Stare at the three dots on the bridge of the nose for one minute without blinking then stare at a blank space on the wall or ceiling and you will see America's Most Captivating Hypnotist

Project the image of the hypnotist upon the wall

A set of these cards is placed on each seat in the auditorium before the show starts.

Each spectator gets a set. On occasion, Jerry Valley uses these as an "ice-breaker" to start the show on. They are fun to do. On one card you are to try to discover how many "Fs" you can find. Try it and see. On the other card, a reversed picture of the hypnotist is given. Perform as instructed and a projected "afterimage" is formed. With your name and address printed on the back of each card, these provide good advertising for future engagements.

Chapter Sixty-One
Ideas From the Pat Collins Show

Pat Collins is one of America's best-known stage hypnotists. Her show has been seen by thousands in personal appearances and by millions on television. Her performance radiates professional show-business, albeit somewhat on the risqué side, as befits the night club situations in which she most frequently performs and her billing as "The Hip Hypnotist".

Pat Collins is a fast-talking woman with a masterful personality who immediately takes charge of her audience. She commands attention and holds spectator interest. That is expert showmanship. As she often performs in a cabaret lounge situation, in which stage space is relatively limited, she uses a small committee of from six to eight persons in the audience who will become hypnotised during her show. Sometimes such persons are invited to join the group on the platform, or else are awakened in the audience to enjoy the show.

As a background to her act, she employs a three-piece combo to furnish music as required during the action of her show. The musicians are well cued. Formerly a singer, she makes use of songs occasionally for added interest. She works with a microphone and likes surrounding the audience in sound: she has speakers placed in front of the stage, directed at the audience in the packed room, and at the sides of the stage for committee coverage.

Pat Collins enters briskly to centre stage and presents her personable introduction to the show, in which she explains the nature of hypnosis, what experiences the volunteers will have when they enter hypnosis, and what the audience can expect to witness as entertainment. She is very direct and honest. Her introduction, in detail, is given in Chapter Six of this text.

Following her introduction, Pat Collins invites persons to come up on stage and be hypnotised, via her classic line: "Come on stage and sleep with me." The chairs are quickly filled, and immediately she goes into a hypnotisation of the group. She uses a rapid form of progressive-relaxation technique related to the following description of the method.

413

The "Progressing to Sleep" Hypnotising Method

Face committee and say: "All right, everyone, let's all try the experience of entering hypnosis together. You have come on stage for the purpose of being hypnotised, so here is your opportunity to get hypnotised. You will find it a very pleasant experience, so everyone give undivided attention and concentrate. You will become hypnotised.

"All ready. Relax in your chairs, place your feet flat on the floor and rest your hands in your lap. Now direct your eyes fixedly at me and you will find your eyes quickly becoming heavy and tired. I will count slowly from one to ten, and by the time I reach ten your eyes will be closed and you will go to sleep, yet you will continue to hear me and will follow my suggestions at all times."

Gesture towards the committee, while giving the suggestions. This appears dramatic to the audience as well as holding the attention of the subjects. Make sweeping passes with your hands. Repeat the committee encompassing gestures over and over until everyone's eyes are closed.

"Notice how pleasant and relaxed you begin to feel throughout your entire body. You will note a sensation of warmth growing all about you, and your eyes feel heavy and tired. All right, I will count slowly from one to ten now, and with every count your eyes will close more and more, so by the time I reach the count of ten, or before, close your eyes down tight together and shut out the light. Ready. One … two … three … four … eyes closing all down tight … Five … six … seven. Close your tired eyes and let them rest. Eight … nine … *ten*. Eyes all closed together shutting out the light. Eyes all closed tight!"

Glance over the entire committee; all subjects' eyes should be closed. Continue: "It feels so good to close those tired eyes. So good, and they are so tightly closed you cannot open them try as hard as you will. See how tightly they are shut together. See how they stick."

In working with the entire committee as a unit, do not make an issue of this "eyelid fixation" but continue directly on: "Forget all about your eyes now and go to sleep. Go sound to sleep. You are dropping down, down deeply to sleep. Sleep. Go sound to sleep. Your breaths are deepening as you drop down to sleep. Breathe deep and free, and every breath you take sends you down deeper and deep to sleep. You are completely relaxed and your head falls forward on your chest and, as your head falls forward, you drop off into deep hypnotic sleep. [Head falls forward onto chest by all subjects; any who do not respond to this action are quietly dismissed. If someone in the audience has responded, that person is invited to come on stage and fill the emptied chair.] You are in hypnosis and will follow instantly my every suggestion."

NOTE TO HYPNOTIST: Observe how this induction compounds one series of suggestions upon another: first, eye closure and dropping asleep; second, breath deepening, producing sleep; third, bodily relaxation and head falling forward on chest; fourth, the suggestion that all suggestions will be responded to immediately. This is a progressive-relaxation method of hypnotising that Pat Collins performs rapidly, directly to the point. She wastes no time and her show is paced for action.

Pat Collins now goes to each hypnotised person in turn and lifts an arm straight up in the air with the command that it is stiff and rigid and they cannot move it; that they cannot lower it try as hard as they will. If anyone lowers their arm that person is immediately dismissed. The emptied chair is immediately filled with another responsive volunteer. All subjects with their arms rigidly upright and unable to move (Pat pulls on each to ascertain the rigidity) are retained. She then suggests:

"All persons with their arm upraised are in hypnosis, and at the count of 'three' your arm will instantly fall relaxed to your side and when it hits your side you will be in deep hypnosis. You will forget all your inhibitions and just have a good time. Just let yourself go! Be prepared to have a free and easy swing time. You will instantly respond to everything I tell you." The count is made, and all arms drop on the moment. The show is ready to roll à la Pat Collins's fast-paced routining.

NOTE TO HYPNOTIST: Observe how the Pat Collins's handling "mentally sets" the subjects to respond rapidly to her suggestions. Further, that suggestions given to hypnotised persons should be clear and direct. Right on target! Pat Collins works on the somnambulistic level of hypnosis, causing the subjects to respond quickly. She expects such reactions, and obtains such accordingly. She often likes to feature the reactions of one subject at a time. When working with a small group in limited stage space, this works splendidly. By way of example, she will call a subject by name, as we'll now see.

The "Hot Seat" Test

The hypnotist asks the names of the various hypnotised persons on stage. This establishes verbal responses from the subjects during tests, a device Pat Collins frequently employs. As her group is small, this establishing of names is accomplished quickly. Touching the head of a subject, she calls the person by name: "Fred, you are sitting on a hot seat!" Fred leaps up! Touch another subject: "Susan, hot seat!" Up goes Susan. Each subject, as called by name, jumps up from their "hot seat". Finally all are commanded to go back to sleep.

> NOTE TO HYPNOTIST: "Sleep" in the show is the equivalent of return to hypnosis. Observe how in the show action is heaped upon action. Pat Collins presents her suggestions in a staccato manner.

A subject is then aroused, and Pat holds a conversation asking the party whether or not they feel they were hypnotised? The response is interesting, as many do not actually know whether they were hypnotised or not. She assures them they were, and suddenly exclaims: "Sleep!" The subject immediately collapses in her arms. She says: "Open your eyes, Don, and look at me. Say, you're naked, Don!" The reaction is immediately to cover private parts, or run to hide behind a chair. Instantly she will say: "You are not naked, Don. I am!" The subject ogles her. She says: "Return to your chair and go to sleep, Don." The test is complete. Pat Collins's show is very personal.

Sexy Reactions

Pat Collins likes to include sexual implications in her show. Such fits the nightclub audience in which she specialises. Using her staccato approach, she will, for instance, say to a hypnotised girl: "Sit still, sister, and watch your boobs grow." Or, she will tell an attractive woman to go and passionately kiss her boy friend in the audience. Sometimes she brings the couple on the stage, so the audience can better enjoy what is going on. She may even suggest that the girl's lips are stuck to the man's and she can't break free. After the amusing reaction: "Now you can. Your lips are free. But my, that man's breath is awfully bad! Try to kiss him now and see how bad it is." The girl's reaction is disgusted aversion. Such a test is always concluded with the removal of the suggestion, and a return to sleep.

The "Missing Finger" Test

This is a favourite routine in Pat Collins's show. A subject is brought to centre stage and aroused with the suggestion that while they were asleep someone in the audience stole one of their fingers, and when they count their fingers they will find that finger number six is missing. The subject counts his fingers, and finds to his dismay that number six is gone. Pat then points to someone in the audience, stating: "That man out there has your finger. Demand its return; even plead for it, if need be."

The ensuing tableau is lots of fun for the audience. Really quite dramatic! Finally, she tells the man in the audience to return the missing finger. Obligingly the man pretends to do so. The subject is delighted. Pat tells him to replace the missing finger, and to count them. The subject counts his fingers finding all ten now in proper order. Everyone is happy, and the subject is returned to sleep.

Serious Hypnosis Consideration

As a central segment to her show, Pat Collins breaks away for some moments from antics to a serious consideration of hypnosis, as is used for hypnotherapeutic work. She demonstrates how pain can be controlled by having each subject hold out a hand. It is suggested that all hands will be immune from pain, and she runs the flame of a match beneath the palm of each. A body cataleptic test of one subject is then performed. The subject being placed suspended as a bridge between two supports. The test concluded, the show then continues on into its lighter side.

Concluding Her Show

Making full use of her three-piece combo, she has the fellows play different kinds of music, and the subjects on stage dance in various manners according to the nature of the music, i.e. Hawaiian music, the hula; classical music, ballet; rock and roll and so on. This fills the stage with diversified music and actions in the entire group participating. Always the showman, Pat Collins keeps her hand upon the pulse of the public, and the tests she presents are in keeping with the tempo of the times.

Drawing Made in 1560 A. D., Showing the Dancing Mania, a Form of Mass Insanity Which Afflicted Thousands in Europe at That Time.

Hypnosis, in one form or another, has always been with us

Chapter Sixty-Two
Ideas From the Martin St James Show

Martin St James hails from Australia, and is Down Under's most popular hypnotist, having played repeated tours of the leading cities of that country. In his long career he has hypnotised over 250,000 people on stage and on Australian television. His box office records have outstripped many of the world's "superstars". A young man of great vigour he presents his show in a mod manner. His dress, his style, his hypnotic presentation directly appeals to the "rock" generation. He is the Elvis of stage hypnotists.

Martin St James works with a line of twenty or more chairs on his stage. He starts his show is a wham-bang manner directly inviting any and all who want to be hypnotised to come on stage. He is so well known in Australian that no further encouragement is needed. The stage is immediately filled, often to overflowing. He presents a rapid hypnotic induction to the group. If any of the volunteers do not go "under" they are dismissed, and his entire stage is filled with responsive subjects. His stage method of hypnotising the group is related to the method given here.

The "Triple Response" Induction

This method of group hypnotising employs first a response to the Handlocking Test. The handlocking demonstration is performed on the entire group. Then going to each subject in turn, the hypnotist pushes the locked hands forcefully into the subject's lap along with the command: "Close your eyes now tightly together and as your hands hit your lap they will come apart but your eyes will become stuck together so you cannot open them." The result of this handling is to cause a transference of the locked-hands to the locked-eyelid response. Its effects are demonstrated by challenging the member of the committee to open their eyes if they can. They find it impossible to do so. Then comes the third hypnotic response which leads directly into the induction of profound hypnosis. The performer states: "As I pass my hand gently over your locked eyelids they will open, and as they open you will pass down instantly into profound hypnosis with your eyes wide open staring blankly into space." One by one the hypnotist passes down the line of subjects and causes the eyes to open, leaving each subject staring blankly into space. The induction is eerie, as this induction of hypnosis, ending with eyes open, is just the reverse of usual procedures. The hypnotist then completes the induction of the group by suggesting: "Your eyes will close now, and you drop down yet deeper into profound hypnosis."

This is a rapid and spectacular method of group induction on stage, as a triple response: 1. locking the hands; 2. transference from hand locking to eyelid locking; 3. transference to eye open to open eye hypnotic induction. One, Two, Three! And finally the yet further deepening of the hypnosis is the closing of the eyes again and dropping into profound hypnosis. "Profound Hypnosis" will be found a powerful suggestion for the stage hypnotist to employ, as it is conducive to somnambulistic phenomena which is manifested best in profound hypnosis. Martin St James uses it well.

Hypnotic Handling in the Martin St James Stage Show

This hypnotist likes to work with the entire group of hypnotised persons reacting to a suggested dramatic situation all together. This makes for a BIG STAGE SHOW filling the stage with action, as this example:

The "Picnic in the Country" Test

This popular routine suggests to the subjects, as a group, that they are going to take a trip out into the Australian countryside and have a picnic. "Come along with me now and experience the trip." The hypnotist suggests: "We are driving an old jalopy along a bumpy road, and you are jogging up and down. Bump, bump, bump as we go along. You jog up and down with the bumps."

The action starts, and the entire stage full of subjects jog up and down in their seats, as the hypnotic trip in the country moves along. The hypnotist continues: "Okay, open the car door and get ready to get out. We are going to have the picnic on the ground. Boy, you sure are hungry and can hardly wait for the spread."

Subjects respond in accordance to their personal reactions to the suggested situation. Hypnotist continues: "Okay, you feel much better now. But what is this: a cloud is passing across the sun and a wind has sprung up. It is a cold wind. Gosh it is sure getting cold. Darn cold! Maybe you had better bundle up or take cover somehow. It is so cold!"

Subjects respond to the "cold" suggestions, each in their individual way. Hypnotist continues: "Good, the cloud has passed by now and the wind has stopped. It is just right for our picnic now. I will spread out the food on the ground before you. Sit on the ground and start to eat. Help yourself to whatever you enjoy the most."

The picnic action starts. Subjects get out of their chairs, sits upon the stage and begin to apparently eat. Martin St James goes to each person in turn and asks them what they are eating, how it tastes, etc. The spontaneous variety of answers the subjects give is very amusing to the audience. The hypnotist continues: "Hey, what is this? Ants have come and got into the food. Flick them away. Smash them. Get rid of those darn ants."

The subjects respond in all manner of ways to this annoying situation. Finally: "Good. The ants are gone. You had a swell time at the picnic. It is time to go back home now, so get back in your seat in the car and return to sleep."

The subjects arise from the stage floor, retake their seats, and re-enter the sleep-stage of hypnosis. The test is complete, and the subjects ready to perform the next dramatised situation the hypnotist suggests.

Martin St James presents such group situation experiences for his subjects to perform. The hypnotic sequences follow each other in logical order. Such theatrical handling makes a very entertaining show. It is action packed!

The "Horse Race" Test

Speaking to the group of "sleeping" subjects, the performer asks: "How would you like to make some money? If so, nod your head. [All heads nod in agreement.] Okay, we are going to the race track now and to bet on the horses. When I tap you on the shoulder, I will give you a number that is the number of the horse you are betting on. As I give you the number you will go deeper to sleep, and you will remember your number perfectly so you can cheer your horse on when it runs in the race."

The performer goes down the line tapping each on the shoulder and giving a number to each: 1, 2, 3, 4, 5, 6, etc. down the row of subjects until all have a respective number.

It is then suggested that on the word "Go!" they will open their eyes, be at the race track and will cheer their horse on by shouting its number with enthusiasm, and that the louder they cheer the faster their horse will run.

Racing music starts, and the hypnotist shouts: *"Go!"* The crowd go wild in cheering on their horse, which the performer encourages by describing, in race commentator style, the scene, calling out the various horses, as they take the lead, etc. The action is played up. Finally, the race is ended with a "photo finish", so no horse is declared a winner; however, the track commission agrees to give each person $500 as their share of winnings. The hypnotist goes to each person in turn and presents them with hallucinated money. The money is grabbed eagerly.

As a tag to the scene, the performer states that there are pickpockets amongst the crowd at the race track, so they had better hide their money away, in as safe a place about their person as possible. It is a lot of fun for the audience to watch the "tucked away" places that are used. All money safely stowed away, the subjects are told to go back to sleep, and the race track scene is complete a la a Martin St James presentation.

The Hypnotic Band

Martin St James uses the same principle of improvisation in his "Hypnotic Band" presentation. It has proved a popular number in his show. In this test, the group of hypnotised subjects are told that they are musicians in a band, and each person will play his favourite instrument when give the command to play.

On command, all start to play, interpreting their instrument each in his or her original way. Some play drums, others a trumpet, trombone, piano, etc. It is a riot to watch, and is an hypnotic demonstration much enjoyed by the spectators.

The hypnotist then goes to each subject in turn and asks them to state what instrument they are playing. Speaking into a mike, each subject names his or her instrument. The use of speech applied to hypnotic tests often increases entertainment value.

For a finale to the demonstration, the hypnotised subjects, each still playing their imaginary instrument, take a march around the theatre, finally returning to the stage, instructed to take a seat and return to sleep. It's a fun test all the way. Appropriate band music (Sousa, for instance) used as a backup to the hypnotic "musicians" completes the production.

NOTE TO HYPNOTISTS: What is to be especially learned from Martin St James's handling of the hypnotism show is the freedom afforded the subjects in allowing them to react to the suggestions in their own individual ways, in accordance with their personalities. Only the rudiments of the situation are suggested, the reactions to such being spontaneous by each individual. No attempt is made to tell the subjects how to react. They react entirely as they elect. This lends great variety to the hypnotism show. Each show is different, each group test then becomes an individual tableau of reactions. Hypnotic improvisation holds great routine-developing potential for the stage hypnotist. Martin St James is to be congratulated for using it so effectively.

Two photos showing hypnotised subjects as imaginary musicians

Chapter Sixty-Three
Dr Flint's Hypnotic Routines Modernised

Public interest in hypnotism is today at a zenith. Hypnotherapists flourish in every community. Pioneer stage hypnotists such as Dr Flint can well be thanked for contributing to an art which has become a science.

Dr Herbert L. Flint was one of the all-time greats of American hypnotists who toured the country with his full-evening stage show at the end of the eighteenth century.

In the book *Leaves From the Note-Book of a Hypnotist*, Eugene F. Baldwin and Maurice Eisenberg give an eye-witness account of the performances of Dr Flint. They toured with Flint to investigate hypnotism, and their descriptions furnish the most complete record of a Victorian hypnotism show extant. Long out-of-print, the book has become a rare collectable.

As the hypnotic routines of Herbert Flint are from an era long gone, it is obvious that they are now out-of-date in many ways; however, basically they are as entertaining as ever when modernised. I present them in this manner. You literally have an entire hypnotism show here. It is so old it is new. The modern hypnotist may well find ideas here that he can directly incorporate into his current shows. Here is a report on Dr Flint's routines:

The show began with the hypnotist entering briskly to the centre of the stage and delivering a brief discourse on hypnotism, following which a request for volunteers to come upon the stage was made. Twenty volunteers were secured and seated in a semi-circle facing the audience.

Dr Flint then passed around the group, stroking each one's head and forehead, repeating the phrases: "Close your eyes. Think of nothing but sleep. You are very tired. You are drowsy. You feel very sleepy, etc." Thus the committee was hypnotised by the verbal suggestion method.

When the Doctor had completed his round and had manipulated all of the volunteers, some of those influenced were nodding, some were sound asleep, while a few were still awake and smiling at the rest. These latter were dismissed as unlikely subjects.

When the stage had been cleared of all those who were not susceptible, suggestions were then given to the hypnotics that they would be responsive to all of the experiments, and the Doctor then passed around quickly to each individual and awoke him.

The committee was now wide awake. Dr Flint then took each subject in turn and had each perform a different waking suggestion test, such as fastening the eyelids together so they would not open, falling over backward, stiffening an arm or a leg, etc. These were interesting phenomena for the audience to watch as they gave an insight into the personality of each individual subject by the manner in which they reacted to the test performed upon them. To conclude this opening portion of his show, the Doctor performed a group "Hand Clasping Test" on the entire committee at the same time, as he repeated the suggestions: "Think of your hands being locked so tightly together that you cannot pull them apart. They are stuck fast. You cannot pull them apart. Try, try hard, but you cannot." All in the committee made frantic efforts to unclasp their hands, but were unable to do so.

The Doctor explained to the audience that this illustrated what the French psychologist, Baudouin, referred to as the "Law of Reversed Effort", i.e. that the extreme effort the subjects were putting into trying to get their hands apart was actually producing the effect of holding them all the more tightly together. (Psychologists now regard this as a pseudo-law. However, it is often quoted to illustrate the point – McGill.) Again facing the struggling subjects, the Doctor snapped his fingers and the subjects' hands came apart. One subject was then brought forward to the front of the stage and hypnotised.

It was suggested that he would not be able to smoke cigarettes for twenty-four hours. The subject was then awakened and he was given a cigarette to try. He took one in his mouth; it made him ill and he flung it away with every expression of disgust.

An experiment was now presented in which the subjects were instructed to rotate their hands around and around each other. As they whirled around faster and faster, the Doctor suggested that they could not stop; that the more they tried to stop them, the faster they would go. Finally, with a command and a snap of his fingers he stopped the rotation. This experiment was performed as a waking suggestion test.

Dr Flint then approached a subject and pointed his finger. The subject began to look steadily before him, at which the rest of the group was highly amused. Presently, the subject's head leaned forward, the pupils of his eyes dilated and assumed a peculiar glassy stare. Under Dr Flint's suggestions he arose from his chair and, following the pointing finger, marched with a steady, gliding gait to the front of the stage. The subject's eyes were staring blankly into the audience. Dr Flint took a lighted match and moved it in front of the subject's eyes which remained unblinking. It was most impressive. A pass of the Doctor's hand and the subject closed his eyes, and was left standing in a profound sleep. This was repeated on half a dozen subjects; the manifestations were the same in each case.

Those selected were now drawn up in an irregular line in the front of the stage. Each was then given a suggestion. One was to be a newsboy and sell papers. Another was given a broomstick and told it was a gun, and he was to hunt in the woods before him. Another was given a large rag doll and told that it was a baby, and that he must look among the audience and find its father. He was informed that he could tell who the father was by the similarity and colour of the eyes. Another was told that he was at the college prom and he was to go out and ask the young women courteously for a dance. Another was told that he was a small lost child and would go crying into the audience looking for his mama, and the sixth subject was told that he was a candy, hot dog and soda-pop hawker who was to go out among the audience and sell his wares.

The command was then given that each subject would open his eyes still in deep hypnosis, and the whole party were started off at once and together. They walked down the steps extending from the stage and mingled with the audience. The one who was impersonating a newsboy went about crying his edition in a loud voice; while the hunter crawled along stealthily and carefully. The newsboy even adapted the well-worn device of asking those whom he solicited to buy to help him get rid of his stock. One man offered him a nickel for a paper, when the price was ten cents. The newsboy sarcastically asked him if he didn't "want the earth".

While this was transpiring, the hunter was engaged in the pursuit of game. He was utterly oblivious of the people in the seats, and, whereas the newsboy had accosted them and argued with them, the hunter seemed to regard them as so many stumps of trees. He searched diligently, and when he had found a bird, carefully flushed it, and, as it rose into the air, he took steady aim at it with his broomstick and apparently fired, for he acted as though he felt the recoil. Then he picked up the imaginary bird and placed it in a side pocket. He then resumed the hunt, peering about, walking carefully along, searching everywhere to the right and left.

During all of this time, the one with the rag-doll was engaged in looking for its father. He sought out every adult man in the audience and carefully compared the doll's eyes, placing the doll against the face of the man in many instances, and looking at them several times. He finally discovered one man whose eyes answered the description, and the look of earnestness changed to one of complete and serene satisfaction, as he placed the doll into the man's arms and turned away.

The other three subjects performed with equal earnestness; the one gallantly asking each young girl who attracted his fancy if he might be favoured with a dance, the other crying through the audience looking for his mother, and the sixth subject loudly hawking his wares as he passed amongst the spectators, calling: "Candy, hot dogs, soda pop. Who wants to buy some candy, hot dogs, soda pop?" The performance was a veritable *Hellzapoppin*!

After the fun had continued long enough, Dr Flint, standing in the centre of the stage, commanded the subjects to march back on stage and form a line. This they did, eyes staring blankly out to the audience. The Doctor passed his hand in front of each subject and they closed their eyes, and he ended the routine by waking each in turn. They acted precisely like persons suddenly aroused from profound sleep.

All subjects again seated in the semicircle, Dr Flint passed to each in turn and instantly put them to sleep in deep hypnosis. The subjects were told that the end of a small riding whip was a bar of hot iron. One by one he touched the subjects with the end of the whip. The moment the subject felt the whip he jumped and shrieked as if it were really a hot iron. Each exhibited the utmost pain and fear. It was an impressive test. (Impressive as it undoubtedly was, I do not personally recommend that the hypnotist make use of such tests that produce pain and fear. These are best avoided, and also such stunts as passing needles through the flesh, etc. The hypnotism show in our modern day is under enough criticism already without heaping coals upon the fire. Further, it must be remembered that the subjects have volunteered to take part in the performance in good faith and there is not reason to inflict distress upon them, even if it is only illusionary. It is my personal recommendation that all hypnotic routines involve situations that are pleasant and interesting to the subjects – McGill.)

Three subjects were then told to play marbles. Two of them were large men, while the third was a small boy. They began the game in good faith. But presently the small boy stole the marbles of the big players and, when they protested, he threatened to thrash them. They both blubbered and went about begging for their marbles.

A number of subjects were told that they were watching a baseball game, and they experienced all the excitement and enthusiasm one would expect from a baseball fan, even to the point of arguing with each other about the capabilities of the imagined participating players. They offered to bet. They perched on their chair-backs in their excitement. They groaned at the imaginary umpire and they cheered the players at the imaginary successful runs. They argued about the rules, and at the suggestion of a "home run" they went wild with enthusiasm. The baseball enthusiasts were recalled to themselves by the hypnotist, and all the subjects were ready for the next test.

This was that of bees. A swarm of bees came by and, after buzzing in the air overhead, they lighted upon the subjects. Their frantic efforts to escape, their blows and dodges were exciting to see, for each one, even in this, exhibited his own individuality. Some fought the bees quietly while others took off their hats and chased the bees about the stage. (Here again is an example of the type of "painful test" that it is well for the modern hypnotist to avoid. Stage hypnotists of the "old school" used to make much use of such distressing experiments as the action is intense. However, they have little place in the repertoire of the modern hypnotist – McGill).

Then one of the subjects was told that he was a vegetable salesman. He mounted his imaginary truck and, with a voice that rivalled a fog-horn, began shouting: "Lettuce, asparagus, cabbage and potatoes for sale!"

Another subject was told that he was a juggler, and he began to juggle imaginary balls with the greatest skill. (In studying Dr Flint's show, it will be noted that some of his effects are currently out-of-date, but at the time they were presented they represented all forms of daily popular activities. Today's hypnotist must do the same, incorporating in his show that which is representative of now! – McGill.)

Performing upon the entire group, Dr Flint then suggested that all of the subjects had rubber noses. Each one began to feel his proboscis, to pull it out and let it go again, to bend it around his cheek, and to fumble it. Some would stretch it out and let it go, and then wait to feel it bounce back.

Two subjects were each given a horse to ride. Seated astride their chairs as though mounted on horses, they urged their horses forward, and it was curious to note their flushed cheeks and strained eyes as they strove to pass each other and go the fastest.

A subject, at the side of the stage, was given a pail of water and told it was a lake. A broomstick was handed him with the suggestion that it was a fine fishing-pole. Sitting down in front of the pail, he held the pole over it. The angler baited the hook and when he had prepared himself he fished. No more attention was paid to him but he fished away with the utmost patience, occasionally rebaiting the hook and removing fish from time to time. It proved a very funny "running gag" used throughout the show. A young man was told that he was a side-show barker in a circus. He at once jumped upon a table and, in a voice typical of the profession, began to expound upon the fat woman, the snake charmer, sword swallower, the wild man from Borneo, and all such attractions that may be seen in such a show. He indulged in side remarks, such as: "This is hot work." He rolled up his sleeves and took off his tie, all the while expatiating upon the merits of the freaks inside the tent.

Another laughable test was performed in which a tall young man was given a broom and told that it was his sweetheart. He accepted the suggestion and sat down by the broom. At first he was shy, but eventually he grew bolder. In a moment of confident response to his courtship, he clasped her around the waist and planted a kiss upon the brushy part of the broom. He was so absorbed in his love-making that he continued to hug the broom completely deaf to the roars of laughter from the audience.

Dr Flint then, using all of the subjects, introduced his big-circus act, in which each subject was given a part to perform in the circus. One was the ringmaster, others were clowns, another was an acrobat, still another a posturist, another a bareback rider and so on. The bareback rider mounted his phantom steed. Every now and then he would leap upon his steed (a table), and apparently ride around the ring. He jumped through make-believe hoops; he pirouetted and stood on one leg and balanced himself, kissing his hand to the audience all the while. The clowns cracked their jokes, varying their wit by turning hand-springs. The posturer started with Rodin's "The Thinker". His poses and attitudes were most laughable. All of the subjects acted out the parts that had been suggested to them. Each performer followed out his own suggestion, and yet there was no confusion.

It was – in truth – a veritable "three-ring circus". One after another the Doctor restored the subjects to their normal condition, and they returned to their seats in the audience. Finally only the bareback rider was alone on the stage. He made one grand spring from his steed, and the Doctor awakened him and dismissed him from the stage amidst terrific applause from the audience.

As a climax to his show, Dr Flint then introduced his daughter and placed her in a deep cataleptic trance. Her entire body was made rigid and she was lain on two supports, one at her neck and the other at her ankles.

A sheet was next draped over her body and a soft rug on that. Dr Flint then invited a man up from the audience to stand upon her cataleptic body, and, for a sensational finish to the test, a large rock was placed on the girl's body. A local blacksmith came on the stage with a ponderous sledge hammer. He swung it in the air bringing it down with all his might upon the stone that lay on the girl. Again and again the massive sledge rained blows upon the rock, while the girl lay like a statue. At last the great rock broke under the blows, each piece falling to the floor with a resounding crash.

The Doctor then stepped to the side of his daughter and lifted her to her feet. He passed his hand lightly in front of her form, and she slowly awoke, looked at the shattered fragments of the rock and smiled at the audience. The blacksmith left the stage shaking his head in wonderment. The curtains slowly closed, and Dr Flint's great show was ended.

NOTE TO HYPNOTIST: There is a secret to the successful presenting of hypnotic routines of the magnitude of Dr Flint's, which may be summed up in the one word, "prestige". By prestige is meant a "sold-in-advance" audience acceptance of the performer and his show that motivates the subjects to do their best to be successful hypnotics. Such motivation brings brilliance to the hypnotism show. When the performer has a reputation and/or is recognised as an outstanding hypnotist as the result of extended engagements, his prestige will make it possible for him to present all manner of hypnotic tests. Conversely, if his work is such that it does not carry this prestige factor so that he literally has to sell his ability as a hypnotist, both to the subjects and the audience, on the spot, as it were, while under fire in actual performance, then he had best omit too complicated tests and content himself with effects more readily produced that he has confidence in and is sure of. The successful stage hypnotist is the adroit showman who correctly sizes up his audience, subjects and performing situation, and adapts his show accordingly. Such is one of the arts of stage hypnotism.

Complete body catalepsy with Marina Flint

Chapter Sixty-Four
A Compilation of Hypnotic
Routines from Around the World

In this chapter, you are given some seventy-plus hypnotism show routines that have been successfully featured in shows around the world. There is valuable material here that will help you in designing your own show.

Routines are the entertainment heart of stage hypnotism. Routines are the "stage play" of the show, and your subjects are the actors on the stage. Hypnosis turns them into actors, as you direct them to perform in following your suggestions, and the suggestions you give are to perform your routines.

The hypnotism show is much like legitimate theatre. But there is a big difference. The actors (subjects) perform through subconscious motivation rather than conscious motivation, i.e. they perform spontaneously often without being aware they are performing. Subconscious behaviour is very basic to human nature for we all react to it.

In suggesting an hypnotic routine to his subject(s), the operator must be precise in giving his instructions so there is no doubt as to what is expected. It is interesting how an audience enjoys knowing what is going to occur and then seeing it successfully occur. Hypnotic entertainment features a big question mark: will it occur? When it occurs everyone is delighted, and the satisfaction is phenomenal.

Subjective Response To Routines

The stage hypnotist has to present his routines in a dual role: one to the subjects and one to the audience, and both are given at the same time. In such regard, the performer must be definite in presenting instructions to his subjects on stage. Some subjects are highly creative and only the bare suggestion is sufficient. Other subjects are unimaginative and lethargic. You deal with all kinds of minds in the hypnotism show so, for success in general, Be specific.

433

Some of the routines you will be given can be effectively handled with one subject, worked with several at the same time or demonstrated on the entire committee. It will be found that some tests are most effective when attention is concentrated upon one person, while others are best with the entire committee performing. Experience is your best teacher of presentation.

In presenting each routine to the subject(s) always include in your suggestions a "cue" to cause each suggested operation, such as suggesting: "When I clap my hands such and such will occur." Or: "When I clap my hands such and such will stop occurring." Planting such a "cue" makes it possible to perform hypnotic tests cleanly and emphasise dramatic points of greatest audience impact.

> NOTE TO HYPNOTIST: This giving a "cue" either for the occurrence or termination of an hypnotic command is important to the stage hypnotist. What occurs when such a "cue" is given is a spontaneous deepening of the hypnosis in responding to the "cue." It is very subtle and passes largely unnoticed, however on "cue" the shift of consciousness which is characteristic of hypnosis does occur.

Routining Your Show

Routine your show using the most effective sequences possible. That is the showmanship of programming. The hypnotism show must be good theatre. You have a fine array of material here to work with, so plan your show carefully featuring the best in entertainment.

Whatever routines you elect to perform, learn each thoroughly so you can present each test with polished perfection. Master every suggestion, every gesture, every bit of staging. Rehearse your entire show so it flows along from beginning to end as one continuous unit of smooth entertainment. Precision in presentation is the mark of the polished performer.

A Compilation of Successful Hypnotic Routines

> NOTE TO HYPNOTIST: Stage hypnotism is funny. It produces unsuppressed laughter. It is truly amazing how a simple action that when seen performed in the conscious state would seem silly, when seen performed in an hypnotic state can convulse an audience.

Tell the subject that when he wakes up he will light a cigarette and that when you snap your fingers he will be unable to draw on it, but that he will blow through it instead.

Tell the subject that he will be unable to drink from a glass of water no matter how hard he tries; that he will spill the water all over in the attempt to drink it.

Tell the subject that he cannot light a cigarette no matter how hard he tries.

Tell the subject that he cannot place a cigarette in his mouth no matter how hard he tries until you snap your finger by his ear.

Place the subject's thumb to his nose and tell him he cannot remove it no matter how hard he tries. The "feeling tone" of this stunt is a bit harsh and such a test should only be presented in the proper situation.

Similar to the above test, tell a subject to place a thumb in each ear and that he cannot pull them away no matter how hard he tries.

Tell a subject that when he awakens he will find his shoelace untied (pull the shoelace loose), and that he will be unable to retie it no matter how hard he tries.

As a posthypnotic, tell a woman subject that her name is John Smith, and tell a man that his name is Mary Brown. Awaken the subjects and ask them to introduce themselves by name to each other.

Tell a man subject (who is actually sitting on the stage next to a woman) that his neighbour is a man and that when he wakes up he will ask the party for a cigar. This is very funny.

Tell a woman subject that she is a little girl in school and that she is to recite her favourite little poem to the students.

Give the subject a piece of rope while you explain that it is a lasso, and get him to lasso an imaginary horse.

Tell a woman subject (seated at the side of the stage) that every five minutes she will come up to you and tell you that your face is dirty; she will take her handkerchief and try to wipe it for you.

Give a subject a wax candle and tell him it is a delicious stick of candy. The subject licks it with obvious relish. This test can be varied by suggesting that the candle is a cigar that the subject will smoke. His expression on finding a candle in his mouth, on being awakened, will produce howls of laughter from the spectators.

Toss your wallet upon the floor and tell the subject that it is full of money and he can have it if he can pick it up, but that he cannot do so because his legs are too stiff.

Tell each subject that he is a musician and will play a certain instrument. Each subject is instructed that on "cue" he will play his instrument (each subject being told to perform on a different type of instrument). One subject is given a baton and is told that he is the conductor of the orchestra. The starting signal is given, and the "musicians" start to play. This routine is a great favourite in the Franquin Show.

Give a woman subject a doll, tell her it is her baby and that she will rock and sing it to sleep.

Give a subject a half a lemon and tell him it is an apple. He will eat it with complete enjoyment.

Tell a man that he is a famous opera star and to sing a song for the audience. You can vary this by having him become a pop singer.

Tell a subject that he is happy and to laugh. Now sad and to cry. If you have a very animated subject, you can suggest that he will laugh on one side of this face and cry out of the other.

Tell a subject that when he wakes, he will dash into the audience and go immediately to sleep in his chair. Go after him into the audience. Suggest that you will awaken him at a snap of your fingers, and that he will dash immediately back onto the stage and go to sleep in his chair up there. There is lots of action in this test.

Toss a $20.00 bill on the floor and tell the subject that he can have it if he can pick it up, but that he cannot do so as every time he reaches for the money his hand will take a wide curve away from the bill. It's sensational!

Tell a group of subjects that they are walking in deep snow.

Tell a group of subjects that they will open their eyes and watch a tennis match.

Tell the subject that there is a window in the centre of the stage, that it is stuffy in the room, and that he will go to the window and open it to let in the fresh air. It is very funny to watch the subject open the imaginary window, especially if you unexpectedly suggest that it is stuck and he is having difficulty getting it opened. The pantomime subjects perform while hypnotised can truly be amazing. Do not expect all subjects to be master pantomimists however, as such skills differ with each individual. Use subjects who have proved themselves animated for such tests.

Tell a girl subject that her boy friend will have disappeared when she awakens; that she will look all around trying to find him, and that after the passing of a couple of minutes he will suddenly appear seated beside her.

Tell a group of girl subjects that they are in Hawaii and that they are learning the Hula. When the music starts they will dance. Start the music and watch the fun. It is even more fun if you perform this with a group of men.

Hand subject a broom and tell him it is a beautiful girl; to sweep her up in his arms and dance with her. When the dance is over, have him wave goodbye to her.

Odd and Even Hypnotic Experiments

This is very professional handling and provides good entertainment. It is excellent to use in many hypnotic tests. What is done is to label the subjects odd and even, and tell them to remember which they are. In the course of presenting a group test, you can call out that all of the odd subjects will do such and such and that the even subjects will do such and such. Obviously, this device can be used to great advantage by the stage hypnotist in many ways. Here are examples:

Odd subjects become hot while even subjects become cold.

Odd subjects laugh while even subjects cry.

Odd subjects are Republicans while even subjects are Democrats.

Hypnotist George Singer uses the odd-and-even handling at the very beginning of his show before he even begins hypnotising. The committee seated on the stage, starting at the right hand side, he has each person call out their number, i.e., first person is one, second is two, third is three, and so on. Each person is then asked to remember their number throughout the entire show. Subjects are then hypnotised and the show progresses. He is then all set to use odd-and-even handling any time he wishes. All he has to say is: "All persons with odd numbers will do such and such, and those with even numbers will do such and such."

There is good psychology in this handling also, as it gets the group of subjects involved in taking instructions, right from the very start of the show, from the performer. Likewise, it gives them something to turn their attention to as they must remember their number. Prof. Singer sometimes makes use of these numbers in an additional way by simply stating: "Subject number so-and-so will do this and that" etc. Designating numbers to the subjects gives him ready access to use whatever subject or subjects he wishes for the performance of different tests, as all he has to do is to call out the relevant number(s).

Give a subject a doll and a handkerchief and tell him he is the father and that the baby needs a change of diapers; that he will try to put the diaper on but cannot fasten the pin.

As a posthypnotic suggestion, tell a woman subject that she is displeased with her husband for wearing such loud neckties and that when she awakens she will turn to the man nearest her, whom she will think is her husband, and will give him a lecture about his ties, but that when you snap your fingers she will be unable to utter another word until you say she can speak.

Tell a subject that her shoes hurt and that she has them on the wrong feet; that she must put the left shoe on her right foot and the right shoe on her left foot to make them comfortable. Awaken her. It's a riot when she tries to walk and notices that her shoes are on opposite feet.

Tell a woman subject (who has a purse on the stage beside her) that when she awakens she will not be able to see her purse and will look all around trying to find it.

Tell a subject that there are robbers in the audience and that he has a bundle of $100 bills which you give him (hand him some blank paper slips) and tell him he had better hide the money in his shoes. Then awaken him, and ask him what he has in his shoes.

Tell a subject that he will smoke a cigarette but that when you snap your fingers it will suddenly taste like burning rubber. This is very funny especially when worked with a group of subjects.

Tell a subject that when you snap your fingers his chair will suddenly get hot!

Having hypnotised a group of subjects on the stage, tell them that you will awaken them now, and that you will then leave the room and will hypnotise them from a distance by "telepathy". Awaken the subjects and exit from the room leaving them seated on the stage. As the audience watches, gradually the subjects fall asleep. You then return and wake them up. This is an interesting example of hypnotic misdirection; actually the response has been caused by a posthypnotic suggestion, but you have given another causation to it by seeming to produce the experiment by telepathy from a distance. It is an amazing effect when presented with strong showmanship.

Hand some subjects each a paper plate, and tell them that they are seated in their car and are holding firmly on to the wheel as they speed along. Tell them to be very careful to watch out for pedestrians and speeders on the highway.

Tell the subjects that you are going to give them a treat and present them each with an ice cream cone. Hand an empty cone to each subject, and tell them to start licking the ice cream.

Many variations on the "eating theme" are possible; subjects can go out into the country and have a picnic eating imaginary sandwiches, drinking soda pop, etc. For a climax, suggest that ants are getting into the food and to brush them away quickly.

Give a subject a broomstick and tell him it is a splendid fishing rod and that he is casting in his favourite stream. You can end the test by suggesting that the fishing rod is getting so heavy that he cannot hold it in his hands. He will drop it to the stage. Then suggest that it is so heavy that he cannot pick it up.

Hand a woman subject a bottle of perfume and tell her how much she enjoys it. Suddenly suggest that you made a mistake, that it is a bottle of ammonia. Her reactions are unmistakable.

The reverse of this experiment can also be performed, in which a bottle of ammonia is handed to the subject and she is told it is perfume. She inhales the ammonia fumes with pleasure. I do not personally recommend the test performed in this manner as, although the reaction of the subject is to enjoy the fumes, actually they are not good to inhale. The experiment is just as entertaining performed in the completely harmless manner as outlined in the paragraph above.

Tell the group of hypnotics that they will yawn, yawn, yawn, and be unable to stop yawning. The suggestion is not only effective with the subjects but with the audience as well, many of whom will yawn in unison.

Tell a group of subjects that there are mice all over the floor. The reactions of the girls and even some of the men is most amusing.

Tell a group of subjects that they are dancing at a crowded disco.

Hand a subject a piece of rope and tell him that he cannot tie a knot in it.

As a posthypnotic, tell your subject that after one minute has passed he will find his right shoe is getting very hot, so hot that he will not be able to keep it on; that he will take it off, and that immediately he gets his right shoe off his left shoe will then become hot and will also have to be removed. You can develop even more fun if you suggest, at the same time, that the subject will try not to attract attention to himself unduly while he takes off his hot shoes.

Tell a group of subjects to go into a beautiful garden and pick the flowers. Then to gather up the flowers into a bouquet and to smell their fragrance. Now tell the girls to take the flowers and go down amongst the audience and give a flower to each baldheaded man they see, and that each time they pass out a flower to give the man a kiss on his bald head.

Hand the subject a glass of water and have him take a drink; then suggest that when you snap your fingers it will suddenly taste like sewer water. The kind with the green scum on top and he will spit it out.

Have two subjects (boy and girl) sit facing each other and tell them they are going to hypnotise each other. The performer stands behind them and gives the suggestions. As each gazes into the other's eyes they fall asleep.

I have found it effective to use the above test in combination with the popular "Heavy Chair Experiment". Hypnotist David Tracy gives an excellent routine that runs along these lines:

Suggest to one of the subjects (who have just hypnotised each other) that when you awaken her she will notice a chair that she will try to pick up, but that she will find it weighs over 1,000 pounds and that she cannot lift it no matter how hard she tries. Awaken the subject and she tries to lift the chair in vain.

Now suggest to the boy subject that when you awaken him he will see a girl trying very hard to move a chair and that he will go to her aid to help her lift the chair, but that he will find the chair weighs 1,000 pounds and that he and the girl simply cannot move it no matter how hard they try.

The fun resulting from this situation is obvious. When the subjects find that they cannot lift the chair, you walk over and lift it easily. Tell the subjects to retain their hold on the chair firmly and you let go; it immediately drops back to the stage pulling them down with it.

Hand a subject a sheet of paper and tells him that he cannot tear it no matter how hard he tries.

Tell a subject to grip a pencil; then tell him it has become sticky with glue and that he cannot throw it away from his hands no matter how hard he tries.

Tell a subject that he is stuck to the seat of his chair and that he cannot rise up from it no matter how hard he tries.

Place a coin on the floor and tell the subject he cannot get a grip on it to pick it up.

Tell a subject as a posthypnotic that a candy bar will taste like gasoline when he bites into it. Awaken the subject and show him a bar of candy. Have a girl take a bite of it and ask her how it tastes. She will say: "Fine." Give the bar to the subject to bite into. What a reaction!

Give a subject a hat and tell him it is a dog. That he is to pet and feed it.

Tell a subject as a posthypnotic that he will discover that his nose is made of rubber and will have a lot of fun stretching it out and letting it snap back to his face over and over. Awaken him and leave this subject seated over towards the side of the stage and he will keep stretching his nose and letting it snap back all through the show. Allow the stunt to ride for awhile until you have milked all of the laughs from it, then end the stunt by returning the subject to "sleep".

Hand a subject an empty bottle to hold by its neck. Tell him that it is stuck to his hand and that he cannot drop it no matter how hard he tries.

Have the subject play "patta-cake, patta-cake", as they clap hands with each other. Tell them they are doing it faster and faster, and that they cannot stop until the hypnotist commands them to stop. It's great fun.

As a hypnotist, the late Morris Maxwell (Dr ZORRO) made effective use of this routine in his shows. A male subject was hypnotised and told that he is a glamorous female movie star making up for her appearance at a premiere. A mirror, lipstick, eye shadow, powder and puff is provided. The fun of seeing the man make up his face with woman's cosmetics is terrific. After the laughs have gone on long enough, and while the subject is still looking at himself in the mirror, he is awakened. The surprised reaction is a riot. To end the test, give the subject a towel so he can wipe his face off, assure him it is all in good natured fun, and have the audience give him a big hand.

Hypnotised subjects are each told that they are famous personalities. Identify each subject with a specific personality (give names of people such as movie stars, political figures, popular personalities in the current news). Tell them that when they awaken they will be the person named, and that the audience will applaud them when they are introduced. They are to acknowledge the applause. Awaken each subject and introduce them to the audience by the name of the famous personality you have identified each with while hypnotised. The impersonations are often amazing; this coupled with the audience applause and response to each make this a truly outstanding test.

Movie star hypnotic tests are always entertaining. Here is an effective one. Tell a male subject that one of the women subjects on the stage is a famous star, and that when he awakens he will see her and, although he is shy, he will go over and ask her for a dance. The humour of the situation can be imagined.

Hand the subject a pair of glasses (without lenses) and suggest that they are "comedy glasses", and that when they look through them they will laugh at everything they see.

Related to the above experiment, hand the subject a pair of glasses and state that when he peers through them out at the audience, the glasses will give him X-ray vision and he will be able to see through the clothes of everyone in the audience.

The hypnotist Franz Polgar uses this test most effectively. Another interesting variation is to give each subject a card with a keyhole in its centre and suggests that when they peer through the hole they will see the audience in the nude.

The "nudity scene" can be presented as a posthypnotic effect in which it is suggested to the subject that, when he awakens and sees the performer make a certain gesture (such as snapping his fingers), his clothes will suddenly disappear and he will discover himself naked. His reaction is very humorous. Add to the suggestion that when you snap your fingers his clothes will be on again. You can develop the situation as you wish.

Another humorous variation of this is to suggest that at the snap of your fingers the subject's trousers will have vanished, or that they have fallen down about his ankles and he must retrieve them quickly and secure them in their proper position.

Experiments of this "embarrassing type" are very funny. However, they must be used with wise discretion as to when and where they are appropriate. For example, in a nightclub situation things that would be entirely out of place if shown to a family audience on a public stage are acceptable as entertainment. Even so, good taste must always prevail, and it is especially important that the suggestions do not produce too distressing an experience for the subject. Some persons are sensitive about being seemingly caught in the "nude", as it were and it can be most disturbing and even traumatic for them. To avoid any such tendencies, I advise using these qualifying suggestions to all such tests:

Having hypnotised the subjects, suggest: "We are here in a nightclub all together as friends and the emphasis of the entertainment is on fun. Everyone here, along with yourselves, is in a carefree mood and is out for a good time to enjoy themselves. Whatever you do, whatever happens to you, you will enjoy. Everything that happens is all in fun. The entire show tonight is all for fun. You, right along with the audience, will have a wonderful time and lots of fun, Fun, *fun!*"

NOTE TO HYPNOTIST: When working shows where your suggestions are going to be bold it is important to take the "sting" out of embarrassing situations and place emphasis that it is all done in the spirit of fun, and everyone is having a good time. Further, only present demonstrations of this type in places where such is appropriate.

Get your subjects in a row on the stage and tell them to start clapping their hands. Then tell them that they can't stop clapping, and the harder they try to stop the louder and harder they will clap. There is something about hand clapping that is very rousing to an audience.

Kreston the hypnotist seats two subjects side-by-side, and places an open book between them. He suggests to the subject on the left that what he reads in the book will be very sad and will make him cry. He tells the subject on the right that what he reads in the book will be very funny and will make him laugh. He also suggests that they will be very puzzled by the entirely opposite reactions that each gets from reading the same book. The hilarious situation resulting can be imagined.

There is a valuable point illustrated here in the successful development of hypnotic routines, and that is to combine a variety of reactions together as in the present instance of one subject crying at what he reads, the other laughing at what he reads, and the puzzlement of both over the different reaction that each has. A man and a woman can be effectively used in this test.

Tell the group of subjects that they will laugh at each other.

Give a subject a pillow and tell him it is a crying baby and that as the father he must try to make it stop crying.

Tell a subject that he cannot button his coat or shirt.

Here is an old classic that for laughs is hard to beat. Hypnotise one subject and tell him that he is a mother and you will place her baby on her lap and she will rock it to sleep. Hypnotise another subject and tell him he is the squawking baby. Seat the "baby" on the "mother" and watch the fun. You can also give the "mother" a baby bottle to feed the "baby" if you wish.

Another old hypnotic classic that is very seldom seen these days is to suggest to the hypnotic that his personality is completely changing and that he is becoming a pussy cat. Have the "cat" get down on its knees and crawl about looking for a bowl of milk. Suddenly call: "Here kitty, here kitty." The "cat" will come over to you and rub against your leg, scratch its head and it will start to purr. Tell the subject that his personality is normal again, have him stand up and awaken him.

Needless to say, a test of this nature should only be performed when

conditions are such that there is a carpet on the floor so the subject will not damage his trousers crawling about. Also a young person should be used to whom such an incident will just be good fun. The use of good sense by the performer in deciding when, what and on whom various stunts will be performed is naturally assumed. Very possibly some stunts should never be performed at all.

Tell the hypnotised subject that he is a famous western movie star who is going for a ride on his trusty horse. Seat him backwards in a chair so he is facing the back, as you suggest that he is riding off at a gallop.

As a posthypnotic, tell your subject that every time he sees you touch your forehead he will shout out loud: *"Cuckoo!"* and, having done so, will promptly forget what he has said. Awaken the subject and touch your head. His reaction will get a good laugh. This can go on at intervals throughout the entire stage performance.

Perform a "Three-Ring Circus"

Hypnotise three subjects and have them stand in a row at the centre of the stage. As a posthypnotic, tell each person that he will perform a specific act upon awakening. One is to tie and untie his tie; the second person is to keep combing his hair; the third subject is to keep buttoning and unbuttoning his shirt. When all three subjects are doing something at the same time, it will have your audience in stitches. It is amazing how such simple acts as these performed by hypnotised subjects can produce such laughs and response from an audience, but it is true. Such is one of the real marvels of the hypnotic show as entertainment.

The "Horse Race" test is a riot. Each subject is given the number of a horse in the race and told that they have bet all their money on their horse. On command, the race starts and subjects are to cheer their horse on as each number is called. Start the race with all of the subjects watching and call out the number of the different horses as each takes the lead. Each time you do, the subject cheers on the horse of his number to be the winner. At the end of the race, all horses that they had bet on lost the race and all lose their money. The complete contrast of elation in spurring on their winner to the dejection of losing their money is terrific entertainment. This is a very exciting test, especially if the performer dramatises it "race-track-announcer" style!

Tell subjects that birds are fluttering around in their hair, and that they are to bat at them and shake them out. This is especially funny when using some of the long-haired generation as subjects.

Hypnotists, in the past, used to frequently present a test in which they told their subjects that a swarm of bees was buzzing about their heads, and to swat them off. That was of course very humorous, but the "Birds in the Hair" test is just as funny and is better because bees suggest a painful experience, while birds are simply an amusing one.

This is a wonderful group test. Subjects are told that the person seated on their right is invisible to them. They know that he (or she) is there as they can feel and hear the person, but they cannot see him. Perform this test as a posthypnotic. When subjects awaken, tell each to try to find the person who was previously sitting on their right; to reach out and try to touch him or her. The resulting confusion is tremendous as each subject gropes "blindly" to their right trying to find the person who they know is there, yet who is invisible to them. End the test with the suggestion: "All right, when I clap my hands, everyone will be visible again instantly."

Yet another variation of the "Invisible Hypnotist" test is to suggest to the subjects that while they cannot see the hypnotist they can see to their amazement the results of his invisible presence. Pick up a small boy and carry him across the stage in front of the subjects. To them it appears that the boy is floating in space and is utterly amazing.

Dr David Tracy presents a detailed handling of a "Taste Change" test. It will serve to show how a routine in hypnotism can be developed into a sequence of happenings.

Hypnotise a woman subject and ask her if she likes fresh peaches, plums and oranges, and which fruit she prefers.

If her desire is a peach, say to her: "I am going to give you one half of a nice fresh peach, and I want you to eat and enjoy it." Hand her half of a lemon and tell her to eat it while you suggest: "My, how you do enjoy eating the nice sweet peach."

After she has eaten about half of the lemon say to her: "Now you've had enough of the peach, I'm going to give you half an orange and I want you to take a bite out of it." Give the subject half an orange and let her take a bite, then suddenly suggest: "Oh I made a mistake, I gave you half a lemon instead of an orange." Her reaction is immediate.

Now say to her: "I was only fooling. That is really an orange, a nice sweet orange that you are eating. Taste it again and you will see that I am right." The subject responds with satisfaction.

For a climax to the experiment, Dr Tracy hands the subject a piece of raw potato while he says: "I am going to give you now a nice juicy apple, and I want you to eat and enjoy it. While still eating with relish the potato, the subject is awakened and her expression at finding herself munching on a raw piece of potato is a masterpiece of humour.

This listing of hypnotic tests could go on and on, as what can be created to entertain in the hypnotism show is without limit, dependent entirely upon the creativity of the hypnotist. I am indebted to many fine performers for this compilation of favourite routines.

NOTE TO HYPNOTIST: Of course, it depends a great deal upon the performer's personality and his style of working, but always show good taste in the hypnotic tests you present.

Hypnotic demonstrations from the past have been more or less of the type to put the subjects in ridiculous situations and make fools of them. For the sake of completeness a few such experiments are suggested in this chapter, but the modern approach to the hypnotic experiment is to use tests that, while amusing, show principles of hypnotism and the variety of effects it can produce without directly poking fun at the subject. Naturally, the type of audience you are working before and the entertainment expected of you are factors in your deciding just what experiments are suitable. As an experienced showman, you can easily resolve such problems but, generally speaking, make it your rule never to use experiments that would later make the subjects regret that they came forward upon the stage. Remember, these subjects are free-will volunteers who came directly from the audience to the stage to help you. That implies a trust and confidence in you, and you must always respect that confidence to the utmost.

Chapter Sixty-Five
Sensational Hypnotic Feats

These are spectacular demonstrations in hypnosis to add to your stage show. They incite awe. Do not use them on volunteer subjects. Perform with your personal assistant while under hypnosis on stage. The volunteer subjects can help you perform the feats by watching closely.

The "Hypnotism Blood" Test

This test works best performed with an assistant who is of the fleshy, pink skinned type. Hypnotise him, roll back his sleeve leaving the right arm bare, and have him stand erect with hands resting at his sides. Then tell him to clench his right hand tightly into a fist. As he does this make contact passes up both sides of his arm while you suggest:

"Blood. Blood. Blood crawl up the arm. Blood crawl up the arm and leave it white and bloodless. Blood. Blood. Blood crawl up the arm!"

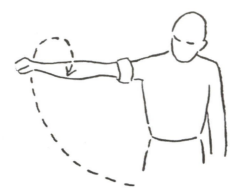

Take your hypnotised assistant's arm and swing the arm upward in a circular motion to the horizontal position, and suggest forcefully: "Arm. Arm. Arm become all stiff and rigid. Arm and shoulder muscles all stiff and rigid, and the blood lessens from the arm!" The effect of this action, with the suggestions, is to cramp the muscles of arm and shoulder, driving the blood from the arm.

Now tell your assistant-subject to open out the fingers of his fist. The arm is seen as white and bloodless. The colour change is most visible when using a subject of the fleshy type, as plump persons tend to have a transparency to their skin that emphasises the effect of bloodlessness.

The feat completed, tell your assistant to close his hand again into a fist; that the muscles of his arm and shoulder are becoming relaxed, and that the blood will flood into his arm. As the muscles relax, the blood rushes back colouring the arm brilliantly.

The "Human X-ray" Test

In this feat you cause your assistant's extended arm to take on an X-ray effect, with the skin becoming transparent and an array of blood vessels clearly seen. While no actual hypnosis is required in the demonstration, genuinely hypnotising your assistant-subject increases the mystery.

The effect is accomplished by rubbing a chemical on the skin of the subject. The chemical used is a mixture of three parts salicylic menthyl ester and one part benzyl benzoate. The compound may be obtained from the Department of Organic Compounds of the Eastman Kodak Company. It is kept in a bottle with a sponge applicator.

In performing the effect, hypnotise the subject and have him bare his arm. Have him extend his arm straight out with palm of hand and underside of arm facing the audience. Announce that you will produce an X-ray effect upon the arm as you apply the chemical. As the skin becomes transparent and the veins show up, it is an effect the spectators will long remember. To conclude the feat, wipe off the compound, roll down the sleeve, relax the arm, and awaken the subject.

The "Heart and Pulse" Test

Your assistant is introduced to the audience. You explain that you will hypnotise him and cause his pulse to stop and start at will. A volunteer subject on stage checks the pulse, and the remarkable results occur.

Your assistant is prepared to perform this test by having a handkerchief with a hard double knot tied in its centre fastened around his arm so the knot comes directly beneath the armpit. Pressure upon the knot under the arm will cause the pulse-beat to stop; releasing the pressure causes it to beat again. By the assistant holding his breath, at the same time, the effect is even more marked.

The assistant has been prepared to perform the feat and conditioned to apply and release the pressure, as the test proceeds. The hypnotism can be genuine. The feat is startling, as indeed the pulse stops and starts at will. Begin the test by having your assistant's pulse taken. Hypnotise him, and suggest: "Your heart will in a moment begin to beat slower and slower. Already it is beginning to slow down."

The pulse beat is felt again. You can cause the pulse to stop and start at will, as all the assistant has to do is press his arm in upon the knotted handkerchief in the armpit and the pulse stops. Releasing the pressure it starts again. When you perform this feat, if possible use a physician to check the pulse. Awaken the subject and complete the test.

The "Pin Through the Flesh" Test

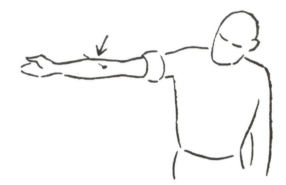

Anaesthesia can be readily induced through hypnosis. Use your assistant for this test. Hypnotise him, roll back the sleeve, make a few contact passes along the fleshy tissue on the side of his arm, and suggest: "All sensation is leaving your arm. There is no feeling in that arm at all. It is completely insensible. The arm feels numb." Repeat these suggestions several times and lift up a fold of flesh and push a sterilised needle directly through.

In performing this test, use a sharp needle and have a strong thread attached to it so you can easily pull it back out of the flesh. A thimble will assist in pushing it through. Pinch the flesh sharply between your thumb and forefinger just before you pass the needle through. Always use medically sterilised needles for this test and apply Band Aids or a similar dressing to the puncture wounds afterwards. The experiment is an easy one to perform, and is most useful in convincing the audience of the genuineness of your phenomenon.

NOTE TO HYPNOTIST: Prior to the advent of AIDS and other diseases transmitted through body fluids, we always got by sterilising our own equipment for this experiment. I would not recommend doing this now and would strongly advise you to always use medically certified materials.

The "Flame-Resistance" Test

Like the foregoing test, this one demonstrates anaesthesia through hypnosis. Your assistant subject is hypnotised and his arm is outstretched palm downward. These suggestions are then given: "Your extended hand is becoming numb to all sensation. It is impervious to heat and pain. You will feel absolutely nothing in your hand except a pleasant warmth, as we perform this test."

Having given these suggestions, take a cigarette lighter and light it, getting a good flame. You then proceed to move the flame back and forth under the hand of the subject. The anaesthesia is complete. The subject is then awakened and the test concluded.

In performing this test, keep the flame moving under the hand. Do not hold it still or in one place or it will cause a burn. By keeping the flame in motion no burning will be experienced, and the test safely performed.

The Famous "Cataleptic Body-Rigid" Test

The feat of rendering a subject's entire body cataleptic and supporting him between two chairs, even while standing on the subject, has been a sensational stunt in hypnotism shows for years. If you use the demonstration, perform it with your personal assistant.

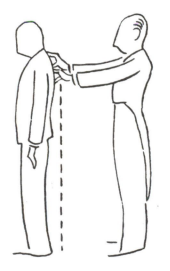

Hypnotise your assistant, have him stand with feet tightly pressed together, and suggest: "Every muscle of your body is beginning to get stiff and rigid. As I pass my hand down your back from the top of your head to your feet, the muscles of your entire body will become cataleptic. Every muscle in your entire body is becoming stiff and rigid." Pass your hand down the back of the subject. You can tell how he is responding as you feel the muscles tensing.

Then go to the front of your subject, face him, place your hands on his shoulders and shout: *"Rigid!"* Follow right on through with a rapid fire of suggestions: "Every muscle in your entire body is rigid! Nothing can make you bend. You are like a solid bar of iron! Nothing can make you bend! You are stiff and rigid like a bar of iron!"

Have a couple of volunteers on stage help you lift your assistant and place him across the back of two chairs, with face of seats inwards. Place the person's ankles on one chair and shoulders on the other. A pillow draped over the top of each chair will help in keeping them from cutting into the subject ... and remember you place the subject's shoulder blades on one chair, not the back of his head. It is important to position the subject safely in performing this full-body cataleptic test.

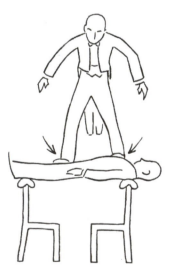

Now with the help of a chair or couple of volunteers step directly on top of the subject. Plant your weight evenly and do not shift about. One of your feet goes in the centre of chest and the other on the lower thigh.

You can stand on the subject for as long as you wish; when ready to come down, take the hand of a spectator and leap to the floor. Have the subject removed from the chairs and stood upright. Release your assistant from the rigidity and awaken him. It is important in this experiment to remove the rigidity gradually and completely, so be thorough about it as you suggest: "All right now, every muscle in your body is again becoming relaxed and at ease. Every bit of tenseness and stiffness is gone. And when you awaken you will feel good all over."

Repeat these suggestions a number of times until you see that every trace of rigidity is gone. Then awaken the subject by the usual counting method.

Joan Brandon and her assistant performing the "Human Bridge" hypnotic test

The Rock-Breaking Test

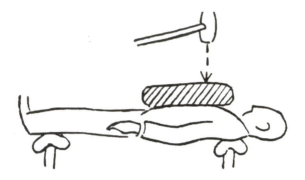

This is a variation of the foregoing cataleptic feat. Use your assistant. Hypnotise him, render him cataleptic and place his body outstretched between two chairs, as in the previous test. A felt pad is then draped over his chest and a large sandstone, about two feet square and six inches in thickness, is placed directly on his chest. Taking a sledgehammer the rock is broken with one sharp blow. Hit it right in the centre and the pieces will go plunging to the stage.

The feat is spectacular and works itself, as the felt pad over the chest of the subject takes some of the blow and the inertia of the rock absorbs the major part. Actually the subject experiences little more than a slight jar, and to your hypnotised assistant such is not even noticed.

Hypnotism Show Stagecraft

In this section, you learn hypnotism stagecraft and mechanical aids for your show. You enter the realm of theatrical production: light, sound and stage dressing are discussed to produce your show, combined with some special hypnotising methods you can use.

Chapter Sixty-Six
Staging the Hypnotism Show

You have studied stage hypnotism in relation to the hypnotising. Now consider stage hypnotism in relation to the staging. The hypnotism show can range from a one-person informal show with no props to staging an elaborate production. It can even be developed into a theatrical production of Broadway scale. We will now consider hypnotic stagecraft.

Show Time

The audience is waiting, expectant. Overture. House lights dim and fade out as red and blue footlights come on front curtain. Front curtain slowly opens. Spotlight. The show is on.

The Chairs

When the curtain opens the first thing the audience sees in the hypnotism show is a group of chairs arranged on stage. Every hypnotism show uses chairs for the subjects to sit on. Usually these are obtained at the place of performance. However if you are aiming towards production you can carry an array of elegant chairs, for the nicer the appearance of the chairs the nicer the stage setting. Attractive chairs attract the volunteers to come on stage to occupy them.

> NOTE TO HYPNOTIST: Did you ever think of elaborately staging the hypnotism show in a regal setting; using elegant chairs in which each subject feels as though seated on a throne. Suggestion is at work, the subjects become kings and queens on stage. The results can be imagined. Hypnosis deserves such treatment. Someday some enterprising showman will create such a production.

Arrange your chairs (whatever kind they may be) in a semicircle on stage. Place them about eight inches apart, so that, while the subjects will be seated closely together, they will not touch each other. Each subject should be an "island" unto him or herself. The number of chairs you have will depend on the size of the stage you are working upon and the size of the audience you are working for. Twenty chairs works fine for a large stage and not less than six for a small one (approximation).

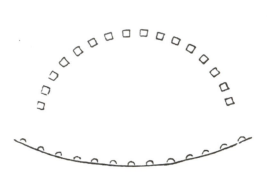

Use as many chairs as you can, as the larger the group the more potential good subjects you have to work with. Also, it provides you with a large cast on stage which increases the importance of the show.

The larger the group the more important the experiments seem to the audience, and the subjects gain confidence by being with many others of similar volunteering status as themselves. There is safety in numbers, plus being mass action in committee size in subject responsiveness.

The Curtains

Usually the show will use whatever curtains the stage provides. However if you elect to carry your own, rich velour curtains of deep blue or deep wine are ideal. The essential thing in colour being that it contrast well with your subjects on stage, and make their actions stand out.

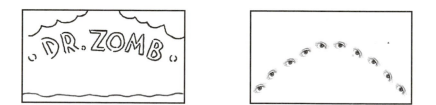

If you have a design on the back curtain keep it simple so as not to conflict with stage action, and leave a good portion of the curtain plain. If you decide to use a design drop, have something which builds up your prestige such as your name in glittering letters or possibly a row of hypnotic eyes. The important thing in selecting a curtain is to have it designed to fit the type of show you are presenting, to form a picture-like setting for the things you do.

The Lights

Curtain opens on stage flooded with red and blue footlights and red and blue border lights. Following white spotlight brings performer on from wings to centre stage. Introduction given in white spot. While action is on stage, house lights out. If any tests are performed on audience, house lights on.

When committee is invited on stage bring both stage lights and house lights full up. Once subjects are seated on stage turn out house lights, but leave stage lights full up for first group test. White spot light remains on throughout the show featuring performer. When white spot is on and house lights are off audience visibility is nil and subjects feel isolated on stage as blackness appears before them. The effect is conducive to hypnosis.

The general lighting pattern through the show is stage reds and blues for each test with a single subject, and full stage lights for group tests. White spot emphasises action throughout the show.

Let the lighting add atmosphere to your show. Here are some special effects:

Have baby spotlight mounted overhead in the grid. Have amber gelatine over lens and focus it vertically downward directly on chair placed beneath it for individual hypnotic demonstrations.

Have baby spotlight in stage wings focused on performer's face when he hypnotises. Try it with green gelatine.

A double-faced mirror mounted on turntable with spot focused on it gives an hypnotic effect as it revolves.

Place the device behind first curtain wing; as it revolves the mirrors reflect out flashes of light above the stage. This is effective to use while hypnotising a solo subject.

Having a revolving globe covered with small pieces of mirror overhead, at stage centre, with a spotlight focused on it, will send you flashes of light about the theatre. It produces a spectacular effect. This device is especially effective while hypnotising the entire committee. Devices such as these enrich the hypnotism show in the style of a theatrical production.

Coloured lights have definite psychological affects on hypnotic subjects: Yellow light increases suggestibility. Purple, blue and green light are sleep inducing. You can apply these principles in hypnotising. Start hypnosis with yellow light on subjects. After eyes close and you suggest sleep, switch to blue light. Coloured lights provide spectacular and effective ways to hypnotise subjects.

The Mike

The use of a public-address system (PA) is essential to the modern hypnotism show. Indeed, the mike forms the heart of your presentation. Using the mike makes clear your speech in addressing the audience and amplifies your suggestions to subjects on stage. Even place a second set of loudspeakers behind the subjects on stage. *Surrounding your subjects with sound is a secret for producing profound effects.*

Arrange your show so mike placement works conveniently for yourself. Mike on stand placed centre stage is useful for direct addressing of audience. Mike can be carried in hand while performing tests with various subjects. The use of a radio microphone is the most convenient of all.

The Music

Musical background is important to the staging of the hypnotism show. If you have a combo or organist to work with you can get some excellent support. Most shows use music on cassettes played over the PA.

The essential thing in selecting hypnotic music is to use pieces that are not too well known and are soothing in nature. Organ and symphonic music is effective. Get pieces that suggest sleep, dreams, moods of quiet and rest, such as New Age music which produces a meditative mood very good for the hypnotic show.

Music played softly behind your voice while you hypnotise adds to the effectiveness of the process and increases presentational value.

Sound Effects

Sound effect cassettes can be purchased. These will be useful in staging your show as sound effects can be played from backstage over the PA to increase the dramatic value of certain routines.

For example, in the "Frankenstein Monster" test, the clanking of dragging chains and the stomp of heavy feet is effective. In the "Flying Saucer" test outer-space sounds build the mood. In the "Aeroplane Ride" test background sound of aeroplane motors get things off for a takeoff. Sound effects not only increase the dramatic value but actually amplify the effect of the suggestions.

In staging the hypnotism show bear in mind that it is a theatrical production, and the more appropriate production you can get into it the better. hypnotic stagecraft does not lessen the scientific value of what you present. It just makes it a better show.

Special Stage Effects

The hypnotic show is theatre. Use whatever special effects you desire to increase dramatic values. For instance, a fog machine, in the wings, can send a carbon dioxide mist rolling across the stage. It produces an eerie effect to have the hypnotist appear out of the fog. A strobe light flooding the darkened stage can be used to emphasise the impact of a science fiction type experiment, as it produces a slow motion effect to action on stage reminiscent of moving under lighter gravity.

A visit to a theatrical supply house will provide many ideas you can incorporate into the production of your show. However, by and large, be practical. Use what enhances your presentation but do not allow production to be a burden or overwhelm your hypnotic effects.

Chapter Sixty-Seven
Mechanical Aids for the Hypnotism Show

The Hypnotic Wand

This is an effective and handy prop to use in the hypnotic show. It adds a dramatic touch of magic to the show and fits well into the stage show. It can also be used as an hypnotising method. At a plastic supply house, get a two foot length of clear, one-half inch diameter, Lucite rod. This forms the wand. It is attractive and catches the lights on stage. It can be used in pointing at the subjects in performing various hypnotic tests. It looks mysterious and captures audience interest. Also, it is effective in waving before the group as the "cue" which returns them to hypnosis during the show.

Here is how to use it to hypnotise a subject. Having seen the hypnotic wand used in pointing up many of your demonstrations, subjects will come to associate it with being hypnotised. Bring a subject forward from the group, and have him stand facing you. Tell him you are going to hypnotise him using the wand.

467

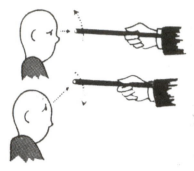

Have the subject stand erect with hands at sides. Ask him to relax a bit as he focuses his eyes on the tip of one end of the wand, explaining that he is to keep his eyes riveted on that end at all times, and to follow it with his eyes wherever you move it, as shown in the illustration.

Hold the wand in your right hand about eight inches from his face, directly on a level with his eyes, and grip the back of his head with your left hand, as in the illustration.

Move the wand upward in a slow arc. As you are holding the subject's head firmly so that it cannot move, only his eyes will turn upwards, and when they reach a point where the pupils are almost hidden behind the upper lids, they will suddenly blink shut. At this point, bring the wand down again level with the eyes, and repeat this up and down motion with the wand ten times.

After the tenth time (if he has not closed his eyes before), when his eyes blink command him to keep them shut tightly.

Now place the wand so that it touches the centre of the top of his head, and tell him to roll his eyes upward under the closed lids as though he were looking back into his head towards the very spot where the wand is touching. Tell him to keep looking upward under the closed eyelids as you press the wand firmly against the top of his head, and suggest that his eyelids are becoming stuck so tightly together by the power of the wand that he cannot open them, try as hard as he will. Keep a series of such suggestions going directly into his ear, associating his responses as being due to the properties of the hypnotic wand. Press firmly on the nape of the subject's neck. This produces a deadening sensation that he will feel throughout his body.

As you perform this eyelid fastening technique, move your left hand down from back of the subject's neck and massage the bony structure behind the right ear. This has a remarkable soothing effect and is sleep-inducing. Follow on into "sleep formula": "Now the hypnotic wand is making you very sleepy. Its power is seeping into your body and is making you go sound asleep in hypnosis while you are standing right on your feet. Go to sleep, go sound asleep now!" The subject will soon be entranced in hypnosis.

Hypnotising with a Flashlight

The mechanical hypnotising aid used in this method is a small "penlight" flashlight or torch of low power. It is used to produce hypnosis via an "after image" effect within the eye caused by the focusing of the light. This technique was developed by hypnotist Charles Cook.

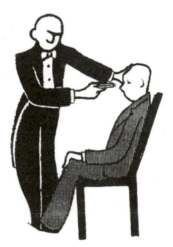

In this technique, the subject is seated facing you in readiness for hypnosis. You lean forward and place the palm of your left hand over his right eye. You shine the penlight directly into his left eye, holding the light about an inch from this eye, as shown in the illustration.

A flashlight of this small size is not powerful, and being a relatively dim light will not bother his eyes. Tell the subject to keep staring into the light, and to relax his body completely, and to close his eyes when you tell him to.

After about thirty seconds, command him to close his eyes tightly together. Due to the light which has been directed into his eyes, he will now experience a very vivid "afterimage", and you describe this effect to him, as it occurs within his eye, thus: "You will see inside your closed eyelids now a very bright spot of light. This spot will change in colour as you watch it. It will fade away altogether, and then it will reappear. Watch this spot of light closely inside your eye. Concentrate your complete attention upon this spot. As you watch it, you will begin to feel yourself becoming very drowsy and sleepy."

Continue on with "sleep formula". This method of hypnotising is very effective. What makes it particularly unique is that the "afterimage" in the subject's own eye is used as "the fixation object" to concentrate upon rather than an external point. The method will swiftly produce deep hypnosis.

Hypnograph Buttons

Print dollar-size cardboard discs of this design. Give one to each subject in your committee. Have your subjects hold the Hypnograph before their eyes, centring their gaze on the white dot. The hypnograph is employed as the "fixation object" in this induction method.

You present the suggestions that as they gaze at the disc it is becoming blurred; their eyes are closing; the hand holding up the hypnograph is dropping to their lap, and when it hits their lap they will be in profound hypnosis. This is a good stage method for the initial hypnotising of the committee when you start the show.

The Hypnotic Spiral

This mechanical hypnotic aid makes an interesting display on stage. The revolving spiral produces an interesting optical effect that is attention compelling. The machine is easily constructed being a black and white spiral disc mounted on a turntable. The device is set up vertically facing the audience. The motor is started and the disc whirls around producing a fascinating effect for the audience to watch. It provides a good method to use for hypnotising the audience.

The hypnotic spiral can also be used as a novel stage method to hypnotise a solo subject. It is first demonstrated to the audience and is then placed before the seated subject to stare at. In using it for solo hypnosis, set the disc about six inches before his eyes. Start the disc revolving and instruct him to stare at it for as long as he can keep his eyes open. As he watches it revolving around and around apply your favourite method of hypnotising. The hypnotic effect of this machine is powerful and will rapidly induce hypnosis.

The Rhythmic Light

This effective mechanical method of hypnotising is made by rigging a light to the tip of the "meter stick" of a metronome. Since the speed of this device can be varied you can easily set its rhythm to a hypnotic pace. The ticking of the machine in time with the swinging light is very hypnotic. Used in semi-darkness, the rhythmic light will quickly induce hypnosis.

Electrical Hypnotism

This novel method of hypnotising will add drama and spectacle to your hypnotism show. It uses the familiar electrical device called "Jacob's Ladder", which is made from a high-tension transformer to the output of which are set two upright metal rods. As these rods are spaced at an angle, when the electric spark arcs across the gap it runs up the rods disappearing at their tops as it breaks. As the arc climbs up the rods, spark following spark, a ladder-like effect of bluish electric flame is produced.

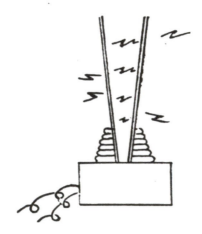

In using this machine on stage, the subject is seated in front and told to concentrate on the perpetual rising sparks, as they climb up the ladder. As they climb up and break, climb up and break over and over, each time they break he is to say "sleep" to himself, and it will put him to sleep. When subject's eyes close, proceed with your hypnotising formula. Performed with dimmed stage lighting it is a very spectacular hypnotising method.

NOTE TO HYPNOTIST: In using this device keep your subjects away from touching it, as there is some 50,000 volts of high tension current passing up "Jacob's Ladder".

The Audio Oscillator

A high-pitched audio oscillator is one of the most unsuspected secrets the stage hypnotist can apply. The sound oscillator is fitted with a "tweeter" type speaker so as to produce an extremely high pitched sound beyond the range of the human ear. Such a sound tends to increase hypnotic responsiveness. Consciously it cannot be heard, but subconsciously it does its job.

The Brainwave Synchroniser

This modern technique of inducing hypnosis comes as near to a mechanically perfect method of hypnotising as has yet been developed. The machine is the product of the Schneider Instrument Company of Skokie, Illinois, with whose permission it is included in this text.

The brainwave synchroniser (BWS) is an electronic instrument designed to induce various levels of hypnosis by subliminal and photic stimulation of the brainwaves. The inventors, a clinician and an engineer, have developed a method of "driving the alpha rhythm". The instrument is designed to increase receptivity to suggestion and has been clinically tested on more than 2,500 subjects. As reported, the apparatus induces light to deep hypnosis in over 90 per cent of the subjects; also it shows remarkable potentialities for deepening a previously fixed hypnotic level and for facilitating and speeding up hypnotic induction, especially in subjects who are difficult to hypnotise.

A major advantage of the device is that it has been reported as effective in hypnotising persons who were not previously hypnotisable. Such is of obvious use to the stage hypnotist. Also the introduction of such a machine in his show is excellent showmanship in bringing a touch of the scientific to his performance. A device such as this carries great audience interest.

The brainwave synchronisers, is most effective because the light flashes synchronise with the patient's brainwave frequency. These controlled photic and auditory stimulations are produced throughout the range of the brain rhythm and thus the instrument causes a fixation effect. The explanation of this technique captures the patient's concentrated attention, and thus the time of induction is cut down. It also helps in inducing good trance depth. This technique definitely lessens the patient's resistance and causes the patient to be highly receptive to suggestions. The operator's comments during the stimulation complete the process of hypnotic induction by providing the rapport necessary for utilisation of suggestions.

There is a great deal of evidence in everyday life that photic stimulation will produce a state of fixation or a trance state: sunlight streaming through the trees as a cyclist pedals down the lane; light rays broken by a whirling propeller. However, these are hit or miss examples, and results are unpredictable. The outstanding characteristic of the BWS is that its pulse is controlled to stimulate the brain pulse in electronic form, and is adjustable in frequency throughout the delta, alpha and beta ranges.

The Brainwave Synchroniser Stage Show Hypnotism Method
Ormond McGill Presentation

The committee of subjects are seated on stage; you stand before them. The hypnotic machine mounted on a stand at slightly above eye height to the seated subjects is rolled out to centre stage as you address the audience.

"Ladies and gentlemen. The science of modern electronics has even entered the psychological field. You might say that it has entered the science of hypnotism. The instrument you see before you is known as the brainwave synchroniser. It is a device especially designed for inducing hypnosis. We shall use it this evening for the initial hypnotisation of the volunteer members of our committee on stage.

"[Turn to the committee.] Members of the committee of hypnotic investigators, I know you will find this a most interesting and pleasant experience as you enter hypnosis through concentrating on this hypnotism machine. I will explain its operation to you. [Turn sideways so that you are addressing both the audience and the subjects on stage at the same time.]

"Members of the committee, I invite you to try this scientific experiment for a very interesting experience. Relax back in your chairs, place your feet flat on the floor, and rest your hands lightly in your lap. Be perfectly comfortable and direct your attention to this machine. When I turn it on, concentrate on the flickering light as I adjust it to your brainwave rhythm. You need not look directly at the light, rather look through it into the reflector behind the light. Your eyes can stare at it much as if you were in a passive, pleasantly relaxed state of daydreaming. You will feel the effect very quickly. Relax completely now and concentrate on the machine as I turn on the brainwave synchroniser."

This has proved an effective presentation as it introduces and explains the operation of the instrument while building up expectancy of its power to induce hypnosis. This is important psychology as the hypnotist well knows; in this instance the instrument has actually been designed to operate as you have described, i.e. to increase suggestibility and to aid the induction of hypnosis. The combining of the hypnotist's suggestions with the physiological effects of the machine are hypnotic.

The stage lights are now lowered so that all attention will be centred on the machine when the BWS is turned on. As the instrument has a removable panel, I take this to a table at the side of the stage, while I explain to the subjects: "I will stand over here at the side of the stage so as to be entirely out of your way and you can concentrate without distractions of any kind upon the hypnotic light."

The machine is now turned on, and every subject is asked to concentrate on the light. I set the dial on the control panel at the lowest level on the alpha scale and turn on the power. I slowly increase the pulsation rate of the instrument while scanning the faces of the subjects. As I am working with a group and not a solo subject, I have to find the frequency that appears to carry the greatest influence upon the most subjects. It will be noted that a subtle cataleptic change seems to occur in the eyes of the subjects and their facial muscles as the range synchronises with that of the specific frequency in the subjects' brain. Experimentation has shown that the range between a setting for alpha 4 to 8 is the most effective. A setting at 6 is a good average to effect the most people generally.

While this operation is going on, my suggestions continue: "Watch the flickering light of the brainwave synchroniser. I will gradually increase

475

the frequency, and when it matches your brainwave frequency you will note a fixating effect. It will grip your attention. The pulsations are increasing now and the effect of its influence is increasing. You can feel it becoming stronger and stronger in its effect. It is holding you; gripping you. It is capturing completely your attention, and you are relaxing, relaxing. The machine is tuned to your brainwave frequency now. Keep watching it. Keep watching it. Take a deep breath and hold it deep in your lungs. That's it. Hold it. Now exhale slowly. Exhale and relax. Inhale again; inhale deep. Hold it. Exhale and relax. Inhale again ... hold it ... exhale and relax. You are beginning to feel sleepy. Your eyes are becoming tired and heavy; they want to close. But don't close your eyes yet, keep staring at the strange flickering light of the hypnotic machine. Breathe deeply and regularly. You may close your eyes now and go to sleep. I will count from one to five. With every count your eyes will become heavier and heavier, and by the time I reach five, or before, your eyes will be shut tightly together. One, two, three ... eyes closed ... all eyes closing ... close your eyes and go to sleep. Four and *five*! All eyes closed down tight together now, yet even through your closed eyelids you can still sense the strange patterns produced by the flickering hypnotic light in tune with the pulsations of your brainwaves, and it is sending you down deep, deeply to sleep. Fast asleep."

At this point you are ready to test for eyelid catalepsy. Suggest: "Your eyes are closed tightly together. They are closed so tightly together that you cannot open them no matter how hard you try. Try, try hard, it is impossible to open your eyes." You have induced eyelid catalepsy and your subjects are in hypnosis. You are ready to deepen the trance, but first a word of advice:

Watch the subject closely. If any open their eyes note who they are and you can shortly request them to return to their seats in the audience and watch the show. At the moment, however, do not detract from your hypnotising process by removing them. That can come a little later after your subjects are deeply entranced. You will find that many in the committee will be influenced by this time and the eyelid catalepsy complete. Continue your suggestions: "Forget about your eyes now, relax and go deeply to sleep. Breathe deep and go to sleep. Every breath you take will send you on down deeper and deeper to sleep."

I have a pocket full of pennies, and at this point go to each subject in turn and pull out their right hand in front of them with the palm up. Comment: "Hold your hand out in front of yourself now with the palm up. In the centre of the palm I am placing a penny. Hold it there still and calm. Your outstretched arm will not bother you in anyway, just continue breathing deeply and go deeper and deeper asleep."

After the arms of all of the subjects have been pulled outstretched, and a penny placed on each palm, continue: "Think about your arm that has been stretched out in front of yourself. There is a penny resting on the centre of your palm. Here is a strange thing. That penny is becoming so heavy it is becoming difficult to support it. It is becoming heavier and heavier. It is so heavy that it is making your palm slowly turn downward towards the floor so the penny will fall to the floor. Your hand is turning, slowly turning. It is turning, it is turning and the penny is going to fall from your hand and hit the floor. When you hear it hit the floor it will send you deep, deep to sleep."

Watch the subjects' hands. You can tell by the way the hands turn in response to your suggestions who your best subjects in the group are going to be. The hands will gradually turn, slowly turn until they are facing downward and the pennies fall to the floor. Follow directly with these suggestions:

"The pennies have fallen to the floor. You have heard them hit the floor and you are asleep. Fast asleep in a deep hypnotic trance. I will show you how deep that hypnotic trance is by making your arm so stiff that you cannot bend or move it no matter how hard you try. You can feel it happening now. Your arm out in front of your body is becoming stiff; it is stiff and rigid as a bar of steel. You cannot bend or move it no matter how hard you try. Try, try hard. It is impossible to bend or move it."

The subjects will try in vain to bend their arms. Here again in this test you can ascertain your best subjects and plan to eliminate any others not responding satisfactorily. Continue: "All right now ... forget about your arm being stiff ... it is becoming relaxed again, and when I reach the count of three it will be so relaxed that it will fall like a limp rag into your lap, and when it hits your lap it will send you on down yet deeper to sleep in complete hypnosis. Ready. One, two, *three*. Your arm falls into your lap and you are fast asleep."

Watch the arms of the subjects fall. Here again you have an excellent chance to judge your subjects. This is one of the factors which makes this method so excellent for the stage hypnotist; it provides repeated opportunity during the induction process to study the responses of the various subjects, and the performer can plan on ahead in his mind which persons he will use for such and such tests in his show. Continue: "You are all sleeping soundly. Nothing will disturb or bother you in any way. Breathe deep and go deeper and deeper asleep."

This is a good time to remove any unwanted subjects. Simply request them to quietly leave the stage and return to their seats in the audience. Your suggestions continue: "You are all fast asleep in deep hypnosis. I will awaken you for a moment now, but first remember these suggestions: next time you will not need the brainwave synchroniser to be hypnotised. All you will need to do to enter deep hypnosis is to look into my eyes. When you look in to my eyes and I touch you lightly on top of the head you will immediately go down into deep hypnosis. You will go instantly asleep in deep hypnosis."

This is a strong posthypnotic suggestion which given at this stage of the induction will make it possible to rehypnotise many of the subjects "instantly" throughout the show. You are now ready to awaken the committee.

"All ready, I am going to arouse you. I will awaken you for a few moments so you can rest a bit, then I am going to hypnotise you again more deeply than ever and you will have a wonderful time responding to the hypnotic phenomena in the show tonight."

"I will count from one to five. With every count you will gradually awaken, and at the count of five be wide awake again and just feeling fine. One, two, three, four, *five*. Awaken now. Wake up. You are wide awake and feeling just fine."

The frequency of the brainwave synchroniser is returned to zero and the instrument shut off. The initial hypnotising of the committee is accomplished, and all subjects remaining on stage are conditioned to respond to the interesting hypnotic experiments in your show.

NOTE TO HYPNOTIST: After the subjects have rested for a few moments, go to each in turn and quickly rehypnotise them via the posthypnotic suggestion you have established which accomplishes this. This instantaneous production of hypnosis to the spectators is astounding. It is a brilliant test in itself and, with the committee members again in hypnosis you are ready to proceed with your show as you have routined it.

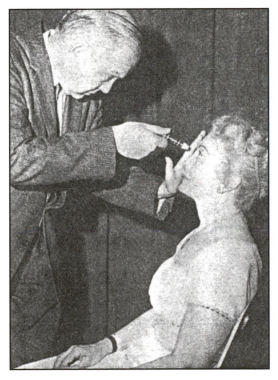

The hypnotic-flashlight method in operation

Chapter Sixty-Eight
Additional Aids to the Hypnotism Show

Presented in this chapter are a number of "tricks of the trade" of use to the professional stage hypnotist.

Stage Accessories

These constitute the extra props needed in working the show. These will vary with each performer and performing situation. Generally speaking, having a table or two, lemon, glass, pitcher of water and the various props used for the different hypnotic effects you present. Have all things handy, placed upon a table at the side of the stage. The hypnotism show must be presented with smooth precision, so know exactly where things are when you reach for them. Nothing looks less professional than to have to grope for props.

Stage Assistants

Although the hypnotism show can be effectively handled on a strictly one-man basis, if you do have assistants they can increase the show's production value. If your male assistant has a good voice he can introduce you and assist in ushering the volunteers to their chairs as they come up on to the stage. Occasionally it will be found good showmanship to leave the stage when the volunteers are coming up to form the committee. This pause will give you a chance to rest in the wings, and provides a chance for the assistant to pass out name tags to each person, have them write their first name on it, and stick it on their suit of dress. Self-sticking name tags are available at stationary stores for this purpose. The name tags make it possible for you to call each person by name when you work with them. This often increases hypnotic receptivity, as it generates rapport. All of these advance details can be tended to by your assistant, while you take an off-stage break. When ready, you re-enter and the show proceeds. (This expedient has been mentioned before in this text.)

An attractive female assistant (and/or assistants) can add a touch of beauty and class to the show. A hypnotism show carries a certain dignity, so have them costumed appropriately. Evening gowns are fine. Your female assistant(s) can hand you the various props as needed, and likewise assist in directing volunteers to their respective chairs.

It is well for the hypnotist showman not to overdo the number of assistants. One boy and one or two girls will be ample and during the action of the show, for the most part, keep them inconspicuously in the background. Well-trained assistants will always direct audience attention to the performer, and never attempt to attract attention to themselves.

Performing Clothes

What type of clothes the hypnotist should wear on stage depends much on personality and style of show. Dress according to the situation: a formal show on stage works well in evening dress. With a young crowd more casual dress can be worn. Businessmen presentations call for a suit. An Oriental approach gains from a suitable East Indian type costume. Whatever you elect to wear, wear clothes of top quality and be clean and neat. Proper personal dress goes a long ways in increasing your effectiveness as a hypnotist.

A Before-the-Show Exercise

Whether or not you give credence to "animal magnetism" or "human energy" theories of hypnotism, this exercise is useful. Before your show, stand erect and inhale deeply. Imagine that you are charging your hands with a "force" just before you walk on stage. To do this, tense up your fingers, shake your hands, turn your palms towards each other, hold them with the fingertip about two inches apart, and visualise in your mind that an electric-like energy is passing down your arms and is sparking out of your fingertips. As you perform this exercise, you will actually seem to experience a tingling in your hands. Get this sensation going strongly, then walk out briskly and start the show.

The Hypnotic Gaze

In stage situations, there is much eye to eye contact between the performer and his subjects. For a more effective hypnotic gaze, use this technique. Focus your eyes at a point on the level of subject's eye about six inches inside of his head! This gives the appearance that each of your eyes is staring directly into his, looking within his very brain, as it were, and is effective in holding attention.

The Magnetic Bowl of Water

An interesting prop to use in the hypnotic show is to have, on a table at the side of the stage, an Oriental-looking bowl containing water. Every so often during the show, between effects, go over and dip your hands in the water and then shake them vigorously dry. Believers in the "animal magnetism" or "magnetic energy" theory say this helps remove depleted magnetic energy and recharges the hands. Whatever the reason, it is powerful and very effective showmanship. If you use this process, do not comment about it to your audience or your committee. Just do it, and let them wonder as they will.

The Taste-Test Secret

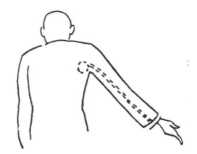

A useful gimmick (a gimmick is a secret device) for the hypnotist to have up his sleeve is the one here described. It consists of a small rubber ball with a hole made in its sides to which is attached a length of thin rubber tubing. Another hole is made in the ball and some grains of powdered saccharine dropped inside. This hole is then covered with adhesive tape. The device is now ready to operate. Have the tubing of a length to reach from under your right armpit to your wrist; insert it in your coat sleeve with the ball placed under armpit. Tie the ball under armpit so it will remain in position, run the tube down your sleeve ending at the wrist just inside of coat sleeve. A rubber band will hold the lower end of the tube in position. See illustration. So prepared you are ready to perform an effective test in apparent taste suggestion. It is very convincing.

Hold up a candy bar and ask each person to imagine how it would taste, as you continue giving suggestions of a sweet taste coming into their mouths. As you give these suggestions, pass rapidly down the row of your seated subjects, waving your right hand in front of the face of each, and as you pass the subject's mouth press your arm sharply against your side. This forces a tiny spray of the powdered saccharine from out of your sleeve, directly toward the mouth of subject. The spray is so fine it is invisible, but the saccharine is so concentrated in sweetness, every subject is bound to experience a very real sensation of sweetness in his mouth. Experiments of this nature, which employ artifice to emphasise your suggestions, can be very useful in secretly intensifying the phenomena and especially helpful when employed towards the beginning of the show.

Perfumes and Incense

Odours have their place in the hypnotism show. For instance your femaile assistant(s) can wear an exciting perfume. And a little pheromone perfume sprayed upon yourself cannot but help increase your sex appeal. Sex appeal is not a bad ingredient to add to your performing charisma.

Incense can also be used upon the stage, with braziers burning on either side. Such add an exotic touch, and incense charms the senses. Devices such as this lend atmosphere to the hypnotism show and increase the anticipation of both committee members and the audience of hypnotic miracles that will be shown.

Challenge Hypnotism

A gimmick apparatus, somewhat similar to that employed in the "Taste-Test Secret" is used in this method of "challenge hypnotism". By this method the performer can issue a challenge that he can hypnotise any person in the audience.

The apparatus used for this purpose is shown in the drawing. It consists of an atomiser bulb attached to a length of rubber tubing that goes into a glass container (bottle) via a cork in its top. A further length of tubing from the bottle passes down the sleeve of the hypnotist, the nozzle end of which is fastened by a strap to the performer's wrist. Some anaesthetic solution (chloroform or ether) is placed in the bottle, which is then tightly corked. The apparatus is positioned on the performer's body as shown.

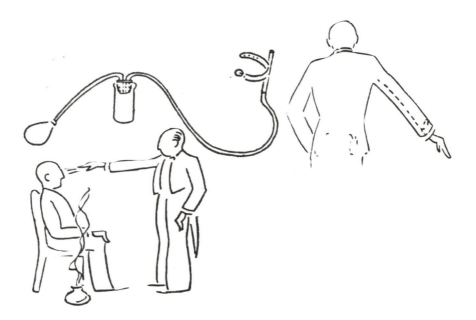

When the atomiser bulb is squeezed the anaesthetic vapour is forced out of the nozzle concealed in the performer's sleeve. The apparatus should be professionally made.

In hypnotising with this apparatus, place a pot of burning incense on the floor near the subject, so the smoke will rise upward towards his nose when the vapour of the anaesthetic is directed toward his face, as shown in the illustration.

In the presentation, explain that the method you are going to apply is Oriental in nature, hence the use of incense. Then proceed to hypnotise the challenger by your favourite method. Place your hands over his eyes to force them closed, and hold them closed with your left hand as you suggest that he will note that the odour from the incense will begin to change, that it is becoming very powerful and is sending him down to sleep in deep hypnosis. Tell him to keep his eyes closed now, as you remove your left hand and casually place it in your pocket. Now wave your right hand in passes before his face, as you repeatedly squeeze the atomiser bulb in pocket. The vapour of the anaesthetic is forced out, and the subject will go to sleep.

NOTE TO HYPNOTIST: In using this apparatus, be sure the tubes within the container of anaesthetic do not touch the liquid. Only the vapour of the anaesthetic should be expelled.

A Stage Presentation of Challenge Hypnotism

The following is a description of how this method of challenge hypnotism was used on the vaudeville stage, as a prelude to a hypnotism show. The hypnotist is wearing the apparatus described. It is ready to operate. A thronelike chair is centre stage with a bowl of burning incense on either side. The performer advances to the front of the stage, and boldly issues a challenge to the audience stating: "If there is any big, strong powerfully willed man in this audience who does not believe I can hypnotise him let him step forward now! Come on stage and take a seat in this chair."

A burly volunteer is forthcoming. The man is duly seated. Standing before the person, the hypnotist looks steadily in to his eyes and, waving his hands before the person, keeps repeating suggestions of how sleepy he is becoming. The challenger's eyes are pressed closed, and the suggestions of "Sleep! Sleep! You are going to sleep!" are repeated over and over. During the process of making hypnotic passes before the subject, the spraying of the anaesthetic is applied. The man goes to sleep. The hypnotist has met his challenge to hypnotise a defiant subject. Needless to say, after witnessing such a demonstration of "hypnotic power" other persons who venture upon his stage quickly succumb to the hypnotic influence this master presents.

The modus operandi of successfully meeting such a challenge to hypnotise even a defiant person is twofold: it is both psychological and physiological in this method. First is the person's attitude in accepting the hypnotist's challenge. Bold as he is, he does not actually know but that he can not be hypnotised by the performer even though he professes he cannot be. Coming on stage and being seated in the special chair with the lights beaming at him, and with the entire audience caught up in the tenseness of this dramatic situation, his uncertainty is even more increased. This very uncertainty renders his mind responsive to the hypnotist's suggestions. The law of reverse effort goes into effect, making the person susceptible to hypnotic induction subjectively, contrary to his objective wish not to be. As long as the performer is confident of success and bold in his presentation, the cards are stacked for success of the demonstration.

The use of the anaesthetic spray further assures its success. Seated in the throne chair, surrounded by pots of incense, that in itself is hypnotic; and, as the performer waves his hand before the challenger's face, the etheric vapour does its job. The rising incense covers the smell of the anaesthetic, and the anaesthetic effect of the drug suffices to ensure entrancing the subject into a sleeping state.

Hypnotising a Vase of Flowers

Using the identical apparatus employed in the challenge-hypnotism demonstration, you can present this surprising effect. The showman explains that even flowers are susceptible to hypnotic influence. He waves his hand over the flowers, while crooning soothing words that they go to sleep. Amazingly the flowers droop and go to sleep. It is not generally known that flowers, too, are susceptible to an anaesthetic. A test of this nature will elicit a great deal of comment when seriously associated in your lecture on possible theories of hypnotism. It is hypnotic magic!

Hypnotism Show Miscellany

In this section, an assortment of material useful to your outstanding performance of a hypnotism show is presented. You are shown how to hypnotise animals, and given a variety of clever "hypnotrix" to add to your arsenal as a showman. The complete Dr Q Hypnotic Act is covered. Attention is directed to performing stage hypnotism in the popular night-club field.

Chapter Sixty-Nine
Hypnotising Animals

Hypnosis in animals is more a physical condition than a mental one. It resembles catatonia. However, as the process renders the animal immobile and it appears asleep, it passes as hypnosis to the audience. There is no need to get too technical. You will find hypnotising animals an interesting entertainment segment to include in the show. If desired, it can be included in the opening lecture prior to discussing hypnosis in humans.

Hypnotising a Frog

Flop the frog over on its back and hold it immobile for a few seconds. Then carefully remove your hands, and the animal will remain as you placed it. To remove the condition, snap your fingers for effect beside the frog's head, and quickly flop it over right side up. It will instantly reawaken and hop about.

Hypnotising a Lobster

This is a spectacular creature to hypnotise. With its big claws it looks as though it might be dangerous. Actually this animal succumbs very easily. To hypnotise a lobster just stand it on its head, using its claws as supports. Hold it in this position for a few seconds, and it will go immediately to "sleep". To remove the condition, set it again on its legs.

Hypnotising a Chicken

Chickens are fun to hypnotise and audiences get a kick out of the experiment as it is funny to see chickens squawk and thrash about, and then docilely go to "sleep".

Use a hen for the experiment. Catch hold of it by the neck and force its head down so it lies flat on the table. Then, take a piece of chalk and draw a line directly out from its beak for about two feet. Hold the chicken still for a few seconds, and it will go to "sleep".

Carefully remove your hands and it will stay in that exact position motionless. To awaken the chicken, clap your hands loudly beside it, and push the hen a bit away from the chalk line. It will "come to", and loudly let you know it on the instant!

Hypnotising a Rabbit

Bunnies are favourite with audiences, as there is something lovable about rabbits. They love to see you put bunny "under". To hypnotise a rabbit, lay it on its back, part its ears with fingers of your right hand flat on the table, and push its hind legs down to the table with your left hand.

Hold the rabbit in this stretched out position on its back restricting its movements for about thirty seconds, and then carefully remove your hands. The rabbit will seem to be asleep, lying motionless on its back. To remove the "hypnotic influence", blow sharply on its nose and push it over on its side. Bunny will immediately awaken and scamper about.

Animal Hypnotism Showmanship

When you present these experiments which appear to hypnotise animals, handle them with care. Many people feel very tender towards animals and will judge you by the way you treat the animals you use. Hypnotising animals calls for finesse in presentation. You make it seem that you are hypnotising the animal but never that you abuse the animal. Be gentle and kind.

In hypnotising animals do not be too casual about it; make it seem a bit difficult. In other words, perform animal hypnotism with showmanship. Make hypnotic passes over the creature which appear to be the cause for it going to sleep. Caution the audience to be quiet while the sleep ensues. Walk around it gingerly as though you do not want to disturb it and when it awakens, pat it and hold it up for the audience to applaud the animal. Properly presented you will find animal hypnotism will add demonstrations to your show that audiences will long remember.

Chapter Seventy
Hypnotrix

Hypnotrix are pseudo ways of simulating hypnotic effects. They are good bits of business for the stage hypnotist to know.

In stage hypnotism the show's the thing. Hypnotrix sometimes provide just "the ace in the hole" the showman needs. Add them to your repertoire and include them in your arsenal of knowledge. What you are able to do with Hypnotrix is often just what an audience believes a hypnotist should be able to do, which is to amaze, mystify and entertain.

As a hypnotist, you may never have occasion to use any of these tricky methods but, if you do, perform them with the same sincerity you do when presenting genuine tests.

Protecting Your Hypnotic Eyes

To this day, the general public tend to associate powerful eyes with the hypnotist. There is something about Svengali! For a dramatic opening to your show, enter wearing a pair of dark glasses and keep them on while you give your opening lecture and get the subjects on the stage. Take them off when you hypnotise.

A Clever Way to Gain Rapport

Rapport between subject and hypnotist is important to hypnotising. It promotes a bond of willingness to be hypnotised by you and a knowing that you can do it. When speaking of hypnotising with a new subject, state it is well to see what kind of a rapport exists between you. You propose a test. You grip the subject's two hands and tell him to think of one of them and that you will try to discern which hand he is thinking of. You do it.

Stand facing the subject and grip his left hand in your right and his right hand in your left. As you speak about checking rapport shift your grip up a bit toward his wrists, so the forefinger of each of your hands will rest on the pulse. You can feel the beats. Take careful note of the rhythm.

Have the subject close his eyes and you close yours; request that he think of one of his hands, right or left. Immediately as he centres his thought in the direction of one of his hands, the pulse-beat in that hand will alter; it will tend to slow down or skip a beat; it will be individual, but it will give you a sufficient clue for you to tell which hand he is thinking about. Name the hand. The subject is impressed with the rapport you have achieved with him.

Making it Impossible for a Subject to Rise from His Chair

Have a person take a seat in a chair and close his eyes. Present a series of hypnotic suggestions that he is stuck to the seat and cannot get up, then place the forefinger of your right hand directly in the centre of his forehead just above the root of his nose; push forcefully upon this point while tipping his head back at the same time. This forces the subject off balance and he cannot stand up no matter how hard he tries as long as you maintain the pressure. To end the test, take your finger away and tell him: "All right, you can get up out of the chair now."

Making it Impossible for a Subject to Rise from the Floor

Have a person lie out flat on the floor, face up. Have him close his eyes, and point your forefinger directly at the root of his nose while commanding that he cannot get up no matter how hard he tries. He tries, but it is impossible. This seems wonderful because although you are pointing at the subject you never actually touch him, yet the influence seems exerted.

The effect is accomplished by securing a black horsehair from a paint brush, and with a bit of Scotch tape fastening it to the nail of your right forefinger. When you point your finger at the prone subject the tip of this hair touches the root of his nose between his eyes. Being black, at even a short distance it is entirely invisible. It is a surprising fact that as the subject tries to rise up from the floor that hair digging into the root of his nose will keep him glued to the spot every time. To end the test, merely remove your finger and the person can get up immediately.

Making a Bug Crawl Around in a Subject's Ear

Here again the black horsehair attached to your forefinger is employed. Have a person take a seat and close his eyes. Perform hypnotic passes over his head and about his ear while you state: "There is a bug crawling about in your ear. You can feel it. It is there. It is crawling, crawling, crawling. Brush it away quickly."

Sure enough, the subject most decidedly does feel the bug crawling about in his ear for as you make the passes you take good aim and tickle his ear with the horsehair attached to your fingertip. It produces a wonderful effect and looks for all the world like the party is responding to your hypnotic suggestions.

When presenting these hypnotrix using the horsehair gimmick you can begin your performance with it already attached to your finger; when you have finished with these particular tests it can at a propitious moment be scraped off and dropped from the finger as the show carries on.

Making a Subject Lose His Sense of Direction

Get a "toy cricket" for this stunt, the type you press and release to make a sharp, snapping sound. Any novelty store can supply this. Seat the person and tell him that you are going to make him lose his sense of direction. Snap the "cricket" about a foot away from his ear, take your hand away, and ask him to point to the approximate spot where you held the "cricket" when it snapped. Repeat the same with the other ear. He points to the spot where you made the sound.

When he understands what he is to do, blindfold him and make hypnotic passes while you state that he is losing his sense of direction and will not be able to locate the source of the sound no matter how hard he tries.

Now snap the "cricket" on either side of him, behind his head, under his chin, near his nose, over his head, etc. and watch the fun. Have him point out the direction in which he believes he hears the snapping sound each time. Rarely will the subject point out the spot of the sound correctly as he indicates where he thinks it is supposed to be. To end the test, remove the blindfold, gently tap the subject as though removing the influence, and thank him for his cooperation.

Making a Subject Faulty in his Observation

Introduce a clothes brush and tell the person that you are going to make it impossible for him to keep track of the number of times you brush his coat. Blindfold the subject and have him stand before you. Now begin brushing the back of his coat over his shoulder-blade, and ask him to keep count of the brushings as you do so. He is wrong completely.

Why? Because, actually, you do not brush his coat at all. You merely draw the side of your right forefinger along the back of his coat in a brushing motion, while, at the same time, you brush strongly your own coat so that the party may hear the sound of the brush upon the cloth simultaneously with the brushing motions of your fingers down his back. To the subject it seems exactly as if you were brushing his coat with a brush. Try it – it's very deceptive.

Making a Subject Lose His Sense of Taste

Everyone will get a big kick out of this stunt. Have the person take a seat. Now show a red apple and a green apple. Tell the subject that you are going to make it impossible for him to guess which apple he bites a piece from while blindfolded. You place the apples in a paper bag. Then blindfold the party.

Now reach in the bag and take out a potato, cautioning the spectators not to laugh by a pantomime gesture. Cut a clean piece out and hold the subject's nose so that he cannot breath through it, place the piece of potato in his mouth and ask him to chew it and see if he can guess which apple he ate. He is wrong in every case. Remove the blindfold and show him the potato. When you hold his nose his sense of taste strangely disappears.

Making it Impossible for a Subject to Bend His Leg

Have the person stand erect before you. Look him in the eyes hypnotic fashion as you place the fingers of one of your hands along the side of his head tipping it to one side. Hold it that way. At the same time place your other hand along the side of his hip, on the side opposite to that which you have tipped his head. For instance, if you tip his head to the left, press on his right hip, and vice versa. Keep pressure on both the side of his head and on his hip. Now tell him that his leg is stiff (the one on the side to which his head is tipped) and that he cannot bend it; that he cannot even move it!

Make him try to move the leg, but he absolutely cannot do so; it is truly stiff like a stick of wood. To end the test, remove the pressure of your hands and tell the subject: "All right, you can walk now" and it is successfully concluded.

Making it Impossible for a Subject to Stand Up

Have the person place his hands on his hips; then bend down so that his head is almost level with his hips. Hold his head with both of your hands, lightly on each side by his ears. Tell him not to move his feet during the test. Now pull him slightly forward. Just a very little bit is necessary so as not to be noticeable to the audience; pull him just enough so that his weight is well forward, then command that he cannot stand up erect no matter how hard he tries. He cannot, and will admit that he can't. To end the test, lift his head right up as you say: "Okay, now you can stand ... the influence is entirely gone."

The Hypnoheat Method

This method was described earlier in which a ball of tin foil, held by the subject, mysteriously becomes hot apparently in response to the hypnotist's suggestions. It was presented as an instantaneous method of hypnotising, for which purpose it has proved eminently successful. However, beyond question it belongs in the category of hypnotrix. It is possibly one of the most powerful of all hypnotrix, the modus operandi being secretly to add the chemical, mercuric chloride, to the foil which causes it to generate heat.

> NOTE TO HYPNOTIST: Mercuric chloride is a deadly poison. Handle with extreme care.

Comments on the Mercuric Chloride Method of Hypnotising by Barry Brilliant, MA

Barry Brilliant has been a student of hypnotism since his high school days. He holds a master's degree in mesmerism from San Francisco State University (first ever issued). He has written these comments on this method, based on his experience in its use, presented entirely as information in this book of encyclopedic scope.

"I have used the mercuric chloride method for twenty years, and I consider it one of the most powerful techniques for inducing hypnosis one can apply. Indeed, its effects are so powerful that it must be used with caution. Not only is it a poison, but the psychological deceptiveness needs to be examined. The paradoxical position of trust and then presenting a magical phenomenon as a genuine phenomenon for the subject's 'best' interest must be thought through by each user of this method. In other words, do the means justify the end? In my opinion, we should use what tools we have with consideration for the good of others to which they are applied.

"The power of this method was impressed upon me in a dramatic way. I was invited to see if I could help a psychotic patient who had the delusion that he was possessed by Satan. Psychiatric help had not been very successful, and it was hoped that hypnosis might be an aid. I will relate my experience.

"The patient was convinced he was influenced by Satan which made him evil. He seemed to feel that somehow Satan had entered him and taken possession of his soul. It might be expressed that in his mind he was a man torn between God and the Devil, as it were. To help resolve this inner conflict I told him straight out that I had the ability to burn Satan out of his consciousness forever. I told him I had a special process to do it. He believed in my ability.

"He smoked cigarettes, so I asked to borrow the pack and tore off a piece of tinfoil from the wrapping. I told him that after I had hypnotised him I was going to send my energy into this foil, while he held it, and make it so hot it would suck Satan from his being.

"I hypnotised him by a progressive relaxation process. He went semi-deep. When he was in this relaxed and receptive state, I told him that I was now going to take the bit of foil I had torn from his cigarette pack, roll it into a ball, and asked him to grip it tightly in his hand. Then I said I would send my energy into the ball of tinfoil, as he held it in his hand, and he would feel it become hotter as Satan left his body, and the very heat he felt would mean that Satan was being burned completely out of his system … and it would become so hot that he would have to toss it away from his hand, as it was just too hot to handle. And in that tossing he would be tossing Satan out of his life for ever.

"The effect was phenomenal. As the ball of tinfoil became hotter and hotter in his hand he squirmed and screamed and finally had to fling it away from himself. At that very moment I shouted: 'Go deep asleep now!' He dropped into profound hypnosis on the instant. I proceeded to give him some further suggestions that he was now cleared of all evil influence from his life for ever, and that the Archangel Michael now stood by him as his friend.

"Who can say for ever? But I can say that when I woke him from hypnosis he gave me a broad smile and said he really felt as though he was in control of his life for the first time in years. It is wonderful how the subconscious works when old ingrained ideas are removed and are replaced with beneficial new ones."

Grant's Hypnotism Over Earphones

This clever act of pseudo-hypnotism was used effectively by the late U. F. Grant. It is given here with permission. First go to your local radio shop and have them fix you up with a pair of headphones with, running from them, a wire with a small microphone attached backstage. Have the outfit rigged so that anything spoken into the backstage mike will be heard by anyone wearing the headphones. Also get a mike; it does not have to work as it functions only as a "prop". The wires from the headphones run offstage to the workable mike in the hands of your assistant backstage, while a fake set of wires run from the headphones to the fake mike you use on stage.

To make the set-up of the device clear it is arranged simply so that while it appears that the person wearing the headphones is hearing your voice when you speak into the fake mike you are holding, he actually is hearing the voice of your assistant speaking backstage over the "live" mike.

When you perform the stunt, bring a subject forward and explain that you are going to perform a little psychological experiment with the voice and that you would like to have him put on the headphones so that you can talk to him in a very intimate and personal manner. You will notice that you have not mentioned a thing about what you are going to do other than that you are going to try an experiment with the voice.

Have the party take a chair and hand him the headphones to put on. Be sure you use a large size pair of earphones with the rubber cups attached so they will fit snugly to his ears so that he can hear no outside voices, just the voice over the phones.

Pick up the fake mike and start talking to the person over it. Actually the subject does not hear a thing being said, but the audience thinks that he does. Now, as you talk, your assistant off stage talks to the person wearing the headphones. In the following ensuing instructions and conversation, (P) stands for the performer and what the audience hears and thinks the subject is hearing. (A) stands for what your concealed assistant backstage says and the person wearing the headphones actually hears:

(P) I shall now endeavour to hypnotise you by the aid of my voice alone. Whatever I tell you to do, try not to do that. Try to work your will against mine. You will have to do exactly as I command. Let's try some tests now and see.

(A) We are here this evening to have some fun so I want you to help me out and do exactly as I say. I am trying out a little experiment.

(P) Your eyes are getting heavy. Try not to close them.

(A) Blink your eyes a few times. That's right. Now close them slowly.

(P) You are getting very sleepy. Soon your head will drop against your chest. It will be impossible for you to keep your head up.

(A) Now please drop your head down on your chest. That's fine. Now open your mouth wide. Don't mind doing this, it's all in fun.

(P) Now I command you to wake up and open your eyes, but you will still be under my control.

(A) That was fine. Now quickly raise your head and open your eyes.

(P) During your short nap you have actually forgotten your name. Try to tell us your correct name.

(A) Please say: "My name is Mary Smith." Please state the name in a very serious manner. (This is very funny since it is a man you have with the headphones on.)

(P) Try not to raise your left arm and hand.

(A) Now raise your left hand and arm high into the air.

And so you can work out most any kind of test you wish. For example, you pass through the audience and force three cards that your assistant knows. You return to the platform and, over the fake mike, ask the person to name the three cards. He does so successfully, with the aid of your concealed assistant.

Hypnotrix are confidential. Use them when you need them. Keep the secrets to yourself.

NOTE TO HYPNOTIST: Hypnotrix are useful to the stage hypnotist if they contribute to his show. Sometimes such methods even lead the subject down the pathway into profound hypnosis. The "Hypnoheat Method" is a striking example of this. Likewise, such is often the case when you perform Dr Q's hypnotic act, described in the next chapter.

Chapter Seventy-One
The Dr Q Hypnotic Act

The act of the famous magician/hypnotist John Calvert was the inspiration for the Dr Q Act, which I wrote in 1944 for William Larsen Sr. It was published by Thayer Studio of Magic and was included in the text of my *Encyclopedia of Genuine Stage Hypnotism*, 1947 edition.

The Dr Q Hypnotic Act is an act of pseudo-hypnotism, yet the presentation is so successful that it advances from what begins as the following of conscious "cues" by the subjects into spontaneously obeying subconscious commands. There is an amazingly thin line between following conscious and subconscious directions. The Dr Q presentation provides an excellent example of this fact.

The basic premise upon which the Dr Q Hypnotism Act is designed leads the subjects from believing they are merely assisting you to entertain the audience to opening themselves to being hypnotised. The Dr Q Method could be referred to as hypnosis by misdirection. Here is the detailed presentation. The act begins by your presenting brief comments on hypnotism.

Introduction

"And now, friends, let us turn our thoughts for a few moments to the wonderful science of the human mind, hypnotism. The study of hypnotism has claimed human thought for centuries, but it has only been in comparatively recent years that a real appreciation of its marvels have come to be recognised for, as you have undoubtedly read in the many current articles now appearing, hypnotism is currently being practised in our foremost hospitals and colleges with almost miraculous results both curatively and psychologically.

"Tonight, in just a moment, I am going to invite a few volunteers up on to this stage to participate in some demonstrations in this remarkable phenomenon called hypnotism.

"First, however, I should like to remove the old superstition that to be hypnotised a person must have a weak mind. Such has now been proved by science to be a complete fallacy. Indeed, some of the very best hypnotic subjects have been persons of very high intelligence and vivid, creative imaginations. So, tonight, when you volunteer for these demonstrations, you may rest assured that you are placing yourself amongst the very best of intellectual company.

"You see, hypnotism is not something dark and mysterious. To explain it simply, and to phrase it in psychological terms, it is purely a state of mind produced through the influence of suggestion, the power of ideas.

"Now, when you volunteer to come up on stage to participate in these demonstrations, I want every person to realise that I shall treat them with the utmost courtesy and respect. And, by the same token, I merely ask that you give me your earnest cooperation and attention.

"And now, without further ado, I wish to invite a few of you gentlemen up on stage to experiment with hypnotism. Will four or five, or possibly even more, gentlemen kindly step forward? Thank you, sirs."

You will find that this introduction convinces your audience almost instantly that you know your subject, and makes them realise that there is indeed something to hypnotism. Also, these opening remarks place the volunteers completely at ease in coming up on to the stage, removes them from any later criticism of being weak-minded and places them in a frame of mind to work along with you. Thus your introduction has not only secured for you cooperative volunteers, but likewise sold your audience on the reality of what you are about to attempt.

The Dr Q Direct Cue Method

Having secured four or five volunteers on the stage, have them stand in a row about two feet apart. Go to the one on the left end of the line (as you face them) and, turning your back deliberately on the audience, place your left hand on the back of his neck, at the base of the brain, and squeeze gently, but at the same time firmly.

In assuming this position you will be facing the subject squarely, so look him directly and earnestly in the eyes while your free right hand makes gentle pass-like gestures in the air, and whisper (simply speak in a low, soft voice … this will carry clearly to the subject but will not reach the ears of the spectators in the audience) to him: "We are going to have some good laughs on the audience and fool them … so when I tell you to do some funny things, do exactly as I secretly tell you. Okay? Swell!"

(Then deliberately wink at the spectator in a friendly fashion.)

The psychological effect of such a proceeding is to render the man a willing dupe to your ends. Your stance, with the pressure upon his neck, puts you in a position of dominance. This coupled with your position as "master of the stage" will render him amenable to doing exactly what you tell him.

Then, too, your words to him are in the nature of a "whispered confidence" of producing laughs on the rest of the spectators in the audience. The volunteer thus begins to feel important that he is in on a secret and is to become "part of the show."

Your boldly stated "Okay? Swell!" implies his automatic acceptance of willingness to follow your instructions, and your parting wink cinches the spirit of "good fellowship" between you. Handled thus, any spectator who happens to come up on the stage quickly becomes "a perfect hypnotic subject" for your demonstrations. Dr Q is certainly to be commended for developing this perfectly brilliant psychological method of "handling" the subjects.

Proceed now to the second spectator in the row, and repeat exactly your instructions. Take the same stance with him, and say the same words, just as you did with the first subject. Possibly this second spectator may have heard a bit of what you whispered to the first person. If so, he will simply "catch on" that much quicker.

Then go to the third spectator and proceed likewise with him. Just before you leave, however, whisper: "After I shake your hand and let go… make your palm stick to mine."

Step a bit to his side, and, as though it were a friendly parting gesture, take his right hand in yours and shake it. Move the hands around a bit, and then open your fingers, at the same time pressing your palm tightly against his. Push your palm up so it forces his arm back. This tends to "set" your whispered instructions in his mind, so when you now pull your hand down, as though to take it away, he will follow right along with you exactly as if his palm were really glued to your own.

This is very funny, and in a second's time the fun will start, and the volunteer will begin to get a "big kick" out of all the laughs he's creating and will really stick to your hand in earnest, just as though he were hypnotically stuck. If you wish, you can even try shaking your hand free from his, but he'll follow right along, stuck tight. The audience will howl! Then suddenly give him a tap on the neck (as though snapping him out of hypnotic influence), and with a loud: "All right!" jerk your hand free.

This demonstration, funny as it is in itself, is performed at this time for a very important purpose. It shows the other volunteers the kind of actions that are going to be expected of them ... and thus gets them all expectant awaiting to follow your whispered commands.

Then quickly proceed to your next volunteers and give them the same whispered instructions to do whatever you tell them ... you are now ready to go into the hypnotic routine.

First, however, let us consider for a moment just what has been the audience's reaction to all of this. To them it looks as though you are hypnotising the subjects, and, since that is what they are expecting you to be doing, it all passes naturally. The audience sees your stern position as you gaze into the eyes of the man, the mysterious passes your right hand is making in the air, and even the mumble of whispers seems to them the expected "hypnotic formula" used in hypnotising.

Since you are whispering so softly that only the subject you are directly in front of can clearly hear your words, the audience has no chance whatsoever of knowing what you are saying ... and since they have no idea as to just what is going to happen, they have no cause for the least bit of suspicion. Their attitude is one of eager interest, waiting for something amusing to happen.

The whole "hypnotising" procedure with the first two subjects takes place so rapidly that it is completed before anyone has had much chance to give it critical thought. And then the funny demonstration with the "stuck hand" is such a big laugh that it covers up the little remainder of the time it takes to get to the rest of the subjects in the line.

After that first test, the spectators will be more than ever on their toes, eager and expectant, to see more of your "hypnotism". This building of audience acceptance is another ingenious aspect of the Doctor's hypnotic method ... for not only does it psychologically handle the subjects on the stage, but it also psychologically handles the audience.

Dr Q's Hypnotic Routine

Having instructed each of the volunteers secretly, as has been described, Dr Q next would dash back to the first spectator in the line and whisper: "When I clap my hands fall down". He would give these quick instructions in a flash without even so much as stopping in front of the first spectator, and then pass right on to the second spectator in the line.

Pausing before this person he would raise his hands and clap them, and the first spectator would fall down. While clapping his hands thus, and during the laugh on this unexpected occurrence, he would whisper to the second spectator: "When I pick him up, you fall down."

The Doctor would then rush over to the first spectator and pick him up from the floor, and the second spectator would fall down. As he picks up the first spectator he would then whisper: "When I pick up this other fellow you fall down again." Then picking up the second spectator, the first would fall down again. He would then shout loudly: "All right, all right ... it's all gone!" and go over and help the first subject back on his feet.

It is impossible to describe how funny this demonstration appears to the audience. You will just have to try it to appreciate its value. You'll find that your audience will positively howl ... and the more they howl, the better your subjects will respond to your whispered instructions.

Dr Q, during this laughter at his "Falling Test", would go to the third subject (the one he had previously used in the "Hand Sticking") and shake his hand while he would whisper: "Make our hands stick again." And the subject's hand would become again stuck to his. Dr Q would then bend over, and placing the subject's right hand flat on the floor would go through the motions of nailing it to the stage while he would whisper: "Make it stick there."

The subject would then vainly try to pull his hand free, until the Doctor would hit him gently on the back of the neck and say loudly: "All right, it's all gone now!" While the subject was trying to pull his hand free of the stage, Dr Q would go to the fourth subject in the line and, while standing directly in front of this spectator, would request him to open his mouth wide. He would then whisper for him to keep it open as though it were impossible to get it closed. Stepping aside, the audience would see the subject with his mouth stuck wide open. Dr Q would even tell the subject to try hard to close it with his hands.

Few things could be funnier, and the audience would howl louder than ever with laughter. During this laughter, Dr Q would release the subject, pulling on his hand stuck to the stage, and rapidly move on to the last subject in the row. Standing in front of this man he would raise the subject's right hand and place its thumb against the man's nose, while quickly whispering: "Hold it stuck there." The subject would then appear to try in vain to get his thumb away from the end of his nose.

Quickly, Dr Q would leave this last subject with his thumb stuck to his nose, dash over to the first subject in the row, and lead him over to the side of the stage or wall. Placing his hand against the wall, he'd whisper: "Keep it stuck." Dashing back to each of the remaining subjects on the stage, he'd command each in turn to open their mouths wide, with a whispered cue to: "Keep it stuck."

By this time, there is so much action heaped each upon the other, and the audience is laughing so loudly, that you will find in working the act that you can almost give your instructions out loud. In fact, your subjects will so have caught on to what is expected of them and be having such a swell time in making the audience laugh that they'll do anything you suggest at the slightest provocation. Indeed, you can abolish the whispered instructions almost entirely and proceed right into the role of a hypnotist giving suggestions as: "Open your mouth wide. It is stuck, you cannot close it!" As you look steadily at the subject while giving such suggestions, give him a wink.

Dr Q would thus go from subject to subject until he had a row on the stage standing with their mouths stuck wide open. Then going quickly to each one, he'd apparently snap them out of it by a gentle tap and a loud: "All right, it's all gone!" At the same time he'd whisper to each: "When I clap my hands fall down."

Dr Q then would thank the subjects for volunteering to help in the demonstrations, and ask them to return to their seats. As they left the stage, he'd watch them carefully, and when some were in the aisles and others on the stairs, he'd clap his hands together loudly … and the subjects would fall down in a heap wherever they happened to be! Thus providing a perfect climax for a perfect act.

The foregoing is the exact hypnotic routine as performed by the celebrated Dr Q. Of course the reader can work out his own routine in any number of countless variations, for in applying this method numerous tests will suggest themselves to you. However, don't make the mistake of performing too many demonstrations. Just do a few and let it go at that.

Frankly, it is to be doubted that Dr Q's own routine can be very much improved upon. Performed with showmanship, it will positively provide a few minutes of utter amazement and humour that an audience will never forget.

> NOTE TO HYPNOTIST: Attention should be called to the subtle manner in which the Dr Q method presents the whispered instructions; note how all instructions are given under cover of some larger action, and how all instructions tends to be "one ahead" of their occurrence … so that while the audience is laughing at one stunt a new one is being "set" to be subsequently performed. Thus, when in transpires it appears to occur spontaneously. This is hypnotic misdirection.

Chapter Seventy-Two
Hypnotism in the Nightclub Field

Many of today's top-flight hypnotists are finding nightclubs the new show-business venues for their acts. The nice part about this is that a solo performer can fill a full hour spot for the club with a presentation that is rousing to the spectators and also builds a following for the club. Successfully presenting hypnotism in nightclubs calls for some special handling.

Nightclub Performing Situation

Nightclubs often present rather cramped performing conditions. Except for de luxe clubs, often the stage provided is quite small; sometimes the stage is nonexistent, and the hypnotist is required to work in the middle of the dance floor surrounded by spectators eating and drinking at tables.

There is little of what is called "aesthetic distance" to be found in the nightclub situation. The spectators being close to the subjects can be distracting. Also there are bar noises, waiters or waitresses serving tables, frequent bits of conversation about the room, etc. These are all things that the nightclub hypnotist must cope with.

To meet such conditions, the performer should limit his committee of volunteers to about ten persons (there is scarcely room for more chairs than that anyway), and should develop as much stage show atmosphere as he can in the room. By darkening the club and concentrating a spot on the subjects, attention on the show can be increased. Under such lighting the spectators can see clearly, yet those within the spot will seem more "cut-off" from the rest of the audience, as all beyond the light seems in blackness. And the use of a good PA system will assist in deleting distracting noises, as will also some soft background music (used occasionally). Usually the club combo or orchestra can provide such music on cue, or the performer can provide his own music played on a tape recorder over the PA by his assistant behind a screen placed inconspicuously at the back of of the floor or small stage. Meeting successfully the performing conditions of the nightclub situation is a good test of the calibre of the showman.

Nightclub Hypnotising

Hypnotising in nightclubs generally calls for a more snappy presentation than does the usual stage show. Drinks flow freely in such places, and the holding of audience attention is a factor to be constantly considered. In planning the nightclub hypnotism show, action and laughs are the essential ingredients. The emphasis must be centred on entertainment.

The show should be planned to run not over an hour in length and be carefully planned to roll along smoothly at a good pace. Every moment must be designed to provide entertainment. In planning your show, consider it much as one would the running of a motion picture that exhibits a set pattern each time it plays. Make your nightclub show so tight, that it rolls along with a precise routine each showing. And keep your opening introduction down to a minimum, making it just long enough to capture audience attention and get the needed volunteer committee formed; then get right down to business rapidly.

It will be found that the longer a performer is at in a club, the easier it will be to get a committee quickly assembled for the show. At first it may take a bit of coaxing, but as the hypnotist becomes known, soon he'll have more subjects than he can use, especially in view of the limited number he has room to accommodate. In inviting the committee, as the spectators are close to hand, often a personal invitation directed towards an individual or couple seated at a nearby table will bring them forward to join the group. The chairs will fill quickly, and try to get up an equal number of women along with the men. It makes for a better show this mixing of the sexes.

Once you have your committee assembled, in the nightclub situation, it is usually best to proceed directly to a hypnotisation of the group and let preliminary waking suggestion tests go. The nightclub show is a concentrated show and this gets things proceeding right into quick action. For nightclub hypnotising use a positive and very definite technique, one that is both precise and almost commanding. Entrepreneur hypnotist Gil Boyne's early adventures in hypnotism were in the nightclub field. He used this handling: the subjects are seated in a row on their respective chairs, the club lights dim and the spot comes on focusing all attention on the subjects. Soft music comes in as a background, the performer faces the committee and begins his comments: "Being hypnotised is a process that requires good concentration. The better you can concentrate and the more intelligent you are, the more quickly you will respond to hypnosis, and the better hypnotic you will be. If you can't concentrate, then I will have to dismiss you; if you can, you'll have a lot of fun.

"Now everyone sit back in your chairs comfortably, place your feet flat on the floor, and rest your hands on your knees so they do not touch. All right, everyone relax and concentrate on me; concentrate on relaxing every muscle of your body; concentrate on relaxing the muscles of your eyes. As you concentrate and look towards my eyes, your eyes begin to feel very tired and heavy. Your eyes are becoming so tired and heavy that they want to close down tight together. At the count of three, close your tired eyes tight together. One, two, *three*. Everyone close your eyes tight together … tight, tight together. Your eyes are all closed so tightly together that they are stuck, they are stuck, stuck together and you cannot open them. Try, try hard, but you cannot open them. Forget about your eyes now and go to sleep. Breathe deep, breathe very deep. Breathe deep and go to sleep. Every breath you take sends you down deeper to sleep. And your head is relaxing now …let your head fall forwards upon your chest. Drop your head forward upon your chest and go to sleep. Go to sleep now. Sound, sound asleep.

"I take your right hand and place it flat on the top of your head. Press your hand tight against the top of your head when I place it there. The hypnotist now goes along quickly from subject to subject and places their right hand flat on the top of their head, pressing it firmly against the head, as he remarks: "Press your hand tight, tightly against your head." When all hands are in position along the line, he continues: "Your hand is pressing in tighter and tighter to your head. It is stuck there! Your hand is stuck so tightly to your head that you cannot pull it away no matter how hard you try. Try, try hard … you cannot pull your hand away from your head no matter how hard you try!"

If any subjects free their hands, unceremoniously dismiss them immediately. After the others have tugged for a moment or two, suggest: "Forget about your hands now. When I say three, your hands will fall from the top of your head down limply into your lap, and when it hits your lap it will send you down deep, deep, to sleep … when it hits your lap you will be sound asleep. Fast asleep. One, two, *three*."

Watch the hands drop and, by the abandoned way some fall, you will know who your best subjects are. Continue on with a few further suggestions: "You are fast asleep. Sound asleep and will follow my every suggestion in deep hypnosis."

Notice how direct and precise this method of induction is. The action starts immediately and there is no mincing of words. The subjects are told exactly what they are to do. They are not asked to do it, they are told to do it. The whole procedure is handled with a command approach, in a businesslike manner that shows the operator knows exactly what he is doing and expects obedience. Be positive. For nightclub hypnotising this presentation will be found especially good.

The show is now ready to get into gear and grind out entertainment. For an opening routine, following this induction, I have found body sensations of hot and cold effective and train the subjects in a hypnotic response that is strongly felt and yet does not call for too much body movement which might snap the subjects in lighter hypnosis awake. The handling runs thus: "You are sleeping deep in hypnosis and you are gaining an amazing control over your body ... so much so, in fact, that you can actually control the temperature of the room surrounding you. Think of how warm this room is becoming, and already you begin to feel the difference. It is starting to get warmer and warmer; it is getting hot. It is so warm and so hot that you cannot sit still in your chairs any more but squirm about to ease the heat. My, it is so hot. Wipe away the perspiration. Fan yourselves to try to get cool. It is so hot, hot, *hot!*"

Watch your subjects and gauge your suggestions to their responses, heaping suggestion upon suggestion as they react. Then suggest: "It is so hot you are taking off your coat to get cool. Take off your coat, take off your jacket. Get cool. Try to get cool to get away from the heat."

There is comedy and entertainment here. Watch your subjects and suggest the actions accordingly. Then suddenly change your tempo and suggest: "The heat is going away now. My, it has suddenly become cold in here. It is cold, cold, *cold!* You feel cold, so very, very cold. You are shivering. Better bundle up, bundle up, snuggle up. Brrrr, it is so cold, cold, *cold!* Better bundle up, snuggle up."

Watch your subjects and see how they respond to the suggestions. Gauge your suggestions to their actions and keep them flowing until you get the desired responses. Heap suggestion upon suggestion and build action upon action. It is very funny and amusing to the audience seeing the subjects first becoming very hot and then suddenly very cold. It seems amazing, but actually these temperature sensations are surprisingly easy for the subjects to experience, and their response deepens the somnambulistic condition in which you have placed them. You can end the experiment simply:"The cold is beginning to go away now. It is becoming warm in this room. It is warm and pleasant. Just the right temperature for perfect comfort to sleep in. You are perfectly comfortable and are fast asleep, deep, deep asleep!"

This opening test has accomplished three things: it has entertained the audience, it has actually functioned as a portion of the initial induction technique in deepening the committee's hypnosis, and it has trained the subjects in hypnotic responsiveness.

Your committee of subjects is now hypnotised and you can proceed with whatever show you have planned. Except for an occasional posthypnotic experiment for variety, there is no special need to awaken them between each test and then rehypnotise. Just go quickly from experiment to experiment, situation to situation with snappy routining; that is the nightclub way to present hypnosis. Know exactly how your show is to run and stick exactly to the pattern. Test follows test precisely as you have programmed it. It will not be attempted to tell the showman what particular routines he should use as that depends upon the individual performer and what experiments he has found most entertaining for his own use. Generally speaking, night, club hypnotic routines should be ones that incite laughter and even occasionally are a bit risqué . Experiments with a touch of sex such as seeing the audience and/or themselves in the nude, or a posthypnotic experience where a woman goes in to the audience and gives her husband a passionate kiss such as she did on her wedding night are examples of such presentations that might well be totally out of place in more staid show places, but are quite acceptable in the nightclub situation. Just remember to keep your show routined along action-laugh lines with the emphasis on entertainment.

Hypnotism and Alcohol

Liquor flows freely in nightclubs, and even some of your subjects may be "under the influence". However, this need not be of too great concern to the hypnotist as the imbibing of some alcohol actually increases suggestibility. It also removes some inhibitions and helps the show. However, remember this means some alcohol not too much alcohol. Too much alcohol depresses responses and befuddles attention, so persons too "high" should not be used as subjects. Should any such volunteer, dismiss them with a friendly pat on the back and jovial comment, "You'll have more fun sleeping it off at your table" – or some such.

Nightclub Showmanship

Keep your show rolling right along with well-oiled precision. Don't be a stuffed shirt; you must match your performing mood to the mood of the place. Never attempt the reverse of trying to make the club come to you ... you must go to it. That is one of the major rules of nightclub entertaining which is the reverse of stage show entertaining.

Keep yourself and your performance relaxed and full of good-natured fun. But, at the same time, let there be no doubt as to who is in command. Do that, and you will be a successful nightclub hypnotist.

Hypnotism Show Business

In this section, you are instructed in the dollars and cents side of hypnotism. You are shown how to advertise the hypnotism show: newspaper ads, window cards and posters, press stories, photos, newspaper interviews, magazine articles, radio spots and interviews. The hypnotism publicity feature of the "Window Sleep" is covered in detail, including hypnotism by radio presentation and other attention-grabbing stunts.

Chapter Seventy-Three
Advertising the Hypnotism Show

Publicity and public exposure is the life blood of the successful stage hypnotist. It is his or her road to fame. All such advertising factors lead the public to his box office, and box-office receipts are the success of show business. This end of hypnotism is vital to the stage hypnotist. In this chapter, we will discuss ways and means of advertising the hypnotism show, and getting the public out.

Newspaper Advertising

Newspapers form the backbone of theatrical advertising. The performer should have a major two-column ad prepared professionally. This should sell the show strongly, yet in a simple and direct manner. On the following pages will be found two examples that I have used for my show: one, when working as Dr Zomb years back, and the other showing my current "Concert of Hypnotism" handling. Both types have proved effective.

In addition to a two-column advertisement, the performer should have a one-column advertisement designed by an artist. The ad-art layouts are then made into cuts of the required sizes from which copies can be made for newspaper use. A one- and two-column ad will usually suffice for the hypnotism show.

Window Cards and Posters

The use of window cards to advertise the stage show is waning in modern usage as it is relatively expensive for what good it does. Especially in large cities, card coverage is expensive because, unless large quantities are used, they do little good in attracting attention to the show, and frequently posting must be handled by union men who charge a fee per card placed, which runs up the advertising budget.

In having window cards and posters printed be sure that a blank dating space is left (usually at the top of card). This is vital, as it is in this space that your dating copy goes, giving date, time and venue of the show. Such copy is imprinted in the blank space on the poster, often in contrasting colours so that it will stand out prominently on the card.

Two column ad layout as used in my "Concert of Hypnotism" show
The same artwork was used both in producing the major newspaper advertising for the show as well as the window cards.

Two-column ad layout as used in my Dr Zomb "Seance of Wonders" show. This layout functioned both as the major ad for the show as well as for the design of the posters used.

Reveen, the Australian hypnotist, took this full-page ad in
Variety Weekly **to thank Canada for his $1,000,000 season**

Current newspaper ads as used by Cole the Hypnotist. All effective advertising must contain complete dating copy, giving clearly the where, when, and time of the show. Such information is important to potential show-goers and is vital to the pulling power of the ad.

Above is a current newspaper ad as used by hypnotist, Pat Collins. Note the modern trend towards simplicity of handling. The rule of successful advertising is to present attractively the product one has to sell to the best advantage and make the public want to buy it. To the hypnotist this means: sell 'em what they're going to see!

For the stage hypnotist, advertising serves a double purpose. Not only is it essential to his obtaining an audience to see the show, but it also begins his actual hypnotising process. From a psychological standpoint, persons somnambulistic in nature who are especially susceptible to hypnosis are attracted to such performances. These people form the best subjects and function as the very nucleus of the hypnotism show. The performer's suggestions of: "Come up, come right up, come up on stage and be hypnotised!" produces a strong urge in such individuals to take part in the performance, and they come flocking onto the stage. Also, advertising increases the performer's prestige, and the "prestige factor" is an ingredient to the successful induction of hypnosis.

Effective advertising is the guarantee of the successful stage hypnotist.

Gimmicks such as offering half-price tickets to the first performance or "two for the price of one" ("twofers"), admitting child or student free to the show when accompanied by an adult, and selling tickets purchased in advance at a discount price are all devices to increase business at the box office. The professional stage hypnotist can use all such show business exploitation to his advantage.

525

In smaller cities, window cards are definitely effective. For my show, I use the same art design that I use for my major two-column newspaper ad. This is a good idea as it tends to associate the advertising of the show in one unit so that the newspaper advertising reinforces the poster advertising and vice versa. Some performers, of course, desire to have as much variety as possible in their advertising and use a different design and copy on their posters from that used in their newspaper ads; some even make use of several different types (design) of window cards that are posted about the city billing the show in much the same way as the old circus handling. Such is effective, but it is also expensive; using a single card design will usually suffice to advertise the stage show in our current times of high prices for everything.

Expense of production on window cards can be cut down somewhat by having the printing done on paper rather than on card stock. The paper posters must be put up in the store windows using scotch tape or some such, to hold them in position, rather than just being placed inside the window, as can be done in the case of regular window cards. Some merchants do not particularly like the use of tape on their windows. However, in most cases, permission will be granted.

> NOTE TO HYPNOTIST: If you use window cards and posters be sure to place enough of them up in the city to make a splash! Otherwise it is best to save your money. They should be well placed in as many store windows as possible and in prominent places such as on public bulletin boards. Posted effectively, they can do a good selling job for your show.

Newspaper Stories

In addition to newspaper advertising, the use of press stories publicising the performer and his show should be used. Such publicity runs free and is very important to the showman hypnotist. A number of such stories should be prepared and Xeroxed so that these can be given out as needed to the local newspaper editors at the same time that the ads are placed. As the ads are paid for, this is an incentive for the editor to run your stories in his paper. Be sure that full dating copy as to venue and time of the show is given to the editor so that this information can be correctly inserted in the story copy.

Along with each press story, it is well to include a photo-mat that can be run in the newspaper. This is simply your photo (action or portrait as the case may be) reduced to one-column and two-column size cuts (use both: there is no point in having any photo-mats made in larger than two-column size as the papers will never use them) and screened correctly for newspaper reproduction. Mats can then be run off from the halftone cuts, and these given to the editor along with your press stories. The use of a photo in connection with a story always increases its interest and reader attention value.

I present a couple of press stories as used in my own show while playing a tour in Australia some years back under the show title of "The Miracle Show". These can function as illustrations for the writing of your own releases. And following is a short press release of the well-known Italian hypnotist, Dr Ceccarelli.

Hypnotic Show by Dr Ceccarelli

Dr Ceccarelli is one entertainer who can put audiences to sleep during his act and brag about it afterwards. Ceccarelli's act isn't all that boring. He's an Italian hypnotist, and putting the audience to sleep is one part of his fascinating show.

The only thing boring about Ceccarelli is his eyes. They can look right through you and, by the time you count to three, your hands which you've been told to clench and raise over your head won't come unlocked until he gives the word. A skill like that could come in handy during a riot, in the hands of the right people.

Ceccarelli's biographical data gives rise to some thought. He claims to have put hundreds of British soldiers "under" via radio so that they could sleep harmlessly through an Italian military operation during World War II.

This may explain why so very few Allied soldiers were endangered by the Italian military during that conflict. Perhaps we should be thankful that the Germans didn't find out about him, too. They only had the SS, the Panzers, the 88s, V-1s and 2s going for them.

All kidding aside, Ceccarelli is mass entertainment at its best.

In planning your personal press releases, don't make the mistake of being modest. Often enough the editor will tone them down anyhow, and every so often you'll be lucky and get them through verbatim.

ORMOND McGILL IN MYSTERY REVIEW FOR LOCAL GROUP

Those attending the exciting road-show attraction, "East Indian Miracles", which will be presented in this city by Ormond McGill, will have the unusual opportunity of witnessing many genuine demonstrations of scientific hypnotism. They will enjoy watching their friends hypnotized on the stage in a riot of marvels and laughs and they may even learn how to hypnotize themselves.

Ormond McGill, "The Man Called Dr. Zomb", is one of America's leading hypnotists and the author of several medical books on hypnotism. He claims that the art of self-hypnotism may be learned by any intelligent person and that with the mastery of that skill, a person can overcome unwanted habits, can increase their memory, and can even abolish the feeling of pain while having a tooth extracted at the dentist's. Using volunteers, from the audience, he will demonstrate such phenomena. [Persons who have previously witnessed an hypnotic demonstration know what a treat is in store for them; those who have not as yet enjoyed such an unique experience are in for a delightful surprise.]

"East Indian Miracles" is really three shows in one. The first part will incorporate spectacular illusions featuring 1001 Magical Wonders gathered from the remote regions of the world. These will include the Girl In The Haunted House Illusion, A Boy Beheaded By Fire, Escape From The Dungeon of Calcutta and The Delhi Sacred Sacrafice. Part two exhibits many feats of Mental Wizardry that have astounded audiences throughout the world. In part three persons in the audience will come up on the stage and actually duplicate many magic feats of the mind. McGill claims that his feats of hypnotism are 100% authentic and he offers $50,000.00 to any person proving that he uses confederates in any of his demonstrations.

Following the regular two and one-half hour show, those interested will be invited to remain for a session of "self-hypnosis". It is believed that many who are nervous, irritable, jumpy or suffering from hyper-tension will benefit by learning how to induce deep relaxation through self-hypnosis.

"East Indian Miracles", now on a world tour, is guaranteed to provide entertainment for the entire family. Ormond McGill and his company of assistants provide a full evening of clean and amazing fun which will long be remembered.

528

TV HYPNOTIST TO APPEAR IN STAGE SHOW

Ormond McGill is one of the pioneers in bringing hypnotism to radio and television. His frequent appearances on such popular coast-to coast network programs as "Life With Linkletter", "Meet The Missus", "G. E. House Party", "Maxwell House Program" and "People Are Funny" have earned for him the reputation of "TV's Mystery Star". Now on a round-the-world tour with his giant two and a half hour roadshow, "East Indian Miracles", McGill combines the hypnotic arts with those of a magician to bring his audiences a delightful fare of fascinating mystery.

Actually three shows in one, the first section of "East Indian Miracles" features spectacular illusions among which will be seen the "Dungeon of Calcutta", a thriller from India being presented in this country for the first time. Part two of the show exhibits feats of mental wizardry for which Ormond McGill is world famous. Part three climaxes the show with the sensational "Seance of Hypnotism".

Ormond McGill maintains that the East Indian mystics and fakirs accomplish much of their wonders through the power of hypnotism. Therefore, he will invite persons from the audience to come up on the stage and actually duplicate these amazing feats of the mind.

Hollywood and Broadway celebrities such as Edward Arnold, Charles Boyer, Bette Davis, Hedy LaMarr, William Bendix, John Wayne and Amos and Andy are among those who have been entertained by "The Man Known As Dr. Zomb". This show has been brought to this city by a local organization and will be presented in a local auditorium at an early date with the proceeds going to a worthy cause.

Tickets for the show will be on sale at the Advance Ticket Sale Box Office and from the members of the local organization which is sponsoring the roadshow here in this city. A limited number of reserved seats will be available and they will be sold only in advance.

Ormond McGill, "The Man Called Dr. Zomb", is the hypnotist and magician who will present the roadshow presentation, "East Indian Miracles" on the stage of a local auditorium. This attraction will feature stage illusions, Fakir Mysteries, mass hypnotism and a session of "self-hypnosis". This show is sponsored by a local organization for the benefit of a worthy cause.

NOTE TO EDITORS:
Please insert name of your city, date of show, and sponsoring organization into stories on this page.—THANKS.

Photo-mat Press Releases

It is well to supply the newspaper editor with various photo-mats of yourself and your show. Give them the mats along with your personal press stories all ready to go. As they say, "one picture is worth a 1,000 words", and good photos used in conjunction with your publicity releases greatly increase advertising values.

Newspaper Interviews

In addition to press stories of his own circulation to the newspapers, in cosmopolitan areas good publicity can be obtained by having a special press interview with a staff writer or columnist who can do a feature story on the performer. These usually have to have a novel slant to give them special reader interest, and are written under the columnist's byline. An example of such an article is shown on the following pages.

The hypnotist will find out that there is one main difference between the press story and the press interview. In the former, he can write up and pass out what he wishes about himself and his show, while in the press interview he is at the mercy of the staff writer. One never knows for sure just what they are going to write, and it is usually the writer's prerogative to add a bit of "bite". Whatever they write, it's all good publicity for the showman.

Magazine Articles

Yet another source of publicity/advertising for the hypnotist via the journalistic field are magazine articles. They are usually not so personal as the press interview, and carry more of a story angle. A theme for such must be sought to make them effective. Usually, the performer can present ideas and photographs for such articles, but the actual handling and what is done with the material is in the hands of the writer.

PACIFIC

STARS AND STRIPES

AN AUTHORIZED UNOFFICIAL PUBLICATION
FOR THE U.S. ARMED FORCES OF THE PACIFIC COMMAND

The Entrancing Dr. Furst

By CPO TOM GSELL
S&S Staff Writer

TOKYO—His eyes stared owlishly as Dr. Arnold Furst's deep voice assured, "Even though hypnotists have no special power, entertainers often try to give the impression that they have a mysterious control over their supposedly helpless subjects.

"Never mind the hocus-pocus, mumbo-jumbo and other baloney," soothed Dr. Furst with mesmeric gestures during an interview between lectures for physicians and dentists in Japan. In 1943 he began as a magician entertaining troops overseas with the USO, but later became serious about hypnosis.

"Hypnosis is not an art nor is it a science," said Furst. "It's a skill which anyone can learn, although some will be better than others.

"There are three kinds of people who come to me asking to be taught hypnosis," he said. "I refuse to associate with charlatans who want to add hypnosis to their fraudulent practice and I'm impatient with individuals who want to use self-hypnosis as a substitute for honest effort. However, I cooperate fully with professional therapists who have a legitimate use."

Presenting one-day courses at U.S. military hospitals and for Japanese medical and dental groups, Furst enables his trainees to immediately apply his rapid induction techniques in daily treatment of patients. He is now on his 14th semi-annual tour of Japan.

"Many leading American

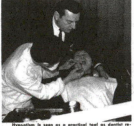

Hypnotism is seen as a practical tool as dentist removes nerve from tooth of entranced subject. During show, a hypnotized subject lies on a bed of nails (right) and feels none the worse for the young lady standing on his chest.

medical and dental colleges include graduate courses in hypnotherapy," Furst pointed out, "and it's also used extensively in veterans hospitals.

"In dentistry," he cited, "the use of hypnosis in therapy, called hypnotherapy, assures painless and bloodless tooth removal without the risk of toxic after effects encountered in other forms of anesthesia."

In a recent case at the 249th General Hospital at Camp Drake near Tokyo, hypnosis may have saved the life of an

American soldier from Vietnam who had previously suffered a heart attack. The patient also had a severely decayed tooth feeding poisons into his blood stream further aggravating his heart condition. The soldier had been receiving anti-coagulants and the dentist refused to extract the tooth for fear of the soldier's bleeding to death.

Dr. George Sardina of the medical department was consulted and he induced hypnosis so the tooth was painlessly removed without loss of blood.

"Minute muscles along arteries and veins respond to the brain's stimulus," explained Furst. He recalled that, "Dr. Sardina had finished my course just the night before and this was his first therapeutic use of hypnosis."

The author of "How to Prepare and Administer Hypnotic Prescriptions," Furst also co-authored the book "Case Histories in Hypnotherapy" with Dr. Lester T. Kashiwa of Maui General Hospital in Hawaii. His books reveal many dramatic cases of hypnotherapy.

"Hypnotherapy has many medical uses," he said, "such as stopping bleeding and treating shock, amnesia, mental illness and even killing pain in childbirth."

At the 106th General Hospital at Kishine Barracks near Tokyo two years ago, Furst aided another soldier from Vietnam. Afflicted with about 40 shrapnel wounds, he was receiving the maximum amount of morphine for nerve damage but couldn't be evacuated to the United States until the intensity of his pain subsided.

"He was amazed and happy, too," recalled Furst, "when I proved to him that he could make the pain go and stay away. His doctor's eyes glistened with tears as he saw his patient's happiness over the prospect of going home."

Do entertainers using hypnosis lower the public's respect? "Does wrestling on television deter young men from entering college and Olympics wrestling?" he countered. A proponent of stage hypnosis, Furst's

tours include night club performances. No pin-eyed Svengali, he finds no need to gesture theatrically nor does he chant mysterious formulas. In his rapid induction technique, he merely talks to his subjects in a friendly and confident manner and they comply within seconds.

Watching Furst perform at the Sands Club in downtown Tokyo last fall, the assistant manager was not convinced. However, he sought out the hypnotist's subjects after the show and was impressed by one man who insisted he sensed no heat from a lit cigarette lighter held under his hand. Another subject testified that he felt refreshed after he rested on a bed of nails with someone standing on his chest.

Furst returned to Japan early this month after performances at the Cafe de Paris in Bangkok and a special demonstration at the home of Thailand's Prime Minister Thamon Kittikachorn. In Osaka, Feb. 11, he assisted a dentist with painless removal of a nerve from a patient's tooth with hypnosis.

"I was confident of success," said Furst, "because I had once used self-hypnosis on myself to aid my personal dentist in removal of a nerve from one of my teeth. But I confess," he said with a chuckle, "having convinced my dentist it was sure to work, I was momentarily apprehensive."

Furst said, he was "willing to talk without charge to any group of U.S. military medical or dental therapists."

Pacific Stars & Stripes 9
Thursday, March 4, 1971

DR. FURST HYPNOTIZES SUBJECT INTO RIGIDITY.

Hypnotic Photographs

Of great use in all aspects of hypnotic advertising are photographs. Pictures tell a story at a glance and their use cannot be over-rated. For booking purposes, newspaper advertising and publicising the hypnotism show they are invaluable.

Hypnotic photos fall largely into two classes: planned photographs and "on-the-spot" shots. Use both. Get a good professional photographer with theatrical know-how to do your portrait and planned work, and then, whenever possible, get others with a camera to shoot your show and catch bits of your hypnotic work under fire, as it were. You will soon have a fine selection of photographs to work with. It is a file that all showmen must build and keep as one never knows when such will be needed in a multitude of useful ways in the advancement of their career.

What It's Like To Be Under Hypnotic Spell

No Memory Of Writing This Story

By JAMES P. BENNETT
Herald-Examiner Staff Writer

"When I count to five you will slowly go under . . . you will feel your eyes growing heavy and you will be asleep . . ."

When hypnotist Ormond McGill said I would be asleep at the count of five the last thing I remember was his soft voice saying "five" and out I went.

This experiment in hypnosis took place in the photo room of The Herald-Examiner yesterday—proving that even hard-headed reporters can succumb to the "great power of suggestion."

What does it feel like?

RESTFUL SLEEP

That's hard to say, because one doesn't really recall what it is like to be under. It was a deep sleep, a sound sleep, a restful sleep.

I am told that at McGill's suggestion, I changed seats several times — but I have no memory of it.

'WHEN I COUNT TO FIVE . . .'
Hypnotist Ormond McGill tells reporter James Bennett

I am told that I held my arms rigid and then rotated them for several minutes — but I have no memory of this, either.

I am also told that McGill suggested that I stay away from rich foods if I want to loose some not-so-needed pounds — but I imagine that this remains to be seen.

McGill is most capable as a hypnotist. His voice is gentle and soothing.

PRACTICAL SIDE

His performance is just as smooth, and can be seen three nights weekly at the Ivar Theater in Hollywood.

There is a practical side of hypnosis if used properly McGill contends.

As far as I'm concerned he's right — it gave me a 20-minute nap on office time.

P.S.—I just woke up.

The above was written under post-hypnotic suggestion by McGill's, and can truthfully be said I don't remember writing a line.

I recall little beyond McGill's fine-grained voice saying "Five" which must prove something or other.

And, I'm not hungry. When this experiment was conducted it was lunch time and I recall thinking that I wanted to get it over with so I could have lunch. Now I have no desire for food.

"I didn't suggest any particular diet for you," McGill now tells me. "I merely suggested that you stay away from rich foods, lower your level of eating."

Who knows, I may become "old Slim Jim" once again.

Mysterious Groovies!

If you haven't met a groovy before, pick up a Sunday Herald - Examiner and see what all the talk's about.

20-MINUTE NAP ON OFFICE TIME!
Reporter Bennett under the hypnotic trance

Radio Spots

The hypnotist will find it well to have a number of prepared radio spots that advertise his show. Radio gives good coverage, and the smaller stations covering local communities are relatively inexpensive. Also, you will find them usually rather generous with their time; if you are a "good fellow with the boys" they will often run extra spots gratis in addition to those you pay for.

You can write your own spots; have them duplicated, and leave with the station. Their announcer will read them effectively. Below are a couple of examples. It is important to be certain that each spot carries, in addition to your message, complete coverage about the time and venue of your show, as getting across the dating message, via radio, is most important. Nothing is more frustrating to a listener than to stir up his interest and then leave him dangling as to where and when the show is going to be. Below are a couple of examples of radio spots as I have used them in my own show:

Radio Spot One ... McGill Show

ANNOUNCER: Have you ever been hypnotised? New thrills and excitement await you. the great "concert of hypnotism" is coming to town. presented by America's master hypnotist, Ormond McGill. This sensational show will play here in this city for [number of nights] nights starting [date of show's opening]. Make a date now to attend this great show for the fun times when you see your own friends hypnotised on the stage. The "concert of hypnotism" guarantees more laughs per minute than any show you have ever seen. Remember the date [insert careful date copy here as to where the show is being presented, what date[s] the show is being presented, and at what time the show is being presented]. Tickets may be obtained at the door.

Radio Spot Two ... McGill Show

Sound of laughter recording ... fade out:

ANNOUNCER: Laughter, fun, excitement and thrills are coming to town when the great "concert of hypnotism" plays at the [name] auditorium on [show dates]. The show is being presented in this city by America's master hypnotist, Ormond McGill. It is entertainment the entire family will enjoy. Ormond McGill guarantees that all of his experiments in hypnotism are genuine and offers a reward of $50,000 to any person proving he uses stooges in any of his demonstrations. Be sure you see this exciting show ... it is totally unlike anything you have ever seen before. Remember the date [repeat dating copy in full].

Radio spots function as specific and repeated reminders of the coming show. They don't have to do a whale of a selling job in themselves. They simply stir up a bit of interest that ties in with the other advertising on the show that has been placed about the city. Let the station management assist you in designing your spots. Used wisely, readio spots are good business boosters.

Radio Interviews

While at the station placing your spots, you can arrange for an interview or two. Radio stations like to interview interesting guests on various programmes, and will be happy to use you. This provides you with a wonderful opportunity to plug your show, but, remember, you must be entertaining when you go on the air.

In planning the radio interview be sure to make it interesting; if you are interesting then the listening audience will be interested in what you have to say and very likely many of them will be interested in later seeing your show. On the other hand, if you are a bore or have a poorly planned interview this can actually kill business for the show.

Hypnotism carries a lot of public interest in its subject matter so there is no reason why you cannot present a very effective radio showing. I have found that a question-and-answer session about hypnotism is most effective for interview use. In this regard, it is well to prepare in advance a list of pertinent questions about hypnotism that you can give to the station interviewer to ask you. He will be pleased to receive these and you can thus have good answers to the questions ready on the tip of your tongue. Following are a few examples of such questions that you can use; these can be elaborated upon as the performer desires:

QUESTION: What is hypnotism?

ANSWER: No one knows for certain exactly what hypnotism is. There are many theories of course. About as close as one can get is that it is an induced state of mind characterised by extreme suggestibility. Hypnotism is the art of creating this hypnotic state.

QUESTION: Who can be hypnotised?

ANSWER: Every person of reasonable intelligence can be hypnotised. Some people can be hypnotised very quickly at the very first attempt, while others have to try it a few times in order to achieve the skill. At the show, I give an equal opportunity to all who may wish to try entering hypnosis.

QUESTION: Does a man or woman make the better subject?

ANSWER: The question of sex does not seem to enter into the matter as to who is the better hypnotic subject. In my program, I try to have an equal number of both sexes on the stage as it makes things more interesting that way.

QUESTION: Is it easier to hypnotise a woman than a man?

ANSWER: I cannot say I have noticed any difference in how quickly one or another subject can be hypnotised. Man or woman, they seem equally as fast, or equally as slow. The description of "easy" is an incorrect definition.

QUESTION: Is a person with a high IQ harder to hypnotise than a person with a low IQ?

ANSWER: I would say that a person with a high IQ would make a better subject generally than one with a low IQ as it requires concentration in order to enter hypnosis, and concentration is a characteristic that goes along with intelligence.

QUESTION: Is age an important factor in being hypnotised?

ANSWER: No, I have not found it to be particularly important. In general, I try to get a mixed group of subjects on the stage from high school, through college to adult age levels.

QUESTION: How long does it take to hypnotise the average person?

ANSWERS: As everyone is individual, he responds in his own individual manner and at his own individual speed. Some persons can be hypnotised in a few seconds, while others take a considerably longer period. In my stage demonstrations of hypnotism, I operate with rapid methods of induction, as pace is important to a good show and entertainment is the thing.

This list of possible questions and answers about hypnotism could go on and on, but these will serve to illustrate the handling. It is well to tie the answers in the direction of your show when you can do it unobtrusively, as building public interest to see the show is the basic purpose of the interview.

Television Interviews

Similar to radio, interviews on guest spots by the hypnotist can be easily arranged at local TV stations. They are always looking for interesting guests.

Television offers an excellent medium for the performer to sell his show; however, TV interviews have to be even more carefully planned than do the ones for radio as the performer's appearance is important here as well as his voice and what he has to say.

Television providing visual entertainment, as it does, will give you the opportunity to show what you can do over the air. If you have an interesting mystery stunt of some kind that you can use in your interviews, use it, but don't let them talk you into hypnotising on these local TV shows; save that for your own show.

NOTE TO HYPNOTIST: The stage hypnotist will do well to be exclusively a stage hypnotist. The only time I recommend he present hypnotic demonstrations off stage is in connection with some publicity feature such as the "Window Sleep" or as a special television guest-spot feature. Such provide excellent opportunity to advance his name and publicise his show.

Chapter Seventy-Four
Hypnotism Publicity Miracles

For more than a hundred years the "Window Sleep" has been used as an effective publicity stunt to advertise the hypnotism show. I used it extensively during the period I was touring the theatres with my Dr Zomb "Seance of Wonders" show.

This is definitely a "wild attraction", and to lift the stunt to the status of dignity that a hypnotism show deserves it must be presented with care. These eight points of handling should be maintained:

1. City Licence and Police Permission

Check at the city hall for any permits required to present a public demonstration feat of this kind. Also arrange for permission from the police department and request that some police be on hand to handle the crowds. Advance attention to these details can save possible conflicts at the time the demonstration is made public had not civic permission been obtained. It will be found that city officials will respond much more graciously to such publicity if they are sought out in advance than if the demonstration is put on "behind their backs", as it were.

2. The Window

Have your personal manager in conjunction with the local theatre manager line up the store window that will be used. Try to obtain the best possible store, located right in the very heart of the city, that has a large display window. Generally speaking, the more prestige the store has the more prestige the stunt will acquire, so try to obtain the city's best. As "The Window Sleep" will attract large crowds and provides much advertising for the store, arrangements are easily made.

3. Setting the Window

The more attractively the window can be dressed for the demonstration the better. A large bed should be in the centre neatly made with crisp sheets and luxurious blankets. A sign with copy similar to this is then placed in the window (as this example used by me):

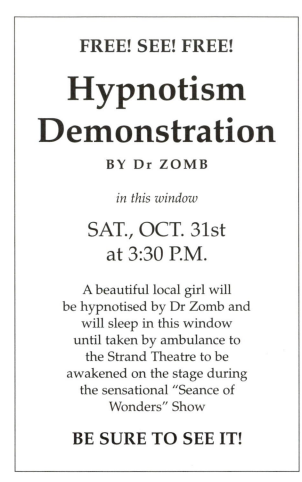

FREE! SEE! FREE!

Hypnotism Demonstration

BY Dr ZOMB

in this window

SAT., OCT. 31st at 3:30 P.M.

A beautiful local girl will
be hypnotised by Dr Zomb and
will sleep in this window
until taken by ambulance to
the Strand Theatre to be
awakened on the stage during
the sensational "Seance of
Wonders" Show

BE SURE TO SEE IT!

Be sure also to have in the store window quarter cards and/or signs calling attention to the hypnotism stage show at the theatre. Always to be alert to your advertising and publicity values is the mark of the real showman.

4. Additional Advertising

Include in a box, under your regular ads on the show, in the local newspapers calling attention of the free hypnotism demonstration in the store window. Give date, time and place. Also such can be included in the show's radio announcements over the air. All of this additional advertising of the "Window Sleep" will be appreciated by the store that has donated its window as it plugs the store at the same time, and such assures a large crowd being assembled to see a free demonstration.

5. The Hypnotic Subject for the Window Sleep

Use a local woman as the subject for the demonstration. Theatre managers frequently use one of their employees for this purpose or else run a small classified ad asking for a girl interested in taking part in the hypnotic demonstration. She is paid for her services. Women are to meet in the manager's office a couple of hours before the stunt is scheduled to take place in the store window, at which time the hypnotist will select the one most suitable. Privately the girls are hypnotised and the one most responsive to hypnosis is selected. Often only one girl will be available, in which event the hypnotist must work with her carefully to entrance her deeply. For this purpose, I personally employed the careful technique outlined in my "Master Method of Hypnotism".

This preconditioning of the girl to be used in the demonstration is important, as the sleep is to run several hours; the success of the feat is vital, as were it to fail, it would greatly harm the success of the stage show. Make it your rule never to enter the store window with a strange, untried subject. By "conditioning" the woman for hypnosis in advance, the performer knows exactly what response he may expect, and the demonstration will run smoothly.

6. Window Sleep Details

The length of the sleep should run not more than five hours. Longer sleeps have been done, but five hours will be found quite long enough to give it full effectiveness and still not be too difficult for the sleeping girl. Arrange to start the demonstration around 3:30 p.m. This is a good time as the children will be out of school by then and will be there to join the crowd to witness the stunt. You want them there as they are good potential customers for the show.

Be sure to have a public-address system set up in the store window (mike inside window and speakers outside) so that the crowd can both see and hear what goes on, and you can talk to them. Over the PA music can be played in advance of the demonstrations and continued on throughout the afternoon and early evening while the girl is sleeping. It adds to the effect. Occasionally, the demonstration can be dressed even more by having a young woman in a nurse's uniform in attendance in the window while the girl is sleeping with an ambulance parked out in front of the store by the curb. Such "medical handling" builds interest. In the window, have both a heater and a fan so you can adjust the temperature to the sleeping girl's comfort. Attention to such small details are important to the smooth running of the demonstration.

7. Presentation of the Window Sleep

When you and the girl enter the window be sure that both of you are well groomed. As the performer, be clean shaven and neatly, but conservatively dressed. And she likewise should be attractively attired. Indeed, the better looking the girl used the more effective will be the publicity stunt. All must look high class.

At the appointed time, enter the window and start talking to the crowd over the mike. Be sure to begin right on the dot as scheduled. Once you are in the window, just take your time and let the crowd build while you talk to them about hypnosis and the interesting demonstration they are going to see. As long as there is something going on, the crowd will stay and a crowd attracts yet a bigger crowd. Just take your time.

Start by saying what you intend to do, i.e., how a local young woman, whom many of them undoubtedly know personally, has volunteered to be the subject in this hypnotic experiment, that you will hypnotise her and she will be left sleeping in full view in the window until 7:30 p.m., at which time she will be taken from the window, by ambulance, directly to the stage of the Strand Theatre (or as the case may be), to be awakened on the stage during the show that evening. In presenting the "Window Sleep", always, thus, tie in the awakening of the subject on the stage during the show, as its value as a business-getter lies especially in whetting the public's curiosity to see the successful conclusion of the feat. You can also make some comments about the exciting things they are going to see at the show to build interest in attending. You have a wonderful chance for direct advertising here.

Handle yourself and your conversation in the window in a dignified manner to lift the demonstration into the direction of class. The woman is then introduced, and over the mike she is asked if she is willing to be the subject to be hypnotised. After she confirms, she is seated on the side of the bed, and you proceed to hypnotise her. Take your time doing this as it is interesting to the watchers and it what they came to see. *In the hypnotising process, and while you are in the window, at no time touch the woman yourself.* After she is hypnotised, have your assistant lower her to the bed and gently cover her. Then suggest to the hypnotised woman:

"Adjust yourself in a position of complete comfort to yourself ... snuggle down into the bed in perfect comfort and sleep soundly now. You will sleep soundly and pleasantly and nothing will bother or awaken you until I awaken you on the stage of the Strand Theatre tonight during the show."

Leave the woman sleeping on the bed, turn to the crowd outside the window and comment that you will return from time to time to check on the subject to see that she is sleeping safely, and then leave the window and go out of the store by the back entrance. It will be found best to handle your exit this way, as you can avoid conversation with watchers which lowers the dramatic value of the demonstration and removes aesthetic distance by being too informal.

Every so often, throughout the afternoon, drop into the window to inspect the sleeping woman. While there, you can give suggestions that she can move her body or turn any way that she desires for perfect comfort. Stay but a few moments after making your professional observations and then leave. The last time you come, you can say to the subject: "You have only an hour or so more to sleep before they come to take you in the ambulance to the theatre where I will awaken you from hypnosis on the stage. As they move you from the bed, it will send you down deeper and yet deeper to sleep in deep hypnosis and you will not be disturbed in any way."

8. Concluding the Window Sleep

At the arranged time, the attendants can come to the store window, place the woman on a rolling stretcher and carry her to the waiting ambulance to drive her to the theatre. You need not be on hand for this removal from the window. Indeed, it is better showmanship if you are not. Have the ambulance turn on its siren as it drives through the city streets to make a good show.

The woman is then driven directly to the theatre in the ambulance, a most effective proceeding as it sirens its way through the streets. She is rolled directly into the theatre lobby and left still sleeping on the stretcher. Attendants are appointed ready to roll her down the theatre aisle and lift the stretcher up on to the stage at the chosen spot in your performance that you desire it, and you proceed to awaken the woman by these suggestions:

"At 3:30 this afternoon you were hypnotised in the window of the such-and-such store and have been sleeping there ever since. It is now [state time as you look at your watch] in the evening and we are on the stage of the Strand Theatre. I am going to awaken you now and you will feel just fine, and here is a very interesting thing. When you wake up it will seem to you that you have but barely closed your eyes and dozed off to sleep. Time will have seemed not to have existed at all for you, and you will awaken feeling wonderfully well, rested and happy. And you will tell your friends how wonderful you feel when they ask you about your remarkable experience."

Awaken the woman from the hypnosis. Help her up from the stretcher gently. Thank her and have the audience give the young lady a nice round of applause for her part in the demonstration. You have success-fully concluded the feat ... and your show moves on.

Effectively advertised and presented "The Window Sleep" will be found to have excellent publicity value that will attract large crowds down to the store window to see it and, what is more important, into the theatre to see your show. Even more effective advertising value can be obtained. If you present the demonstration via television or radio.

The "Window Sleep" via TV or Radio

If there is a television station in the city, you can present the stunt over TV by having the station's remote truck cover the window while you are on camera at the station. The programme can be monitored to switch back and forth from the camera at the store to that in the studio to make an effective show. Handle it as a news event. Or, if there is no television station available, you can likewise present it very effectively via the local radio station. There are two ways to do this:

1. A radio set is beside the bed in the store window. Your assistant tends to the initial details in the window explaining to the watching crowd that you are at the local radio station and that at such and such a time you will hypnotise the woman over the air. He arranges all details of introducing the woman, seats her on the side of the bed, holds a crys-tal ball (or a flaming lamp) before her eyes to gaze into, etc.

    When you come on air, be sure the radio set in the window by the bed has a mike (PA) placed by it so that the watching crowd can hear what you say as you hypnotise the subject via radio. Attention to such details is important. My script for this handling runs thus:

    Music fades out ... end of hypnotising by Dr Zomb.

    ANNOUNCER: We have just received a phone call from the _____ store advising that the young woman is fast asleep. According to the report, at the beginning of the experiment, the woman directed her eyes into the flame of an oriental lamp and followed exactly Dr Zomb's commands. Gradually her eyelids flickered and closed as the

Doctor counted. Next she collapsed, her body being then stretched out on the bed and carefully covered … and now she is sleeping peacefully dead to the world.

Remember, ladies and gentlemen, this hypnotised young woman will be sleeping here in this window from now until eight o'clock tonight, at which time she will be taken to the _____ Theatre to be awakened on the stage during the "Seance of Wonders". You are all most cordially invited to come on down to see for yourselves the startling result of this demonstration in radio hypnotism which has our whole city talking … and then, tonight, witness the astounding awakening of this hypnotised woman, which will take place right during the "Seance of Wonders" on the stage of the _____ Theatre. This is but one thrill among the thousand and one wonders that you will see tonight when you witness the internationally famous "Seance of Wonders" conducted by Dr Zomb. Make your plans now to attend! The theatre management reports that this great show has been playing to capacity business everywhere, so if you wish to be certain of a good seat, it is suggested that you purchase your tickets early. Tickets are now on sale at the box office.

This is your announcer, _____, now signing off. Dr Zomb is on his way to the window of the _____ store to check on the hypnotised young lady. We will be seeing you.

Mysterious mood music … rise up, establish, fade out.

2. An even more effective way of handling this "Hypnotism via Radio" feature is to arrange for the station to have a line and a studio announcer in the store window. Then the announcer can broadcast right from the store window and can give a man-on-the-street approach asking various spectators in the crowd what they think of the demonstration, what they think of hypnotism and such like, and handle the broadcast right on the air as a news event. He can then transfer controls over directly to the studio where the performer is, and the hypnotising proceeds.

When the woman is asleep, the announcer in the window then takes it back and tells the audience, both on the spot and over the air, just what happened and builds it up as an event of real public interest. An announcement about the stage show can then be given; mention being made that tickets are now on sale at the theatre's box office, and for everyone to be sure to come and get theirs early as tickets for the show will undoubtably be sold out?

In your enthusiasm and attention to detail to successfully present the "Window Sleep" demonstration, don't forget the importance of selling tickets to the stage show: after all, this is the real purpose of the whole proceedings.

Here is my script for this line in the window handling.

Radio script for Dr Zomb's "Hypnotism via Radio" programme (to be used when working with line and announcer in store window):

ANNOUNCER (at studio): Ladies and gentlemen, your attention please! For the next fifteen minutes we will present one of the most unusual broadcasts ever attempted in the history of radio. A programme personally conducted by Dr Zomb of the internationally famous "Seance of Wonders"… hypnotism via radio.

Mysterious mood music … rise up, establish, fade out.

ANNOUNCER: At this moment, here beside me in our _____ studios is Dr Zomb, and in the window of the _____ store is a young woman, who, of her own free will, has volunteered to be the subject in this sensational experiment in modern hypnotism. She is a local woman, a resident of _____; undoubtedly many of you know her personally.

We have just received word that a huge crowd is gathered before the store's window to witness this thrilling demonstration, and the young woman is seated upright on a luxurious bed inside the window itself. Beside her is a radio set tuned to the station to which you are now listening, and over this set shortly will come the voice of Dr Zomb in an attempt to hypnotise over the air. Dr Zomb has asked me especially to mention that no person listening to this programme need have the slightest concern that they will become hypnotised, as only the young woman towards whom he is directly concentrating will be influenced.

And now, just before Dr Zomb takes over the microphone here in the studio of _____, we shall first transfer controls to the window of _____ store, where _____ is on location to give you a first-hand account of what is taking place down there. Come in _____.

ANNOUNCER (in window): This is _____ reporting from the window of _____ store. A gigantic crowd has gathered down here today to witness this exciting experiment. People are crowding and pushing up against the window, and I see them perched on car fenders and in every conceivable position as they strive to get a better view into the window. Everyone seems strangely tense and expectant as if somehow a spell of mystery were beginning to hang over them, as they eagerly await the culmination of this amazing demonstration in hypnotic science.

Miss _____, the young woman who has volunteered to be the subject in this hypnotic experiment, is here in this window seated upright on a luxurious bed. Where do you live, Miss _____?

Woman answers question.

"How do you feel about participation in this feat, Miss _____? Do you have any qualms or misgivings?"

Woman answers question.

Well, we sure do consider you a mighty brave woman, and anxiously await the outcome of this fascinating exhibition. We have also in the window with us today Dr Zomb's personal assistant, Mr _____. Sir, can you tell us some details of what we may expect to see in this demonstration, and a few words as to just what hypnotism is?

ASSISTANT: Well, hypnotism is a condition produced through the concentration of the mind along certain directed lines that produces a mental state in which ideas are accepted and acted upon automatically. This hypnotic state of mind differs from normal behaviour in that the hypnotised subject does not respond to their own conscious thoughts, but rather responds subconsciously as directed by the mind of the hypnotist.

In this particular demonstration, Dr Zomb will entrance the young woman, not by personal contact as is usually the case in most experiments with hypnotism, but instead he will hypnotise her by a remote control process of his own, which is what makes this experiment so unique. As his thoughts and his voice come to her over the radio, you will witness some most intriguing mental transfigurations.

ANNOUNCER: That is certainly most interesting. Tell me, has Dr Zomb been successful in performing such a hypnotic feat over radio before?

ASSISTANT: Yes indeed, hypnotism via radio has become an exclusive feature with Dr Zomb, and so closely associated with his name that he has become internationally known as the one man who has powerfully cultivated this unique ability to hypnotise over the air.

ANNOUNCER: Thank you, Mr _____. I notice a number of spectators crowding in close to the microphone to get in a position for a better view of the demonstration. Here's a gentleman over here. Tell me, sir, what is your name?

Spectator gives name.

And what is your reaction to all of this excitement?

Spectator answers question.

How would you like to be the subject in a hypnotic demonstration such as this?

Spectator answers question.

Various additional questions can be asked of different persons standing close by in the watching crowd as time allows.

Well, it looks as though we are ready to proceed with the actual experiment, so come in once again _____ at our _____ studios.

ANNOUNCER (at studio): This is _____ back at the control room of our _____ studios. You have just heard a first-hand account of what is going on at the _____ store's window, and now that all is in readiness for this experiment in hypnotism via radio, it gives me great pleasure to present the man who has so modernised and streamlined hypnotism that he has become acknowledged America's premier hypnotist, Dr Zomb!

Music "Claire de Lune" … rise up, establish, fade to background behind voice Dr Zomb hypnotises woman over the air (maximum time five minutes).

Music fades out. End of hypnotising by Zomb.

ANNOUNCER: We take you now once again directly to the window of _____ store, where _____ is standing by to give you a report as to what has occurred down there. Come in, _____.

ANNOUNCER (in window): This has certainly been one of the most amazing things it has ever been our pleasure to witness. At the start of the experiment, the woman directed her eyes into the flame of the oriental lamp which was held by Dr Zomb's assistant and followed exactly

Dr Zomb's commands. Gradually her eyelids flickered and closed as the Doctor counted. She then seemed to somehow collapse, and her body was stretched out upon the bed, and carefully covered. She seemed to be responding automatically to Dr Zomb's every suggestion. Her breathing deepened, and one could observe her sinking deeper and deeper into the hypnotic trance. And now, here she is sleeping peacefully before us. If ever I saw a person dead-to-the-world, this woman is that person!

Remember, ladies and gentlemen, this hypnotised young woman will be left sleeping here in this window from now until _____ o'clock tonight, at which time she will be taken to the _____ Theatre to be awakened on the stage during the great "Seance of Wonders". So you are all most cordially invited to come on down and see for yourselves the startling result of this demonstration in radio hypnotism which has our whole city talking ... and then tonight witness the astounding awakening of this hypnotised woman, which will take place right during the "Seance of Wonders" on the stage of the _____ Theatre. This is but one thrill among a thousand, and one wonders what you will see tonight when you witness the internationally famous "Seance of Wonders" conducted by Dr Zomb. Make your plans now to attend! The theatre management reports that this great show has been playing to capacity business everywhere so, if you wish to be certain of a good seat, it is suggested that you purchase your tickets early. Tickets are now on sale at the theatre's box office. I return you now to our main studios. Come in,_____.

ANNOUNCER (at studio): This is your announcer, _____, now signing off. Dr Zomb is on his way to the window of the _____ store to check on the condition of the hypnotised young lady. We will be seeing you.

Mysterious mood music ... rise up, establish, fade out.

NOTE TO HYPNOTIST: These radio scripts can easily be adapted to television presentation when such is desired. However, many countries have specific rules governing the transmission on television of this nature. In the USA, the FCC will not allow such an experiment on national networks, but as a local broadcast it can usually be performed. In the UK, the transmission of the actual process of induction is forbidden. Be sure to include in your handling mention that only the woman will be influenced by the hypnotism and that viewers will not be affected in any way.

The use of this hypnotising-over-the-air feature is highly recommended used in conjunction with the "Window Sleep", as through this handling you can greatly increase the value of the stunt as you reach a much larger audience over the air than you could possibly via the window alone; also by presenting it in connection with either radio or television you increase the prestige of the entire demonstration. This radio and/or television tie-in will likewise be of interest to the station, as it gives them a chance to get in on the local advertising value with the result that they will frequently give you advance plugs calling attention to the demonstration in hypnotism that is to be presented over their station at such and such a time, all of which is just that much more publicity for the show.

Other Hypnotic Publicity Stunts

In addition to the sleeping woman in the window, I have on occasion tried other such stunts; all have proved effective. Here are some.

The Hypnotic Bicycle Ride

For this, have a bike placed in the store window mounted upright in a stand so it will be solid and yet have the rear wheel supported so it will revolve freely.

The subject is seated on the bike, hypnotised, and is commanded to start pumping the pedals. It is suggested that he is taking a long, enjoyable ride in the country and will travel up hill and dale until he is awakened from the hypnosis. Suggest that he will not become tired in any way, that he will rest and coast when he wishes to, and then will continue on his trip entirely as he chooses.

The hypnotised subject then begins pumping the bicycle and you leave him in the window peddling the hours away until he is removed, still sleeping, from the bike by the attendants and is taken on a stretcher to the theatre to be awakened on the stage during the show.

The Hypnotic Fisherman

The subject is hypnotised in the store window and is seated in a chair. In front of him on the floor is a tin bucket and he is handed a rod to which is attached a length of fishing line with a weight on its end. It is suggested that he is seated on the bank of a stream and is enjoying himself fishing. Suggestions are given that he will play with the fish every strike he feels and will reel in the fish when he hooks one, remove it, and place it in the fishing basket at his side. Thus he will continue fishing throughout the entire afternoon until he is awakened on the stage. Conclude the demonstration upon the stage as explained under the "Window Sleep".

The Hypnotic Three-Ring Circus

When the store window is large in size and the necessary subjects are available, all three of these demonstrations can be conducted at the same time. Usually it is best to use boys for the "Bicycle Ride" and the "Hypnotic Fishing" and a young lady for the "Sleeping" in the bed. Stage it with the bike at one end of the window, the bed in the centre spot and the fishing at the other end. This presentation gives the watchers much to see and attracts great interest. It is a great business-builder for the show.

Another stunt I have found effective is to hypnotise a good piano player and have him play tunes throughout the afternoon until dehypnotised on the stage. For the Manila Grand Opera House in the Philippines, a hypnotised three-piece combo was used in the window. Very sensational. Such publicity stunts have a real place in successful stage hypnotism.

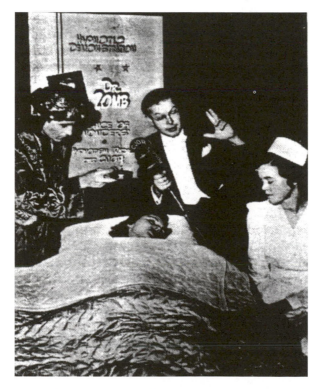

The "Window Sleep" via "Hypnotism Over Radio"

(This demonstration was conducted in the main display window of the gigantic Hudson Bay Store, Vancouver, BC, Canada by Ormond McGill as Dr Zomb.)

In Conclusion

Chapter Seventy-Five
How to Avoid Hypnotic Lawsuits

I have dealt elsewhere with the subject of the stage hypnotist's relationship to hypnotherapy and the American Medical Association's position regarding hypnotism as entertainment. Doctors Sylvanus and Evelyn M. Duvall sum up "the anti-hypnotic show attitude" pretty well in their syndicated column, "Explore Your Mind", in this paragraph.

"Question: Can hypnotism cause emotional disturbances? Answer: In the hands of an amateur, hypnosis can bring on serious emotional disturbances, depressions and panic. For these reasons, hypnotism for entertainment is condemned by medical experts. One of the problems of allowing the unqualified use of hypnosis for the treatment of disorders, is that it may mask a serious problem and delay the patient's getting proper treatment before it is too late. So beware of the self-styled hypnotist, and stay with what your own doctor orders."

Such comments are perhaps a bit harsh, as the stage hypnotist is anything but an amateur, and the magician learning hypnotism is in no way attempting to treat disorders, but it does tend to show the current attitude of the medical profession to discourage the public away from hypnotism as entertainment and also tie-in unprofessional hypnotherapeutic treatment with such entertainment.

I present these comments to re-emphasise the importance of the stage hypnotist steering entirely clear of all hypnotherapy situations. The stage hypnotist must remain exclusively the entertainer.

Actually, such press comments condemning hypnotism as entertainment only serve to increase the hypnotist's box office, as these are times in which many people rebel from any attempt of "the Establishment" to tell them what they should or should not do. However, by the same token, these are also times in which many people seek the opportunity to bring a lawsuit to bear in the hope of picking up some money, and such anti-hypnotic publicity makes the stage hypnotist particularly vulnerable.

As an example, a crowd of teenagers will attend a performance by a famous popstar or band, and may become hysterical, swoon and faint, and no one gives it the slightest thought, but let a similar experience occur during the hypnotic show and the operator is immediately blamed. Such hysteria is, of course, self-induced, but that isn't the point. If such occurs, or an accident of any sort occurs during his show, the hypnotist is in an especially susceptible position in relation to lawsuits.

Many people go out of their way to find causes on which they can slap a suit on the gamble that they can collect a cash settlement either in or out of court. The hypnotist is literally asking for trouble when he invites all who wish to volunteer on to his stage to experiment with the phenomenon of hypnosis ... for, as sure as the sun rises in the east, eventually will join his group that person who has the hope and plans of making some money by claiming mental injury.

The total knowledge that the average person possesses about abnormal psychology is concerned with the fear of insanity and to be aware that the mind is capable of becoming damaged. Hence, when a person who has been subject in a hypnotic experiment reports him, or herself, as behaving abnormally as the result of mental tampering by the hypnotist, jury sympathy is spontaneously with the "abused" subject, which verdict is all the more fostered by adverse publicity against hypnotism for other then medical purposes by a qualified physician. Yes, truly the cards are stacked against the hypnotist faced by lawsuit charges. What then is the stage hypnotist to do to protect himself?

The most logical answer is for the hypnotist to take out an insurance policy safeguarding himself against specific charges of injury and a possible law suit. However, premium rates versus the percentage of chance of suit are so closely in balance that the operator might almost be better off financially to take the occasional risk of lawsuits rather than meeting the costly rates of such insurance, so this hardly provides an answer.

As a practising hypnotist who must be concerned with the very problem under consideration in this chapter, I have adopted a dozen rules of conduct to my presentation that can be of value to stage hypnotists in protecting their interests from lawsuit threats. These are principles which I have repeatedly stressed in this course as correct hypnotic stage show conduct and which I sum up here for this very practical purpose to the performer.

Rule One
Avoid all forms of hypnotherapy or treatment of your subjects in any way. Also do not keep subjects under hypnosis for too long periods at a time; such can cause fatigue in just the same way as a prolonged period of concentrated study can cause mental fatigue and resulting distress.

Rule Two
Avoid age-regression experiments or attempts to probe the subject's psyche.

Rule Three
Avoid all hypnotic tests that in the eyes of the law could cause the subject pain or bodily harm. Experiments such as passing a pin through the subject's flesh or burning him with a match are examples of such tests that are wisely omitted if the hypnotist wishes to stay clear of possible suit charges. Also such feats as making the subject into "A Human Bridge" supported between two chairs while someone stands upon him should be avoided. As hypnotists, we well know that the subject can be rendered immune to pain sensations and that his body can be made cataleptic to support considerable weight but, from the standpoint of the courts, the operator deliberately puncturing or burning a volunteer's flesh, or standing upon him while in an abnormal position, without even so much as bothering to secure the person's permission, scarcely builds sympathy for the hypnotist's side of the case in the jury's eyes.

Rule Four
Avoid hypnotic tests that produce in your subjects symptoms of psychological abnormality. Causing deliberate amnesia, producing neurotic and psychopathic behaviour are examples of the abnormal-behaviour type of hypnotic experiments it is often wise to leave alone. Such tests leave open ground for suit charges. Justified or not, it would take very little persuasion on the part of a lawyer to convince the jury that his client suffered a continuation of mental lapses if he had been subjected to a test of having all memories of his identity removed by the hypnotist. Mental injury is unquestionably a most pertinent factor in hypnotic lawsuits, so stay clear of all experiments that lead in that direction if you wish to operate safely.

Rule Five
Temper your routines with courtesy and avoid rough-house tactics. Experiments such as causing the volunteers to drop onto a dirty stage, or piling them up like a cord of wood are examples of the rough-house type of hypnotic demonstration that you will do well to avoid if you wish to stay clear of criticism. As the hypnotic show gets rolling, with both the subjects and the audience responding to your presentation, there is

always a great temptation to go to the limit and build the laughs, but such may also build grounds for a lawsuit, and that wouldn't be so funny. The volunteers who come on the stage, in response to your request, show an implied trust in your good treatment of them that you will do well to heed if you desire to continue profitably functioning as a stage hypnotist.

Rule Six

Keep your hands off your subjects. Scrupulously avoid any head snapping, neck twisting, nerve pressing or rough handling of your subjects if you wish to stay out of trouble. Also avoid all tests that endanger your subjects physically in any way. Hypnotising and conducting all hypnotic tests in a genteel manner is your best insurance for protecting your bank account from hypnotic lawsuits.

Rule Seven

Make use of waking suggestion experiments in your presentation. It is only in the deeper stages of trance hypnotic experiments that a person would stand much chance of collecting on a claim of "mental injury" ... thus the entire gamut of waking suggestion experiments are open to the operator with perfect safety.

Rule Eight

Slant your presentation along the lines of self-hypnosis rather than operator-subject domination. You are taking the "teeth" right out of hypnotic lawsuit charges when you place the emphasis for the phenomena in the subjects' laps by stressing the fact that you are teaching them how to perform the various hypnotic feats themselves through their learning the skill of self-hypnotism.

A lawsuit charge of "harmed by the hypnotist" becomes obviously ridiculous and trumped-up were a person to make such a charge who had been specifically informed that every experiment presented was done entirely through his own choosing and personal accomplishment. And does such presentation undermine the entertainment value of hypnotism? Far from it!

Modern audiences, in general, are far more interested in what they may be able to do for themselves than in witnessing the exclusive "power" of an outsider. In many ways, the slanting of your demonstration of hypnotism in the direction of teaching the volunteer the art of self-hypnosis will ensure your safety of operation while, at the same time, modernise your presentation.

Rule Nine

Make your subjects important in the audience's eyes. There is solid psychology here that will go a long way to ensuring you against the possibility of lawsuit by any volunteer ... for, if a person is made to feel that he has accomplished something important, it is unlikely that he will deliberately go about undermining his own self-esteem.

The hypnotist is in an excellent position to build up the subjects' importance by stressing the enviable ability of mastering such and such an experiment, and then publicly complimenting the subjects (or subject) on their mastery after the successful completion of the test. Not only is this a safety valve from possible lawsuits, but it is also sound showmanship in making your subjects want to accomplish successfully each hypnotic experiment you suggest.

Rule Ten

Let your subjects take the bows. Directly related to Rule Nine is this one of letting your subjects take the bows at the conclusion of each successful demonstrated experiment. Play this rule for all its worth, even to the extent of deliberately commenting on the remarkableness of the subjects' accomplishments and by leading the audience in the applause directed at the volunteers for what they have accomplished. Such presentation may not bolster the operator's personal ego as much as if he himself should take the bows at the end of the experiment, but what he may lose in ego-boosting will be more than compensated for by what he may be able to retain in his bank account by avoiding lawsuits through this handling.

Rule Eleven

Avoid lawsuits in hypnotic publicity demonstrations. A detailed discussion of the "Window Sleep" demonstration has been given. Performers who indulge in such sensational hypnotic publicity demonstrations will do well to make it a firm rule always to have the subject (or subjects) in such a feat sign a release to the effect that he (or she) enters into the demonstration of his own free will, is fully informed of the nature of what is involved in the demonstrations, is to receive a predetermined amount of compensation for services rendered in performing the feat, and that he will not hold the hypnotist or any other parties involved in the demonstration in any way responsible.

Such a release will probably be all that will ever be required to safeguard against suits resulting from such publicity stunts, but, if it is wished, the form may even be made stronger in having the party agree (in the contract) not to sue. And be sure that the subjects used in such demonstrations are of legal age when they sign such a release, or else get the parents of the subjects (or subject) to sign the release in agreement also; otherwise, you may find the parents swooping down on you with a charge that you intimidated a minor, and find yourself involved in a defamation of character suit.

Rule Twelve
Be wary of countries or towns within countries where public exhibitions of hypnotism are unlawful.

There is legislation prohibiting public demonstrations of hypnotism in several countries in the world, such as Switzerland. This is also the case in North America in the states of Oregon, Montana, South Dakota, Nebraska, Kansas, Tennessee, and in the Province of Ontario in Canada. Also, the United States Air Force bases now have rulings against hypnotism shows on their premises.

While such legislation is frequently lax, it is still well for the stage hypnotist to have knowledge of such "sensitive spots" as repercussions from lawsuits in such places can be additionally serious. When playing such areas he must work with great care. As much as is possible, it is well for the hypnotism show to book in places where it is officially accepted.

It may seem that these twelve rules of conduct here suggested in order that the performer may steer clear of hypnotic lawsuits rather cut into the scope of the hypnotic stage show. Very possibly such is true to some extent, but if the modern hypnotist is interested in staying in business without being "victimised" by lawsuits he will simply have to make the concessions. Actually, however, with a little creative thought the practical operator will find that the entertainment values and instructive aspects of his programme have not been much undermined by this rigid tightening of the rules governing modern hypnotic demonstrating, and that the "law-suit-free presentation" of hypnotism actually increases the dignity of his art.

As a clever performer, plan your show so it does not present opportunities for anyone to sue.

Chapter Seventy-Six
The Stage Hypnotist and Hypnotherapy

This is largely a chapter on opinions. You must form your own on these matters. The stage hypnotist will inevitably run into persons who will seek his help to use hypnosis to correct some unwanted condition or to produce a desired one. Persons from the audience frequently come backstage and make such personal requests. Requests such as wishing to stop smoking and overeating are common.

In my opinion, it is well for the hypnotic showman to steer clear of such requests, since they are time consuming, and it is really not his field. He can handle such matters diplomatically by simply stating that he does not practise hypnotherapy and by recommending those who do so specialise. On the other hand, some hypnotists do not hold to this opinion, and even offers to aid persons with problems after the show if they prove to be responsive subjects.

Also, it is well for the stage hypnotist not to get involved in hypnoanalysis experiments in which he tries to pry out sources of complexes and psychological difficulties. Such can be touchy situations. As the psychologist Andred M. Weitzenhoffer comments on the matter of regressions:

> In my judgement, regressions probably are potentially the most dangerous of all hypnotic phenomena insofar as the mental health of the subject is concerned, for one usually does not know what sort of traumatic experiences the subject may have gone through in the past. Thus, as one explores the subject's past, there is always the danger of inadvertently regressing the subject to just such a nuclear point in his life. When this happens, anything can take place, but only the clinically trained person is competent to handle the situation adequately. Only sheer good luck and, in a few cases, an innate intuitive ability, will permit the untrained hypnotist to smooth over the resulting disturbance. Once regression has returned the subject to a highly traumatic situation, it may become imperative to transform the hypnotic situation into a psychotherapeutic situation or else the risk is run of having a seriously disturbed individual on one's hands. I believe that, without exaggeration, every regression experiment should be labelled "DANGER POTENTIAL HIGH TENSION".

Hypnoanalysis and regression can be commented upon on the stage, but do not deal with real cases. Audience understanding is well satisfied with imaginary situations in such regard. Such imaginary regression experiences are harmless as they touch upon no traumatic experiences in the subject's past. Martin Roberts PhD, a well-known British psychologist who has made a specialisation of the study of altered states of consciousness, has this to say in 1995 on the subject of hypnotic regression:

> All forms of regression, clinical or non-clinical, hypnotically induced or otherwise carry with them the inherent risk associated with what has fashionably become known as "False Memory Syndrome". The European and American legal systems are already bursting at the seams with cases awaiting hearings where therapists are accused of creating false memories in their patients. The cost of defending an action in this highly contentious area are enormous and a full hearing will more than likely exceed the limits of the average therapist's professional indemnity insurance, possibly leaving the therapist with huge personal costs, not counting the worry, inconvenience and damage to the image of his or her practice even when they have won the action. My advice is simple. Don't do regression work without first checking your insurance policy and preferably only do regression work in a proper clinical setting where all the necessary safeguards are present, e.g. a hospital or clinic.

The American Medical Association and the Hypnotism Show

The American Medical Association (AMA) has gone on record as accrediting hypnosis as a useful therapeutic tool, and in general has opposed its use in/as entertainment.

It is but natural that the professional stage hypnotist should not be pleased to have his show curtailed in this manner. Still, the AMA does have a point when they stress that the practice of promiscuously hypnotising on the stage does not provide a means of screening as to who should be hypnotised and who not.

Ninety-nine times out of a hundred the hypnotist will not run into any difficulty, but there does occur an occasional subject in which hypnosis does bring forth mental abnormalities. Such abnormalities, of course, are innate to the respective personality of the individual and are not a product of the hypnosis, but the hypnotic condition does tend to aggravate them in some instances, and when such occurs such must be dealt with correctly and not played upon as "funny" by the psychologically untrained showman.

Every skilled hypnotist should have enough knowledge of psychology and abnormal psychology to recognise such symptoms immediately and screen out such subjects from his committee of volunteers. The symptoms of abnormality are readily recognised by evidences of hysterical-type behaviour such as head and body extremity shaking, gasping breathing, lethargic or unexpected responses not under the direct instruction of the hypnotist, and conversely over intensified responsiveness to the suggestions.

Abnormal subjects are often very responsive to hypnosis and enlist much laughter from the audience in the extreme things they do, so there is a temptation on the part of the performer to use them in many of his demonstrations. **This is exactly what should not be done!**

Immediately a subject shows any abnormal symptoms they should at once be carefully removed from the hypnotic state and dismissed from the stage. Such intelligent handling can do much to prevent what might be psychological damage to the subject as well as disastrous results to the reputation of the hypnotist and his show.

Actually, when properly handled, the hypnotic stage show can be one of the very best ways to interest persons in the audience in hypnosis for useful hypnotherapeutic applications. Likewise, the hypnotic has an unusual opportunity to pin-point abnormalities in persons in early stages which otherwise might go unnoticed for years. When it is possible, such persons should be recommended for psychological and/or psychiatric attention.

If the stage hypnotist is also a professional hypnotherapist, any requests for therapeutic help can be referred to his office. In such regard, the hypnotism show can be extremely useful in building clientele for office practice. A hypnotism lecture with a few demonstrations included presented for service clubs in a community, such as Rotary, Lions, Kiwanis, women's groups etc., can be especially productive.

Chapter Seventy-Seven
The After-the-Show Show

On occasion, I have found it advantageous to add an after-the-show show to my stage show. An audience likes this. Some stay and some do not, but it is a gesture that all appreciate. It gives the customers more for their money, and what you offer in this attraction is decidedly worthwhile to all who choose to participate. At this late hour performance, you present a form of Oriental hypnotism called *yoga nidra*.

Yoga nidra is a method of self-hypnosis that originated in India, designed for the purpose of increasing the awareness of the true nature of oneself. It provides an advancing in consciousness and emphasises that the participant should remain awake and not go to sleep. However human nature is such that the very suggestion not to go to sleep creates just the opposite effect in many. Amusing, but not important, for asleep or awake all benefit from *yoga nidra*.

The Performance of Yoga Nidra

Assemble your audience who remain for this after-the-show session down at the front of the auditorium, and you stand in their midst. Explain that these few moments spent in the meditation of *yoga nidra* will benefit them in every way. All try it together.

Each person sits relaxed on their chair, feet flat on the floor with hands resting loosely in laps, palms cupped upwards. Have them close their eyes, take three deep breaths as you direct and relax all over. Turn out the lights.

In the darkened room you now present *yoga nidra*. You can do it personally speaking into mike or make and use a suitable amplified audio cassette.

The Formula of Yoga Nidra

"Everyone sit relaxed and become motionless and listen with great attentiveness to all that transpires about you. Listen with care and become aware of the sounds outside the room in which you are. Allow your sense

563

of hearing to range into the distance, and then gradually draw it back into the room in which you are ... and hear the sounds in the room about you ... develop your awareness of the room in which you are ... and become aware of yourself performing *yoga nidra*.

"In this performing of *yoga nidra* you are not to go to sleep, as your purpose is to become more awake than ever by advancing your consciousness of all that is. *So do not go to sleep!*

"Turn your attention to your breathing, and become aware of your breath as it goes in and out of your body. Become fully conscious of your breathing along with your awareness of your body ... and remember your purpose in performing *yoga nidra* is to not go to sleep no matter how sleepy you feel; your purpose is to increase your awareness.

"State to yourself this resolve: I am advancing my consciousness and heightening my awareness in every way. I am advancing my consciousness and heightening my awareness in every way. I am advancing my consciousness and heightening my awareness in every way.

"Now, as you relax with attention, sitting comfortably in your chair in this dark and pleasant room, allow your consciousness to rotate throughout your body, as I direct it. Let your mind jump freely from one part of the body to the next, in this order:

NOTE TO HYPNOTIST: In presenting this, allow timing between each suggested experiencing of each part for adequate experiencing.

"Think of your right hand. Become aware of your right hand and experience your right hand. Now experience your right thumb. Experience your right forefinger. Experience your right middle finger. Experience your right ring finger. Experience your right little finger. Experience the palm of your right hand.

"Experience your right wrist ... your right elbow ... your right shoulder ... the right side of your waist ... your right hip ... your right thigh ... your right kneecap ...your right calf ... your right foot. Experience the soul of your right foot. Experience your right big toe ... your right second toe ... your right third toe ... your right fourth toe ... your right little toe.

"Move your awareness to the left side of your body. Experience your left hand ... your left thumb ... your left first finger ... your left middle finger ... your left ring finger ... your left little finger. Experience the palm of your left hand.

"Experience your left wrist … your left elbow … the left side of your shoulder … your left waist … your left hip … your left thigh … your left kneecap … your left calf … your left foot. Experience the soul of your left foot. Experience your left big toe … your left second toe … your left third toe … your left fourth toe … your left little toe.

"Move your consciousness to the top of your head.Experience the top of your head. Experience your forehead … your right eyebrow … your left eyebrow … the space between the eyebrows. Experience your right closed eye … your left closed eye … your right ear … your left ear … your right cheek … your left cheek. Experience your nose … your upper and lower lips. Experience your chin. Experience your throat … the right side of your chest … the left side of your chest, and the middle of the chest. Experience your navel, your abdomen, your genitals.

"Move your awareness to your back, and experience the sole of your right foot … the sole of your left foot … your right heel … the back of your right calf … the back of your left knee … the back of your right thigh … the back of your left thigh. Experience your right buttock, your left buttock, your right hip, your left hip. Experience your whole spine … experience your right shoulder blade and your left shoulder blade … experience the back of your head and the top of your head.

"Now experience your whole right leg … your whole left leg. Experience both legs together. Experience the whole front of your body. Now experience your entire body – all together.

"Become aware of the meeting points between your body and the chair upon which you sit. Think about where you sit.

"Consciously experience the skin on the soles of your feet … experience the skin on the souls of your feet from the heels to the tips of your toes.

"Move your consciousness to your hands, and become aware of the skin on the palms of your hands … experience the skin on the palms of your hands and fingers. Feel the skin and become aware of the lines on the palms of your hands … experience the skin of your hands intensely with full awareness.

"Now move your consciousness to your face, and experience the skin of your face. Develop your awareness of the skin on your face, on your forehead, on your cheeks and chin. And as you contemplate and experience the skin on your face become aware and feel the meeting points where your closed eyelids meet. And now feel the meeting points where the lips of your mouth meet. Feel the meeting of your lips with full awareness.

"Bring attention to your breathing, and become aware that you are breathing quietly and slowly. Become completely conscious of your breathing ... and concentrate on the flow of your breath as it goes into your lungs and on way down deep inside of you, as far down as your navel. Feel the breath moving along this passage as you inhale. Become aware of the in breath entering your nostrils ... entering and flowing through both of your nostrils, and visualise the flowing in through both nostrils and meeting at the top to form a triangle.

"Think of your breathing as starting separately from a distance, and drawing near and uniting in the space between your eyebrows. This is your eyebrow centre, and behind it lies your 'third eye'.

"Now think of the breath coming in through your right nostril and exhale it through that nostril. Then think of inhaling and exhaling the breath through your left nostril. Go on thinking of inhaling through alternate nostrils. Think breathing in and out of your left nostril, as you inhale and exhale your breath. Continue this thinking of alternating your breath in and out ... in and out ... in and out ... in and out. And do not become sleepy as you do this remain fully aware at all times.

"Become aware of the inner space which appears before your closed eyes, as your screen of mind. Move this space from in front of your eyes yet deeper inside yourself, so you see it as though inside your forehead. This space now surrounds completely your 'third eye'. Develop your awareness of this inner space as an infinite space that extends as far as you can see. Become intently aware of this space; be totally aware but do not become involved ... just be aware that you are watching whatever you are watching that occurs in this space as though you are watching a movie upon a screen ... and you are just witnessing it.

"Bring your consciousness, your attention, your awareness to your eyebrow centre, and focus your attention there upon your 'third eye' at this centre. And in this contemplation of this centre become absolutely still and listen ... and you will hear the "god sound" of *AUHM* radiating from your third eye centre. Visualise the reverberations of the *AUHM* being projected by you through your 'third eye' out into the universe.

"Stop your radiating and bring your attention to your third-eye centre, and return to witness your screen of mind which appears before you as infinite space. Now watch this space carefully for any colours or patterns that may emerge. Make no effort in doing this. Just be a watcher. Become totally aware of your watching your inner space without involvement. Continue watching this space and become aware of any images and any spontaneous thoughts that may emerge.

"Relax, relax, relax, now more deeply than ever, and again say to yourself your resolve three times: I am expanding my consciousness in every way. I am expanding my consciousness in every way. I am expanding my consciousness in every way.

"Return your consciousness again to your third eye centre between the eyebrows ... and focus your attention there and as you do this become aware of a golden door. Visualise it as a large, solid, golden door ... and try to open that door. Push ... push ... push ... push with your mind and it opens before you. Now you are on the other side of the door and visualise yourself now standing at the entrance of a dark cave. And deep within the cave you can see a flaming light. Go towards the light. Move your consciousness towards that light and discover what you find. And you will see within that light there is a golden egg. It is very bright and it dazzles your eyes. Become aware of that golden egg which is housed within the flame, as it is symbolic of your soul which resides at your centre of being.

"Leave the golden egg and the flaming light, and pass back out through the golden door and close it behind yourself as you exit, and become aware again of your third eye centre which lies behind the space between your eyebrows.

"Become a witness to your screen of mind upon which appears your inner space and think of it as becoming like an ocean. Think of a dark-blue ocean and become aware of the waves. This ocean lies within your inner space, and the rolling waves represent sleep the manifesting of the unconscious state of your mind. Now, without going to sleep, become aware of sleep, and try to visualise this state of unconsciousness within you which is like the waves upon this ocean ... and you are becoming the master of these waves so you can ride upon this vast ocean with ease. For, in your mastery, the waves become calmed and the ocean serene to your experiencing, and with the lessening of unconsciousness more and more consciousness arises within you.

"Imagine and visualise upon your screen of mind a well, and you are looking down into the depths of this well. The well is dark and deep it appears as a cylindrical tunnel into the depths of the earth. There is a bucket on a chain, and you lower it into the well, and it drops down into abysmal darkness ... you can still feel the weight of the bucket on the end of the chain, but you cannot see it. Now pull the bucket up, up out of the darkness into the light. Now visualise yourself as getting into the bucket and winding yourself down into the darkness of the well ... as you descend deeper and deeper into the well more and more intensely does the darkness surround you. You are moving in complete darkness ... into the unknown all-pervading darkness. Complete darkness and emptiness surrounds you, and it is so dark that you cannot even see yourself, but even so you find that you can know and feel that you are. For your discover that there is no need to see yourself to discover your self. This revelation becomes yours, and you begin to realise who you are deep inside yourself.

"Start winding yourself up and pull yourself back out of the well. Up and up you rise from out of the darkness and again you come into the light. And you feel changed somehow for now that you are again in the light and can see yourself on the outside you know you have had a glimpse of your real self on the inside. Get out of the bucket now ... get out of the well now. What bliss you feel.

"Bring your awareness to the present, now, and make sure you are not sleeping, for as many objects are now named visualise them upon your screen of mind upon that inner space into which your 'third eye' peers. As fast as the images are described to you visualise and experience them upon all levels of feeling, of emotion, of imagination. As fast as you are told so fast you move your mind in full awareness. So witness now upon your screen of mind:

"See the face of Buddha smiling. See Christ standing. See a flickering candle. See a weeping willow tree. See a tall palm tree. See a car moving along a road. See coloured clouds gathering in the sky. See yellow clouds; blue clouds; red clouds. See a starlit night. See a moonlit night. See the full moon in the sky. See a dog standing. See a cat reposing. See an elephant moving through a jungle. See a horse racing. See a rising sun. See a setting sun. See an ocean with waves upon it. See a big pond of clear water. See a blue lotus flower; a white lotus flower; a pink lotus flower. See a golden spider's web. See a sandy bank of a wide river. See a boat sailing on the ocean. See yourself as lying naked upon the sands of a beach by the ocean with a silver cord extending from yourself into the sky. Visualise yourself as the immortal being that you are.

"Visualise yourself as floating outside your body. Imagine that you are on the ceiling of the room in which you now sit. Now see your body get up from the chair and tiptoe to the door of the room in which you are.

568

Quietly open the door and go outside the room, and then close the door behind you. See your body walking outside of the room you were in. See many things with which you are familiar about you. And note how freely you can move. You experience complete lightness. It is wonderful this feeling of lightness. And it may be that you will see some people that you know on this mental journey. You can see them but they cannot see you, as you make this astral out-of-body flight.

"Suddenly you see your body floating out over the sea. See this clearly and become completely aware of the experience. See the dark blue waters of the ocean glistening below you, as you float above it so lightly. Your body floats like a cloud, and wherever the wind blow the clouds your body is likewise blown. Feel the wisps of clouds that brush past your face as you rise up higher amongst the clouds and you observe the sunlight reflected off the banks of white clouds through which you are passing. Now your body is lifted by currents of air and is carried over the land, and you descend closer to earth and, as you float along in this out-of-body experience you see farmhouses, carefully laid out fields, thick forests, winding rivers that reflect the sun. Pause a moment in your astral flight and look closely at yourself, and note how totally relaxed you are, and on your face is an expression of peace and calm of utter blissfulness. See your body suddenly immersed in colour as it passes through a rainbow ... and feel yourself washed and purified by the subtle colours of yellow, green, blue, violet, red, orange and gold. You can even feel these colours penetrating your entire body nourishing and invigorating you."

Returning from **Yoga Nidra**

You can now leave the midst of your relaxing audience to whom you have given the direction. With mike in hand go upon the stage and continue ... "Slowly return to your body. See your body return to the outside of the building in which you are. See again the familiar surroundings of the room in which you are. Quietly open the door to the room and walk inside, and close it after you. Return to the chair in the auditorium in which you sit. In fascination you can see your relaxing body still sitting in the chair exactly as you left it. Now sense yourself floating above this seated body, and visualise yourself as slowly descending into it ... to mesh again with every fibre of that body which again is you, and you are home once more in the home in which you dwell in this immediate space and time. And you rest quietly in the chair.

"Relax completely your whole body now, and prepare yourself to return again to the here and now. Relax all effort and bring your attention again to your natural breath. Maintain for a few moments now your awareness of your breathing and, at the same time, develop your awareness of the state of physical relaxation you are in. And you have not been asleep. You have not dreamed. It has happened to you. It is a wonderful experience you have been through, and you are now aware of yourself from a new position of higher consciousness.

"Now become aware of your physical existence, and visualise yourself seated in your chair in this auditorium. You feel so good and vital and alive in every way. Now with your mind visualise the surroundings of the room in which you are, and in doing this allow your mind to become completely external. You are coming back, but do not open your eyes yet. Come back slowly. Just sit quietly for a few moments yet becoming externalised, and I will disappear from the scene now and you are alone feeling wonderful and fine and with a new awareness of yourself."

EXIT

Leave the stage of the darkened theatre now and go backstage, yet through the mike you can still address the relaxing participants of *yoga nidra*.

"You are ready to come back out of *yoga nidra* now, so start moving your body and stretch yourself. Move gently and just enjoy your body in this pleasant arousal. The lights will come back on now and with the lights you will be fully awake, but do not open your eyes just yet. Just rest a few moments longer.

Turn on the lights in the auditorium.

"The lights are on and you are fully back in your body in the here and now, so open your eyes any time you wish. You are back in the here and now feeling wonderful and fine with a remarkable awareness of the true nature of yourself, and this session in *yoga nidra* self-realisation is complete. Arise and shine! The after-the-show show is over, and have a safe trip home."

NOTE TO HYPNOTIST: *Yoga nidra* is a yogic form of self-hypnosis. It provides a remarkable after-the-show session for those staying on to try. The effect is profound. The spectators return to the here and now to an empty stage. You are gone! It is impressive. And the ones who leave the theatre after Yogi Nidra are changed from how they were when they came in. *Yoga nidra* is an experience never to be forgotten. It provides the pinnacle of your hypnotism show. You will for ever be remembered.

Exit! Exit! Exit!

You now have the know-how to become a master stage hypnotist and present a marvellous show.

Remember always, true art conceals art. There are so many fascinating things you can do in demonstrating hypnotism there that is a temptation to overdo presentations and length of show. Do less not more. A little bit of miracle goes a long ways.

So I can now make my exit. I take my exit in three ways ...

Exit No. 1
I complete the writing of this book by stressing again that you be an original in your performing of stage hypnotism. Learn from others but do not copy others. Create your own masterpiece.

Remember ...

A good artist may make a good copy of a Van Gogh painting. He would be lucky if he could sell the copy for $50, while an original Van Gogh would sell for over a million.

Exit No. 2
When you conclude your hypnotism show, how do you take your exit? Here are two ways:

(a) Be sociable. Go out and meet your spectators personally. Many will engage you in conversation about hypnosis, and some may even ask you to help them stop smoking, etc.

(b) Disappear after the show. Not being able to find you makes them exit talking about you rather than you talking about yourself. Somehow by your not being there after having presented a hypnotism show makes you "bigger than life".

Best wishes for a successful career in stage hypnotism
with your very own hypnotism show!

THE CONCERT OF HYPNOTISM on ABC-TV
A pioneer presentation of hypnotism on television, 1945

Appendix I
The Sensational Gil Boyne Hypnotism Stage Show

Complete Presentation and Routines

Gil Boyne is a driving force in hypnotism throughout the world. His Hypnotism Training Institute in Glendale, California, has advanced to international scope. Numerous Hollywood stars have taken his training. His connections in Washington, DC, caused hypnotherapy to be legalised as an established profession in the United States. This is the first time the Gil Boyne Hypnotism Show has ever appeared in print. I am pleased to be able to include a detailed description of his show as a special appendix in this *Encyclopedia*: his presentation, routines, and observations are of great value to stage hypnotists.

The Gil Boyne Show
Initial Comments

Gil Boyne performs in a forceful manner, working rapidly. He adapts his show to the performing situation, sometimes working with as few as six subjects in a nightclub to a stage overflowing with subjects filling the largest theatres.

Opening

Curtain open on fully lit stage revealing a row of chairs from side to side (number of chairs depending on size of stage). Follow white spot on performer. Gil Boyne enters briskly to stage centre directly into ...

Introduction

"Good evening, ladies and gentlemen, tonight we are all going to sleep together. In just a few moments, I will invite on stage as many of you as would like to participate in the hypnotism demonstrations. I call it 'demonstrations' rather than performance, as we never quite know what is going to happen.

"You will find the experience of being hypnotised fascinating, and it may prove a help for some to overcome habits like smoking, drinking, or sex. [Laugh pause.] As we go along, just let me know what I can help you with while you are in hypnosis.

"We have a stage full of chairs up here, so if you wish to be hypnotised and take part in the show, come right up and fill them now."

Volunteers come on stage, being ushered to appropriate chairs, i.e. couples coming up together being separated and seated next to strangers etc. The performer talks to the audience:

"It may have been that some of you were reluctant to come on stage and be hypnotised, but these people [indicate committee on stage] have been willing to volunteer, learn about hypnotism by being hypnotised, and entertain you. So, it is fitting that we show our appreciation to them by a nice round of applause."

Audience applauds the volunteers. Speaking to the committee, the performer says: "See, you haven't done a thing yet, and they love you already."

Speaking to the audience the performer says: "All on stage are going to enter hypnosis now, and I request that even if there are persons on stage you know, please do not wave to them or talk to them. They have to concentrate and must not be distracted while being hypnotised. So, for the next few minutes please remain quiet while they enter trance. While hypnotised they are going to explore some of the wonders of their subconscious mind, so I ask you to extend to them the same courtesy you would expect were your positions reversed. [Pause for silence.] All right, we are ready."

Gil Boyne's Rapid Stage Hypnotism Induction

Speaking to the committee the performer says: "Now, everyone, look directly into my eyes, as I stand before you. Concentrate on my eyes and do not look away. Look directly into my eyes and do exactly what I tell you to do and nothing more.

"And ...

"If I tell anyone to leave the stage, immediately go quietly back to your seat and watch the show. If I send anyone back go their seat, it simply means that the person is too tense right now to take part in the demonstrations. Understand. All right, get ready to be hypnotised.

"I want everyone to begin by extending their hands straight out in front of themselves, with the palms facing each other about twelve inches apart." The Committee members do as directed. All extend their hands outwards.

"Now, keep looking at me. I am going to count backward from three to one, and when I reach one close your eyes and bring the palms of your hands inward towards each other until the palms of your hands touch together.

"Get ready to close your eyes. Three, two, *one*. All eyes closed. Now slowly bring your hands together until the palms touch."

The committee does as directed. All eyes are closed before proceeding. "All eyes closed; now squeeze your hands tightly together. Interlock your fingers so they become a solid mass like a block of wood. They are so solidly enmeshed you cannot get them apart even when you try. Try! Pull with all your strength, but you cannot get your hands apart for they have become like a solid mass."

The committee find their hands so tightly fastened together that they cannot get them apart. Should anyone separate their hands they are immediately dismissed from the stage.

"Now, as I push your locked hands down to your lap let your head fall forward on your chest and go to sleep. Sleep and relax!"

The subjects respond accordingly. Gil Boyne then goes to each person, in turn, and forcefully pushes their locked hands down into their laps, while exclaiming repeatedly: "Sleep and relax! Sleep and relax!" All directions are positive and dominant! Any person not responding is dismissed from stage, with a gesture to leave. Every person is given personal attention in this pushing the hands into lap process. The entire procedure is handled with action and verve, and is quickly accomplished. Every person on stage is seen with their head bowed on chest, eyes closed as though asleep. It is a rapid induction technique which is now intensified via a continuance of the suggestions, as each person is approached. "That's it! Go way down! Go way down deep to sleep! Go to sleep! Go to sleep, way, way down sleep to sleep." The entire committee is hypnotised.

"Sleep deep, everyone. For the balance of this evening you will remain with your eyes closed until I tell you to open them, and even when you open your eyes you will still remain hypnotised even though you may appear to be awake."

NOTE TO HYPNOTISTS: Throughout the entire Gil Boyne Hypnotism Show never once is it suggested that the subjects will awaken from trance until the very end of the show. This maintains a hypersuggestible state of mind causing spontaneous responsiveness to the performance of all suggested experiences.

Hypnosis Deepening

"Now, do exactly what I tell you to do, and you will continue to go deeper and deeper to sleep in hypnosis; much deeper even than you are right now. Right now your fingers on your lap are beginning to relax and your hands are separating, and your right arm is becoming very light and is beginning to rise up from your lap into the air. Your right arm is coming up, up, up until it is pointing towards the ceiling."

Suggestions of arm rising are continued until arms of everyone in the committee are up and pointing towards the ceiling, i.e. the fly loft above the stage. "Good. Now your right arm is becoming very stiff, so stiff you cannot bend it. Even your fingers are stiffening out. Your arm is becoming like a bar of iron, and you cannot bend it, try as hard as you will. Try! It is impossible to bend your upraised arm, and you are going down deeper and deeper to sleep in hypnosis the more you try. You are going deep to sleep in hypnosis. [Subjects respond.] Your arm continues to get stiffer and stiffer, and you go deeply to sleep in hypnosis."

NOTE TO HYPNOTIST: Observe how suggestions of relaxation, sleep and hypnosis are continuously associated throughout the entire performance. Gil Boyne keeps emphasising going deeper and deeper to sleep in hypnosis. Thus, a deep trance level is achieved and maintained.

"Now, when I snap my fingers your right arm will lower to your side while your left arm will rise up to point to the ceiling. Then, when your left arm is fully up it will start descending, and your right arm will again rise up and point to the ceiling. Then, when that arm is fully up it will start descending, and your left arm will then rise up, as it was before. In this manner, your arms will see-saw up and down over and over and over."

NOTE TO HYPNOTIST: All directions for performance in hypnosis are presented by Gil Boyne in a clear manner, often repeated, so subjects know exactly what performance is expected of them.

The performer snaps his fingers as a "cue", and subjects respond by arms alternatively moving up and down see-saw fashion. "Faster and faster your arms move alternately up and down, up and down like a see-saw, and you are going ever deeper into hypnosis."

The subjects' arms are rising and falling at a rapid rate. While the stage is filled with this action, Gil Boyne goes to a few of the most animated subjects and lifts person's leg holding it outstretched and commanding that it is stiff and will not bend or move. A number of subjects are thus left with extended legs along with the see-sawing of the arms. More action is then heaped upon action. "Now, when I snap my fingers your hands will stop rising and falling, and will drop limply into your lap. And all legs that are suspended will, also, drop down relaxed to the floor … and you are going down continuously deeper and deeper to sleep in profound hypnosis."

The performer snaps his fingers for the "cue" and subjects respond. All action, on-stage, is quiet in sleep for an impressive moment. "Now, left up hour hands, bend at the wrist so your fingers are pointing towards each other. Move your hands closer together and start revolving them around and around each other. That's it. Around and around they go, and they are revolving faster and faster, and every revolution sends you deeper and deeper into hypnosis." The subjects respond in a wild revolving of arms.

> NOTE TO HYPNOTIST: An important technique for intensifying hypnosis is demonstrated here in associating sleep-suggestions with response to action-suggestions, and vice versa. It has a compounding effect productive of hypnotic responsiveness.

"Now, when I stamp my foot you arms will revolve in the opposite direction. The revolving of your arms is becoming automatic like the beating of your heart. Ready now!" The performer stamps his foot for the "cue" and subjects' arms immediately revolve in reverse direction. "Now, when I stamp my foot your arms will take on lateral movements going in all manner of oblique directions. Zigzag. Around in circles. Every which way. Anyway they want to go. Ready now!"

The performer gives the foot stamp "cue", and one-arm action proceeds. This change is very amusing. This change is very amusing as the subjects vary in their responses. all responses are allowed to build. "When I stamp my foot your arm movements will cease entirely, your hands will become quiet in your lap, and you will drop down deeper and deeper to sleep … asleep in profound hypnosis. You are ready to proceed on to adventures in this show having a wonderful time."

The foot stamp "cue" is given and the subjects respond by becoming quiet in sleep ready to proceed with the show. All is silent on stage. Allow the silence to hold for some seconds. The induction is complete.

> NOTE TO HYPNOTIST: Gil Boyne considers all procedures up to this point in his show has been related to deeply hypnotising the subjects, and "conditioning" them to be actively responsive to the hypnotist.

On Into the Show

The performer says to the hypnotised committee: "You all did so well that I am going to give you a real treat now, and take you on a vacation trip to Hawaii. We are in an aeroplane ready for the trip. This is Flight 804 with United Airlines, so observe the NO SMOKING sign and fasten your seat belts." (The subjects go through the actions of fastening seat belts.)

"Good. We are taking off now and starting the flight. We are in flight now. We are flying across the blue Pacific Ocean on our way to the Hawaiian Islands. The performer suddenly seem to notice a change in temperature in the plane's cabin. Very casually he says: 'Hmmmmm, somehow it seems to be getting rather stuffy in this plane. It is getting kind of warm.'"

The performer approaches a few of the hypnotised subjects, and says: "Open your eyes and look out of the plane's window; tell me what you see."

This questioning action is repeated with several of the subjects. It is productive of a speaking response. Mike is held near mouth so audience can hear comments. Often they are quite interesting. After responses, subjects are told to re-close eyes and go down deeper to sleep.

The performer again refers to the increasing heat in cabin: "Say, the air conditioning in this plane seems to be off. It is getting awfully warm. *Wow!* It is getting positively hot. It must be over 100 degrees in here now. Everyone, you'd better fan yourself to keep cool! Wow, but it is hot! Wipe away the perspiration. Take off your jacket, if you wish. Do anything you please to get cool. It is so darn hot in this plane!"

The subjects react in a variety of manners in responding to the suggestion of becoming very hot. These actions continue for a time. Then: "Ah good, it is better now. Guess they got the air conditioning going okay now. The temperature seems perfect, and here comes a flight attendant with a cool drink for us all. Hold out your hand and take the cup given you. Gulp down the drink and throw the cup away."

During these comments, hypnotist pretends to hand a cup to each person, rapidly down the line. Saying: "That's it. Gulp it down and throw the cup away. It tastes so good and cools you off. Hmmmmmmm good! Say, this is 'giggling water' they gave you. It is like champagne. It works like laughing gas, and makes you giggle and laugh. Everything seems so funny and tickles your funny bone. You are laughing, laughing, laughing. What a time for laughter this is."

The subjects respond so everyone is laughing. Laughter is contagious so the audience will laugh in equal measure. Right at the height of the laughter, suddenly shout: "Sleep! Go to sleep, everyone!" Instantly there is a transformation from boisterous laughter to the quiet of sleep. The entire committee returns to somnambulistic trance on the moment, and it is very impressive!"

NOTE TO HYPNOTISTS: In presenting dramatic scenes like this, the performer must enter into the situation. It must be dramatised. Gil Boyne does a continuous job of dramatising, even inclusive of "aside remarks" to the audience at every opportunity. Remember, the Hypnotism Show is a form of theatre. Make it theatrical.

The flying scene continues as the hypnotist goes to each subject in turn, and tells them to relax more and more completely. Some subjects relax so completely they start to drop out of their chair, and are gently lowered outstretched to the floor where they lie quietly. An arm or leg is pulled upwards and allowed to drop limply just to show how perfectly relaxed they are while in hypnosis. Other subjects are tipped to rest against each other. Heads meet. It is a cosy scene.

Then suddenly: "Say, them must still be having trouble with the air conditioning. It is getting awfully cold in here. Brrrrr, it is so cold. I am sorry it is so cold on our flight, but I can't help it. We are all shivering. Brrrrrrr! Better snuggle together to increase your mutual body warmth. It is so cold!"

The subjects react in a variety of ways to adjust to the cold. They are allowed to shiver for a while. Then suggest: "Guess they've got it fixed now and the cold snap in the cabin is ended. Thank goodness. It is becoming all comfortable on our flight now. The temperature is just right. It feels great, and we are flying along. Here comes that flight attendant again. And this time, let's see ... she has ice cream cones for each of us. Hold out your hand and take an ice cream cone when it is given you."

Down the line the hypnotist goes pretending to pass out a cone to each person. "Better eat your cone quickly as the ice cream seems to be getting pretty soft. It is melting and is dripping." These suggestions are played up, lending amusement to the situation. Everyone knows how messy a melting ice cream cone can be.

"Say, did you notice what an alcoholic taste that ice cream has. This must be a champagne flight we are on, as they sure seem to like champagne on this plane, as this sure is champagne ice cream. Tastes good though, but it does make one feel like it is New Year's Eve, when people all join in to sing that favourite song, 'Auld Lang Syne'. What fun this is. What a party, feeling a bit drunk on champagne ice cream and wanting to sing. Let's all sing it together."

The subjects chorus the song, the hypnotist joining in with them. The audience is invited to join in with the singing. Everybody knows "Auld Lang Syne". If a tape of that music is available, it can be played as background to the singing. A nice production touch. "Say, this is lots of fun. Let's try another song together. How about 'Show Me The Way To Go Home'? Okay, let's start."

Singing starts (and the music, too if it is available) ... the hypnotist commences the singing, and all the subjects joining in. The song ends by hypnotist telling the subjects to hold the last note in "Barbershop Harmony". The pure abandonment with which hypnotised people perform is pure enjoyment.

"Okay, everyone. You did great. And here we are just about ready to land in Hawaii, but they seem to be having trouble with the engine. It is getting kind of bumpy. Looks like they are going to have to make an emergency landing on a beach strip. It will be okay, but better prepare yourself for an emergency landing anyhow, as it could be bumpy.

"Best thing to do is to buckle your safety belt up tight; then lower your head between your knees and brace yourself by pressure of your arms against the seat in front of you. Do it now, and get ready for a bump landing. Bump! Bump! Bump! We're landing. Good. All safe and sound now. Let's get out of the plane and stretch ourselves, and enjoy some fresh air on this sandy beach, while they fix the plane.

"We are all out of the plane now and are on the beach. There is a pleasant breeze coming in from the sea, so stretch yourself and breathe in deeply that nice fresh air. Hmmmmmmm it is so refreshing."

NOTE TO HYPNOTIST: Observe how the various suggested scenes flow along smoothly in procession and dovetail into each other. The hypnotised subjects get caught up in this flow. The skilled performer knows his show thoroughly so as to present a perfect performance each time, yet presents it so spontaneously it always seems fresh and new. Allow sufficient time for the subjects to react and develop each suggested situation to the fullest. By this time in the show the reactions of the hypnotised subjects will be more or less spontaneous; the bare outlined suggestions of a situation will be sufficient motivation to begin its improvisation. Allow the subjects freedom to express themselves without overly direction. Sometimes the improvisations are remarkable. That's entertainment! As commented upon, observe how Gil Boyne allows each suggested situation to flow smoothly into the next. That's routining!

"Look at those palm trees swaying back there on this tropical isle. Here comes a group of beautiful Polynesian womans to greet us. They are all dressed in hula skirts, and, by crikey [if you use any slang be sure it is natural to your way of speaking], they are going to teach us all how to do the hula. We want to learn before we get to Honolulu, so everybody stand up to attention, and get ready to learn how to hula. [All subjects stand up.] You all know how in dancing the hula the swaying hands tell a love story. At the same time, get some hip movement into it. Watch the

581

womans and do what they do, as the music plays." The offstage music comes in: "Lovely Hula Hands".

"Okay, go ahead and practise the hula now everyone. Right along with the womans; sway your hands, wriggle your hips. Hula, hula, hula." The subjects all commence to hula, with varying degrees of perfection. Some dance splendidly, some clumsily. All are funny. In the midst of the fracas, suddenly.

"Stop! Hold it right where you are. The native womans are all leaving now, so wave and blow kisses to them as they go, and whoop out loud: 'Aloha! We all had a great time.' The subjects respond accordingly and whoop a big 'Aloha!'

"Just stand still for a moment, for it looks like more fun is on its way to entertain us. Here comes the warriors and they are going to show us how to do the Hawaiian war dance, when the music starts. You know how that goes: stamp your feet, pound your chest. Whoop it up! Watch the warriors and do what they do. Get into the spirit of the exciting music when it starts, and let yourself go in town. Here we go!" Off stage, the music "Hawaiian War Chant" starts.

"Great! Go to it and whoop it up!" The subjects go to town dancing the war dance in a frenzy on the stage. In the midst of the fracas the music suddenly stops.

"*Stop!* Hold it right where you are, and let's give the boys even a louder 'Aloha' than we gave the girls." The subjects shout "Aloha!" In the midst of the shouting the hypnotist shouts "Sleep!" The stage becomes silent on the instant!

"We are now going to resume our journey as the plane is fixed and ready to take off for our landing at the airport in Honolulu. We are back inside the plane so go back carefully to your seat; feel the edge of your seat behind you and sit down." The subjects gingerly resume their seats. You are now ready to "set up" a group of subjects for some posthypnotic antics. Use your most demonstrative subjects for these.

"We have all safely landed in Honolulu now. It has been quite a trip, so it seems good to just sleep for awhile. Meantime, here are some interesting things some of you will perform. Only the person I touch on the shoulder are involved, the rest of you just continue to sleep right on. All is so nice and pleasant now, here in Honolulu." The hypnotist approaches a responsive subject and touches him on the shoulder.

"Sir [or, if known, use the person's first name], you hear me well and I must tell you that there is an electric buzzer attached to the chair you are sitting on, and every time you hear me say the word 'hypnotism' the buzzer will go off, and, boy, will it make you jump! When you feel the buzzing you just can't leap out of that chair fast enough!"

The hypnotist goes to another sleeping male subject, and touches him on the shoulder: "You hear me well, and every time you hear me say the word 'hypnotism', you will jump to your feet and shout at the top of your voice: 'The British are coming!' "

The hypnotist goes to another sleeping subject, a lady this time, and touches her on the shoulder: "You hear me well and understand: every time you hear me say the word 'hypnotism', you will rise from your chair, dance up and down, and shout: 'I'm the last of the red-hot mamas!' " The hypnotist goes to another sleeping male subject, and touches him on the shoulder: "Sir, you hear me well. We are liable to have some of these people causing a disturbance on this stage, so I want you to be on guard and be prepared to restore order. This is your responsibility. When I say the word 'hypnotism', if anyone on this stage causes disturbance, please stand up and try to quiet them by telling them in no uncertain terms: 'Sit down, you fools!' Make them go back to their seats and be quiet. You are in charge. When order is restored then go back to your seat."

The same is done with another male subject, i.e., posthypnotically appointing the man as "stage orderly".

NOTE TO HYPNOTIST: By this handling, you have "conditioned" some subjects to respond as suggested when a "cue" is given (in this instance, the word "hypnotism"). The spontaneous responses of subjects to posthypnotic suggestions provides some of the hilarious episodes on the stage. The suggested situations can be played several times, and each time to increasing merriment.

"Everyone sleep on for a few moments longer now, as we rest on our arrival in Honolulu. All rested? Good. Every one open your eyes now and remain quietly in your seat deep in hypnosis. Pardon my back while I address the audience. [To the audience.] Ladies and gentlemen, I want to tell you about a show I presented some while back in New York City. It was real exciting. Sometimes a show of hypnotism [emphasise the word] can be very exciting."

Upon hearing this hypnotic "cue" the conditioned subjects will leap up to perform their various actions. One man leaps from his chair complaining of an electric buzzer operating under his seat. Another stands up and shouts: "The British are coming!" The woman sings out: "I'm the last of the red-hot mamas!" Pandemonium reigns on stage. The two appointed orderlies have their hands full regimenting the subjects back to their seats shouting: "Sit down, you fools!" Others on stage stare blankly into space oblivious of what is going on. The stage is restored to order, and the performer turns to address the audience again.

"Friends, please pardon this interruption. As I was saying before I was so rudely interrupted, sometimes a hypnotism show can be exciting."

Again the posthypnotic responses occur. The second time is even more fun than the first, as the suggested fracas ensues on stage until the "orderlies" again restore order. The hypnotist faces the group and with a sweep of his hands commands: "Sleep, everyone!" And the entire committee goes to sleep on the instant. Quiet reigns upon the stage.

Performing Some Individual Tests

The hypnotist goes to a sleeping woman and tells her to stand. He stands before her and suggests she cannot say the letter "P" no matter how hard she tries. When she tries to say the letter "P" she stutters. The woman is told to open her eyes and repeat the old rhyme: "Peter Piper Picked a Peck of Pickled Peppers". The hypnotist says it first, then requests her to repeat it. She stutters all over the place.

The test is repeated a couple of times. Then she is told to close her eyes and sleep with her head resting on hypnotist's shoulder. He tells her: "You are all calm now and your speech is free and flowing. Perfect in every way. The letter "P" gives you no trouble at all in saying it. You speak perfectly. Go ahead and repeat: 'Peter Piper Picked a Peck of Pickled Peppers' now." And the woman repeats it perfectly.

"You can say 'P' okay now, but somehow you can't remember the number five. Five somehow drops right out of your mind every time you come to that number. Open your eyes, stand up straight, and let's count slowly from one to ten." The subject does as directed. One, two, three, four all come out fine, but when five is reached she goes blank. The only way she can get beyond it is to jump to number six and on through to ten. The performer advances the test a step further.

"Let's try it this way. What is one and one?" The subject says 'two'. What is two and two? The subject says 'four'. What is three and two?" The subject goes blank and right in the middle of this blank space the hypnotist continues:

"Would you like to know how to recover your memory of the missing number?" The subject nods affirmative. "Okay, I will show you how. Just touch your right forefinger to the tip of your nose and you will recall the number five instantly. The only trouble is that when you remember the number your finger will become stuck to your nose, and you can't get it off. Try it and see." The woman does as instructed, and the hypnotist tells her to count from one to ten. She does it perfectly, but her finger has now become stuck to the tip of her nose. The hypnotist asks her if she would like to have a way to free her finger from the tip of her nose. The woman, assuredly, says "Yes".

"Okay, all you have to do is push your left forefinger into your ear and it will push your right forefinger right off your nose. Try it and see, but the only trouble is that when your finger comes free from the tip of your nose, your left forefinger will become stuck in your ear, and you can't get it loose. Try it and see." The woman puts her finger in ear and off comes the finger from her nose, but now she is stuck with a finger in hear ear. It is a paradoxical situation.

The hypnotist tells her to try it a few times. First a finger is stuck to her nose and when it comes off a finger is stuck in her ear. Back and forth and action goes. It is an extremely whimsical test. Finally, the hypnotist shrugs his shoulders and says: "Well, I guess I will just have to leave you for a while and let you figure it out for yourself. Keep trying."

The hypnotist turns away from the woman to approach another female subject, leaving the first woman to solve her own dilemma for a time. Going to the new subject, he tells her to open her eyes and stand up before him. He tells her to clasp her hands around his neck and that her hands have become locked so tightly together she cannot free them from about his neck, try as hard as she will. The woman tries and tries but to no avail. Her arms remain locked around the hypnotist's neck.

The hypnotists turns and addresses the audience: "Well, ladies and gentlemen, I guess that concludes the show for this evening, so I will have to leave the stage." The hypnotist tries to take his leave, but there is no way to do so except to drag along the woman. It is a very awkward situation. Finally, he apparently gives up. To the clinging woman he says: "I will show you how to free your hands from about my neck. To do it, just stamp your right foot firmly on the floor and your hands will instantly come free. The only trouble is that then your right foot will become stuck to the floor, and you cannot budge from that spot. Go ahead and stamp your foot."

The woman stamps her foot. Her hands come free from about hypnotist's neck. He moves across the stage and tells her to come to him. She cannot because her foot is stuck. The hypnotist tells her that to free her foot she will have to press the palm of her right hand against his, but while it will free her foot she will then become stuck to his hand. The woman tries the experiment. Her foot is freed but now her hand is stuck to the hand of the hypnotist. With a smile, he has her close her eyes and says: "When I tap you on top of your head, you will be completely free and you can return to your chair and rest."

A tap on the head and she is free. The performer tells the audience to give her a nice round of applause, as she resumes her seat upon the stage. The audience applauds. The hypnotist then returns to the woman with the nose-ear dilemma. He looks into her eyes and tells her to go to sleep and rest her head on his shoulder. Instantly, she does. The suggested tap on the top of the head causes all to be pleasantly free and clear. The hypnotist taps her on the top of her head and arouses her. He asks her to test for herself to see if the strange influence is gone entirely. It is. She returns to her seat as the performer requests a round of applause for her.

> NOTE TO HYPNOTIST: These individually featured hypnotic tests are very effective. And, the more the hypnotist can enter into the drama of each situation, the more effective such becomes. Gil Boyne is a master at this dramatisation to capture audience interest throughout his show. It is the finesse of hypnotic showmanship. For successful stage hypnotism the performer must not only be a good hypnotist but also a good actor. That's show business.

Speaking to the audience, the performer says: "Ladies and gentleman, I hope you are finding these experiments in hypnotism [again emphasise this word very strongly] interesting." On the "cue" word "hypnotism all the posthypnotically conditioned subjects erupt again into action. At this time, this unexpected happening comes as such a surprise it leaves the spectators limp with laughter.

After the group has once more been calmed, the hypnotist goes to the subject with the "buzzing in the seat of his chair", and asks what is the matter? The subject explains as best he can.

Suddenly grasping the subject's hand, a quick pull forward is performed with the command to *"Sleep!"*. Instantly, the subject is re-entranced. The test is easily accomplished, as actually the originally induced state of hypnosis has never been removed, so hypnotic suggestibility remains intact – in whatever direction the performer wishes to guide it. To this subject, the following is suggested.

"Actually, the buzzer in your chair is not the source of what you feel, as the party on your left has pinched you on your buttock. Now don't get mad about this, but should it happen again you certainly have the right to tell the person to get off it! Open your eyes now, and resume your seat."

Again the hypnotist mentions the word "hypnotism", and while all react, it is the "buzzing chair" individual with the pinched behind who is the star of the show this time. He directly complains in no uncertain terms to the person seated on his left that he wants the intimate pinching to stop. The person emphatically denies the accusation. Sometimes almost an argument ensues which the performer has to quiet. This is an ambiguous situation that the audience enjoys thoroughly.

When all has quietened down, Gil Boyne turns and addresses the audience: "Ladies and gentlemen, I am now going to show you a demonstration in hypnotism that is seldom attempted. It is called 'telepathic hypnotism' and is a demonstration of mental power you will long remember. In this experiment, I am going to hypnotise the entire group on stage from a distance by sending a mental thought of 'sleep' through space from far across the room, causing them to become entranced in response to my mental command. To present this demonstration under test conditions, I will leave the stage and have a volunteer accompany me to the far side of the room, and we will them attempt the experiment. Please remember this is an experiment, and experiments sometimes work and sometimes they do not. It will be interesting to see how this works tonight."

Before leaving stage, hypnotist explains to the committee what he is going to attempt – hypnotising them from a distance by telepathic thought. To them it will seem that they can hear his voice speaking to them inside their head. "All ready, eyes open and alert. Sit up in your chair, and make yourself receptive to my thoughts. As you receive my thoughts you will return to sleep within the next three minutes, as the experiment proceeds. Altogether, let us try it now."

The hypnotist leaves the stage and goes to a corner of the room (auditorium or theatre) accompanied by a volunteer selected by the audience. Standing in the corner he puts his hands to his temples in a position of intense concentration. Amazingly, those on stage go to "sleep" under his mental command! One by one they drop off to dreamland! The performer returns to the stage seemingly exhausted by his mental effort. It is an unusual demonstration of hypnotism and one the audience will long remember.

> NOTE TO HYPNOTIST: The experienced hypnotist will, of course, recognise that this demonstration is accomplished by the use of "hypnotic misdirection". In the performance, the audience is given an imagined cause for the hypnosis occurring from a distance via telepathy. Being already preconditioned, the suggestion of "mental influence" acts as a "cue" to return to trance, as the hypnotist presents such a happening through his apparent concentration. (This concentration should be real and truly does intensify the results.) A demonstration of this nature adds a touch of mystery and novelty to the show.

Returning to the stage, and with the row of hypnotised (sleeping) subjects behind him, the hypnotist is ready to present the hilarious conclusion to the show. Gil Boyne refers to it as the "subconscious power of imagination".

Climaxing the Show

As with all types of theatrical productions, the hypnotism show follows a pattern of beginning, central body of the drama and concluding climax. The show has all manner of light-and-shade along the way, leading up to a crescendo climax. Gil Boyne climaxes his show in the following kaleidoscope of hypnotic action:

Speaking to the audience, he says: "The subconscious phase of mind is highly responsive to imagination. As a concluding spectacle to the show, I will now show you a variety of demonstrations illustrating the remarkably degree to which the imagination stimulated – by hypnosis – can manipulate the body, even to the degree of impersonating things.

To his hypnotic subjects he says: "Go ever deeper and deeper into hypnosis now, and prepare yourselves for some amazing experiences. You are going to be motivated through your imagination to become a variety of THINGS. When I stamp my foot, you will imagine you are a perculating coffeepot! You will impersonate a perculating coffeepot even to the extent of boiling over!"

The performer stamps his foot and says: "Go to it and become a coffeepot perculator!" Everyone on stage now impersonates a perculating coffeepot. It is a riot – and some of the impersonations are remarkable – each and every one being based upon the imagination of each individual subject. After sufficient time has been allowed for the audience to enjoy and marvel at these actions, the hypnotist tells the group to cool off and stop "perculating". All action subsides.

"Now, when I stamp my foot you will all start impersonating a washing machine in operation." A stamp of the foot and the stage becomes filled with human washing machines. Whatever the subjects imagine washing machines to do, the subjects do, each in their own individual way. The stage is filled with action and thrashing about, until the hypnotist commands them to stop.

"Now, when I stamp by foot, you will imagine are a typewriter". A stamp of the foot and the stage overflows with typewriters. Clicketly, clickety, click! Stimulated imagination via hypnosis can do wonderful things. The action stops upon command.

"Now, when I stamp my foot you will become a vacuum cleaner." The stage gets swept-up in motor-purring vacuum cleaners. They turn off when the hypnotist says "Turn off!" The last imaginary impersonation is now performed.

"When I stamp my foot you will all become a tree. Each person will transform into a tree. You will grow straight and tall. Your roots will sink deep into Mother Earth, while your branches reach up high into the azure sky above. And, as a tree you will bud and blossom." A stamp of the foot is the hypnotic "cue" for transformation, and everyone on stage becomes a tree, with surprising beauty. The subjects are then all returned to deep trance.

> NOTE TO HYPNOTIST: The use of appropriate of accompanying sound effects can make these impersonating of things sensational. Tape the sound of a perculating coffeepot; a washing machine; a typewriter; a vacuum cleaner in operation, and play the sounds over the sound system as background to the various hypnotic impersonations. And think of the beautiful idea of using the lovely poem "Trees", set to music and used as an accompaniment when the subjects form a forest of trees on stage. It's great theatre.

Gil Boyne now introduces a unique climactic segment in his show, suggesting the subjects will all shortly return to their normal waking self *with* a memory of what hypnotic experience meant the most to them while hypnotised on the stage. The entire committee is then aroused from hypnosis. With microphone in hand, the hypnotist goes to each person, in turn, and has them tell what they liked best. It is very interesting to the audience to get these personal slants, as they are indicative of the personality of each subject. This technique promotes close human relationship between the subjects and the audience. Significantly, the majority usually express that they most enjoyed the experience of being a tree.

After all interviews are completed, the group if rehypnotised for the final awakening, completing the show. "Everyone stay wherever you happen to be, and look up towards a spot on the ceiling. Concentrate upon it. Now close your eyes and return to sleep."

The entire group becomes entranced. Gil Boyne now concludes his show in a graceful manner of wakening. First, however, just prior to the formal awakening, he sets a "topper" for an after-the-show bit of merriment. A male subject is selected. "You whom I now touch upon the shoulder will do what I tell you to do after you are dismissed from the stage and return to your seat in the audience. When you hear me say 'Thank you, ladies and gentlemaen,' you will turn about and look at all the people surrounding you and everyone will strike you as extremely funny, and you will *laugh, laugh, laugh* at everyone you see. You are so tickled and overcome with all the funny faces you just can't stop laughing, until I come down beside you in the audience and tell you to cease." This posthypnotic suggestion having been established, the formal awakening of the committee proceeds.

Gil Boyne has international recognition for his outstanding work in hypnotherapy. He brings to his stage work his expertise, being concerned that every person who participates in his show leaves the stage feeling better than when they came up. Such is the obligation of the conscientious stage hypnotist. Sometimes he makes this announcement at the very beginning of his show.

"I guarantee that every person taking part in the hypnotism show will leave the stage at the end of the show feeling better than when they came upon the stage at the beginning of the show."

Further, it will be noted that Gil Boyne, while presenting an extremely entertaining show, does not involve his subjects in any possible danger stunts, such as the "Human Bridge", "Pins Through the Flesh" etc. Subject safety runs paramount through his entire presentation. It is the way of the expert.

Gil Boyne keeps his promises and his final arousal of the subjects clears fully all residual effects of any suggestions given during the show and produces a euphoric sense of well-being for all participants. (The only exception being the posthypnotic of the one subject laughing.)

The Gil Boyne Awakening

"I am now going to count from one to five and by the time I reach the count of five, you will be wide awake feeling wonderful and fine, you are cleared, except for the one person who will laugh at all the funny faces, of each of the suggestions given you, and when you leave the stage they will have no further influence over you. You will remember as much or as little of your stage experiences, as you wish. It is entirely up to you. You will know it was great fun!

"All right now, get ready to come back from hypnosis, wide awake and feeling fine, as I count from one to five … One, you feel fine. You feel relaxed and good all over. Two, you experience a wonderful calmness in both your mind and body. Three, you feel refreshed in every way. This has been a wonderful experience for you. You have enjoyed every moment of it. Four, open your eyes now. Your eyes are sparkling and clear. They feel like they have been bathed in fresh spring water. Five, you are wide awake now and feeling splendid in every way. You feel wonderful as you leave the stage and return to your seat – while your friends tell you of the fascinating things you performed in the show. They marvel at you."

The committee members are dismissed from the stage amid the declaration from the performer: "Friends, let's stand and give these remarkable people a rousing applause for they are the real stars of the show!" A standing ovation is the case, as the committee members return to their seats in the audience.

Gil Boyne advances to the front of the stage, while the curtain closes behind him. He holds up his hand for silence. Immediately a hush descends upon the applauding audience. He speaks: "Ladies and gentlemen, it has been a pleasure performing for you this evening. I hope I have been able to bring you some appreciation of the magic of the mind, for the human mind is the most magical thing in all the world. Thank you, ladies and gentlemen, and good night."

The Posthypnotic Topper

On the words "Thank you, ladies and gentlemen," the posthypnotic "cue" for the topper of the show occurs, and the preconditioned man, in the audience, starts to *laugh, laugh, laugh* at everyone he sees.

Pandemonium – right in the middle of the audience!

591

Leaving the stage, Gil Boyne goes directly to the laughing man in the audience. He stops his laughter, thus ending his show amongst the spectators. A very personal touch – and that's showmanship!

Appendix II
The "State of the Art" in 1996

We are indebted to Paul McKenna and his publishers, Boxtree Limited, for permission to produce this extract from Paul's excellent book – Paul McKenna's Hypnotic Secrets. Paul has become world famous during the last four years as a hypnotic performer on stage and television. Since his debut on television in Great Britain in 1992, his series of shows, The Hypnotic World of Paul McKenna, *has been sold to more than fifty countries.*

This extract provides an interesting insight into what goes into developing, refining and finally delivering a successful routine on television. However, it must also be remembered that Paul's stage shows go through a very similar process from initial concept through to delivery. Paul will happily tell you that there is no excuse for not being "professional" in all aspects of presentation, whether you are working with just a handful of people or with a TV audience of many millions. He will also freely tell you that his greatest secret for success in this field is practice, practice and even more practice.

Now the Bits You Don't See on TV
by Paul McKenna

As most of the routines on my TV show don't last for more than four minutes, I can quite understand why some people are staggered when I tell them just how many weeks of work and the number of people that go into putting just one of them together. Sometimes I can't help wondering myself why it takes so long! For instance, preparation on routines for my August Bank Holiday Special, 1995 – featuring the ten best ever subjects – started six weeks before it was filmed. My manager Clare and I began by getting together with the seven programme associates who work permanently on the show to thrash out ideas in a small office in London's Covent Garden. It is where about half the routines begin their life, the rest are designed by Clare and myself. Coming up with a good hypnotic routine isn't like writing ordinary linear comedy, it's more like building a hologram. For that reason, our programme associates are not traditional writers, but people with a weird surreal way of looking at the world.

For eight hours, we chucked ideas for routines back and forth, dumping many because they were either too complicated or not funny enough.

One of the definite winners was a sketch in which a subject, whose dream car is a Testarossa, is hypnotised to think a plastic kids' car is his gleaming red Ferrari. I explain it has no insurance, but allow the subject to take it for a spin with tragic consequences. A hard-man character – we instantly thought of soccer star Vinny Jones – rams into the back of him in another plastic kids' car, but accuses the subject of reversing into him. A policeman, who has arrived on a toy bike, takes Jones's side, pointing out: "How can I disbelieve such an upstanding member of the community?" Of course, we never know how a subject is going to react, but it's most likely he would by now be in a complete panic, remembering he has no insurance. Then the sketch finishes with the PC telling him that his vehicle must be removed – and a JCB digger rolls on and crushes it. We all agreed the routine would be a hit. One of the production assistants immediately set about booking Vinny Jones and, for the policeman's role, TV presenter Ross King who had shown me how funny he could be when I hypnotised him on BBC1's *Children In Need* special in 1994. Both agreed immediately – Vinny was particularly keen because he had seen me in a stage show. Now we write their scripts and send them off to them. These are only ever outlines of what we believe might happen, because with hypnotised subjects you can never really tell until the night. The same is being done for all the other eight sketches on that show.

A week later the real work starts when everybody the set designers, programme associates, producer, director, costume lady and props man as well as ten volunteers – arrive at the rehearsal rooms in Brixton, South London. We spend an exhausting day testing all the routines with the volunteers – they're imaginative subjects from my stage shows who are keen to be hypnotised again but they won't be used in the TV show. We try out a routine, with different subjects, five or six times over the next fortnight to find ways of improving it, as every subject interprets it in their own individual way. Some have to be drastically re-worked, but the "Vinny" sketch, as it has become known, is hilarious every time so is hardly altered.

The Day of Filming

10:00 a.m.
I arrive, ready for a twelve-hour day, at the London Television Studios on the South Bank of the Thames. We film in the largest studio, No. 1, seating 500 people, which is the home of many of ITV's biggest family shows including *Barrymore*, *Blind Date* and *Surprise Surprise*. For most of the day, we are locked in rehearsals, estimating where we think the subjects will move, though we are not always right. Luckily, our director, Martin Scott, is never fazed. We can not afford to run overtime because just a few

minutes extra costs thousands of pounds. I rehearse all the routines with ten young actors and actresses standing in for the hypnotised subjects. Obviously, I never use them on the real shows but I'm always intrigued by the way that the actors behave so differently from the people who are genuinely hypnotised. I take this to be positive proof that these routines could not be faked as sceptics have suggested.

11:30 a.m.
We run through the "Vinny" routine so the director can tell the cameramen exactly what shots he is looking for.

3:30 p.m.
The celebrities starring in the routines arrive to rehearse their roles. Also in the line-up for the show are Roy Barraclough (*Coronation Street*'s Alec Gilroy) and former *EastEnders* star Leslie Grantham. We had been a little nervous about Vinny, particularly because he's not an actor. But he turns out to be a pro – arriving on time, word perfect – while Ross is the part in his uniform. Many stars who have appeared in the show have told me how fascinating they found it sharing the stage with "amateurs" because of their unpredictability. On a lot of occasions the celebrities have found it hard to keep straight faces to some of the reactions of the subjects, especially as they so earnestly believe what they are saying. During one routine, Gareth Hunt was playing a vicar conducting the marriage of a hypnotised couple. The bride was given a suggestion that she found the vicar very attractive, but after the cameras stopped rolling she carried on professing her undying love to him, with her arms wrapped tightly around his neck. He had to walk over to me with the young lady literally hanging from him to get me to wake her from the suggestion.

5:00 p.m.
Martin Scott and I go through technical aspects, such as where to stand at particular times and which camera to talk to. Scene shifters are setting up the road scene for the Vinny sketch, complete with a T-junction and traffic lights. A JCB is also being manoeuvred into position behind a piece of scenery. Meanwhile, Vinny and Ross join the other stars in the make-up room, mainly to take the shine off their faces.

5:25 p.m.
Break from rehearsal for dinner with the guests in the delightful canteen. I usually eat nothing more exotic than fish and chips with baked beans!

5:55 p.m.
In my dressing room, I change from jeans and casual shirt into a suit. We have wardrobe assistants who work on our show, but Clare always has

the final say on my ties. I also grab the chance to read my suggestions for the show for the final time.

6:00 p.m.
Studio staff open the doors to the 500-strong audience, all over eighteen years old because of television guidelines. Unlike many shows, we never advertise anywhere for our audience. They have all been found at our live shows, where they have filled in forms asking for tickets, which means that they know what to expect.

6:15 p.m.
I put myself into trance for fifteen minutes to prepare for the long evening ahead. I create images of the evening going really well, and the relaxation helps give me energy to get through the evening. To me, fifteen minutes of hypnotic trance is equivalent to two hours of conventional sleep.

6:30 p.m.
Off to the make-up room. This wasn't something I had to face when working on radio!

6:35 p.m.
Paul Alexander, the script editor, makes some last-minute changes to my lines which are typed into the Autocue (electronic word prompter). Of course, we never have any idea what the subjects are going to say or how they will react during the show. So the opening link is the only bit of script for me.

6:40 p.m.
Top TV warm-up man Ray Turner cranks up the audience with some gags and get them used to laughing and applauding.

6:50 p.m.
Dr Chris Pattinson, a respected medical doctor who uses hypnosis in treatment of his patients, takes his seat in the audience. He is hired by ITV as an independent observer at all the shows to see that everything is done exactly by the book.

6:55 p.m.
Ray introduces me to give a preliminary talk where I explain a few simple studio rules, such as, "If you see yourself on one of the monitors during the show, don't point and say. 'Oh, I'm on telly.' "

7:00 p.m.
The music starts, I walk out and do my first introduction to camera for real.

Hypnotising the TV Subjects

I know many viewers are fascinated by how I put the subjects into a trance, but we are not allowed under the TV rules to broadcast what I say during the induction. I believe that this is with good reason because, otherwise, some people watching at home could be hypnotised. The last thing I want is Granny leaping about like Elvis in the living room. There is one story, probably apocryphal, about a hypnotist sending thousands of viewers into a trance on Italian TV, then having to snap each one of them out of it for hours on the phone afterwards.

Before I ask for volunteers, I always stress that those who suffer from epilepsy, clinical depression, any psychiatric condition or are hyperglyceamic, pregnant, or extremely stressed should not volunteer. Here is a guide of how I put the subjects into trance. The only time I didn't follow this pattern was for the August Bank Holiday show in 1995 because we usually feature the best subjects from the previous series.

7:10 p.m.
First, I ask for volunteers. Around sixty people rush down to the stage from the audience. I have noticed the number has got greater, particularly at the stage shows, the longer the TV series has been going. At one time there used to be only about a dozen people wanting to take part.

7:20 p.m.
Next, I do a handclasp with the volunteers. I ask them to clasp their hands together and imagine that they are locked, bolted, glued, cemented together and that they cannot open their hands however hard they try. This is a suggestibility test. It shows me which people are good at concentrating and have good imaginations, these are essential keys to a good subject for stage or TV hypnosis.

7:30 p.m.
I sit some of the volunteers on chairs before carrying out "rapid inductions" on a couple of people. A rapid induction is a dramatic way of putting somebody into trance and acts as a powerful suggestion to the other people on stage.

7:35 p.m.

During the rapid induction I stand next to the subject and ask them to close their eyes. I tip their head backwards, which disorientates them, then get them to fall backwards as I catch them and lay them on the ground. I then begin the induction for the rest of the volunteers, asking them to count backwards from 300 and systematically relax their bodies.

7:45 p.m.

All this time I am sorting out the people who are concentrating, looking for physiological signs of trance such as rapid eye movement and deep relaxation of the facial muscles. By the point at which I actually start giving the subjects small suggestions I probably have about thirty volunteers left. I do some small routines, asking them to carry out simple tasks using their imaginations. Clare, the producer and I watch them and discuss which subjects we think are the best. When we have agreed on the final ten volunteers I ask them, whilst hypnotised, to raise their hand if there is any reason why they should not take part in the show. If they all indicate that they are happy to continue we have our ten stars for the evening. Now I can relax for five minutes as I wake the subjects up to be fitted with radio microphones.

This particular show was an hour long, but a half-hour show takes almost as long to film. About 45 minutes of this is the induction where we choose the ten volunteers. The actual routines are fairly quick to film but there are so many changes to the set, lighting and cameras that the evening takes a lot out of everyone involved, probably with the exception of the subjects who tend to think that they have only been there ten minutes. It often feels more like ten hours to me and the crew.

Sometimes the routines don't work out exactly as planned. One subject called Billy was given the suggestion that the glove puppet on his hand was insulting him. He started to argue with it before punching it to the ground. He was rolling about on the floor thumping the puppet and at one point the cameraman was laughing so hard he collapsed. I quickly jumped in and woke the subject. We were laughing for days as was Billy when he saw the video of himself.

Another time I gave a young lady a suggestion that she was cementing the studio floor and she was to get irate at anyone who walked on it. We had to stop filming for a technical reason and the producer wandered onto the set. She went crazy, screaming and shouting at him to "get off my wet cement" as she manhandled him onto an area that she apparently hadn't done yet. The poor producer looked at me for help but I was too busy laughing. He got his revenge when I gave two men the suggestion that I was the American President and they were my burly bodyguards. At one point the producer let off a loud bang which they thought was a gun shot. Hurling me to the ground, the two men threw themselves on top of me "for my protection". I couldn't move or speak to tell them to "sleep".

8:00 p.m.
Tony, Clare and I take a break to discuss the filming.

8:30 p.m.

At last it's time to put the Vinny routine into operation. Will all those weeks of planning pay off? Fortunately the subject is superb. He is horrified when PC King sides with Vinny, guilt-ridden when he suddenly remembers he has no insurance and just mortified when the JCB crushes his "dream" car, throwing his arms in the air, shaking his head and shouting "no". The audience are in hysterics.

10:00 p.m.
It's the end of the evening. I wake everybody up and make sure they are all back to normal.

10:30 p.m.
I join Vinny, Ross and the other celebrities and subjects who have taken part for a well-earned drink together in the hospitality suite behind the studio.

A couple of days later we get all ten volunteers back to a smaller studio and show them the footage of what they did, film their reactions and ask them what they remember and what they felt. We then cut their reactions into the show, edit, add music and you see the finished product on your screen a few weeks later. This show is first screened in Britain but then shown in 42 other countries to over 200 million people!

Paul periodically runs a number of hypnosis workshops in different parts of the world for those interested in developing skills in this area. For more information please contact:

Paul McKenna Productions
PO Box 5514
London
W8 4LY
United Kingdom

Paul has also produced an interesting range of products including a range of self-help hypnosis tapes and a number of tapes for sports hypnosis. Most of the products are available from good bookstores and other outlets. However, if you experience difficulty in obtaining them please contact Paul McKenna Productions at the address above.

Bibliography

Allen, R. P., *Scripts & Strategies In Hypnotherapy*, Crown House Publishing Ltd, Carmarthen.

Alman & Lambrou, *Self-Hypnosis: The Complete Manual for Health & Self-Change*, Brunner Mazel Publishers, New York.

Balduc, H. L., *Journey Within: Past-Life Regression and Channelling*, Independence, Inner Vision Publishing, Virginia.

Bandler & Grinder, *Patterns of Milton H. Erickson* (2 Volumes), Meta Publications, Capitola, California.

Boyne, G., *Transforming Therapy: A New Approach to Hypnotherapy*, Westwood Publishing, Glendale, California.

Edgette & Edgette, *Handbook of Hypnotic Phenomena in Psychotherapy*, Brunner Mazel Publishers, New York.

Elman, D., *Hypnotherapy*, Westwood Publishing, Glendale, California.

Erickson, M., & Rossi, E., *Experiencing Hypnosis: Therapeutic Approaches To Altered States*, Irvington Publishers, New York.

Erickson, M., & Rossi, E., *Hypnotherapy: An Exploratory Casebook*, Irvington Publishers, New York.

Hammond, D. C., *Handbook of Hypnotic Suggestions & Metaphor*, W. W. Norton Publishers, London.

McGill, O., *Power Hypnosis Hypnotherapy*, National Guild of Hypnotists, Merrimack, New Hampshire.

McGill, O., *Professional Stage Hypnotism*, Westwood Publishing, Glendale, California.

McGill, O., *Seeing the Unseen: A Past Life Revealed Through Hypnotic Regression*, Crown House Publishing Ltd, Carmarthen.

McKenna, P., *Hypnotic World of Paul McKenna*, Faber & Faber, London.

Rossi, E. (ed.), *Collected Papers of Milton H. Erickson* (4 Volumes), Irvington Publishers, New York.

Tebbets, C., *Self-Hypnosis and Other Mind-Expanding Techniques*, Westwood Publishing, Glendale, California.

Watkins, J. G., *Practice of Clinical Hypnosis, Volumes I & II: Hypnotherapeutic Techniques*, Irvington Publishers, New York.

Yapko, M., *Trancework: An Introduction to the Practice of Clinical Hypnosis*, Brunner Mazel Publishers, New York.

The above represents only a very small number of books available on the subject of hypnosis and are intended as a starting point for further research. It has been estimated that over four hundred books on hypnosis are available in the English language. Most of the books currently in print are concerned with the hypnotherapeutic applications of hypnosis and only a very small number are dedicated to stage hypnosis. However, hypnosis is hypnosis in whatever environment it is applied, and I would strongly recommend that all stage hypnotists should gain a good understanding of the therapeutic aspects of this intriguing subject.

The distributors of this book are specialist suppliers of books and audiotapes to the world of hypnosis. Very comprehensive and descriptive catalogues are available to anyone wishing to learn more. Please contact:

The Anglo-American Book Company
Bancyfelin
Carmarthen
Wales
SA33 5ND
UK

Telephone: +44 (0)1267 211880
Fax: +44 (0)1267 211882
Email: books@anglo-american.co.uk
Home Page: http://www.anglo-american.co.uk

Ormond McGill's
Self-Realisation Audio Cassettes

Over the last twenty years or so Ormond has become famous for his self-help series of audiotapes. These tapes have helped many thousands of people to resolve their problems, from stopping smoking through to quite complex psychological problems. Ormond has produced a set of four individual audiotapes to accompany this book.

MASTER METHODS OF HYPNOTISM

This tape and booklet are designed to introduce the stage hypnotist to the therapeutic use of hypnosis. Ormond believes that the best place to start is with yourself, and listening to the audiotape will accomplish this. The booklet is entitled "Superlative Hypnotism Secrets", and this is just what it is, the inside track on doing therapy really well. Ormond includes many short cuts and tips you will not read anywhere else. This set provides an excellent addition to this book. £14.95

FOUNTAIN OF YOUTH

This cassette trains your mind in the use of self-hypnosis directed towards longevity through the use of Hunza methods of breath control. On side one Ormond presents a simple self-hypnosis induction method called the Sandy Beach. Side two tells you how to imbibe of the Hunza Fountain of Youth. Both sets of instructions combine together in a superlative process for health and long life. Ormond uses these techniques on a regular basis and at a sprightly eighty-two years of age is perhaps living proof of the efficacy of his techniques. Complete with instruction booklet. £12.95

HYPNOYOGA: Touch Technique Hypnotherapy

On Side A, Ormond begins with an invitation to relax deeply and enter a state of hypnosis. He then invites you to explore and find your true self on a journey to greater awareness and wholeness. On Side B, Diana England takes you through some simple Yoga exercises suitable for everyone. She links these with the Yoga breathing technique in order to access a state of altered consciousness. She finishes with meditation where you are invited to centre yourself whilst in a state of deep hypnosis. Comes complete with a forty-four page manual of instructions with drawings. Price £12.95

VITALITY HYPNOSIS

Increasing your vitality is important to everything you do in life. Lack of vitality in handling the stress of modern life is a major cause of illness. This tape is designed to give you a superlative method for bringing vitality from the universe to yourself. Included are processes on how to direct the energy generated to developing your ESP powers of mind, stimulate your inner etheric (astral) body and create thought forms with power behind them. Complete with instruction booklet. Price £12.95

All the above can be obtained from the distributor, The Anglo-American Book Company, contact address on page 604.

Hypnotic Language

Its Structure and Use

John J. Burton, EdD
& Bob G. Bodenhamer, DMin

We each shape our own reality. Perceptions and cognitive processes unique to each of us determine our individual perspective on the world, and we present to ourselves what we are programmed to see. But what if we could change our perceptions and cognitive processes – and consequently our reality?

One way of achieving this is by harnessing the power of hypnotic language. This remarkable book examines the structures of the hypnotic sentence, and the very cognitive dimensions that allow hypnotic language to be effective in changing our minds. Defining the three facets that allow the mind to be susceptible to hypnotic language patterns, *Hypnotic Language* puts these insights into practice in case examples that demonstrate the application and effect of hypnotic language. Teaching us how to create the most effective hypnotic scripts, it provides new language patterns that address beliefs, time orientation, perception, spiritual matters and states of mind, and devises new hypnotic language applications that emphasise the importance of *Gestalt principles* and *cognitive factors*.

An invaluable resource for hypnotherapists, psychologists, NLP practitioners and counsellors, *Hypnotic Language* promotes a new and deeper understanding of hypnotic language, clearly defining the divide between the conscious and unconscious mind – and those language paths that link the two. Providing a wealth of scripts for hypnotic trance, it presents innovative and original ways to induce cognitive change that enable you to access your unconscious mind – and the infinite resources it holds.

Hardback / 320 pages / ISBN: 1899836357

Hypnosis

A Comprehensive Guide

Tad James, MS, PhD
with Lorraine Flores & Jack Schober

Research shows that many people react differently to different kinds of hypnotic induction – yet many hypnotherapists are confined to using only one technique. This book makes three radically different and significant types of hypnosis easy to use in daily hypnosis work, examining in detail the techniques of *Erickson, Estabrooks* and *Elman*. Exploring methods that employ Direct Authoritarian and Indirect Permissive approaches, *Hypnosis* progresses beyond these approaches to describe the inductions pioneered by Dave Elman: a technique that places responsibility for hypnosis *on the client*. An invaluable resource for all trainers and therapists, *Hypnosis* is a comprehensive and lucid manual that incorporates powerful inductions for producing deep-trance phenomena, sections on the application of metaphor and hypnotic language patterns, and scripts for a variety of hypnotic inductions.

"This book is an excellent introductory text for students just beginning to study the art and science of hypnosis. For those already knowledgeable about hypnosis, there are many nuances that will enable you to increase the elegance of your work."
– David Shephard, PhD, Master Trainer of NLP, Director of Research and Training, The Performance Partnership, London, UK.

Hardback / 240 pages / ISBN: 1899836454

Scripts and Strategies in Hypnotherapy

The Complete Works

Roger P. Allen, Dp, Hyp, PsyV

Scripts and Strategies in Hypnotherapy Volumes I and II have been combined to create the single most comprehensive source of scripts and strategies that can be used by hypnotherapists of all levels of experience to build a successful framework for any therapy session. It covers inductions, deepeners and actual scripts for a wide range of problems from nail-biting to insomnia, sports performance to past life recall, pain management to resolving sexual problems. There is a particularly comprehensive section on smoking cessation. All scripts can be used as they stand or adapted for specific situations.

"Scripts and Strategies in Hypnotherapy: The Complete Works *combines Roger Allen's previous books into one accessible volume providing an imaginative source of scripts that cover the most commonly met cases. For the newly qualified therapist, it is a useful addition and for the more experienced it is a source of inspiration.*"
— Peter Mabbutt, FBSCH, FBAMH,
Director of Studies, London College of Hypnosis

"*Imaginative, practical and, quite simply, essential for anyone getting started in hypnotherapy.*"
— Martin Roberts, PhD
author of *Change Management Excellence*

Hardback / 352 pages / ISBN: 190442421X

Presenting Magically

Transforming Your Stage Presence with NLP

David Shephard & Tad James

Have you ever been enthralled by a masterful presenter or trainer? Have you longed to effortlessly entertain and motivate your audience just as they seemed to do? At one time it was considered that such captivating performances were possible only if you were one of the fortunate, 'natural-born' presenters. Now, with the application of advanced human communication technologies such as NLP (Neuro-Linguistic Programming) and Accelerated Learning, *everyone* can learn to present magically.

Whether you are a newcomer or a seasoned professional, *Presenting Magically* will provide you with masterful tips and techniques that will transform your presenting skills. Introducing you to the secrets of many of the world's top presenters, this, *the most comprehensive book available on the application of NLP to presentation,* explores:

- **how to** adopt the beliefs and attitudes of master presenters
- **how to** become calm, balanced and centred
- **how to** connect with your audience
- **how to** structure your language for optimum effect
- **how to** handle hecklers
- **how to** use metaphor
- **how to** use gesture to access the unconscious minds of viewers
- **how to** use and own the stage
- **how to** elicit states from your audience and anchor them
- **how to** structure presentations to fit everyone's learning style
- **how to** to grab the audience's attention – and keep it.

Hardback / 300 pages / ISBN: 1899836527

Precision Therapy

A Professional Manual of Fast and Effective Hypnoanalysis Techniques

Duncan McColl

Encapsulating the work of this highly respected British therapist, *Precision Therapy* is an extremely practical book that describes how to initiate healing processes. It is eclectic in nature, free from dogma and jargon, and designed for the therapist-healer who does not have the need, the time or the inclination to subject clients to protracted mindgames. Its practicality is illustrated in the training material: each page is a script or a prompt-sheet that can be adapted easily to deal effectively with most problems in a matter of hours rather than weeks or months. A comprehensive manual of fast, effective hypnoanalytic techniques.

"Duncan McColl has provided us with a fresh look at how we do our work. It is insightful and provocative. It is scholarly yet remarkably free from the language which constantly calls out for the use of a dictionary. It is fresh and invigorating."

– The Hypnotherapist

Paperback / 248 pages / ISBN: 1899836187

USA, Canada & Mexico orders to:
Crown House Publishing Company LLC
6 Trowbridge Drive, Suite 5, Bethel, CT 06801
Tel: 203-778-1300 Fax: 203-778-9100
E-mail: info@CHPUS.com
www.crownhousepublishing.com

UK, Europe & Rest of World orders to:
The Anglo American Book Company Ltd.
Crown Buildings, Bancyfelin, Carmarthen, Wales SA33 5ND
Tel: +44 (0)1267 211880/211886, Fax: +44 (0)1267 211882
E-mail: books@anglo-american.co.uk
www.anglo-american.co.uk

Australasia orders to:
Footprint Books Pty Ltd.
Unit 4/92A Mona Vale Road, Mona Vale NSW 2103, Australia
Tel: +61 (0) 2 9997 3973, Fax: +61 (0) 2 9997 3185
E-mail: info@footprint.com.au
www.footprint.com.au

Singapore orders to:
Publishers Marketing Services Pte Ltd.
10-C Jalan Ampas #07-01
Ho Seng Lee Flatted Warehouse, Singapore 329513
Tel: +65 6256 5166, Fax: +65 6253 0008
E-mail: info@pms.com.sg
www.pms.com.sg

Malaysia orders to:
Publishers Marketing Services Pte Ltd
Unit 509, Block E, Phileo Damansara 1, Jalan 16/11
46350 Petaling Jaya, Selangor, Malaysia
Tel : +03 7955 3588, Fax : +03 7955 3017
E-mail: pmsmal@streamyx.com
www.pms.com.sg

South Africa orders to:
Everybody's Books CC
PO Box 201321, Durban North, 4016, RSA
Tel: +27 (0) 31 569 2229, Fax: +27 (0) 31 569 2234
E-mail: warren@ebbooks.co.za